is   may

APPLETON-CENTURY HANDBOOKS OF LITERATURE

Albert C. Baugh, Editor

ENGLISH LITERATURE
of the VICTORIAN PERIOD

ENGLISH LITERATURE

of the VICTORIAN PERIOD

JOHN D. COOKE *&* LIONEL STEVENSON

Professors of English
The University of Southern California

New York

APPLETON-CENTURY-CROFTS, INC.

PRINTED IN THE UNITED STATES OF AMERICA

PREFACE

>>

The arrangement of material in this book follows both thematic and chronological principles. The first part of it presents the political and social background of the seventy years from 1830 to 1900, the social history being subdivided according to the principal categories affecting literature.

The remaining part of the book deals with literature, classified as to its main types—Poetry, Prose Fiction, Drama, Expository Prose, and finally a few minor types. Each type is discussed in a general chapter tracing its development during the period and indicating the interrelationships of the authors. After each general chapter the lives and works of the principal writers in that *genre* are presented in some detail. These are in chronological sequence, not strictly as to date of birth but as to date of achieving literary importance. At the end of each group, short notes on authors of lesser stature are arranged alphabetically.

For the sake of unity, all the writings of each author are discussed in one section, even though he may have done significant work in several *genres*. Any one of the preliminary chapters on literary types will therefore be found to contain references to some authors whose detailed consideration is presented under other categories. The principal examples of these necessary dissociations are as follows:

POETRY. Meredith, Hardy, Stevenson (discussed under Prose Fiction), Wilde (discussed under Drama)

PROSE FICTION. Kipling (discussed under Poetry)

DRAMA. Bulwer-Lytton (discussed under Prose Fiction),
Yeats (discussed under Poetry)

EXPOSITORY PROSE AND CRITICISM. Arnold (discussed under
Poetry), Butler, Stevenson (discussed under Prose Fiction)

The bibliographies also combine chronological with topical grouping. For general chapters, if the topic is a simple
one, the entries are arranged in order of publication, except
that inclusive works are listed before specialized ones; but
if the topic is more complex, the entries are divided into
groups, without subheadings. For example, the bibliography
for "Science" begins with general works, then lists references on the separate sciences (alphabetically from Astronomy to Zoölogy), and finally gives biographical studies of
individual scientists (alphabetically by the scientists' names).
The bibliographies on "Religion" and "Art" follow a similar system.

For an individual author, the bibliography begins with
the title of any published bibliography on the subject; then
lists any concordance, dictionary, or handbook to the author's work; next gives the principal collected editions and
the volumes of letters; and concludes with the biographical
and critical studies. In each of these subdivisions the material comes chronologically.

Although not claiming to be complete, the bibliographies
have attempted to mention all significant works in book
form and a selection of outstanding briefer studies. Particular care has been taken to include the most recent biographical and critical data.

Throughout the preparation of this book, much assistance
has been derived from the wise counsel of the general editor
of the series, Professor Albert C. Baugh.

J. D. C.
L. S.

CONTENTS

>>

ILLUSTRATIONS

>>

ENGLISH LITERATURE
of the VICTORIAN PERIOD

INTRODUCTION

>>

The word *Victorian* has acquired so many connotations that a detailed definition is needed. Originally a convenient label for a distinct period in English history, it later came to suggest certain wide ideas in such fields as morality and the arts. In these usages it has been applied far beyond the limits of its British origin and its historical precision. In architecture, interior decoration, costume, and so forth, "Victorian" has been made to imply elaborate ornamentation that has little meaning in relation to the object upon which it is imposed. In manners and ideas, "Victorian" has been made to imply self-righteousness, prudery, narrow conventionality, or hypocrisy.

To a great degree these unfavorable interpretations were due to the principle of revulsion that governs human opinions and tastes. Every generation seeks to establish its independence by defying the authority of the preceding one, scorning established habits, and setting up new ideals to be pursued. The more successful and impressive the older generation has been, the more violently the next one must break with it. For a few decades, everything connected with the immediate past era is "old fashioned" and "absurd." With the third generation a reaction sets in: enough time has elapsed to give perspective, and the once-despised era becomes "quaint," "picturesque," and at last "historically significant."

With regard to the Victorian era this change of attitude is now occurring. People who allowed the junkman to cart away their parents' heavy carved furniture are paying large prices to antique dealers for the same walnut dressers and horsehair sofas. The hoop skirts and poke bonnets that were laughed at as dowdy are winning admiration in costume plays. High-ceilinged mansions with fretwork trimmings and wrought-iron fences are being carefully "restored." In the change of fashion, people have begun to look back to the "horse and buggy days" or the "gay nineties" with a sentimental nostalgia.

In any consideration of English history and literature of the period that extended over most of the nineteenth century, sentimental affection might become as serious a distortion as cynical contempt has recently been; but an objective evaluation ought to be more nearly possible now than at any previous date.

The chance that one ruler occupied the English throne during approximately all this distinctive epoch made her name a usefully brief title for it. Perhaps too much personal responsibility has thereby been attributed to the Queen as an individual. The best-known traits of Victoria were the result of Victorianism, rather than the cause of it. As a matter of fact, at the beginning of her reign the Queen possessed few of the habits and ideas that are popularly considered "Victorian," and even in her later life she was by no means a perfect exponent. The characteristics of the era would have been essentially the same if half a dozen monarchs had held sway in England during its span.

No agreement as to the exact dates of the Victorian period has ever been reached. The years of the Queen's reign (1837-1901) are seldom accepted for it, as no other important event happened in either of those years, and some of the main trends of the period had begun before she ascended the throne. Sometimes the date of the first Reform Bill, 1832, is adopted as a starting point, and the death of Tennyson, 1892, as a conclusion, he being the last major survivor of the literary group that dominated the era. On the other hand, some historians argue that the final phase of Victorianism continued until the outbreak of war in 1914. Decades being easier to remember than specific years, it is logical to select 1830 and 1900 as the limiting dates. Within those seventy years all the significant literary and historical events of Victorianism are included.

The intellectual phenomena of the Victorian age were common throughout Western civilization in the nineteenth century, but circumstances gave them fuller and more immediate expression in England than elsewhere. There the capitalistic, bourgeois culture that emerged from the Industrial Revolution reached its culmination; there the theories of science provoked the most vigorous controversies over rationalism and faith; there the moralistic individualism of the Protestant reformation found its final fulfilment. On the European continent these developments had been delayed by the half century of turmoil and destruction centering upon the French Revolution and the Napoleonic campaigns. In the United States they were only slowly emerging from the practical necessities of establishing a government, exploring a continent, and acquiring a population.

Great Britain, self-contained and prosperous, was a laboratory for social, political, and moral experiments that the rest of the world faced under more violent and confused conditions in later years. The literature of Victorian England is the accurate record of those experiments. For that reason it can be fully appreciated only when accompanied by some study of its religious, scientific, economic, and philosophic background.

In its historical relationships, the Victorian age was a necessary sequel to the age of revolution that preceded it. During the half century after 1775 the European and American continents were torn to pieces and reconstructed. Old dynasties went down to death or exile, the long-weakened structure of feudal aristocracy at last collapsed, the agricultural economy of centuries gave place to industrialism. All these profound changes were accompanied by a welter of theories, arguments, proclamations, and assorted propaganda.

The events of the fifty years were so vast and so speedy that no human mind could evaluate them while they were happening. Literature, which is supposedly a mirror of contemporary life, scarcely even attempted to chronicle the upheavals. England fought Napoleon for twenty years, and yet no major work of English literature, written during those years, did more than mention the war. The country went through the Industrial Revolution during the same decades; but to find a positive reference to the migration from the fields to the factories, the growth of the cities and the slums, the sudden power of the wealthy businessman, one has to go back to *The Deserted Village,* in which Goldsmith caught a prophetic glimpse of these trends before they happened, or else come forward sixty years to the early Victorian authors who suddenly awoke to what had occurred. Almost the only author in the interval who showed any perception of what was going on about him was William Blake, the humble visionary who was easily discounted as "crazy."

The English authors of the Romantic generation were chiefly noteworthy for their unrestrained individualism. All keenly interested in ideas, they expressed their opinions with enthusiasm. So much personal emotion entered into their thinking that what they wrote was stimulating to the reader's mind but was often extreme in its bias and sometimes inconsistent in its assortment of ideas. The "big nine" of English Romanticism—Wordsworth, Coleridge, Scott, Lamb, Hazlitt, de Quincey, Byron, Shelley, Keats—had little in common except their intensity of feeling and their frankness in revealing their own personalities. No two of them were in full agreement upon many topics, and several were openly antagonistic to one another.

In short, the age of political revolution and literary romanticism filled the world to the saturation point with new experiences and new theories. If the balance of civilization was to be retained, a period of adjustment had to follow. People needed to pause for analysis and correlation. What was valid in the recent developments had to be consolidated; what was excessive had to be rejected, once the necessary function of iconoclasm came to an end.

There followed a century in which the elements of European civilization were put together again in a new pattern. Politically it was marked in some countries by reaction. England, however, which had escaped violence during the era of revolution and war, proceeded with a steady expansion of democratic processes. The Industrial Revolution was fulfilling itself in great material comfort and prosperity and the world was exceptionally free of large-scale wars. As England had been able to continue its industrialization during the Napoleonic period—in fact, to expand more rapidly under war-time conditions—she was the unchallenged economic leader of the world. Not since Elizabethan times had English prestige been so high. Consequently, English literature was rich and positive.

The Victorian authors did not break away from the influence of the immediate preceding generation, the Romantic. On the contrary, they deeply admired it. The fame of Wordsworth and Coleridge, of Lamb and Hazlitt, of Shelley and Keats, was enhanced by the praise of the younger authors. Nevertheless, the Victorians were not mere slavish imitators. While basing their literary techniques upon those of their predecessors, they adapted and selected as they chose. Tennyson borrowed traits of Wordsworth, Coleridge, Keats, and others, but wove them into new effects too complex to be termed imitative. Dickens started as a disciple of Lamb and Leigh Hunt, but transformed the "Cockney essay" into vast and varied novels. Whereas the Romantics had proclaimed their beliefs passionately but not always rationally, the Victorians tried to compare one theory with another and to work out logical answers to the problems of existence.

Hence developed their attitude that G. K. Chesterton later named "the Victorian compromise." This was a prominent element in the disrepute that overtook them in the twentieth century. They were accused of inconsistency and of opportunism, of preaching handsome ideals and yet condemning political or spiritual extremists. It is possible, however, that these Victorians can set a useful model for the present age. They believed in the wisdom of looking at all sides of a question, and they were not convinced that truth was simple enough to be condensed into a single dogma. Each author, each philosopher, each politician, had his own beliefs, to be sure; but they were intensely concerned with one another's views, and their controversies were more in the nature of coöperative experiments than campaigns of mutual extermination. An interminable town meeting or panel discussion went on for half a century, every writer contributing his share. For this reason no author or group of authors can be fully understood without constant reference to what their contemporaries were saying at the same time.

It was not a dramatic, vivid situation. The lines of attack were seldom clearly drawn. Many of the most significant contributions were long, exhaustive books. The modern student, depending upon anthologies and books of readings, cannot get a fully adequate conception of the ideas and influence of Carlyle, Ruskin, Morris, or the novelists. It would be doing the Victorians an injustice to assert that the study of their writings is always easy.

On the other hand, these same writings contain more

energy and entertainment than they are given credit for. There is little basis for the impression that all Victorian authors were solemn, didactic, and preoccupied with moralistic discussions to the exclusion of normal human feelings. Because most of them lived to old age, and their best-known portraits were taken in their later years, the modern student has been apt to get a vague idea that they must have worn long grey whiskers from infancy. Those beards in the portraits of Tennyson and Browning and Dickens and Ruskin became symbolic of a supposedly complacent superiority to the emotions of daily life, an oracular repetition of trite ideals.

When the works of those same Victorians are read honestly and without preconceived bias, their solemnity proves to be diversified with sharp wit and hearty humor, and instead of being complacent they often reveal an anxious and almost humble desire to thrash out their problems in debate with an intelligent reader.

Those problems are just as vital and just as far from solution today. The unwillingness of the recent generation to read Victorian literature was part of an instinctive effort to ignore the uncomfortable difficulties and moral dilemmas of modern life. The world has now come to a crisis in which such easy evasion of responsible thinking is no longer possible. Our answers may not be identical with those of the Victorians, but even at points of sharpest divergence we can clarify our own opinions or embark upon further topics under the stimulus of their statements.

One of the trite generalizations about the Victorians has been their "shallow optimism." Not one of the major authors can be fairly convicted of such an outlook. They were acutely aware not only of the existing evils of their day but also of the possibility that worse evils might ensue. Their so-called "optimism" was a persistent belief that human intelligence might apply itself successfully to the prevention of such a disaster. From the Romantics they inherited the concept of progress; but they gave up any naïve faith that progress was inevitable or that a sudden millennium might be achieved in a single revolutionary transformation. Influenced by new scientific concepts of natural processes that occupied millions of years, the Victorians thought that the human race might possibly have acquired enough intelligence and will-power to make some valid contribution to a gradual evolutionary trend.

The Victorian essayists, historians, poets, and even novelists undertook the function of philosophical commentators because they felt that the duty was forced upon them. At a time of rapidly changing conditions and discoveries, the public seeks for advisers who can be trusted to explain difficult ideas in simple terms, to connect strange and novel developments with stable familiar standards, and to suggest attitudes for the baffled layman to adopt. Normally, these services are performed by certain recognized professions: in matters of spiritual belief and moral principles, by the clergy; in matters of social responsibility, by the politicians.

In Victorian England these two professions proved inadequate to their opportunities. The official religious body, the Church of England, was handicapped by internal conflicts among at least three factions, which hated and condemned each other almost more bitterly than they hated their various external rivals—the Nonconformist sects on one side and the Roman Catholic church on the other. When the leaders of religion realized that their whole prestige was endangered by the growth of scientific rationalism, many of them responded with the assertion that science must be an evil force if it dared to invade any corner of religion's prerogatives. No good Christian, it was declared, could accept the scientific view of the universe. Many scientists understandably retorted that if religion thus sought to blockade a process that was making great contributions to knowledge and to man's mastery of his environment, religion was an enemy to progress and human welfare.

The bewildered public, equally anxious to retain some form of spiritual faith and to accept the advantages and enlightenments of science, was unwilling to accept either of these mutually exclusive points of view, and yet felt that if trained minds were so antagonistic, the average intelligence had no hope of comprehension.

In the practical problems of economic and social change, there were equally baffling challenges. Contrasts of great wealth and abject poverty, of national prosperity and individual hardships, of democratic theory and oligarchic practice, made the average citizen uncomfortably aware that something was wrong. The politicians were not much more helpful here than the churchmen were in spiritual affairs. The two old parties, Whig and Tory, which had comfortably alternated in power for a century, had no place in their ranks or in their policies even for the newly-rich city businessman, let alone for the inarticulate masses of labor. Both parties, in their intensified struggle for power, adopted changes of policy that obscured their old identities. A vague third party, the Radicals, never reached the stage of separate organization. Abortive proletarian movements died for lack of leadership. Some of the bitterest parliamentary crises concerned almost extraneous matters, such as Home Rule for Ireland; seldom did debates in Commons come to grips with economic and social fundamentals. The English representative system did prove adequate to promote a gradual program of needed legislation, but in a blundering manner that gained little public confidence. Few political leaders were able to hold the sincere respect of even their own partisans.

In the midst of so much confusion and controversy, the only informed minds that could offer dispassionate analysis and recommendations were to be found in literature. Throughout the Victorian period, therefore, the career of almost every author illustrated a single phenomenon: a gradual and almost unwilling conversion to a concern with spiritual and social discussion. A writer might begin as a humorist (Dickens), an art critic (Ruskin), a verbal musician (Tennyson, Swinburne), a medievalist (Morris); but sooner or later his conscience told him that he was shirking his duty if he did not offer his quota of advice. The eager acceptance of his views was enough to convince him that he was doing the right thing. As the public insisted upon treating authors as prophets and seers, no author could entirely avoid assuming something of the appropriate portentousness.

Their contributions were far from temporary. The chief reason that they often seem to us to be elaborating the obvious or exciting themselves over trivialities is that much of their doctrine became accepted and now forms part of our basic religious and social assumptions. We may be able to estimate these assumptions of ours more clearly if we investigate their Victorian origins.

By too much discussion of the ideas in Victorian literature one is in danger of ignoring another and equally important aspect. No matter how much these authors concerned themselves with the debating of opinions, they never forgot that they were literary artists. Inheriting all the experiments and achievements of centuries, they possessed a greater range of literary forms and verbal devices than any previous generation had enjoyed. The novel became preëminent in scope and variety, historical writing gained new color and drama, lyrical and reflective poetry was rich in imagery and music, even long narrative poems by means of new techniques appealed to a wide public. Except in the drama, Victorian authors were masters of craftsmanship.

Their technical skill was not entirely balanced by a sense

of concentration. Because they had so much to say, and because the mood of their time was leisurely and spacious, the authors did not stint their words. The novels of Dickens, the histories of Carlyle, the monologues of Browning, even the passionate lyrics of Swinburne might have been greater works if they had been condensed. And yet for the harassed modern reader one of the lasting values of the Victorians is their expansiveness. People are turning back to the novels of Trollope with assurance that life can there be savored with fullness and without strain. The student of Victorian literature must be urged to avoid cramming and skimming, to read slowly, a chapter or a poem at a time. The authors wrote with the expectation of being read aloud to a family circle that had no radio or motion pictures to provide entertainment of more rapid tempo.

The Victorians came so near to perfection in handling their accepted techniques that the writers of the next generation were obliged to attempt radical new departures in order to escape detrimental comparisons. In literature, as in the other arts, the vogue of "modernism" is now ceasing to be exclusive, and the merits of the ornate and traditional Victorian artistry are receiving due recognition.

POLITICAL HISTORY
>>>

The history of England in the reign of Victoria is "political history" in a stricter sense than it was in any previous era—that is, there were fewer major wars, international complications, or startling public events, and a greater concentration upon a sequence of legislative acts which profoundly influenced the life of the nation.

The first significant event, nearly a decade before Victoria came to the throne, was the passage of the Catholic Emancipation Act. When the Irish Parliament had been abolished in 1800, and one hundred Irish members had been added to the English House of Commons, a promise was given that the laws against permitting Roman Catholics to hold public office would be abrogated. This change, however, was not carried out, and consequently the majority of Irishmen could not be represented in Parliament by members of their faith. The matter came to a head in 1828, when an eloquent and bold Irish Catholic, Daniel O'Connell, insisted on being a candidate. Upon his being elected, the Prime Minister, the Duke of Wellington, at the head of a reactionary Tory cabinet, refused to admit him. Threats of an Irish uprising, however, forced the Prime Minister to change his mind, and the new law, granting civic rights to Catholics, was pushed through Parliament in 1829.

This encouraged the proponents of other reform measures, and when the death of King George IV caused a general election, the Whig party was brought into office for the first time in almost thirty years, on a platform of extensive revision of the electoral system, which was long overdue.

Although the members of Parliament were nominally elected by all property-owning citizens, the number of voters had decreased since the eighteenth century, so that the power of electing a member was often confined to a small group or to a single powerful landlord. The buying of votes was openly practiced. During the great shift of population resulting from the Industrial Revolution, no readjustment of constituencies had been made, and so there were many rural "rotten boroughs" which still had the right to a seat in Parliament, though there were practically no inhabitants; whereas the new industrial cities of the Midlands were unrepresented.

The Tory party, representing the old land-owning aristocracy, favored continuance of this system which perpetuated their power. The Whigs were more closely related with the newly powerful class of businessmen in the cities, who had grown rich through the Industrial Revolution and the Napoleonic wars and who were eager to obtain more influence in the government of the country, as well as to win the social prestige that their wealth entitled them to.

In 1831 Lord John Russell, on behalf of the new Whig cabinet, introduced a Reform Bill in the House of Commons. After a long series of filibusters and other parliamentary maneuvers, including two resignations of the cabinet (each of which only strengthened its position), the bill was finally forced to passage in June, 1832. It disfranchised towns under 2000 inhabitants, and the seats thus released were allotted to the large centers of population. The vote was extended to every man who occupied property with an annual rental value of ten pounds, thus giving a voice to the lower middle class but not yet to the workers. Only one-twentieth of the population could vote.

Other social legislation was adopted in the next few years. An efficient force of police, first organized in London in 1829 by the Tory Sir Robert Peel (and hence nicknamed "Bobbies" or "Peelers") was extended throughout the country. Slavery was abolished in the British Colonies. A new system of workhouses for able-bodied paupers replaced the antiquated "poor laws." Municipal government, which had been in the hands of the guilds ever since the Middle Ages, was turned over to elected officials. The significance of these breaks with past custom seemed to be symbolized by the fire which in 1834 destroyed Westminster Palace, in which Parliament had sat for five hundred years.

The Whig government also took a strong stand in international affairs. Lord Palmerston, as Foreign Secretary, lent England's support to the new "People's Monarchy" of Louis Philippe in France, and gave active help to revolutionary movements in Belgium, Spain, and Portugal. In the Near East, however, he upheld the obsolete Turkish empire in order to prevent Russian expansion. Palmerston's policy withdrew England from the "Concert of Europe" in which she had participated since the Napoleonic wars, and he used his country's power as a free agent for preventing any continental nation from growing too strong. When France threatened reprisals against British intrusion in the Near East, which was regarded as a French "sphere of influence,"

SIR ROBERT PEEL

Palmerston coolly defied the threats and called the French bluff. Until 1837 the British foreign policy was complicated by the fact that the King of England was also King of Hanover; but as Victoria could not inherit the Germanic crown, Britain's last link with the Continent was severed.

When Victoria came to the throne, therefore, she found her country well launched, both internally and externally, on a program of cautious liberalism. Lord Melbourne, who had become Prime Minister shortly before, was an agreeable gentleman who gained strong ascendancy over the young Queen's mind.

New political forces, however, once they were set in motion by the Reform Bill, soon complicated the comfortable old arrangement by which Whigs and Tories alternated in power, both equally identified with the old hereditary aristocracy. Businessmen who believed in Adam Smith's laissez-faire theories of economics, with the accompanying utilitarian philosophy of "the greatest happiness of the greatest number," became something like a third party, known as "the Manchester school" because it centered in that rapidly-growing industrial city and was led by Richard Cobden, who used the pseudonym "A Manchester Merchant." The basic tenet of this party was Free Trade, because they realized that England was in a position to profit by heavy exporting of manufactured goods, whereas both Tories and Whigs clung to protective tariffs on the old theory of sheltering local producers from foreign rivals. The Free Traders believed also in disarmament and isolationism in England's foreign relations, in contrast to Palmerston's venturous policy. They had welcomed the Reform Bill because they expected it to give them enough political power to force the introduction of Free Trade; and they became disgusted with the Whig government for its retention of tariffs.

The "Manchester Men" were sincere in their devotion to public welfare and world peace. In particular, John Bright, who shared the leadership with Cobden, was an eloquent moralist and an earnest Quaker. But their capitalistic doctrines insisted that prosperity for everyone could be gained only through unfettered competition, mass production, and low wages. Therefore they regarded any humanitarian legislation suspiciously if it implied government interference with industry or with individual liberty. They opposed efforts toward reform of factory conditions, hours of labor, and so forth; they approved of the new police system as a safeguard against disorder among the lower classes; and they insisted that the new workhouses should be too uncomfortable to encourage any able-bodied laborer to avoid the distasteful working conditions by going on relief. For these reasons the "Manchester Men" won the contempt of idealistic reformers like Carlyle and Dickens, who accused them of being greedy, heartless, and hypocritical.

The problem of the welfare of the poor loomed large in the arguments of another trouble-making group, the Radical

RICHARD COBDEN

JOHN BRIGHT

FREE TRADE HALL, MANCHESTER

party, political philosophers who had supported the Reform Bill on ideological rather than on material grounds, and who now, under the leadership of Francis Place, Joseph Parkes, and Joseph Hume, demanded the extension of the franchise to include the working class. As their supporters were chiefly the people not entitled to vote, the Radicals held few seats in Parliament; but they kept up vigorous propaganda and they managed to win office in many of the new municipal councils.

The underprivileged labor class began to seek direct channels of action on their own behalf. Both in the country and in the cities, working conditions were miserable. The agricultural laborers, goaded by unemployment and hunger, had been poaching, rioting, and burning farmers' haystacks at intervals for a decade. In the huge new cities the factory workers suffered from dangerous conditions, long hours, and unhealthy slum housing. Child labor, both in factories and in mines, was an atrocity.

The possibility of remedying these abuses had been shown by Robert Owen, a successful cotton-mill owner of Manchester and Lanark, who had introduced improved working conditions in his own factories and who as early as 1815 drew up a parliamentary bill to control child labor, hours of work, and so on. He also proposed an elaborate scheme of coöperative communities for workers. Although these suggestions produced only slight practical results, they called public attention to the situation.

In 1824 Trade Unions were legalized, but they were denied the right to strike. During the next ten years they began, under Owen's guidance, to group themselves into large inter-craft organizations, until in 1834 a Grand National Consolidated Trades Union was formed with half a million members. Adverse forces quickly came into action, and as a test case six laborers of Dorsetshire were brought to trial for "administering unlawful oaths." When these "Tolpuddle martyrs" (as they came to be called) were sentenced to the penal colonies, the Union movement temporarily collapsed.

Another line of action was then attempted. Beginning as an agitation in northern England against the severity of the new Poor Laws, working men's associations were formed everywhere to demand a further Reform Bill. The demands were formulated in 1838 as "the People's Charter," embracing six points—universal franchise, secret ballot, equal size of all constituencies, annual elections, eligibility of any voter to be elected to Parliament, and salaries for Members. The Chartists assembled in a "People's Parliament" in London and Birmingham in 1839, and gathered signatures to a petition to the government, with noisy threats of revolt if it were rejected. Through inexperienced leadership, however, the uprising disintegrated and its leaders were imprisoned. The movement was renewed in 1842, when a petition with several million signatures was presented in Parliament, but it was overwhelmingly voted down.

All this ferment had its effect upon the Tory party. Its younger leaders realized that they could never return to the old reactionary principles; the only way to regain power would be by showing a stronger concern for popular welfare than did the capitalistic Whigs. When a revulsion of public feeling brought defeat to the Whig government in the election of 1841, the Tories, under the premiership of Sir Robert Peel, had a chance to prove their change of heart.

Anthony Ashley Cooper (later Earl of Shaftesbury) forced the appointment of a Royal Commission to investigate child labor, and its report horrified the public so deeply that Cooper was able to put through a bill prohibiting the employment of girls and women in the coal mines. Against violent opposition both from the Manchester liberals and from his own Tory Prime Minister, he went on to agitate for a ten-hour working day for adults, eight-hour for children.

Peel, meanwhile, was faced with desperate economic problems. Because manufacturers could not afford to pay the duties on raw materials, unemployment was rife in the cities; and as the revenue from tariffs dwindled, the national budget showed a heavy deficit. Peel promptly won favor with the Free Traders by removing the duties on a number of imports; but he annoyed the businessmen when he compensated for the loss of revenue by introducing an income tax. His attitude toward Free Trade soon involved a more fundamental issue. One of the most conspicuous protective tariffs was on wheat, as a safeguard for British farmers. Since their production was inadequate for the enlarged population, the exorbitant price of bread contributed largely to the semi-starvation of the poor. The "Corn Laws" therefore became bitterly hated by the lower classes, and the Free Traders seized this public unrest to strengthen their cause. Cobden and Bright had organized the "Anti-Corn-Law League" in 1838 and kept up a torrent of propaganda. For several years Peel opposed their arguments, but in 1845 a failure of the English harvest and an outbreak of potato blight in Ireland meant a threat of actual famine. Peel announced his conversion to the Free Trade theory and finally carried the repeal of the Corn Laws, with the support of most of the Whigs and against the opposition of many of his own colleagues.

This split marked the end of the old Tory party. Ever since Catholic Emancipation, the balance of power in the House of Commons had been held by the Irish Members, who used every parliamentary device to strengthen their own campaign for restoration of Home Rule in Ireland. In 1843 there was so much friction that Peel indiscreetly sent Daniel O'Connell to prison; two years later the potato famine brought Irish unrest to a crisis which Peel tried to curb by a "Coercion Bill." On this issue the Whigs combined with the Irish Members and the anti-Peel faction of the Tories to force him out of office.

The change of economic policy was already justifying itself. English trade had recovered so rapidly after the removal of duties on raw materials that by 1845 a budget surplus could be applied to the national debt. Thereafter for many years the pound sterling was the undisputed standard of international finance and English factories supplied the markets of the world.

The revolutionary movements which swept Europe in 1848 left England almost immune. The Chartists made another effort to gain their ends, this time echoing the continental disturbances by demanding that England should become a republic; but once again their monster petition was rejected by Parliament, and the Chartist leaders soon fell out among themselves.

While times were good the Trade Union movement was able to rebuild itself. Local trade clubs united on a national basis, but these were restricted to the separate crafts and aimed chiefly to provide mutual benefit insurance. The Amalgamated Society of Engineers, founded in 1851, became a model of a well-planned and responsible union.

This era of prosperity was enhanced by the development of such conveniences as the telegraph, steamships, and railways. As well as contributing to the expansion of trade in general, these innovations brought wealth to their own promoters. Railway speculation in particular was so rife in the forties that some spectacular bankruptcies resulted; but times were so good that the railway companies were able to reorganize and overcome their failures.

The acknowledged commercial preëminence of England, with its corollary of world peace, was symbolized by the great International Exhibition of 1851, which brought visitors from all nations to the huge Crystal Palace in Hyde

Park, where they inspected the products of British industry and listened to optimistic speeches about human brotherhood and the abolition of war.

The years of prosperity meant long tenure for the political party in power. The Whig government, with the popular Lord John Russell as Prime Minister, and Viscount Palmerston back in the Foreign Office, lasted from 1847 to 1852. Its fall was caused by one of Palmerston's typically headstrong actions. Louis Napoleon, who had led the formation of the second French republic less than four years before, now made himself dictator and Emperor of France. The English government was horrified, but Palmerston on his own initiative announced approval of the violent *coup d'état*. He was removed from the office of Foreign Secretary, but in the upheaval the government was defeated. For a few months the strife-torn Tories tried feebly to govern the country, only to give place to a potent coalition of Peelite Tories and Whigs. Peel himself had died in 1850, but two of his strongest followers were in the new cabinet—Lord Aberdeen, as Prime Minister, and William Ewart Gladstone, as Chancellor of the Exchequer (the English term for Minister of Finance).

The other wing of the Tory party, claiming a new title as "Conservatives," was under the leadership of the brilliant writer, orator, and political strategist, Benjamin Disraeli, who had somewhat ruthlessly strengthened his own position by leading the overthrow of Peel. The landowning aristocrats and squires, who comprised Disraeli's party, remained suspicious of his dramatic manners, mischievous wit, and alien background, but by his audacity in Parliament and his appeal to the voters at elections he proved himself indispensable.

In the new cabinet Palmerston could not be reappointed as Foreign Secretary; but in the supposedly harmless office of Home Secretary he remained the strong man of the government, with an immense influence over public opinion. He very soon had a chance to exercise it, in an international crisis which arose to discredit the idealists who had recently been proclaiming the obsolescence of war.

Russia had resumed a war of nerves against the feeble Turkish empire which still ruled the whole of the Balkans and the Near East. As a pretext for intervention, the Czar seized upon a squabble between the Roman Catholic and the Greek Orthodox churches over the administration of the Christian shrines in Jerusalem, which the Turkish government allowed them to control. The Czar demanded recognition as legal protector of all Christians in any part of the Turkish territories. When the British Ambassador encouraged the Sultan to reject the claim, the Russian army invaded Turkey's northern frontier.

As England was not directly concerned in the dispute, Russia felt safe in her aggression. Palmerston, however, was still obsessed with his idea that if Russia won access to the Mediterranean England's life-line route to India would be destroyed. He used all his power to drive the reluctant English government into a show of force, and his efforts were strengthened by his friend across the Channel, Napoleon III, who was eager to justify his seizure of power in France by some spectacular victory. When the English fleet was ordered to the eastern Mediterranean, the French Emperor sent his warships too, and made warlike gestures that intensified the crisis. Palmerston used the well-worn device of resigning from the cabinet in order to rouse public sentiment against the Prime Minister's cautious policy. In November, 1853, a Turkish squadron was sunk by Russian ships. A few weeks later, England and France declared war on Russia.

British public opinion had begun by supporting Palmerston's belligerent attitude because of long-standing confidence in his successful waging of cold war and also through loyalty to the nation's pledges of aid to Turkey. But when hostilities actually started there was a change of mood. Any war would have been repugnant to the humanitarian ideals of the time; but there was further humiliation in being allied with the degenerate overlords of a non-Christian tyranny and with the aggressive dictator of England's traditional rival, France.

FLORENCE NIGHTINGALE

Besides, the country was totally unprepared for waging successful war, which required modern equipment, adequate supplies, and military experience. The British army had taken part in no full-scale fighting for forty years. The high command consisted of officers who had been subalterns at Waterloo and had made no further progress in military science. The war was particularly difficult because of the long supply line between England and the Crimea, where the campaign was being fought. The severe Russian winter caused great hardship.

In the year-long siege of Sebastopol and the fierce battles of Alma, Balaclava, and Inkerman, the troops showed admirable bravery; but inept generalship cost heavy casualties, and even greater suffering arose from disease, frostbite, infected wounds, and bad rations. The only person who won credit in the war was the indomitable Florence Nightingale, who not only organized the first modern nursing service, and improved the intolerable conditions in many respects, but while doing so exposed the stupidity and arrogance of some of the political and military leaders.

Growing public disfavor toward the mismanagement of the war caused the removal of Lord Aberdeen from the premiership. He was replaced by the one man who could restore the morale of the nation, Lord Palmerston, who was seventy but still full of vigor. By that time some of the logistic problems were being solved, and the antiquated officials replaced by men of action. Heavy reinforcements reached the Crimea, and Italy joined the allies. In September, 1855, Sebastopol fell and the war was over; but the Russians owed their defeat as much to their own incompetence as to the skill of their enemies, and England felt no great jubilation in the victory.

Palmerston, however, was the hero of the occasion, and the international prestige of Britain was higher than ever. It was largely through English encouragement that Garibaldi was able to unify Italy without intervention from other European powers. As far afield as Afghanistan and China English expeditionary forces asserted the authority of their nation.

This authority was soon challenged by a crucial uprising in India. The British control of the huge sub-continent had begun as a form of commercial penetration, and still much of the administration was in the hands of the East India Company, which had organized an army of native troops ("Sepoys") under British officers. Large matters of policy were determined by a committee of the English Privy Council, with a Cabinet Minister as chairman.

During the first half of the nineteenth century vast additional areas came under British dominance, although the numerous native princes kept a semblance of local authority. The English were not unaware of the problems and responsibilities of ruling three hundred million people of varied languages, religions, and racial strains. As early as 1836, Thomas Babington Macaulay, while serving on the administrative council of Calcutta, introduced plans for Westernized education for natives so that they could eventually take part in the management of the country. Railways, telegraphs, and other modern facilities were introduced, and laws were enacted against such practices as suttee and thuggery. The strict caste distinctions were regarded by the British officials with disfavor. Christian missionaries preached the superiority of their creed over Islamism, Hinduism, and Buddhism.

These interferences with habit and tradition were resented by the Indian people. Withdrawal of English troops for the Crimean war left the little groups of officials almost defenseless. In 1857 a bloody revolt broke out among the Sepoy regiments. Many Europeans were imprisoned or slaughtered, and several forts withstood long and desperate sieges before reinforcements could make the slow voyage around the Cape of Good Hope from England. When the Mutiny was broken by the end of 1858, the English government avoided extreme reprisals, terminated the rule of the East India Company, and set up a new administrative system with all responsibility centered in a department of the British government in London.

This was one aspect of a profoundly important change that was occurring almost unrecognized. While Palmerston remained chiefly interested in England's relationship to the balance of power on the Continent, a world-wide British empire was coming into being. The Canadian colonies demanded self-government in the year Queen Victoria came to the throne, and in the sixties were making plans for union into a single large entity. Australia, regarded as so remote from the rest of the world that Botany Bay had seemed ideal as a place of exile for convicts, assumed sudden economic importance with the discovery of gold in 1851, and the various states organized responsible government within the next decade. Self-government came to New Zealand in 1856. In South Africa British control since the beginning of the century had spread northward from Cape Colony. As abolition of slavery in 1833 had driven the Dutch farmers to migrate further into the wilderness, the British government in 1854 recognized the two Dutch republics—the Transvaal and the Orange Free State—but ensured the retention of Cape Colony and Natal in the empire by granting them representative government. In addition to all these extensive dependencies, England had a chain of Crown Colonies all around the world, from the West Indies to Singapore.

Palmerston, remaining largely oblivious to these remote developments, also ignored demands for further political freedom within England. The last of the old-school Whigs, he complacently assumed that English social and political conditions were perfect and therefore fully justified the nation's paternalistic attitude toward the rest of the world. Disraeli and his energetic Conservative party became much better aware of the implications of the overseas empire.

In 1858 Palmerston's cabinet was unexpectedly defeated over a minor issue connected with his support of the French Emperor, who was growing more and more hated in England. The Earl of Derby, titular head of the Conservative party, became Prime Minister, with Disraeli as Chancellor of the Exchequer and leader of the House of Commons. A bill to grant civic equality to Jews was passed, and early in 1859 Disraeli introduced a new Reform Bill along the lines now-a-days termed "the corporative state," with votes allotted to various professions and social groups. On this issue the government was defeated and Palmerston came back into power after only a year in opposition.

The connection of British prosperity with her overseas trade was emphasized by the American Civil War, which, by cutting off the supply of cotton to the Lancashire mills, brought immediate unemployment, hunger, and unrest. Employers' associations had come into existence to fight the growing power of the unions, strikes and lockouts led to bitter riots, and some attempt was made to establish arbitration boards.

Public opinion was painfully split on the American war. English humanitarianism dictated sympathy for the abolitionists, but the embargo on cotton aroused anger against the Northern States, and it was intensified by their violation of British neutrality in the *Trent* incident, which roused Palmerston to threats of war. A little later the *Alabama* affair gave equal cause for rage against England on the part of Lincoln's government. In both crises, wise statesmanship in the two countries averted hostilities that seemed imminent.

Lord Palmerston died in 1865, still leading the government in his eighty-first year. He was followed by the former Lord John Russell, who by this time had inherited the family earldom. Old tradition still favored a nobleman as Prime Minister; but more and more of the actual party control was coming into the hands of the leader of the House of Commons, a post now assumed by William Ewart Gladstone. Originally a Peelite Tory, he had remained an ally of the Whigs after the coalition of 1852, and when he became Chancellor of the Exchequer again under Palmerston in 1859 it was obvious that he would never go back to his former party. He had come to be the chief adversary of Disraeli in the House of Commons, his puritanical integrity, austere manner, and exhaustive accuracy making an extreme contrast with Disraeli's brilliant rhetoric and exotic appearance. Both men had ability in authorship, but Disraeli's talent ran to fiction and satire, Gladstone's to ancient history and theological theory.

Gladstone's budgets extended Free Trade to its fullest possible extent; and by successive reductions of the income tax he hoped (though vainly) to abolish it altogether. He opposed expenditures on military armament. In 1866 he proposed a new Reform Bill, which was defeated in Parliament, bringing a Conservative ministry into power. Disraeli then persuaded Lord Derby to put through another Reform Bill, which went further than the one recently rejected. It canceled all property qualifications for voters in the cities, and sharply reduced them for those in rural areas. About a million new voters, all of the laboring class, were thus added. Disraeli believed in a mutual obligation between the aristocracy and the workers, and he thought that the latter should realize that the Conservative party was more concerned for their welfare than were the capitalistic Whigs—or Liberals, as they were now more often called. In 1868 Lord Derby resigned through ill-health, and Disraeli's ambition was at last rewarded with the premiership. His party, however, lacked a clear majority in Parliament, and he had to call a general election, which brought the Liberals back into power and put his rival, Gladstone, in his place as Prime Minister.

Gladstone faced serious problems. Discontent in Ireland had reached such a crisis that he felt obliged to pass a Coercion Act, as Peel had tried to do (disastrously for himself) over twenty years before. In compensation, Gladstone sought to improve the conditions of the Irish masses by "disestablishing" the Episcopal Church in Ireland and by a Land Act that forced absentee landlords to grant favors to their tenants. Although Gladstone was himself a devout Episcopalian and a rich landowner, his policies horrified Englishmen of those categories, who feared that he might proceed to similar innovations in their own country. Fanatically insistent upon governmental economy, he set the reduction of the national debt above other matters which many people considered more essential to the country's welfare. In the course of his career he had changed his opinions on many questions; and while his admirers held that this proved the sincerity of his "Liberal" attitude, his opponents accused him of being a hypocritical opportunist. The religious and industrial middle class idolized him, while the aristocrats hated him as a traitor to his own rank.

His administration was notable for passing the Education Act of 1870, which established a state-supported system of schools; but it alienated some strong supporters among Nonconformist sects by prohibiting the teaching of religion in the "national" schools while permitting it in those supported by the Church of England. In 1872 another significant piece of legislation introduced the secret ballot for all elections.

WILLIAM EWART
GLADSTONE

In foreign policy Gladstone's government failed to hold the public confidence. In contrast with Palmerston's constant jealousy for British prestige, and Disraeli's romantic pride in the vastness of the empire, Gladstone could be called an isolationist. The Franco-Prussian war forced him unwillingly to approve enlarged grants for maintaining the army and navy, but he still insisted that England ought to avoid every possible entanglement in continental power politics.

During the Franco-Prussian war English sympathy tended toward the German cause. The Queen's German husband had won wide popularity before his untimely death, and their eldest daughter was married to the heir to the new German throne. Thomas Carlyle had helped to popularize German philosophy and scholarship. With the oppressive terms inflicted upon France, however, some Englishmen began to wonder whether the elimination of the belligerent Emperor Napoleon might not merely have substituted one dangerous rival for another.

Having lost the respect of the public, Gladstone's ministry was soundly defeated in 1874. Though the Con-

servatives had held office briefly on three occasions since the downfall of Peel in 1846, this was the first time in those thirty years that the party had enjoyed a real majority in Parliament and an opportunity of enforcing a consistent policy. An unusually able group of ministers formed the new cabinet; and the Queen, who had begun to dislike the rigid Mr. Gladstone, was warmly sympathetic to Disraeli's imaginative enthusiasm.

BENJAMIN DISRAELI,
LORD BEACONSFIELD

On internal matters, the principal legislation was a Housing Bill granting power to local authorities to rebuild slums, a Factory Act which regulated working conditions, and a Trade Unions Bill which at last legalized the right to strike. In foreign affairs Disraeli pursued an interest in Asia which had been a leading element in his thinking throughout his career. With picturesque ceremonies Queen Victoria was proclaimed Empress of India. England bought a controlling interest in the French-sponsored canal through the Isthmus of Suez, which was not only a great advantage in world trade but also a safeguard of Britain's military access to her Far Eastern domains.

In 1878, when the Balkans revolted against the Turkish empire, Disraeli maintained Britain's old support of the Sultan, though in the face of scathing denunciations from Gladstone, who eloquently condemned the Turkish cruelty in Bulgaria and championed the oppressed nationalities. When Russia intervened, Disraeli openly hinted that England was ready for war, whereupon several of his cabinet, recalling the miseries of the Crimean campaign, resigned. In the Congress of Berlin, which convened after the end of the Russo-Turkish War, Disraeli took the lead (along with the German delegates) in thwarting Russian claims to influence over the new Balkan states.

In spite of this triumph, Disraeli was losing public support. A depression hit the English farmers, and the government was also blamed for misfortunes in remote corners of the empire. The British consular staff in Afghanistan was massacred. The Dutch settlers in South Africa got into trouble with their Zulu neighbors, and when Britain tried to control it by annexing the Transvaal republic, the only result was increased fury among the Zulus, who in one battle massacred a whole British battalion. In the election of 1880 the Liberals won a large majority, and Disraeli (who had been raised to the peerage) retired from politics, and died a year later.

Upon returning to power, Gladstone confronted difficult and dangerous situations growing out of the rapid expansion of the empire and lack of coördination in its system of government. Nearest to home, unrest in Ireland had reached a new pitch under the leadership of Charles Stewart Parnell, who organized a "Land League" which began to use terroristic methods in the hope of driving the hated landlords out of the country. Gladstone hastened to pass a law reducing rents for Irish tenants, but the Home Rule agitators were unappeased, and two prominent English officials were murdered in Dublin. Once again a Coercion

Act was considered necessary to control the reign of violence.

On the northern frontier of India, forays of native bandits kept the English troops in a recurrent state of guerilla war, and the occupation forces in Afghanistan suffered a humiliating defeat in 1880. In South Africa there was trouble not only with the Zulus but also with the Dutch ("Boer") farmers, who declared war on the colonial government and wiped out a British detachment at Majuba Hill in 1881. Insisting on a conciliatory policy, Gladstone granted full freedom once more to the Boer republics, and thereby was accused of weakness.

The most serious misfortune, however, was in North Africa, where the British support of the Khedive of Egypt (a corollary of controlling the Suez Canal) led to involvement in suppressing native insurrections. A picturesque and popular hero of the time, General Charles Gordon, was sent to the Sudan to deal with a fanatical rebel, and exceeded his orders by occupying the town of Khartoum, which was at once besieged. For months Gladstone refused to send aid, while the British public became hysterical with anxiety. By the time a belated relief expedition reached Khartoum, the fort had surrendered and Gordon had been killed.

All these conflicts were peculiarly embarrassing to a party which claimed to disapprove of war and to protect minorities. Almost unperceived in the uproar over imperial policy, the government enacted the Third Reform Bill, granting the vote at last to all householders—an increase of almost two million voters. This gesture was no longer so progressive as it would have seemed fifty years before, for new radical ideas were in the air. The theories of Henry George were rousing the workers to challenge the rights of property, and Marx's assaults on capitalism were accepted by the Democratic Federation, founded by H. M. Hyndman in 1881. Three years later a faction under the poet, William

Morris, preferring anarchistic ideology to Marxian, broke away from it to form the Socialist League. At the same time another group, favoring a moderate, evolutionary socialism, derived from John Stuart Mill and William Stanley Jevons, organized the Fabian Society to spread Socialist ideas among all parties instead of demanding sudden revolution—a policy more attractive to the British temperament. The Trade Unions became interested in the new theories, and James Kier Hardie took the lead in establishing the Independent Labour Party (1893) to give working-class Socialists a political voice.

Gladstone, meanwhile, in 1886 tried to settle the Irish problem with a bill granting Home Rule to Ireland. Again he was blamed for weak surrender to agitators, and a large number of prominent Liberals refused to support the bill. Upon its rejection in Parliament he appealed to the country in a general election, and was heavily defeated. The triumphant Conservatives even changed the name of their party to "Unionist" to signify their determination to keep Ireland and England united.

The remaining years of the century were politically uneventful. When the Liberals returned to power between 1892 and 1895, Gladstone, now over eighty, introduced another Home Rule Bill, which passed the House of Commons but failed in the Lords. For the rest of the time the Unionists, with Lord Salisbury as Prime Minister, maintained their emphasis upon the expansion of the empire, as symbolized by the pageantry for the Queen's golden and diamond jubilees (1887 and 1897).

In spite of the glow of patriotic pride and the continued British domination in international affairs, the great age of Victorian supremacy was waning. Germany now, rather than Russia, was the foreign power suspected of fomenting every disturbance aimed at undermining British ascendancy. Unrest still seethed intermittently in Ireland, India, and

Egypt, but it was South Africa that brought the empire to its most disturbing peril. The northward expansion of the colonies, under the aggressive leadership of Cecil Rhodes, threatened the Dutch areas with encirclement, and the development of rich diamond and gold mines in the Transvaal brought economic pressures. In October, 1899, the Boer republics declared war on Britain.

In spite of the great disparity of strength, the "embattled farmers" had the advantage of fighting on their own soil, and of adapting their methods to the peculiar nature of the terrain, whereas the disciplined British troops were far from home and unfamiliar with the conditions. As in England's previous war, half a century before, supplies at first were inadequate and leadership was in the hands of elderly officers not adaptable to modern methods. The war dragged on, with prolonged sieges of Mafeking and Ladysmith, until reinforced British troops, under Lord Roberts, crushed the organized opposition, and after many more months of guerilla fighting, the Boers surrendered in June, 1902.

In spite of the imperial pride and patriotism that had sustained England through the war, many people felt uncomfortable about the violence that had been necessarily employed against a non-militaristic, God-fearing adversary. Although the Boers had been disappointed in their hopes of armed intervention by Germany or other nations, England had enjoyed little sympathy from her continental neighbors. The death of Queen Victoria in the middle of the war seemed ominous of an uncertain and frustrative future for the empire that had enjoyed growth, prestige, and prosperity during her sixty-four years on the throne.

Cambridge Modern History, XI, XII (London, 1909-10); *Cambridge History of the British Empire,* II-VIII (London, 1929-37); C. A. Fyffe, *A History of Modern Europe* (3v, London, 1880-90); G. P. Gooch, *A History of Modern Europe, 1878-1919* (London, 1923); C. J. Hayes, *A Political and Cultural History of Modern*

Europe, II (New York, 1936); J. McCarthy, *A History of Our Own Times* (5v, London, 1879-97) ; E. Halévy, *Histoire du peuple anglais aux XIXe siècle* (5v, Paris, 1912-28; Engl. trans., London, 1924-34) ; H. Paul, *History of Modern England* (5v, London, 1904-06); S. Low and L. C. Sanders, *The History of England During the Reign of Victoria* (London, 1907); J. A. R. Marriott, *England Since Waterloo* (London, 1913); *Social England,* VI, ed. H. D. Traill (London, 1898) ; T. H. S. Escott, *Social Transformations of the Victorian Age* (London, 1897) ; G. M. Young, *Victorian England: Portrait of an Age* (London, 1936); G. M. Trevelyan, *British History in the Nineteenth Century* (London, 1922; rev. ed., 1938); A. Bryant, *English Saga, 1840-1940* (London, 1940); H. V. Routh, *England Under Victoria* (London, 1930); *Early Victorian England,* ed. G. M. Young (2v, London, 1934) ; E. L. Woodward, *The Age of Reform, 1815-70* (London, 1938); S. Walpole, *The History of Twenty-five Years, 1856-1880* (4v, London, 1904-08) ; R. C. K. Ensor, *England, 1870-1915* (London, 1936); O. F. Christie, *The Transition to Democracy, 1867-1914* (London, 1934) ; D. C. Somervell, *Modern Britain, 1870-1939* (London, 1941); J. A. R. Marriott, *Modern England, 1885-1932* (London, 1934); J. H. Clapham, *An Economic History of Modern Britain* (3v, London, 1930-38); A. B. Keith, *The Constitution of England from Victoria to George VI* (2v, London, 1940); G. M. Trevelyan, *Lord Grey and the Reform Bill* (London, 1920); B. Newman, *Lord Melbourne* (London, 1930); J. L. and B. Hammond, *The Age of the Chartists* (London, 1930; rev. ed. with title *The Bleak Age,* 1947) ; M. Hovell, *The Chartist Movement* (Manchester, 1918) ; P. Guedalla, *Palmerston* (London, 1927); T. Lever, *The Life and Times of Sir Robert Peel* (London, 1942); J. Morley, *Life of Gladstone* (3v, London, 1903); D. C. Somervell, *Disraeli and Gladstone* (London, 1926); H. M. Lynd, *England in the Eighteen-eighties* (New York, 1945).

LIFE OF QUEEN VICTORIA

>>>

A sudden and violent change in the lives of the English royal family was caused by the death, at the age of twenty-one, of Princess Charlotte, on November 6, 1817. As the only child of the Prince Regent (later George IV) she had been the heir to the throne. Although six sons of George III were living, none of them had legitimate children. In order to save the dynasty from being diverted to a remote branch, three of the elderly princes hastily married suitable German princesses. One of them, Edward, Duke of Kent, fourth son of George III, chose as his wife Princess Maria Louisa Victoria, widow of the Prince of Leiningen, and the mother of two children. It was perhaps not a coincidence that she was the sister of the ambitious and astute Prince Leopold of Saxe-Coburg-Saalfeld, who had been the husband of the unhappy young Princess Charlotte.

Alexandrina Victoria, only daughter of the Duke and Duchess of Kent, was born at Kensington Palace on May 24, 1819. Her father died when Victoria was eight months old. His place as adviser was filled by her maternal uncle, Leopold, who lived in England until she was twelve and who thus found an opportunity of being almost as influential in English affairs as he would have been if his wife had lived and he had become Prince Consort. He was determined that Victoria should be expert in statecraft; her mother, horrified at the moral laxity of George IV and his brothers, was equally determined that the little girl should learn to be severely virtuous.

When Victoria was five, a thoroughly competent governess, named Lehnzen, was imported from Coburg to supervise her training. The girl's imperious spirit was chafed by her mother's fussy control; as she grew up she became more and more devoted to Fraülein Lehnzen, showing a proper respect toward her mother but no strong affection. Because of the antipathy between her mother and the English princes, Victoria seldom saw them, and lived under Coburg influences almost as fully as if she were not in England at all.

Subjected to a rigorous discipline in education, Victoria

never exchanged a word with any adult except when her mother or her governess was in the room, and until she was twelve she did not know of her future prospects as queen. When, according to the plan of her Uncle Leopold, the fact was revealed to her in the course of a history lesson, she said quietly, "I will be good."

Early in the morning of June 20, 1837, William IV died after a reign of only seven years. Victoria was awakened with the announcement that she was Queen of England. At eleven o'clock, in the presence of the Privy Council, the members of which were delighted by her self-possession, she read a speech prepared for her by the Prime Minister, and took the oaths of office. The Salic law, in force in continental countries, required that the crown of Hanover pass to a male heir, and so, after 123 years, it was separated from the English monarchy and was assumed by King William's younger brother.

As Victoria was practically unknown to the English public, an aura of romance and mystery surrounded her. In revulsion from the dissolute kings who preceded her, the people were eager for decency and dignity, and welcomed the innocence and the obvious sincerity of the eighteen-year-old queen. Lord Melbourne, as Prime Minister, became her tutor in political matters and acted with patience and insight. Being almost the first man she had known, the worldly, handsome, middle-aged Melbourne was fascinating to her; but he discreetly diverted his influence toward political ends rather than personal emotion. Thrilled with her power, even in the smallest details of routine, Victoria was equally delighted with her freedom from previous restraints. She loved to dance and to ride; she fed upon flattery and stayed up for late parties; she was inclined to mock at older people who were strait-laced. Though plain of face and tiny of stature, she had a rosy freshness and bright-eyed enthusiasm that made her attractive.

ALBERT, PRINCE CONSORT

QUEEN VICTORIA IN 1837

Her uncle Leopold, who had been elected king of the newly-established Belgian nation in 1831, assumed that he would now enjoy a controlling influence in English affairs; but Victoria tactfully warned him that no foreign advice could be accepted. He remained, however, the only person to whom she could freely express her secret feelings.

The Duchess of Kent was also excluded from any political influence upon her daughter; and as a result petty quarrels and scandal-mongering developed between the Duchess's ladies-in-waiting and the ardently Whig ladies with whom Melbourne had encouraged the Queen to surround herself. In spite of the loyal enthusiasm over the Coronation ceremonies on June 28, 1838, English society was inclined to be incensed over the squabbles at the court. This feeling was intensified by the so-called "Bedchamber crisis" in May, 1839, after Melbourne's Whig government had been defeated and Sir Robert Peel had been called upon to form a Conservative ministry. Unwillingly obliged to give up her favorite adviser, Victoria insisted upon retaining the Whig ladies of her personal household. As this was equivalent to a display of political bias on the queen's side, Peel insisted that the Mistress of the Robes and one or two Ladies of the Bedchamber should be replaced by wives of Tory noblemen. Although Melbourne himself urged the Queen to conform, she obstinately refused, and Peel in his turn declined to take office. Melbourne had to resume the premiership in this embarrassing situation. Radical agitators seized the opportunity for denouncing the Queen's autocracy. In 1841 Melbourne's government was defeated in a general election, and the Queen was obliged to invite Peel once more to become Prime Minister. It was now agreed that the Mistress of the Robes should be of the prevailing party, the other attendants being selected without regard to political affiliation.

Ridiculous though the whole episode appears, it was a

significant lesson to Victoria as to the subordination of royal whims to the political representatives of the people. The change in her attitude during the two years may have been partly due to a new influence that had entered her life—her husband.

The question of her marriage had been much discussed, but in the first years of her reign the Queen had refused to show much interest in various suggested suitors. Her Uncle Leopold, however, had long ago decided that as he could not control her directly, he must install one of his family in the key position of Prince Consort. He had two good-looking nephews, sons of the Duke of Saxe-Coburg-Gotha, and even before Victoria succeeded to the throne these two first cousins had been brought over to England to make her acquaintance. As she showed some signs of liking Albert, who was three months younger than herself, he was taken home to Germany and placed under the tuition of the able Baron Stockmar, who had been confidential adviser to Leopold. For three years Albert was coached in the science of administration. When he visited England in 1839, Victoria promptly fell in love with him and proposed to him, as etiquette demanded. On February 10, 1840, they were married.

The English court and public were naturally suspicious of this foreigner who suddenly assumed a place of so much potential authority in their country. Although Albert was handsome and intelligent, he was studious to the point of pedantry, awkward in meeting people, and indifferent to sports. He spoke English with a German accent. For the first two years of their marriage, the Queen allowed him little voice in public affairs, but by the time Peel came into power Albert by quiet tact and persistence was gaining ascendancy over his wife's mind and was beginning to win public respect. He liked Peel's steady-going bourgeois outlook better than Melbourne's aristocratic boldness, and he soon overcame Victoria's prejudice against her new Prime Minister. Thereafter, under Albert's tutelage, she devoted herself seriously to the business of the realm. The Prince was fond of art, music, literature, and science; a tremendous worker, he proved to be sagacious, far-seeing, and temperate.

The royal couple increased their hold upon the affections of the English people as they acquired a large family and conscientiously fulfilled all the duties of parenthood. Their nine children were:

1. Victoria, the Princess Royal (1840-1901), who in 1858 married the Crown Prince of Prussia, later Kaiser Frederick of Germany. Their son was the Kaiser Wilhelm II who waged the first World War.

2. Edward, the Prince of Wales (1841-1910), who succeeded to the throne as King Edward VII.

3. Princess Alice (1843-1878), who married the Grand Duke of Hesse in 1862.

4. Prince Alfred (1844-1900), who was created Duke of Edinburgh in 1866. When he succeeded to the Dukedom of Saxe-Coburg-Gotha in 1893 he relinquished his British nationality and titles.

5. Princess Helena (1846-1917), who married Prince Christian of Schleswig-Holstein in 1866.

6. Princess Louise (1848-1939), the only member of the family to marry a British nobleman. Her marriage in 1871 to the Scottish Marquess of Lorne (later Duke of Argyll) was very popular.

7. Prince Arthur (1850-1942), who was created Duke of Connaught in 1874.

8. Prince Leopold (1853-1884), who was created Duke of Albany in 1881.

9. Princess Beatrice (1857-1944), who married Prince Henry of Battenberg in 1885.

Under Albert's unobtrusive control, Victoria became the embodiment of the middle-class ideal of wife, mother, and queen. Her good intentions, her tireless devotion to duty, and her stability of character were obvious. These traits, however, were of the type that could harden into obstinacy and prejudice. She was devoted to the Established Church and had little patience with either the Anglo-Catholic movement or the scientific-materialistic tendencies of the age. In literature and the arts her taste was for the obvious, the sentimental, and the didactic.

The everyday activities of the royal household formed a glorified counterpart of what any average prosperous family in the realm was doing and thinking. The Queen and Prince Albert attended concerts and decorous plays, patronized charities, gave receptions and dinner parties, entertained relations and friends from foreign nations, spent holidays at their country residences. In 1846 Osborne in the Isle of Wight was purchased as a vacation home, and two years later a lease was taken upon Balmoral, in the Highlands of Scotland. When the latter estate was purchased in 1852 Albert designed for it a baronial mansion, which was completed within the next three years. The Queen became particularly fond of Balmoral, and her long visits there increased her popularity with her Scottish subjects. Her extended visits to Balmoral and Osborne caused trouble to the prime ministers of successive cabinets, as she insisted upon being personally consulted with regard to all decisions, especially in foreign policy, and cabinet ministers were obliged to make inconvenient railway journeys to interview her. After 1860 the difficulties were diminished when Balmoral was connected with London by telegraph.

The determination of Victoria and Albert to supervise foreign policy led to friction with Lord Palmerston, when he became Foreign Secretary in the Whig cabinet of 1846. As Palmerston was highly respected by the public, this discord made the Queen and the Prince unpopular. The Chartist uprising of 1848, with its avowed purpose of establishing a British republic, was loudly adverse to the royal family. In 1851, when Palmerston's support of Louis Napoleon caused the Prime Minister to dismiss him from the cabinet, Prince Albert and his German adviser Stockmar were regarded as responsible.

Meanwhile Albert had worked hard upon all projects intended to promote international prosperity and peace. He was largely responsible for organizing the great exhibition of 1851. His efforts to preserve peace in the growing controversy with Russia led to a crisis of unpopularity in 1854, when Palmerston resigned from a coalition government. There were wild rumors that Prince Albert was in the pay of Russia, and that he and the Queen were to be arrested for treason. Upon the actual outbreak of the Crimean War, however, the royal couple's patriotic behavior won approval; the Queen visited wounded soldiers in hospitals, encouraged Florence Nightingale in organizing a nursing service, and established the Victoria Cross as an award for heroism. As Lord Palmerston had become Prime Minister, his relations with the Queen and Prince were somewhat improved.

In 1861 Albert had another opportunity of using his influence in behalf of peace. After the outbreak of the American Civil War the arrest of two Confederate envoys on board a British ship caused the Foreign Secretary, Lord John Russell, to draft an angry protest to the Northern government, which might easily have provoked a declaration of war. By Albert's urgent intervention, the message was modified, and the crisis was averted.

At the same time, in spite of uncertain health, the Prince was active in the preparations for a second international exhibition. Weakened by overwork and anxiety, he caught typhoid fever and died on December 14, 1861.

In a frenzy of grief the Queen withdrew into seclusion. She did not, however, give up any of the tasks of rulership;

on the contrary, she decided to dedicate herself to Albert's memory by governing the country in strict adherence to his principles. Although her son, the Prince of Wales, was twenty years old, she felt no confidence in his pleasure-loving, good-natured character, and refused to allow him any share in the duties of government. Some of the ornamental and social functions of the royal office were undertaken by the Prince of Wales and the beautiful Danish bride he married in 1863, while the Queen stayed away from London and conducted the affairs of state by conferring with her cabinet ministers at her country residences. The public complained of the absence of customary royal ceremonies, and condemned the Queen for hoarding her wealth instead of spending it in displays for the gratification of the people. There were muttered suggestions that she ought to abdicate in favor of her son, or that the country should become a republic. Many people repeated absurd gossip that she was in love with John Brown, a faithful Highland servant who acted as her bodyguard when she was at Balmoral and who won her favor by his blunt common sense.

It was during this period that the Queen gained her reputation for being solemn and prudish, the very reverse of the gay girl who had ascended the throne. With middle age she grew stout, and to compensate for her short stature (she was under five feet) she sought for dignity by slow motions and an expressionless face. For the forty years that she survived her husband she always wore the somber weeds of widowhood.

In reply to all demands for less austere social behavior she replied that her health was not equal to public ceremonies, and that all her energy must go to the heavy responsibilities of state. Suspicious of politicians, she felt that her main duty was to protect the true welfare of her subjects from any rash schemes of Parliament and the cabinet. In foreign affairs she also had firm views, derived from her family connections. During the first few years after Albert's death the principal problem was England's attitude toward Germany in the annexation of Schleswig-Holstein. The English people, and Palmerston and Russell in particular, sympathized with Denmark. Victoria, mindful of Albert's conviction that the German states should be united under the Prussian monarch, and influenced somewhat by her eldest daughter's marriage to the Prussian Crown Prince, exerted her influence for the annexation by Prussia. The subsequent policy of aggression under Bismarck, however, was a shock to her; many of her relations were rulers of the principalities that Prussia attacked in 1866, and her offer to mediate was roughly rejected by Bismarck. At the time of the Franco-Prussian war he was disgusted by her success in influencing the Prussian royal family toward leniency in treating the defeated French.

Victoria sometimes showed a progressive attitude in home affairs. When a further extension of the franchise was demanded, she favored the measure, partly no doubt because she feared popular discontent, and she was satisfied when Disraeli cleverly secured its passage. Although she had little understanding of Irish grievances, and regarded the suggestions of Home Rule as treason, she discreetly decided that the disestablishing of the Irish Church, as proposed by Gladstone in 1868, must be approved in spite of all her Protestant prejudices. She also promoted much-needed reforms in the army, by using her royal authority over the head of the House of Lords.

In general the Queen had little appreciation of Gladstone, who treated her with chilly respect and who often opposed her wishes. On the other hand she responded to the homage and lavish flattery of Disraeli, who realized that her age, her bereavement, and her royal dignity had by no means deprived her of feminine instincts. For the first time since the early days of Lord Melbourne, she had a minister who revealed susceptibility to her charm. She was beginning to fancy herself as an author, having published a volume of selections from her diary in 1868, and Disraeli wrote to her as one author to another. In consequence, Disraeli could tactfully suggest ideas that would soon reappear as Her Majesty's own. When he became Prime Minister in 1868 and again in 1874 she was delighted; she praised the acquisition of control of the Suez Canal in 1876, and enjoyed her new title of "Empress of India." So fully did she identify herself with Disraeli's imperialistic policy that she regarded Gladstone's vigorous opposition as personal affronts. When the Conservative government was defeated in 1880 she made a vain effort to find a new Liberal leader and exclude Gladstone from office.

The Liberal government of 1880-1885 brought to a head her habit of scolding and threatening her ministers; there were several disasters that gave her the opportunity of saying, "I told you so." When the Home Rule Bill was defeated and the Conservatives returned to power under Lord Salisbury, her happiness broke down much of her twenty-five-year mourning. In view of preparations to celebrate the golden jubilee of her reign, she spent more time in London and made gracious appearances in public. The imperialistic policies, originated by Disraeli, were now at the height of their popularity, and she was becoming the symbol of national pride almost as much as Elizabeth had been. The great majority of her subjects could remember no other ruler upon the throne. The jubilee celebrations in 1887 were an unprecedented display of loyalty and patriotism.

The tributes of affection from all parts of the world helped her to realize that she was ruler over a more diversified and influential empire than history had ever known. As this growth of British power had largely occurred during her reign, she could hardly avoid feeling proud of it.

In a strange way the plain little old woman acquired a dignity that made her an adequate embodiment of this vast empire. And yet, retaining the unpretentious personal habits and opinions of an average housewife, she treated her statesmen and governors like children to be praised or rebuked, and the other nations like neighbors to be criticised or approved.

Ten additional years of peace and prosperity made her diamond jubilee in 1897 even more impressive than the preceding one. Still energetic after passing her eightieth year, she supported the vigorous prosecution of the Boer War. The gallantry of the Irish regiments, in particular, inspired her to overcome her suspicion of Ireland and display her gratitude by a three weeks' visit to Dublin in

QUEEN VICTORIA IN 1895

1900. Having outlived the nineteenth century, of which she had become the recognized symbol, she died after a brief illness on January 21, 1901. Her reign had been the longest in English history. By the marriages of her children and numerous grandchildren she was represented in many ruling dynasties of European nations. At the time of her death she had thirty-seven living great-grandchildren, the eldest being twenty-two years of age. Her son Edward, at last assuming royal authority, was sixty.

The Girlhood of Queen Victoria, From Her Diaries, ed. Lord Esher (2v, London, 1912); *Letters of Queen Victoria, 1837-1861,* ed. A. C. Benson and Lord Esher (3v, London, 1907); *Letters of Queen Victoria, 1862-1885,* ed. G. E. Buckle (3v, London, 1926-28);

Letters of Queen Victoria, 1886-1901, ed. G. E. Buckle (3v, London, 1930-32); *Further Letters of Queen Victoria*, ed. H. Bolitho (London, 1938); *The Queen and Mr. Gladstone*, ed. P. Guedalla (2v, London, 1933-34); T. Martin, *Life of the Prince Consort* (5v, London, 1875-80); L. Strachey, *Queen Victoria* (London, 1921); F. B. Chancellor, *The Prince Consort* (London, 1932); H. Bolitho, *Albert the Good and the Victorian Reign* (London, 1932); *Victoria the Widow and Her Son* (London, 1934); *Victoria and Albert* (London, 1938); A. Ponsonby, *Queen Victoria* (London, 1933); J. A. R. Marriott, *Queen Victoria and Her Ministers* (London, 1933); E. F. Benson, *Queen Victoria* (London, 1935); F. Hardie, *The Political Influence of Queen Victoria, 1861-1901* (London, 1935); E. Sitwell, *Victoria of England* (London, 1936); M. W. Flexner, *The Young Victoria* (London, 1939); E. Graham, *The Making of a Queen* (London, 1940); H. Bolitho, *The Reign of Queen Victoria* (London, 1948).

SCIENCE

>>

The nineteenth century is often described as an age of science—the epoch when mechanization finally took full control of human ways of life and scientific rationalism assumed almost equal predominance in man's thinking.

Scientific ideas being international, there would be no point in discussing English science of the Victorian period apart from that of the world in general; and many of the leading theories in the physical sciences originated in France, Italy, Germany, the United States and elsewhere. England, however, had been the first country to take full advantage of the Industrial Revolution; and her advanced stage of mechanization in the early years of the nineteenth century, followed by a long period of prosperity and tranquility while continental nations were handicapped by wars, revolutions, and depressions, and the United States was still spending much of the national energy on expansion into new frontiers, gave English science, both theoretical and practical, a peculiarly favorable environment.

All the major inventions which marked the change to modern mechanized society had been completed by the beginning of the Victorian age. The steam engine, with its application in mine and factory machinery, in railroads, in steamships, in printing presses, and so forth, was a commonplace by 1840. Gas lighting had replaced oil lamps and candles in city streets and homes. The telegraph had revolutionized communication. Even photography was reaching a high pitch of skill during the forties. In the next half century, to be sure, great improvements were introduced in all these techniques, and countless new mechanisms were added; but it was not till near the end of the century that the public was introduced to a fresh round of fundamentally important inventions—the automobile, electric lighting, the telephone, the phonograph, and wireless telegraphy.

The years spanned by the Victorian period are therefore less important for applied science than for theoretical. In scientific research and scholarship, the various modern sciences were steadily separating themselves more and more clearly from one another and from the old general caption of "Natural Philosophy"; and yet, paradoxically, the scientific thought of the era was most significant for a wide synthesis which drew evidence from all the sciences to establish an essentially modern concept of the physical universe.

One basis of this concept was laid in astronomy by the nebular hypothesis of Laplace (1796). Steady astronomical progress followed, such as the discovery of the planet Neptune through mathematical calculation by John C. Adams in England and Urbain Leverrier in France (1846). Another important type of research was popularized by Baron Cuvier, whose studies of fossils not only established the science of paleontology but also revealed the many primitive species of plant and animal life no longer existing. In interpreting these data, however, Cuvier clung to the notion of a series of separate creations.

Sir Charles Lyell's *Principles of Geology* (1830-33) laid the modern foundations for this science, and gave names to the major epochs—Eocene, Miocene, Pliocene. Soon afterwards Sir Roderick Murchison and Adam Sedgwick set about mapping the strata of Britain. In physical geography, seminal new ideas were advanced by Baron von Humboldt, explorer, geologist, meteorologist, and botanist, who demonstrated how the configuration of the continents determined climate, plant and animal life, and even human habits. Although his great five-volume *Kosmos* was not published until 1845-62, his basic theories were announced much earlier.

Another epochal investigator was the Chevalier de Lamarck, French botanist and zoölogist, whose studies of invertebrates led him to the theory that living species tend to become gradually larger and more complex, developing new organs to gratify new desires and transmitting these acquired characteristics to later generations.

The aforementioned great stimulators of modern thought, in the closing years of the eighteenth century and opening decades of the nineteenth, represent the same force in the scientific field that their contemporaries the revolutionists exerted in politics and the romanticists in literature. They demolished old assumptions and opened exciting imaginative vistas. People in general became familiar with the vast extent of the physical universe and the eons of time through which it has existed. In one way or another, most of the new theories implied a process of change by which the universe as we know it gradually assumed its present traits.

Botanical and zoölogical research was also progressing. Exploring expeditions were sent out to all corners of the globe to collect specimens. On one such journey, Charles

Darwin spent five years observing the geology and fauna of South Atlantic and South Pacific areas, and thence derived his concept of the mutations of species. From reading the writings of Thomas Robert Malthus, who had alarmed the preceding generation by predicting that population would increase more rapidly than food supplies, Darwin envisioned the struggle for survival as the force which de-

CHARLES DARWIN

termined the disappearance of incompetent species. During the twenty years that elapsed while he was pondering the evidence, a younger scientist, Alfred Russel Wallace, went out on insect-collecting expeditions to South America and Malaya, and arrived at a theory exactly similar to Darwin's. When he sent a report of it to Darwin, the coincidences were so amazing that Darwin hastened to present a statement of their joint views at a meeting of the Linnaean Society in 1858, and the next year he published his book, *On the Origin of Species by Means of Natural Selection, or the Preservation of Favoured Races in the Struggle for Life*.

The idea of "evolution" was far from new. It had been foreshadowed by ancient Greek philosophers, suggested in the eighteenth century by Kant and Goethe, and developed fairly fully by Lamarck. Herbert Spencer, approaching the subject as a philosopher rather than as an experimental scientist, stated clearly in his first book, *Social Statistics* (1850), that natural phenomena as they now exist developed slowly from elementary origins. Two years later, in *The*

Developmental Hypothesis, he pointed out the difficulty of reconciling modern scientific data with the biblical story of a single act of creation; and in *Progress, its Law and Cause* (1857) he stated that each individual form proceeds from simple to complex struc-ture—a principle first stated by the German embryologist, Karl Von Baer.

Darwin's book, however, for the first time revealed the full significance of the concept to the general public. Although in this book he did not specifically discuss the human race, readers could not avoid the implication that mankind, like all other living creatures, was an accidental outgrowth of unimaginably long processes by which he emerged from lower forms of life. Furthermore, the idea of the "survival of the fittest" (Spencer's phrase) depicted all the processes of nature as cruelly competitive and blindly wasteful. In the public mind Darwinism was summed up in the inaccurate simplification that "men are descended from monkeys." Although upholders of orthodox religious belief flayed the new hypothesis, scientific men were soon converted to it. In 1863 Lyell provided further evidence in its support with *The Antiquity of Man.* Darwin elaborated his views in *The Variation of Animals and Plants Under Domestication* (1868) and *The Descent of Man* (1871).

Another proponent of the evolutionary theory was

ON

THE ORIGIN OF SPECIES

BY MEANS OF NATURAL SELECTION,

OR THE

PRESERVATION OF FAVOURED RACES IN THE STRUGGLE
FOR LIFE.

By CHARLES DARWIN, M.A.,

FELLOW OF THE ROYAL, GEOLOGICAL, LINNÆAN, ETC., SOCIETIES;
AUTHOR OF 'JOURNAL OF RESEARCHES DURING H. M. S. BEAGLE'S VOYAGE
ROUND THE WORLD.'

LONDON:
JOHN MURRAY, ALBEMARLE STREET.
1859.

The right of Translation is reserved.

FIRST EDITION
TITLE-PAGE

Thomas Henry Huxley, who—like Darwin and Wallace— had studied living species in the tropics during a long voyage of exploration. Although acquainted with Spencer and Darwin in the early fifties, he retained the concept of separate archetypal species until the evidence in Darwin's *Origin* converted him. The vivid style and forceful arguments in his book, *Man's Place in Nature* (1863), did much to further the

theory. Francis Galton also became a disciple of Darwin, who was his cousin, and began researches in anthropology. After publishing *Hereditary Genius* in 1869, Galton went on to further studies in heredity that led to the new sciences of anthropometry and eugenics.

Experts never agreed upon all the details of the evolutionary process as stated by Darwin. Later in the century

THOMAS HENRY HUXLEY

the amateur scientist, Samuel Butler, assailed the element of accident in the process of "natural selection," and revived Lamarck's concept of "creative evolution." As a general principle, however, evolution provided the key to so many secrets in all the biological sciences, and was consistent with so many phenomena of the other physical sciences, that it remained the basis of all later research.

Although none of the other scientific fields provided as spectacular a controversy, progress in them all was immense. Medicine and surgery showed the most incontrovertible achievements. Anaesthetics revolutionized surgical processes: the use of ether was developed in the United States in the early forties; and in 1847 an Edinburgh surgeon, Sir James

Simpson, who had been experimenting with ether, discovered the properties of chloroform. Of parallel importance was the contribution of another Edinburgh scientist, Joseph Lister, who in 1865 announced the importance of antiseptics in preventing infection. These two aids made possible many types of major operations, while research in anatomy and physiology provided the necessary knowledge of what the operator might achieve. Understanding of the nervous system and the brain was particularly improved during this era.

Lister's realization of antisepsis had been an outcome of the researches conducted in Paris by Louis Pasteur, who established the importance of bacteria as the cause of infection and disease. After Pasteur announced his discovery, during the sixties, medical scientists made immense headway in controlling the worst scourges of human health. During the eighties the microbes of many diseases were identified, and helpful treatments, as well as preventive measures, resulted. Cholera, for example, which had ravaged Europe periodically for centuries, was serious in the British Isles in 1830-31, and several milder outbreaks occurred during the century. In 1883 Robert Koch, who had already discovered the bacilli of anthrax and tuberculosis, identified the micro-organism which caused cholera; and in consequence the next epidemic, in 1892-95, was successfully controlled, and the disease thereafter was kept out of western Europe and greatly reduced in Asia.

In chemistry and physics the most influential discoveries were concerned with atomic and electrical phenomena. Michael Faraday, who had made his first fame in chemical experiments such as the liquefaction of gases, moved on to electricity, and in 1831 discovered the principle of induced currents, which led to the invention of the dynamo. Later he investigated the effect of magnetism on polarized light, and formulated the theory of diamagnetism. The mathematical interpretation of Faraday's discoveries was contributed in 1873 by James Clerk Maxwell, who also made great contributions to the kinetic theory of gases. The other leading figure during the middle years of the century was William Thomson (later Lord Kelvin), who began his studies of thermodynamics in 1847, elaborating the theories of J. P. Joule, and defined the principle of the conservation of energy. He then turned his attention to electricity and his inventions were largely responsible for the successful trans-Atlantic cable of 1866. In the later years of the century the leading English physicists and chemists were Lord Rayleigh, Sir William Ramsay, and Sir William Crookes. The sciences had not yet become too specialized for each of these men to make significant discoveries in several almost unrelated fields.

Toward the end of the Victorian age the social sciences also assumed prominence. Anthropology, psychology, and sociology, using the inductive methods of the physical scientists, and creating an impressive technical vocabulary, began to analyze the individual human being and his relationship to society.

Throughout the Victorian era science was largely responsible for the prevailing optimism of the general outlook. Though religious leaders might complain that the spread of scientific knowledge was leading to gross materialism and rationalistic skepticism, the average man was disposed to reply that in material things science had unquestionably made life happier and therefore had contributed to spiritual welfare. The progressive conquest of disease and pain, the invention of countless physical conveniences, the extension of human power through mechanical contrivances and of human knowledge about every aspect of man and his universe, all suggested that the race had at last vanquished its environment and that the victory would continue to expand through an unlimited future. The theory of evolution seemed to be positive proof of the principle of progress that had prevailed as a philosophical abstraction since the preceding century. If the mere blind workings of natural forces had produced so complex and relatively efficient a mechanism as the universe and so intelligent a race of beings as *Homo sapiens,* the process ought to become far more rapid, now that mankind had become aware of it and could direct all his abilities to its furtherance. Thus the discoveries of physical science became merged with the new "religion of humanity" for which Swinburne gave a slogan: "Glory to man in the highest, for man is the master of things."

W. C. Dampier-Whetham, *A History of Science and Its Relations to Philosophy and Religion* (Cambridge, 1929; rev. ed., 1942); J. T. Merz, *European Thought in the Nineteenth Century,* I, II (Edinburgh, 1896-1903); A. R. Wallace, *The Wonderful Century* (London, 1898); M. Foster, "The Growth of Science in the Nineteenth Century," *Smithsonian Institution Annual Report for 1899,* 163-83; R. H. Murray, *Science and Scientists in the Nineteenth Century* (London, 1925); J. G. Crowther, *British Scientists of the Nineteenth Century* (London, 1935); F. S. Taylor, *The Century of Science, 1840-1940* (London, 1941); *Smithsonian Institution Annual Report for 1900, passim;* W. C. Dampier-Whetham, *The Recent Development of Physical Science* (London, 1904); E. A. Burtt, *The Metaphysical Foundations of Modern Physical Science* (London, 1925); A. M. Clerke, *A Popular History of Astronomy During the Nineteenth Century* (London, 1885; rev. ed., 1902); R. L. Waterfield, *A Hundred Years of Astronomy* (London, 1938); W. A. Locy, *Biology and Its Makers* (New York, 1908); L. C. Miall, *History of Biology* (London, 1911); E. Rádl, *The History of Biological Theories* (London, 1930); J. R. Green, *A History of Botany, 1860-1900* (Oxford, 1909); *A History of Botany in the United Kingdom* (London, 1914); F. W. Oliver, *Makers of British Botany* (Cambridge, 1913); T. E. Thorp, *History of Chemistry,* II (London, 1910); W. J. Hale, *Chemistry Triumphant* (Baltimore, 1932); A. Findlay, *A Hundred Years of Chemistry* (London, 1937); C. L. and M. A. Fenton, *The Story of the Great Geologists* (New York, 1945); C. Singer, *A Short History of Medicine* (London, 1928); W. E. B. Lloyd, *A Hundred Years of Medicine* (London, 1936; rev. ed. New York,

1943); W. Hale-White, *Great Doctors of the Nineteenth Century* (London, 1935); H. Graham (pseud.), *Surgeons All* (London, 1939); C. T. Chase, *The Evolution of Modern Physics* (New York, 1947); M. Foster, "Recent Progress in Physiology," *Smithsonian Institution Annual Report for 1897,* 437-52; L. von Graff, "Zoölogy Since Darwin," *Smithsonian Institution Annual Report for 1895,* 477-91; W. A. Locy, *The Main Currents of Zoölogy* (New York, 1918); E. E. Fournier d'Albe, *Life of Sir William Crookes* (London, 1923); *Life and Letters of Charles Darwin,* ed. F. Darwin (3v, London, 1887); *More Letters of Charles Darwin,* ed. F. Darwin and A. C. Seward (2v, London, 1903); G. Bradford, *Darwin* (Boston, 1926); H. Ward, *Charles Darwin* (New York, 1927); E. B. Poulton, *Darwin and the Theory of Natural Selection* (London, 1896); *Darwin and Modern Science,* ed. A. C. Seward (Cambridge, 1909); S. P. Thompson, *Michael Faraday: His Life and Work* (London, 1898); L. Huxley, *Life and Letters of Thomas Henry Huxley* (2v, London, 1900; rev. ed., 3v, 1903); E. Clodd, *Thomas Henry Huxley* (Edinburgh, 1902, "Modern English Writers"); S. P. Thompson, *Life of William Thomson, Baron Kelvin* (2v, London, 1910); A. Russell, *Lord Kelvin* (London, 1938); R. J. Godlee, *Lord Lister* (London, 1917); R. Truax, *Joseph Lister* (Indianapolis, 1945); *Life, Letters, and Journals of Sir Charles Lyell, Bart.,* ed. K. M. Lyell (2v, London, 1881); T. G. Bonney, *Charles Lyell and Modern Geology* (London, 1895); A. S. Eve and C. H. Creasy, *Life and Works of John Tyndall* (London, 1945); J. Marchant, *Alfred Russell Wallace, Letters and Reminiscences* (2v, London, 1916); L. T. Hogben, *Alfred Russel Wallace* (London, 1918).

RELIGION

The state-supported religious body of England bears officially the title "the Church of England," and is known elsewhere as the Anglican or the Protestant Episcopal faith. Because the English Reformation under Henry VIII had renounced the authority of the Pope but had not otherwise organized a new creed, the term *Catholic* (without an accompanying word *Roman*) is also regarded as applying to the Church of England, though it is seldom used by the public.

The Archbishop of Canterbury has authority over the Church of England in all parts of the British Empire. Most of the English bishops hold seats in the House of Lords and thus fill an active legislative function. All appointments to ecclesiastical posts are under the jurisdiction of the Prime Minister. Church funds are derived from "tithes" collected like taxes from all landowners, whatever their individual affiliation may be. In these respects the special prerogatives of the state church are still in force. At the beginning of the Victorian period the same privileges prevailed in Wales and Ireland. In Scotland, however, the state church is Presbyterian. As the King of England is officially head of both churches he nominally changes his religious faith every time he crosses the border between the two countries.

In the early nineteenth century the privileges of the Church of England were more extensive. Its members had enjoyed exclusive rights of sitting in Parliament or holding any other public office. These prerogatives were extended in favor of other Protestant faiths in 1823 and in favor of Roman Catholics in 1829. Members of the Jewish faith, however, were not allowed to enter Parliament until 1860; and another bitter contest was waged, more than twenty years later, to permit a freethinker to hold a seat without taking a religious oath. Until 1871, only members of the Church of England could be admitted as students or teachers in the universities of Oxford and Cambridge. And until 1868 every individual had to pay a "church rate" in his local parish, whether he belonged to the established church or not. In defense of the latter practice, however, it must be pointed out that the Church was still largely responsible for various forms of local social service, such as elementary education, orphanages, and poorhouses, which later were taken over by government agencies.

The gradual disappearance of many special privileges of the Church of England during the Victorian era is evidence of the growing power of the other religious elements in the country. From Puritan days onward, a large number of English people had belonged to various Nonconformist or Dissenting faiths. Many Roman Catholics also survived, although since 1559 the Roman Church had enjoyed no official status in the country.

During the eighteenth century the clergy of the Church of England had tended to become worldly and irresponsible. Secure in their guaranteed incomes, some of them gave more time to sports or to social amusements than to their parish duties. The social status of the Church made it one of the few professions which could be adopted by the sons of gentlemen without loss of caste. As appointments could be obtained through family influence, some clerics practiced "pluralism," holding several lucrative offices and leaving poorly-paid curates in charge of all of them. Many of the clergy, of course, were conscientious in their duties, and many others took advantage of their academic training and their isolation in rural districts to devote their spare time to scholarly research. A great number of learned works in the eighteenth and early nineteenth century were produced by clergymen, and could not otherwise have been produced at all.

As a result of their social superiority and their economic security, the clergy were apt to be somewhat out of touch with the spiritual needs of their parishioners. Therefore the nonconformist faiths were likely to enjoy more active support. The development of Methodism, which broke away from the Church of England in the later years of the eighteenth century, greatly increased the numbers and the influence of the dissenting forces. Still more significant, however, was the rapid rise of the relative status of the dissenters in terms of wealth and political power. The bourgeois middle class, which for centuries had been the chief strength of the Puritan and later of the nonconformist forces, had grown prosperous through the Industrial Revolution and the Napoleonic wars.

By the opening of the Victorian period, then, the Church of England was beset by strong rivalry, and was also showing signs of discord among several factions within its own ranks. The old comfortable sense of security was giving place to an anxious awareness that something must be done to justify the Church's claims to leadership. By a typically English process of compromise and slow legislative reform, the change in the religious "balance of power" was gradually accepted throughout the period by the various acts of Parliament which repealed the old restrictions—a display of distinct democratic enlightenment, since the Members of Parliament who passed the new legislation at each stage were extending to competitors the privileges which they already enjoyed themselves. By the end of the century all creeds enjoyed identical civil rights. The Episcopal Church in Ireland was "disestablished" (i.e., deprived of public endowment) in 1869, and the same change occurred in Wales in 1914.

The disagreements among the various parties within the Church of England were more complicated. By the middle of the nineteenth century three distinct groups had manifested themselves, all pulling in opposite directions and all causing discomfort to the large "middle of the road" element which would have preferred to retain the old easy-going atmosphere. It was characteristic of the Church of England that these contending factions managed to remain in it and to accept the authority of the Archbishop of Canterbury, no matter how much they all argued with him and with each other.

One of these factions was known as the Low Church or Evangelical movement. Closely in sympathy with the Methodists, the Low Churchmen laid strong stress upon "personal salvation" and upon the Reformation origin of the Church as embodied in its "Thirty-nine Articles." They regarded the episcopacy as relatively unimportant. Joining hands with the Methodists, Quakers, and other humanitarian

organizations, they worked for Temperance, anti-slavery legislation, Sunday Schools, and foreign missions. Their puritanical severity, however, alienated many, especially younger people; and their insistence upon literal interpretation of the Bible made inadequate provision for theological study or for intellectual activity.

An opposite extreme, emphasizing the Catholic antecedents of the Church of

JOHN KEBLE

England, was inevitably nicknamed the High Church party. It was also known as the Oxford Movement (because it originated at that university), the Tractarian Movement (because its first propaganda was a series of pamphlets entitled *Tracts for the Times*), or Puseyism (from E. B. Pusey, one of its leaders). Beginning among a small group of devout thinkers in Oriel College, Oxford, it first came to public notice on July 14, 1833, when the Rev. John Keble preached a sermon at St. Mary's Church, Oxford, on "National Apostasy." Apart from Pusey and Keble, the principal leaders were John Henry Newman, Richard Hurrell Froude, H. J. Rose, and W. G. Ward.

The basic purpose of the High Church movement was to

defend the authority of the episcopacy and the sanctity of the "apostolic succession," thus deriving from Archbishop Laud and the other royalist ecclesiastics who had been removed by the Puritans in the seventeenth century. A strict interpretation of the "Thirty-nine Articles" was considered less important than adherence to the English prayer-book, which in many respects was a translation of the Roman Catholic ritual. Such doctrinal matters as baptismal regeneration and the "real presence" of the body and blood of Christ at Holy Communion were regarded as essential.

If the movement had confined itself to these questions of theological debate, it would not have attracted either the wide support or the violent opposition which soon developed. The founders of the movement, however, were eager to take full advantage of the emotional and imaginative appeals of religious ritual, the dignity, beauty, and traditional connotations of solemn music, stained-glass windows, candlelight, embroidered vestments, and the odor of incense. They introduced such picturesque practices as processional and recessional pageantry, gestures of veneration toward the Blessed Sacrament, and frequent celebration of the Eucharist. The hearing of confession was instituted, and before long Anglican monastic orders came into existence.

These impressive ceremonies appealed to a public which had been brought up on Sir Walter Scott and other romantic devotees of medievalism. The movement coincided with the Gothic revival in architecture, which provided appropriately ornate settings and mysterious shadowy vaults. Lovers of poetry and of history were especially susceptible to the new observances.

On the other hand, the deep-rooted Protestantism of the English public was aroused by the obvious similarities to the practices of the Church of Rome. Newspapers kept up a bombardment of condemnation and ridicule, and mob violence was sometimes threatened, although it never actually occurred.

The adversaries of Tractarianism felt that all their warnings were justified when Newman decided that he could no longer maintain his "middle way" between English Protestantism and Papal Catholicism, and in 1845 announced his conversion to the Roman Church. A number of other Anglo-Catholics followed his lead, the most notable being Henry Edward Manning, who made the change in 1851. On the other hand, some adherents withdrew from the High Church party in protest. In spite of the temporary setback, however, the movement proved strong enough to survive as one of the positive elements in the English Church.

HENRY EDWARD, CARDINAL MANNING

The third active movement during the Victorian age came to be known as the Broad Church. It is also sometimes described as Latitudinarianism. Just as the Low Church party was roughly equivalent to what is now termed "fundamentalist," so the Broad Church was "modernist." Its supporters declared that acceptance of all the complex doctrines of the English Church was less important than intelligent contact with the problems of contemporary life. This concern divided in two directions—progressive social experiments and acceptance of new scientific theories. One of the early leaders, Thomas Arnold, was a pioneer of educational reform at Rugby School and also a proponent of Niebuhr's revolutionary methods in historical research.

The most striking manifestation of the Broad Church point of view was the "Christian Socialism" which was promulgated in 1848 under the leadership of Frederick Denison Maurice, Charles Kingsley, and Thomas Hughes, all of whom were able writers. Their intention was to salvage the Chartist revolt, which had just collapsed, by putting economic equality and social justice alongside of purely political objectives. The leaders were accused of dangerous radicalism because they preached "sermons for working men" and circulated pamphlets depicting the miseries of the under-privileged classes. To put their theories into practice they founded a working men's college, coöperative stores, and community workshops. Their influence thus merged with that of Ruskin and Morris in paving the way for the growth of the English Labour party.

Since tolerance was the keynote of the Broad Church, its members tried to be generous toward their adversaries of the high and low factions and toward the other creeds in the country. Their attitude was far from consistent; Kingsley, for instance, who was more outspoken than discreet, was almost as much a Tory as a radical, and his rabid Protestantism precipitated one of the major conflicts of the era when he wrote that Newman did not make a virtue of "truth for its own sake." Newman's *Apologia pro Vita Sua*, written as a rebuttal, did much to win back for him the public favor he had lost at the time of his conversion.

Another typically inconsistent Broad Churchman was Arthur Penrhyn Stanley, Dean of Westminster. He defended the High Church movement against official condemnation, but opposed it in several crucial controversies. He proclaimed the subordination of the Church of England to the laws of the country as represented by the government, and in opposition to High and Low Church alike he advocated liberalizing the interpretation of both the Thirty-nine Articles and the Prayer Book. In the face of bitter protests he administered Holy Communion to nonconformists (including a Unitarian).

One of the major liberal revolts in the Church, which Stanley defended although he did not join it, centered in the publication in 1860 of a volume entitled *Essays and Reviews*. Six of the seven contributors were clergymen, and two of them were suspended from their duties because of the alleged rationalism of their interpretations of the Bible. Their reinstatement, upon appeal, brought the matter into the newspaper headlines. Shortly afterwards a similar controversy burst out over Bishop J. W. Colenso, of Natal, who was publishing books that questioned the historical accuracy of the Old and New Testaments, notably *The Pentateuch and the Book of Joshua Critically Examined* (1862).

These various publications were examples of a new trend known as "higher criticism," which applied the methods of scientific scholarship to the study of the biblical text. The Church of England liberals were merely traveling with a rationalistic current which was flowing strongly throughout Europe. David F. Strauss's *Life of Jesus,* which was translated from the German by Mary Ann Evans (George Eliot) in 1846, startled the English public by regarding Christ as a historical figure instead of a divine being. In France Ernest Renan wrote a similar book which made a similar sensation twenty years later.

The most notable literary expression of the new theories in England was Matthew Arnold's *Literature and Dogma*. Going far beyond the cautiously Broad Church tenets of his father, he insisted that Christianity must survive by its moral validity and not by belief in miracles. Defining religion as "morality touched by emotion," he asserted that "the object of religion is conduct," and stated his concept of God to be "a stream of tendency, not ourselves, that makes for righteousness."

All these attempts to apply logical and practical considerations to Christianity showed a dawning consciousness that the various controversies within the Church of England, and the mutual suspicions among Anglicans, dissenters, and Roman Catholics, were insignificant in comparison with the danger which was beginning to menace the very existence of any religious faith. This danger was the expanding influence of physical science.

The threat had been latent ever since Bacon established the inductive method. It had prompted deism and other varieties of "rational religion" in the seventeenth and eighteenth centuries.* But in the nineteenth it gained immense momentum. The general attitude of science was unsympathetic toward religious belief in that science insists upon physical evidence for all opinions and accepts nothing upon the strength of tradition or revelation. Hence the existence of an immortal soul in human beings, the existence of God, and the miracles of Jesus, were among the features of Christianity which science was unable to verify. Specifically, as the sciences of geology, astronomy, biology, and archaeology began to investigate the origins and antiquity of the universe, the earth, and the human race, the story of creation in the book of Genesis could no longer be accepted as literal fact. Even the events of Jewish history, as narrated in the Old Testament, were challenged. Later the ethnologists studied primitive religions and placed them on an equal footing with Christianity as manifestations of a psychological urge to worship, a fear of the forces of nature, or a wish-fulfillment to compensate for frustrations.

The challenge to religion came to a head with the publication of Darwin's *Origin of Species* in 1859 and *The Descent of Man* twelve years later. These books were widely read, and made clear beyond cavil that the scientists regarded human beings as essentially identical with all other animals. Furthermore, Darwin's hypothesis of "natural selection" and the "struggle for survival" implied cruelty and blind chance throughout nature, hard to reconcile with belief in an all-powerful and merciful God. At a meeting of the British Association for the Advancement of Science, in 1860, Samuel Wilberforce, the High-Church Bishop of Oxford, attacked the theory as atheistical, and Thomas Henry Huxley defended it in a dramatic debate.

Many of the leading scientists, to be sure, were orthodox in their religious beliefs; Darwin remained a member of the Church of England. Others sought a compromise by assuming that science and religion dealt with separate realms that had nothing in common. Huxley gave currency to the word *agnostic* to express the idea that science could neither prove nor disprove spiritual concepts. Most ecclesiastics, however, whether High Church, Low Church, or nonconformist, assailed scientific rationalism as godless and immoral. Many scientists retorted that if organized religion opposed the progress of human knowledge it betrayed itself as a harmful and obsolete prejudice.

The controversy, though still far from settled, wore itself out before the end of the century. The efforts of the Broad Church party—and still more, perhaps, those of many poets and essayists who strove to reconcile the opposing views—led most people to an attitude of "live and let live" or a dualistic philosophy that assumed both religion and science to be somehow true.

The debate definitely affected most of the religious bodies in England. It was probably partly responsible for the revitalization of the Roman Catholic church there. Many people sought refuge from all the contradictions and altercations by turning to the form of Christianity which was the oldest in tradition and the most positive in telling its adherents what to believe. After the Catholic Emancipation Act of 1829, there was no longer any barrier to the reëstablishment of a full Roman Catholic hierarchy in England. In 1850 the Pope divided the country into twelve episcopal sees, with Westminster as an archdiocese, and appointed Dr. Nicholas Wiseman, an Irish theologian, as the first archbishop, with the rank of cardinal. The militant Protestantism of England was outraged by these events, and the newspapers were full of violent protests; but by patient diplomacy Wiseman gradually won the confidence of the public. Converts from the Oxford Movement strengthened the new hierarchy, and one of them—Manning—was Wiseman's successor as archbishop and cardinal. Newman also became a cardinal.

While the Roman Church was doubling and redoubling the total of its communicants, the nonconformist forces were intensifying their methods of "saving souls." Great revival campaigns were organized, using all the appeal of impassioned eloquence. In London the Baptist minister Charles H. Spurgeon drew such immense congregations every Sunday that they overflowed Exeter Hall, and impelled the building of the vast Tabernacle in 1861. After 1870 Dwight L. Moody, the American evangelist, paid visits to England and attracted huge crowds with his forthright and colloquial sermons, aided by the gospel hymns of his associate, Ira D. Sankey. The crusade was carried to the slums and the taverns by William Booth through the Salvation Army, which he founded in 1878.

If the growth of scientific rationalism drove some people into the ancient shelter of the Church of Rome, and others to the emotional stimulation of revivalism, it encouraged also the emergence of new religious creeds which claimed to be more consistent with the concepts of science. Spiritualism was a fashionable pseudo-scientific craze during the middle years of the century, when Daniel D. Home and other picturesque mediums held séances in wealthy drawing-rooms. Later spiritualism took on some of the features of an organized religious sect. Deeper intellectual tenets marked Theosophy, promulgated in 1875 by Helena P. Blavatsky, a Russian aristocrat, who undertook to interpret scientific theories by the light of Oriental mysticism.

A knowledge of the various religious movements and controversies of the century is essential to a clear understanding of Victorian literature. The public mind was so vitally affected that almost every writer reflected the concern. Dickens, Thackeray, George Eliot, Trollope, and other novelists portrayed many types of clergymen; Newman, Arnold, Spencer, and many more wrote influential discussions of their beliefs; Tennyson, Browning, Swinburne, George Meredith, and Hardy were among the poets who tried almost too persistently to suggest compromises or new creeds that might reconcile religion with science.

A. D. White, *History of the Warfare of Science with Theology* (2v, New York, 1896); T. A. Bonney, *The Present Relations of Science and Religion* (London, 1913); F. Warre-Cornish, *The English Church in the Nineteenth Century* (2v, London, 1910); S. C. Carpenter, *Church and People, 1789-1889* (London, 1933); V. F. Storr, *The Development of English Theology, 1800-1860* (London, 1913); C. C. J. Webb, *A Study of Religious Thought in England from 1850* (Oxford, 1933); T. K. Cheyne, *The Founders of Old Testament Criticism* (London, 1893); J. E. Carpenter, *The Bible in the Nineteenth Century* (London, 1903); G. R. Balleine, *A History of the Evangelical Party in the Church of England* (London, 1908); R. W. Church, *The Oxford Movement: Twelve Years, 1833-1845* (London, 1891); W. J. S. Simpson, *The History of the Anglo-Catholic Revival from 1845* (London, 1932); Y. Brilioth, *The Anglican Revival* (London, 1925); B. C. Boulter, *The Anglican Reformers* (London, 1933); C. Dawson, *The Spirit of the Oxford Movement* (London, 1933); G. Faber, *Oxford Apostles* (London, 1933); E. A. Knox, *The Tractarian Movement, 1833-1845* (London, 1933); J. L. May, *The Oxford Movement* (London, 1933); W. G. Peck, *The Social Implications of the Oxford Movement* (New York, 1933); H. P. Liddon, *Life of E. B. Pusey* (5v, London, 1893-99); W. P. Ward, *William George Ward and the Oxford Movement* (London, 1889); *William George Ward and the Catholic Revival* (London, 1893); P. Thureau-Dangin, *La renaissance catholique en Angleterre au XIXe siècle* (3v, Paris, 1899-1906; Engl. trans. rev. by W. Wilberforce, 2v,

London, 1914); E. E. Purcell, *Life of Cardinal Manning* (London, 1896); S. Leslie, *Henry Edward Manning: His Life and Labours* (London, 1920); W. Ward, *The Life and Times of Cardinal Wiseman* (2v, London, 1897); C. R. Sanders, *Coleridge and the Broad Church Movement* (Durham, N. C., 1942); C. Noel, *Socialism in Church History* (London, 1910); C. Raven, *Christian Socialism* (London, 1921); J. E. Maurice, *Life of John Frederick Denison Maurice* (2v, London, 1884); B. H. Alford, *Frederick Denison Maurice* (London, 1909); G. W. Cox, *Life of John William Colenso* (London, 1888).

FINE ARTS

>>>

Painting, sculpture, and architecture at the opening of the Victorian period were firmly controlled by influences which had been established in the preceding century.

Architecture was still in the neo-classical or "Georgian" style; but the Gothic revival was about to begin. It came simultaneously with a period of wealth and urban expansion, when huge new public and commercial buildings were being erected, residential suburbs were spawning around every city, and old churches were being remodeled or replaced. In the resulting demand for architects, many men of inferior ability found opportunities. Their employers wanted display and impressiveness rather than sound taste or functional efficiency. Hence the Victorian Gothic was usually artificial and pretentious, with elaborate decoration and meaningless conventions applied to the surface of buildings of mediocre design. Sometimes sham effects were produced with plaster or even cast-iron imitating stonework.

The Gothic revival was a late outcome of the Romantic movement, which affected the visual arts more slowly than it affected literature and music. The British Museum, for example, built between 1828 and 1852, and the National Gallery, 1838, were strictly classical. After 1830, however,

THE CRYSTAL PALACE, 1851

the classicists were giving way to the medievalists. The first great example, in which Gothic lines were applied to a classical plan, was the Houses of Parliament, designed by Sir Charles Barry and built between 1840 and 1860. Other important London buildings in the Gothic style were Philip Hardwick's hall of Lincoln's Inn and G. E. Street's immense block of the Law Courts (1874-1882).

The widest application of the Gothic revival was in church building, abetted by the High Church movement and also by the medievalism of Ruskin and the Pre-Raphaelites. Augustus N. W. Pugin, who joined the Roman Catholic Church in 1833, became the leader of the movement, designing sixty-five churches and influencing many other architects. University buildings also followed the Gothic mode, notably Glasgow University, designed by Sir Gilbert Scott, and the University Museum at Oxford, which—at the insistence of Ruskin—imitated the Doges' Palace in Venice.

Never during the Victorian age, however, did Gothic achieve complete dominance. For new types of large buildings, with steel frameworks, such as railroad terminals and the Crystal Palace (built for the Great Exhibition of 1851), an adaptation of the classical proved necessary. Charles R. Cockerill, who had studied classical antiquities in Italy and Greece, led in applying "neo-Greek" style to banks and other financial buildings.

In domestic architecture the desire for social prestige led to showy and insincere styles, such as pseudo-Italian "villas" and streets of city residences with Gothic windows and gargoyles. After 1860 a more pleasing trend set in, with modified renaissance effects or a return to the comfortable "Queen Anne" style of the early eighteenth century.

Sculpture had remained almost entirely loyal to the classical models established by the archeological explorations of Stuart and Revett in Greece in the late eighteenth century, followed by the arrival of the Elgin Marbles at the

British Museum. Such sculptors as John Flaxman (1755-1826), Sir Francis Chantrey (1781-1841), and John Gibson (1790-1866) were disciples of the two popular continental classicists, the Italian Canova and the Danish Thorwaldsen. Later a more naturalistic and vigorous style was introduced by Thomas Woolner and especially Alfred Stevens (1818-1875), whose monument to Wellington in St. Paul's Cathedral is often called the greatest English sculptural achievement of the century.

English painting, after a long period of insignificance, had become eminent in the late eighteenth century through the magnificent portraiture of Reynolds, Gainsborough, Raeburn, and Romney, and the landscapes of Constable. Their impetus gradually declined in the next generation. Sir Thomas Lawrence, who had a European reputation in portraiture until 1830, was a master of technique rather than a great artist; and his successor as official portrait-painter, Sir Martin Archer Shee, brought no innovation. Even the vigorous and gifted sketchers in satiric black-and-white, George Cruikshank and John Leech, followed the tradition of Hogarth and Rowlandson.

The most popular style of painting in the Victorian age was the "picture that tells a story." Events from history, scenes from Shakespeare's plays and Scott's novels, sentimental episodes of rural life, were painted in vast numbers and sold at high prices. The spectators enjoyed identifying the details and reconstructing the action in their minds. This type of elaborate realism had its culmination during the fifties in the large canvases of William Powell Frith, who depicted scenes of crowded contemporary English life, such as "Ramsgate Sands" (1854), "Derby Day" (1858), and "The Railway Station" (1862). Another immensely popular artist was Sir Edwin Landseer, who brought sentiment and drama into his paintings of dogs, cats, stags, and other animals.

THE CROSSING SWEEPER—FRITH

In the early Victorian era the work of the successful painters was less important than the development of opportunities for the public to see and enjoy works of art. The National Gallery was built in 1838, and good collections also became available to the public in Manchester, Bristol, Liverpool, and other cities. Important works of art received prominence in the great Exhibition of 1851. Engraved reproductions of famous paintings were much in demand, to be framed and hung on the walls of homes that could not afford original works. *The Art Journal,* established by Samuel Carter Hall in 1839, was a handsome periodical, lavishly illustrated. Art education had been stimulated in 1827 when the government opened classes in art, under the control of the Royal Academy, at Somerset House. Before the end of the century, efficient art schools were functioning in all the principal cities.

From these forces, new vitality inevitably flowed into the work of the painters. Actually, the one great original painter of the early Victorian age, J. M. W. Turner, had started his career in the preceding century; but he did not reach the fullness of his powers until 1830. The rich color and mysterious vagueness of his landscapes, both in oils and in water colors, and his persistent experiments in showing the play of light on the sea or through mist, were derided by many critics who preferred more obvious scenes and drab hues. In 1843 John Ruskin set out to write a defense of Turner, and his intended pamphlet expanded into five volumes, *Modern Painters,* which not only proclaimed Turner one of the greatest landscapists of all time but also laid down the principles upon which a new generation of English painters developed.

The vigorous young group who called themselves the Pre-Raphaelite Brotherhood was one of the manifestations of the same romantic medievalism that showed itself in the High Church movement in religion and the Gothic revival in architecture. Because its most magnetic leader, Dante Gabriel Rossetti, was a poet as much as a painter, the Brotherhood was equally important in art and in literature, Rossetti forming the connecting link between his two bands of disciples, the writers and the painters.

The manifesto of the "P.R.B." was issued in 1848, and the group remained united for only five years. Of its seven members, the most important as painters were W. Holman Hunt and John Everett Millais. Ford Madox Brown, equally prominent, never officially became a member of the group. The announced theory of these young radicals was that European painting took a false turn when the followers of Raphael devoted themselves to his devices of technique, instead of keeping the honesty and naïveté of the earlier Renaissance generation.

The modern observer finds difficulty in understanding why their pictures created such a furore. Most of them are of the "story-telling" type which was already in vogue— Hunt's "Two Gentlemen of Verona" and "The Light of the World," Brown's "Work" and "The Last of England," Millais's "Ophelia" and "The Huguenot," Rossetti's "Girlhood of Mary Virgin." Millais insisted that the purpose of the Brotherhood was merely "to present on canvas what they saw in nature." In contrast with the accepted painters of the time, they used brighter coloring and harder outlines, so that each figure stood out strongly instead of melting smoothly into chiaroscuro. Even the smallest details, such as individual flowers, were treated with the same precision.

The horror of the public at these unconventional pictures was exemplified by Dickens's attack upon "Christ in the House of His Parents," by Millais:

In the foreground of the carpenter's shop is a hideous, wry-necked, blubbering, red-haired boy in a nightgown, who appears to have received a poke in the hand from the stick of another

THE GIRLHOOD OF MARY VIRGIN—ROSSETTI

boy with whom he had been playing in an adjacent gutter, and to be holding it up for the contemplation of a kneeling woman so horrible in her ugliness that (supposing it were possible for a human creature to exist for a moment with that dislocated throat) she would stand out from the rest of the company as a monster in the vilest cabaret in France, or the lowest gin-shop in England.

Such hysterical abuse as this aroused Ruskin to write an essay in defense of the Pre-Raphaelites, and his prestige helped to turn the tide in their favor.

After a few years the original group began to disintegrate. Millais, in particular, gave up some of its distinctive mannerisms, and gradually became the most popular painter of his generation, ending as President of the Royal Academy. Thus the Pre-Raphaelite movement came more and more to be identified with its articulate spokesman, Dante Gabriel Rossetti. And Rossetti was the only one of the seven who had been less interested in clarity and almost harsh realism than in a vaguely symbolic quality which may have resulted from his literary proclivities. His preference for the frail Elizabeth Siddall as a model caused him to depict tall, thin, sad-eyed women who were eventually regarded as typically Pre-Raphaelite. He also chose his subjects more often from medieval times. These elements in his work strongly influenced the two most important disciples who later joined the movement—Edward Burne-Jones and William Morris. Burne-Jones followed Rossetti's example in painting willowy, long-necked women in flowing robes. Soulful young ladies imitated their styles of costume, hair-dressing, and posture. Burne-Jones also acquired international fame as a designer of stained glass, tiles, tapestries, and so forth. Morris also, after he had decided that he would never become a first-rate painter, turned his talents to the production of arts for household decoration and church equipment, such as draperies, carpets, wall-paper, furniture, printing, and bookbinding. In all of these he used predominantly medieval motifs. Through this transition the Pre-Raphaelite Brotherhood merged into the "Aesthetic" cult which prevailed in the eighties and nineties. But also the example of Morris spread into the commercial world and profoundly affected the developing arts of "interior

A LADY'S BOUDOIR, 1884

decoration" and "industrial design," which counteracted the deadly effects of mass production.

Several artists who had begun with some affinity with the Pre-Raphaelite school, such as Frederick Leighton and Lawrence Alma-Tadema, later followed a pseudo-classical trend, with cool, formal paintings of scenes from mythology and ancient history. Another very popular painter, George F. Watts, began with classical and historical subjects, but made his great fame with portraits of his leading contemporaries (including most of the authors) and with symbolic pictures expressing his mystical concepts of hope, love, and death.

The only stimulating fresh force to affect English painting in the later years of the century came through the American-born James McNeill Whistler, who brought into England the techniques of the French impressionist school and also reflected the newly-recognized beauty of Japanese color-prints. These influences worked against the long-established eminence of "story-telling" pictures. Whistler simplified the subjects and devoted most attention to the harmonies of color and mood. Avoiding the meticulous detail and vivid coloring of the Pre-Raphaelites, he produced subdued, misty scenes and restful portraits. Attracted to media in which color was entirely replaced by tone, he did much to popularize etchings and lithographs.

Whistler aroused dislike and ridicule, not only by his innovations in art but by his affected mannerisms, dandiacal dress, sarcastic epigrams, and impudent essays. Ruskin, whose taste was growing reactionary in his old age, condemned him severely; but the young generation of Aesthetes, led by Oscar Wilde, became Whistler's champions. During the eighties the exhibitions of the new style of art, usually at the recently-opened Grosvenor Gallery, were the Mecca of all the clever young sophisticates.

Whistler's tendency toward black-and-white was carried further during the eighties and nineties by a group of illustrators and decorative designers. Some, like Walter Crane, followed the Pre-Raphaelite tradition; but the most original of them, Aubrey Beardsley, applied a formal, semi-Oriental technique to morbid and decadent subjects which revealed, even more strongly than did the writers whose stories and poems he illustrated, the futile defiance which in the closing years of the century struggled against the dying control of a long and positive age.

J. Fergusson and R. Kerr, *A History of Architecture in All Countries,* v (London, 1902); R. Sturgis and A. L. Frothingham, *A History of Architecture,* IV (London, 1915); H. H. Statham,

Modern Architecture (London, 1897); T. D. Atkinson, *English Architecture* (London, 1904); C. Davenport, *Architecture in England* (London, 1924); J. Betjeman, *Ghastly Good Taste* (London, 1933); T. E. Tallmadge, *The Story of England's Architecture* (London, 1935); C. L. Eastlake, *A History of the Gothic Revival* (London, 1871); K. Clark, *The Gothic Revival* (London, 1928); B. Ferrey, *Recollections of A. N. Welby Pugin* (London, 1861); M. Trappes-Lomax, *Pugin, A Medieval Victorian* (London, 1932); R. de la Sizeranne, *La peinture anglaise contemporaine* (Paris, 1895; Eng. trans., 1898); C. Monkhouse, *British Contemporary Artists* (London, 1899); M. H. Spielmann, *British Sculpture and Sculptors of Today* (London, 1901); D. S. MacColl, *Nineteenth-Century Art* (Glasgow, 1902); W. Bayliss, *Five Great Painters of the Victorian Era* (London, 1902); W. Armstrong, *Art in Great Britain and Ireland* (London, 1909); H. MacFall, *A History of Painting*, VII (London, 1911); J. Rothenstein, *Nineteenth-Century Painting: A Study in Conflict* (London, 1932); E. Underwood, *A Short History of English Painting* (London, 1933); *A Short History of English Sculpture* (London, 1933); M. F. de Montmorency, *A Short History of Painting in England* (London, 1934); R. Fry, *Reflections on British Painting* (London, 1934); S. Sitwell, *Narrative Pictures* (London, 1937); G. Everitt, *English Caricaturists and Graphic Humourists of the Nineteenth Century* (London, 1885); G. White, *English Illustration, 1855-70* (London, 1897); F. Reid, *Illustrators of the Sixties* (London, 1928); J. Thorpe, *English Illustration: The Nineties* (London, 1935); W. M. Rossetti, *Fine Art, Chiefly Contemporary* (London, 1897); *Ruskin, Rossetti, Pre-Raphaelitism* (London, 1899); *Pre-Raphaelite Diaries and Letters* (London, 1900); W. B. Scott, *Autobiographical Notes* (2v, London, 1892); P. H. Bate, *English Pre-Raphaelite Painters* (London, 1899); W. H. Hunt, *Pre-Raphaelitism and the Pre-Raphaelite Brotherhood* (2v, London, 1905); F. M. Hueffer, *The Pre-Raphaelite Brotherhood* (London, 1907); W. Crane, *William Morris to Whistler* (London, 1911); F. Bickley, *The Pre-Raphaelite Comedy* (London, 1932); W. Gaunt, *The Pre-Raphaelite Tragedy* (London, 1942); *The Aesthetic Adventure* (London, 1945); A. Symons, *Aubrey Beardsley* (London, 1898); R. Ross, *Aubrey Beardsley* (London, 1908); H. MacFall, *Aubrey Beardsley, the Man and His Work* (London, 1928); G. Burne-Jones, *Memorials of Edward Burne-Jones* (2v, London, 1904); F. M. Hueffer, *Ford Madox Brown* (London, 1896); A. C. Gissing, *William Holman Hunt* (London, 1936); E. I. Barrington, *The Life, Letters, and*

Work of Frederick Leighton (2v, London, 1906); J. G. Millais, *Life and Letters of Sir John Everett Millais* (2v, London, 1899); K. R. Towndrow, *Alfred Stevens* (London, 1939); W. Armstrong, *Turner* (2v, London, 1902); B. Falk, *Turner the Painter: His Hidden Life* (London, 1938); A. J. Finberg, *The Life of J. M. W. Turner* (Oxford, 1939); M. S. Watts, *Life of George Frederick Watts* (3v, London, 1912); R. Chapman, *The Laurel and the Thorn: A Study of G. F. Watts* (London, 1945); A. Woolner, *Thomas Woolner, R.A., Sculptor and Poet* (London, 1917).

MUSIC

≫≫

English music of the Victorian era produced no composers of genius and no eminent performers; but during the seventy years music made positive progress in social status and artistic competence.

In the early nineteenth century glee-singing was practically the only form of music that was general in England. A few lonely and romantic young men rehearsed flute solos, and most young ladies learned to play the harp as a graceful accomplishment. In the course of the century this instrument gradually yielded to the piano.

A season of ballet and Italian opera at Covent Garden was well attended every year, but the public interest seemed to be attracted by the temperamental behavior of the singers, or the pretty figures of the dancers, more than by the artistic qualities of the performance. Musicians were socially even less acceptable than actors, for as well as being emotional people, suspected of moral laxity, they were usually of foreign birth and therefore seemed fantastic in demeanor. A long-standing theory that music was effeminate discouraged young Englishmen from studying the art.

Royal patronage did much to break down the social barrier. Queen Victoria and Prince Albert were sincere patrons of every branch of music, appearing regularly in the royal box at operas and concerts, and receiving foreign musicians of distinction, such as Mendelssohn and Liszt, at Windsor and at Buckingham Palace. The Prince Consort's taste naturally ran especially to German music, and in this respect he followed the tradition of the previous century, when the early Georges had been the chief patrons of Handel. The Prince's interest in promoting public appreciation of music was symbolized by the fact that the chief memorial to him in London was a great concert hall, the Royal Albert Hall, opened in 1867.

Musical organizations were formed to sponsor public concerts. The Philharmonic Society, which had been founded in 1813, usually gave seven concerts each season, under outstanding conductors. Among the foreigners who came to England for this purpose were Ludwig Spohr, Felix Mendelssohn (who visited England ten times between 1829 and 1847), Hector Berlioz, and Richard Wagner, who made a great success with his concert in 1855. Some of these artists composed important works at the invitation of the Society.

In 1852 Henry Wylde founded the New Philharmonic Society, which presented a richer repertoire and made a special feature of introducing works by contemporary English composers. At the Crystal Palace, when it was moved to Sydenham, a London suburb, a young German bandmaster named August Manns started in 1855 a series of Saturday concerts which he continued with immense success until 1900. With the help of George Grove, the secretary of the Crystal Palace, he did much to create a love for orchestral music in English audiences; he made Schubert and Schumann popular idols, and familiarized the public with the symphonic works of Haydn, Mozart, Beethoven, Weber, Brahms, Rubinstein, and many others. Native work was by no means neglected, as about one third of the composers represented on the programs were British.

In 1859 the music publishing firm of Chappell & Co. started a series of "Popular Concerts" at St. James' Hall on Monday evenings. Six years later the Saturday afternoon rehearsals were opened to the public and in 1876 these were established as "Saturday Pops." These concerts did as much for the appreciation of chamber music as the Sydenham programs did for symphonic. One of the members of the firm, William Chappell, was also largely responsible for reviving an interest in English folk-songs, through his book, *Popular Music of the Olden Time* (1855-59).

Nor was the growing enthusiasm for music confined to London: many of the provincial cities organized music festivals and concert series. The Birmingham and Norwich festivals had been in existence since the eighteenth century, and another important one was started in Leeds in 1858. Later in the century some of the festivals promoted extensive competitions in choral and other types of music.

Side by side with the development of concerts and orchestras went that of musical education. The Royal Academy of Music, founded in 1822 with the King as patron, was intended to train native musicians sufficiently for them to compete with foreigners. From its original enrollment of forty boys and forty girls between the ages of ten and fifteen it grew steadily in numbers and curriculum, offering many scholarships through which gifted young musicians received their training. The certificates of this and the other institutions formed later in the century became the professional credentials of music teachers throughout the British empire.

The Royal College of Organists was established by R. D. Limpus in 1864, and the Guildhall School of Music, supported by the Corporation of the City of London, came into existence in 1880 to spread musical knowledge as widely as possible, with particular attention to the amateur performer. To provide specialized training on a more advanced level, the Royal College of Music was founded in 1882 with the Prince of Wales as patron and George Grove as director.

The growth of these institutions had an effect upon the universities, which had not been enthusiastic about offering musical instruction on the same basis as other subjects, although chairs of music had existed for generations, as practically honorary posts. At Cambridge the reform was led by Charles Villiers Stanford, who became organist of Trinity College in 1873, conductor of the University Musical Society, and eventually Professor of Music. He revised the requirements and demanded residence as requisite for the degrees. Similar reforms were made at Oxford under the professorship of Sir John Stainer. The universities of Manchester, Edinburgh and Birmingham installed courses of instruction and required practical tests of all candidates for musical degrees.

The teaching of music in the schools also developed slowly. In 1841 John Hullah, who had studied in Paris under Guillaume Wilhem, the founder of musical education, started classes in Exeter Hall for the instruction of school teachers. As qualified teachers became available, the London Board of Education incorporated musical instruction in the curriculum of every school.

With an expanding audience and a supply of trained performers, it might be expected that English composers would flourish. Although they increased in numbers, however, few achieved permanent importance. Sacred music, such as hymns and oratorios, perhaps approached nearest to distinction, and the closely related forms of the glee and the madrigal were significant as sustaining an old English tradition. Robert Lucas de Pearsall (1795-1856) was the leader in the revival of the madrigal. John Goss (1800-1880) composed glees and two orchestral overtures, but was best known for his anthems. Sir George Alexander Macfarren (1813-1887), author of standard treatises on musical theory, wrote oratorios, cantatas, operas, symphonies, anthems, and songs. The leading composer of the mid-century, however, was Sir William Sterndale Bennett (1816-1875), who was admired by Mendelssohn and Schumann, served as Professor of Music at Cambridge and Principal of the Royal Academy of Music, and wrote a symphony, cantatas, sonatas, and overtures.

British composers were ambitious to win fame with operas, most of which were in the tradition of the English ballad opera, with an admixture of Italian melodic extravagances. The only one now remembered is Michael William Balfe (1808-1870), an Irishman, of whose numerous operas *The Bohemian Girl* (1843) is still performed. Vincent Wallace (1814-1865), also Irish, composed *Maritana*. Later in the century Arthur Goring Thomas (1850-1892) won a European reputation with *Esmeralda* and *Nadeshda*.

The most distinctive contribution made by English music during the nineteenth century, however, was in light opera. At the beginning of the era burlettas and other species of musical play were being composed extensively by John Hullah, John Barnett, and others. These reached a wide public because they could be performed at unlicenced playhouses where legitimate drama was banned. They paved the way for the witty comic operas, with librettos by W. S. Gilbert, which brought world-wide fame to Arthur Sullivan (1842-1900), somewhat to his embarrassment, as he would have preferred to be known for his serious music. Of Irish and Italian ancestry, he was trained at the Royal Academy of Music and at Leipsic. Upon his return to England in 1861 some of his music was performed at the Crystal Palace concerts, and he became a sensation overnight. From 1875 onward the Gilbert and Sullivan operas, produced at the Opera Comique Theater, and later at the Savoy, delighted the public year after year. Occasionally the collaborators quarreled and Sullivan wrote several scores for other librettists, such as Sidney Grundy, F. C. Burnand, and Basil Hood. He attempted one grand opera, *Ivanhoe*, to words by Julian Sturgis. Outside of this field, Sullivan was successful with a vast range of compositions, such as overtures, cantatas, ballets, oratorios, a "Te Deum," the sentimental song "The Lost Chord," and the hymn "Onward, Christian Soldiers."

During the later years of the Victorian period a new generation of English composers emerged, with greater intellectual and technical endowments than their predecessors. The most prominent of these were Charles Hubert Hastings Parry (1848-1918), Charles Villiers Stanford (1852-1924), Frederic Hymen Cowen (1852-1935), and Edward Elgar (1857-1934). The work of these men won respect for English music throughout Europe and America, and some critics consider that they established a genuine "national school" of music.

The progress of English music since 1830 could be attributed to several main causes: (1) close intercourse with the great musical centers on the Continent; (2) extension of musical education and organizations; (3) improvement in the economic and social status of musicians. The royal patronage furthered this last change by conferring knighthoods upon prominent musical personages. Beginning with Henry Bishop in 1842, almost every outstanding composer and musical expert received the rank of knight before the end of his career.

It is not to be assumed, however, that the development was wholly in the direction of technique, intellect, and social prestige. Vulgar music also flourished. In the early part of the century the chief centers of popular music were the open-air amusement parks, Vauxhall, Ranelagh, and Cremorne Gardens. Also, a crude sort of night-club existed in many London taverns, where soloists or small groups supplied entertainment for all-male audiences, some of the performers gaining great reputations. From these origins emerged the Music Halls, the English equivalent of vaudeville, which drew enthusiastic audiences of all social classes. The songs from their programs, whether comic ("Tommy, make room for your uncle"), patriotic ("We don't want to fight, but by Jingo if we do"), or sentimental ("Paddle your own canoe"), were carried to the farthest corners of the English-speaking world.

Oxford History of Music, vi, vii (London, 1905-34); F. Hueffer, *Half a Century of Music in England, 1837-87* (London, 1889); H. Davey, *History of English Music* (London, 1895; rev. ed., 1921); J. A. Fuller-Maitland, *English Music in the Nineteenth Century* (London, 1902); E. Walker, *A History of Music in England* (London, 1907); J. Bennett, *Forty Years of Music, 1865-1905* (London, 1908); E. Ford, *A Short History of Music in England* (London, 1909); P. M. Young, *Pageant of England's Music* (Cambridge, 1939); F. Corder, *A History of the Royal Academy of Music* (London, 1923); C. L. Kenney, *A Memoir of Michael William Balfe* (London, 1875); W. A. Barrett, *Balfe and His Works* (London, 1882); J. R. S. Bennett, *The Life of William Sterndale Bennett* (Cambridge, 1907); H. S. Wyndham, *Augustus Manns and the Saturday Concerts* (London, 1909); A. Lawrence, *Sir Arthur Sullivan: Life Story, Letters, and Reminiscences* (London, 1899); H. S. Wyndham, *Arthur Seymour Sullivan* (London, 1926); H. Sullivan and N. Flower, *Sir Arthur Sullivan: His Life, Letters, and Diaries* (London, 1927); P. A. Scholes, *The Mirror of Music, 1844-1944* (London, 1947).

BOOK PUBLISHING

>>

The business of publishing, in the modern conception of the word, developed slowly during the eighteenth century. Prior to that time, the manufacture and the distribution of books were in the hands of two separate tradesmen, the printer and the bookseller. The most important books were produced in London, with a large secondary center in Edinburgh; but throughout the country many books and other printed items were brought out locally in the smaller cities. From the beginning of the eighteenth century a few London booksellers became so enterprising in their methods of hiring authors and advertising books that they can be regarded as functioning somewhat like modern publishers; but in general, book production was still a by-product of the bookseller's trade.

Under these conditions authors were likely to be hired as "Grub Street hacks" to prepare some sort of material that the booksellers considered profitable. The author of a more ambitious literary work or a more scholarly treatise had to depend for financial support either upon some single rich patron or upon a group of subscribers who would agree in advance to buy the book when it should be printed.

With the steady increase in the reading public during the eighteenth century the business advantages of book production became more conspicuous. The prosperous middle class was looking for both entertainment and instruction through reading. Circulating libraries became common both in London and in the provincial towns, to supply a steady stream of books, chiefly for ladies who had much leisure time for reading and who did not want to accumulate a large, expensive collection of privately-owned books.

By the beginning of the nineteenth century several booksellers had definitely evolved into powerful publishers. The firms of Longmans and Murray in London, and Constable and Blackwood in Edinburgh, gained a preëminence that lasted through the Victorian period and lends them continued prestige today. The huge success of such authors as Byron and Scott not only enriched their publishers but also changed the business relationship with authors. The old patronage system had been dying ever since Dr. Johnson's assault upon it. Now publishers began to vie with each other in offering clear-cut financial contracts to writers. As a result the profession of authorship assumed an entirely new status in the Victorian age.

As the market grew wider and competition increased, publishers discovered the value of advertising. Among the enterprising new firms were those of Richard Bentley and Henry Colburn, who were bitter rivals in bidding against each other for authors' work and in intriguing to obtain favorable reviews for their books. Formerly book reviews had been long and critical analyses in the solemn monthly and quarterly periodicals; but between 1820 and 1830 several literary weeklies were established, gaining their financial support from the extensive advertising of the various publishers. In 1833 the weekly *Publishers' Circular* came into existence as the official trade mouthpiece of all the London firms. Besides Bentley and Colburn, other notable publishing firms at the beginning of the Victorian age were Taylor and Hessey, Moxon, and Pickering.

The changing conditions also had their effect upon the physical form of books. Until the Victorian period books of any consequence were intended for the handsome and permanent environment of a gentleman's library. Printed in artistic type, on hand-made paper, with widely-spaced lines and generous margins, they were bound in leather and often illustrated with steel engravings. A novel would require anything from three to six neat little volumes, costing twenty shillings or more. At the other extreme, cheap printed matter for the populace consisted of chapbooks and broadsheets of the crudest typography and woodcuts.

The new publishers, however, catered to people who wanted reading matter of adequate form and content but who could not afford to buy expensive books in many volumes. Neat one-volume editions of the standard poets and essayists multiplied. Some of them were miniature books with eye-destroying typography. Bentley, Colburn, and others published reprint series of popular novels at five shillings each. Other firms brought out extensive series of informative volumes in all branches of knowledge, written by competent authorities. Typical were the *Cabinet Cyclopedia* edited by Professor Lardner of the new University of London, and the reprints of Greek and Latin Classics published by Henry G. Bohn, whose various "Libraries," begun in 1846, eventually extended to 766 volumes.

As a medium for issuing new novels, the use of "monthly parts" became important at the beginning of the Victorian era. In this form most of the novels of Dickens, Thackeray, and other authors reached the maximum number of readers. People who would not be willing to pay out a pound or more for a single novel would unhesitatingly spend an equivalent sum divided into a shilling a month over two years. Each installment, containing several chapters and stitched in a paper cover, was sold at bookstalls, and could be bought by busy people to read during a train journey or a quiet evening at home. Prosperous customers could subscribe to the whole work in advance and have the monthly parts delivered to them. Most copies were discarded when read, or worn out by frequent handling. If someone became specially fond of a novel he might have the separate parts bound into one or two volumes in a form to suit himself; and after the year or two of serial publication reached an end, the publisher issued the whole thing in bound form for customers who had not obtained the parts individually.

The present-day value of first editions of those novels is affected by their form of publication. One of them in the original paper-covered parts, all in good condition, commands a high price because few readers preserved all the parts carefully. The identical parts, if stripped of their paper jackets and bound in leather or cloth, have far lower value; and the first edition brought out in book form, though produced by the same publisher from the same type, is now cheaper still.

The method of publication in parts, both for novels and for extended character studies, flourished between 1835 and 1865. Some attempts were made to issue weekly parts at a lower price, but this proved less successful. The monthly parts at a shilling, with several well-engraved illustrations, suited the public better.

The illustrations contributed to the popularity of these works, as such artists as George Cruikshank were famous in their own right for their humorous drawings. It has sometimes even been asserted that the public concept of the characters in the novels was determined by the artist more than by the author. In fact, the method of publication developed partly out of an older system in vogue among printsellers, who issued drawings by favorite comic artists at regular intervals with some continuing topic or group of characters. It was thus that an enterprising new publishing firm, Chapman & Hall, planned a series of burlesque drawings of amateur sportsmen, decided to have some letterpress narrative to accompany each picture, and engaged the young journalist Charles Dickens to write the script. The chance of the artist's death meant that the series of essaylike episodes changed into a continuous narrative, and thus *The Pickwick Papers* became the first widely successful novel in monthly parts.

This form of publication influenced a novelist's technique. As he was usually still writing the next installment when the preceding one was issued, he could be guided by the reactions of the public much as a playwright can revise a play after the first performance. If one installment proved effective, recommendations would spread by word of mouth, all copies would be quickly sold, and the public would clamor for more. Thus the author would know that he had pleased his readers' taste, and he could build up the charac-

No. I.   DECEMBER.   PRICE 1s.

LITTLE DORRIT

BY
CHARLES DICKENS.

WITH
ILLUSTRATIONS BY H. K. BROWNE.

LONDON: BRADBURY & EVANS, BOUVERIE STREET.
AGENTS: J. MENZIES, EDINBURGH; MURRAY AND SON, GLASGOW; J. M'GLASHAN, DUBLIN.

☞ The Author reserves the right of Translation.

COVER OF *LITTLE DORRIT* IN MONTHLY PARTS

ters or develop the episodes in subsequent numbers. On the other hand, if interest fell off, monthly sales would decline and unfavorable letters would reach author and publisher, giving warning that a change of plot was desirable. The outcome was a rambling, unplanned, lively and vigorous type of narration, crowded with varied characters and digressive episodes.

The chief rival of Chapman & Hall in publishing novels in parts was the firm of Bradbury & Evans, which was also successful with magazines. Other new publishers were also assuming prominence. Macmillan & Company, established in 1843, began with educational books, but soon grew strong through issuing the poetry of Tennyson, the novels of Kingsley, the children's books of Lewis Carroll, and many prominent works in the social sciences. The firm of Smith, Elder & Company, which began in 1819, assumed importance in the 1840's under George Smith, Jr., son of the founder; he published the works of Ruskin, Charlotte Brontë, and the Brownings, the later novels of Thackeray, and some of the writings of Darwin, Matthew Arnold, and many other leading Victorians. Typical of the increasing prestige of publishers was Smith's eventual decision to sink some of the proceeds of his business in *The Dictionary of National Biography*, a work of patriotic and scholarly value that would not earn a profit.

The business of issuing cheap reprints in standardized format became increasingly significant. Charles Knight and the Chambers brothers in the middle of the century, George Routledge later, and finally J. M. Dent with his "Everyman's Library" brought good books into the hands of people with small homes and limited incomes. Uniform series of elementary handbooks, such as "English Men of Letters," were available for readers who wanted to expand their educations.

As magazines of fiction had become more numerous and

prosperous, the novels of the most popular authors came to be serialized in them instead of being issued in independent monthly parts. Book publication of novels was then standardized in a three-volume form; and, because this was too expensive for the average buyer, fiction readers depended upon the circulating libraries. Mudie's library gained almost a monopoly. When George Moore's first novel, *A Modern Lover*, was published in 1883, Mudie's banned it as immoral. Moore then arranged with his publisher to bring out his next novel in one volume, at a much lower price. The reduction being compensated by vastly increased sales, the one-volume format became general so quickly that by 1894 Kipling could write his nostalgic poem, "The Three-Decker," on the theme that "the three-volume novel is extinct."

Another important trend in the closing years of the century was toward more attractive physical form of books, one result of William Morris's campaign to bring artistic beauty into everyday life. Morris's own printing and bookbinding, at his Kelmscott Press, while setting a new standard of perfection, was too expensive for the general public; but he influenced the productions of commercial publishers. As part of the "aesthetic" cult of the eighties and nineties, new firms such as John Lane and Leonard Smithers specialized in "exquisite" books with illustrations by Beardsley, Crane, and other designers. New mechanical methods helped toward the production of artistic books which could be sold at a reasonable price.

The financial interests of authors had been fairly well guaranteed by the Copyright Act of 1842. Previous copyright law had been solely for the protection of publishers, but the Act of 1842 protected every book until seven years after the death of the author or for forty-two years from the date of publication, whichever period should be longer. In 1883 the Society of Authors was founded to safeguard

A PAGE FROM THE *KELMSCOTT CHAUCER*

authors' rights and to advise them on contracts, and so forth.

The commercial importance of publishing had meanwhile assumed international aspects. Works of contemporary foreign authors were translated wholesale; such French writers as Sue and Dumas were best-sellers in England. Similarly, works of English authors were translated abroad; and with the increasing knowledge of English upon the Continent it also became profitable to circulate English books there in the original language. An enterprising German publisher, Bernhard Tauchnitz, started to issue cheap reprints of English books in neat pocket-sized volumes. English residents when traveling abroad discovered the Tauchnitz editions to be so much cheaper and handier than the original editions that they brought copies home in such numbers as to evoke protests from English publishers.

A more serious financial competition came from across the Atlantic. As the American reading public increased, large publishing firms developed in New York, Philadelphia, and Boston, using current English literature as their staple. English authors became annoyed when they realized that their books were circulating by the thousand in the United States without any profit for themselves. Dickens, Captain Marryat, and other popular writers crossed the ocean in an effort to arrange financial contracts, and a few of the more reputable American firms agreed to pay for so-called "exclusive" rights; but this did not protect the publishers even from unscrupulous competitors in their own country, who continued to "pirate" the same English books. To some extent the problems became reciprocal, when some American writers such as Fenimore Cooper and Washington Irving, and—later—Mark Twain and other humorists, became popular with English readers.

Prolonged agitation for an international copyright act

gradually brought results. Representatives of several nations met in Switzerland in 1886 to draw up "the Berne Convention," which was ratified by a number of governments, including the British, and which granted reciprocal protection for authors' rights. The United States remained outside of this "Copyright Union," but in 1891 an act of Congress provided for mutual copyright arrangements with various countries, including Great Britain.

The improvement and enlargement of the publishing business had meant a great increase in the number of professional writers, who thus reached a vastly wider public than ever before. This, and the better legal protection of their rights, made authorship a recognized career instead of a precarious indulgence in originality. Competing for such substantial profits, the rank and file of authors undoubtedly advanced in technical facility and in ability to gratify readers' demands. Whether the new conditions also acted as a barrier to the emergence of supreme literary genius is a question open to debate.

F. A. Mumby, *The Romance of Bookselling* (London, 1910); H. Jackson, *The Printing of Books* (London, 1938); M. Plant, *The English Book Trade* (London, 1939); M. Sadleir, *The Evolution of Publishers' Binding Styles, 1770-1900* (London, 1930); T. Constable, *Archibald Constable and His Literary Correspondents* (3v, Edinburgh, 1873); S. Smiles, *Memoir and Correspondence of John Murray* (2v, London, 1891); G. Paston, *At John Murray's* (London, 1932); M. O. W. Oliphant, *Annals of a Publishing House: John Blackwood and His Sons* (3v, Edinburgh, 1897-98); W. Tinsley, *Random Recollections of an Old Publisher* (London, 1900); L. Huxley, *The House of Smith, Elder* (London, 1923); A. Waugh, *A Hundred Years of Publishing* [Chapman & Hall] (London, 1930); F. A. Mumby, *The House of Routledge* (London, 1934); H. G. Merriam, *Edward Moxon, Publisher of Poets* (New York, 1939); C. Morgan, *The House of Macmillan, 1843-1943* (London, 1943), I. R. Brussel, *Anglo-American First Editions, 1826-1900* (London, 1935).

NEWSPAPERS AND MAGAZINES
>>>

The opening year of Queen Victoria's reign was also the first year in which English newspapers attained anything like their modern form and importance. Previously they had been small in size and limited in circulation. In 1836 *The Times*, fifty years old, had the largest circulation of the London dailies, ten thousand. None of its numerous competitors exceeded six thousand copies per day. The chief restraint to expansion was the high price of all newspapers, largely due to a government "stamp tax" of fourpence on every copy. There was also a heavy tax upon each advertisement. The stamp tax, which had been instituted in the eighteenth century as an indirect form of government censorship, was bitterly resented, and during the early 1830's the authorities were defied by numerous unauthorized newspapers that were issued without the tax stamp. Edward Lytton Bulwer as a young Member of Parliament took the lead in having the tax reduced to one penny. At once the prices of newspapers were sharply reduced, the sales expanded vastly, and the papers doubled and redoubled their size. More space for well-written articles being provided, and better salaries being paid, many able writers joined the staffs of the papers, and journalism soon became recognized as a respectable profession.

Such papers as *The Times*, the *Morning Post*, and the *Morning Chronicle* became influential in political comment and literary criticism. Improved communications, provided by the steamship, the railway, and the telegraph, resulted in fuller coverage of foreign events. In 1849 Reuter's international news agency was founded in Paris, and thereafter supplied English papers with world-wide despatches.

Several prominent authors were temporarily attracted by

the new prosperity of journalism. Thackeray was involved in one of the unsuccessful ventures that sought to take advantage of the reduction in the stamp tax. Later he reviewed books for *The Times* and contributed to several other newspapers. Dickens, who had started his writing career as a reporter for one of the smaller papers before the repeal of the tax, afterwards served on the staff of the *Morning Chronicle*, and in 1846 for a few weeks he was editor of a new Liberal paper, the *Daily News*.

In 1855 the remaining penny tax was finally abolished, and the papers again cut their prices. In that year the *Daily Telegraph* was started, selling at one penny a copy, and most of the other papers soon found themselves obliged to follow suit, though the ever increasing prestige of *The Times* enabled it to hold its price at two pence. It gave fuller and more dependable news than any other paper, and gradually came to be regarded as an official mouthpiece of the government.

The Crimean war of 1854-55 offered newspapers their first opportunity of melodramatic reporting, and the "war correspondent" became a recognized journalistic phenomenon, William Howard Russell being the first to win fame in this capacity. Toward the end of the century the power of the newspapers over public thinking, and the tendency of some of them to exploit sensational stories of scandal and crime, began to disturb orthodox minds. In Tennyson's poem "Despair," a man driven to attempted suicide by the materialism of his time is depicted as exclaiming bitterly, "These are the new dark ages, you see, of the popular press."

In 1896 an ambitious young journalist, Alfred Harmsworth, founded the *Daily Mail*, to sell for a halfpenny and to bring the news in simple, vivid form to the widest possible audience. By his use of columnists, his sponsoring of vigorous political and social crusades, his publicity "stunts," he introduced into English journalism much of the energy that was already prevalent in American newspapers.

The larger provincial cities, of course, had also developed noteworthy newspapers, the most famous being the Manchester *Guardian* and the Edinburgh *Scotsman;* but the restricted area and centralized population of the British Isles gave the London papers a nation-wide distribution that increased their power.

Weekly papers were less influential in politics and news-reporting, but were of prime significance in intellectual matters. The *Examiner,* which had been founded by Leigh Hunt and his brother to express their radical opinions, was one of the leading weeklies of social and literary commentary during the mid-Victorian period. The *Literary Gazette,* established by William Jerdan in 1817, was the first important weekly to be devoted primarily to book reviews and news of authors. It provided a practically complete record of current literary events; but as the proprietor was impecunious he began to be accused of allotting space and praise in proportion to the advertising space purchased by publishers. To set a higher standard of literary ethics, James Silk Buckingham in 1828 founded the *Athenaeum.* Under the editorship of Charles Wentworth Dilke this paper quickly gained prestige, and for the whole of the Victorian period it retained its leadership by the dependability of its information and the soundness of its criticisms. Its reviews were contributed by many of the leading authors of each generation.

Established in the same year as the *Athenaeum,* the *Spectator* was less concerned with literature and more with current events. Non-partisan in politics, it discussed the great issues of social and administrative reform throughout the century. Although book reviews occupied only a small proportion of its pages, they were influential because of the high reputation of the contributors. Its nearest rival in the later years of the century was the *Saturday Review*, which began in 1855. A literary weekly which included some important scholarly articles as well as reviews of current literature was the *Academy*, which began publication in 1869.

A special place among weekly journals must be accorded to *Punch*, founded in 1841 as a humorous magazine with considerable serious social purposes of radical political criticism and concern for the welfare of the masses. Illustrators such as John Leech, Richard Doyle, and John Tenniel, essayists and poets such as Thackeray, Douglas Jerrold, and Thomas Hood, gave it a success that has lasted through more than a century, though with a gradual tendency toward more conservative opinions. Its political cartoons were effective, and its reviews of books and plays, while witty, were also soundly critical. A file of *Punch*, by reason of both its pictures and its letter-press, provides perhaps the best as well as the most entertaining week-by-week record of the whole Victorian period.

Monthly magazines also took on their modern identity about the beginning of Victoria's reign. Prior to that time, the most prominent literary periodicals had been the "Reviews," most of which were issued quarterly; as their title indicated, the contents were limited to long and detailed criticisms of books, chiefly those of informative material. The two leading examples throughout the nineteenth century were the *Edinburgh Review* (established in 1802) and the *Quarterly Review* (established in 1809). Originating as the organs of the Whig and Tory parties, respectively, these were disfigured in their earlier years by prejudice; but by the time the Victorian age began they had adopted a more responsible and restrained attitude.

By that time, however, they were meeting strong competition from the monthly magazines. When adopted in the eighteenth century, the word *magazine* had retained its meaning as a "storehouse" and was applied to periodicals that summarized the month's news and selected the best items of current literature. Gradually they accepted a greater proportion of original contributions, but poetry and fiction remained subordinate to literary criticism, political comment, and expository articles. In 1814 the enterprising publisher Henry Colburn founded the *New Monthly Magazine* and tried to give it popular appeal by various fresh devices, such as attaching the authors' names to their contributions and appointing prominent writers to the editorship. When Edward Lytton Bulwer, young and ambitious, was editor in 1831-32 he brought in a number of well-known contributors.

Blackwood's Magazine, founded in Edinburgh in 1817, brought a new note of witty satire, and made frequent use of fictitious dialogues to convey its contributors' opinions, which were highly partisan (on the Tory side) and sometimes scurrilous. *Fraser's Magazine*, established in London in 1830, followed the same pattern. It was *Bentley's Miscellany*, beginning its publication in 1836 with the youthful Charles Dickens as first editor, which shifted the major emphasis for the first time to fiction. Maintaining a large proportion of light and humorous material, illustrated by Leech, Cruikshank, and other favorite comic artists, *Bentley's* appealed to a public that would have been repelled by the heavy appearance and factual or controversial contents of the older magazines. By printing his own novel, *Oliver Twist*, in it in installments, Dickens set a precedent for the serial publication of novels. Essays and poetry by popular authors also figured largely in *Bentley's*, which finally went out of existence in 1869. William Harrison Ainsworth, another prolific novelist, who succeeded Dickens as editor of *Bentley's*, set up a rival periodical of the same style, *Ainsworth's Magazine*, in 1842.

Attempts were also being made to provide magazines at a lower price and on a simpler level of literacy, to reach the wide public that was resulting from the spread of elementary education. Most of these publications were issued weekly and sold for not more than two pence. The most successful were *Chambers' Journal*, founded in Edinburgh in 1832, the *Penny Magazine*, edited by Charles Knight from 1832 to 1845, and *The Family Herald*, founded in 1843. Knight's *Penny Magazine* reached an unprecedented circulation of 200,000.

Dickens, whose taste for editorship had been whetted by his three years in charge of *Bentley's*, became convinced that a cheap weekly magazine could be immensely influential if it had the prestige of good literary contents. Accordingly in 1850 he founded *Household Words*. As he was at the pinnacle of his fame, he was able to enlist excellent contributors, and his magazine was read by people of cultured taste as well as by the wider public for whom it was intended. Fiction and informal articles on topical subjects predominated, and among the contributors (whose work was all printed anonymously) were Mrs. Gaskell, Wilkie Collins, Coventry Patmore, and other great Victorian writers.

After nine years, because of a quarrel with the publishers, Dickens discontinued *Household Words* and replaced it with *All the Year Round*, identical except in title. When he died his son carried the publication on until almost the end of the century.

Newer publishing firms were eager to have a share in the profitable magazine market. *Macmillan's Magazine*, a monthly which compromised in the matter of price by charging a shilling, less than half the cost of preceding monthlies, was started in 1859, and a few months later the rival firm of Smith, Elder & Company brought out the *Cornhill Magazine* at the same price. With the distinction of having Thackeray as its first editor, the *Cornhill* immediately gained a huge circulation of 120,000 copies. Concentrating upon fiction by first-class authors, the *Cornhill* serialized novels by Trollope, George Eliot, Charles Reade, Thomas Hardy, and many others. After Thackeray was succeeded by his son-in-law, Leslie Stephen, a leading critic and literary historian, the magazine also became outstanding for its publication of essays by such authors as Matthew Arnold and Robert Louis Stevenson.

A rival magazine, established in the same year, was *Temple Bar*, on a somewhat lower level of literary distinction. Beginning in 1882 *Longman's Magazine* published the work of a younger generation of authors such as Hardy, Andrew Lang, and Kipling. Before the end of the century new methods of reproducing photographs and other illustrations, including even color-plates, helped the development of a sizable group of handsome shilling magazines that were able to pay good prices for the work of popular writers.

The improved techniques of photo-lithography also widened the scope of the weekly pictorial news-magazines, of which the oldest, the *Illustrated London News,* dated back to 1842. The files of this magazine are of immense value to the student of the history and manners of the Victorian era.

The two senior critical reviews, the *Edinburgh* and the *Quarterly,* retained much of their prestige until the end of the Victorian epoch. They widened their scope by introducing essays on various topics, no longer necessarily based upon some newly-published book. Several rivals shared the field with them. The *Westminster Review,* founded in 1824, became the mouthpiece of the political third party, the Radicals. John Stuart Mill was one of its early editors, and contributors included Carlyle, Froude, George Eliot, and Walter Pater. In 1865 George Henry Lewes established the *Fortnightly Review,* modeled upon the French *Revue des deux mondes.* Assuming that the term *review* could apply to a survey of the current world as well as to criticism of books, the *Fortnightly* (which actually was published monthly except during its first year of existence) devoted itself chiefly to social, political, and international topics. All contributions were identified as to authorship. Somewhat similar in form were the *Contemporary Review* (begun in 1866 with a primarily religious emphasis, and later devoted to social reforms) and the *Nineteenth Century*, which was founded in 1877 and which printed many poems of Tennyson, Arnold, and Swinburne, as well as articles by Froude, Gladstone, Ruskin, Arnold, and other political and literary leaders. In strong contrast, *The Yellow Book* (1894-97) was the organ of the "Aesthetes."

The significance of the periodical press in the literary picture of the Victorian age cannot be over-emphasized. Not only did the book reviews invest critics with new influence, but sale of contributions to newspapers and magazines became a major resource of most authors. A large proportion of the century's literature appeared in periodicals before being republished in volume form. Writers consequently acquired new habits of brevity and informality. Their readers' familiarity with daily newspapers enabled the authors to deal vigorously with current events and problems. Detailed analysis of any Victorian author's work ought always to be accompanied by consultation of the files of major periodicals covering the relevant years.

J. Grant, *The Newspaper Press* (3v, London, 1871-72); H. R. Fox-Bourne, *English Newspapers* (2v, London, 1887); *Progress of British Newspapers in the Nineteenth Century* (London, 1901); T. H. S. Escott, *Masters of English Journalism* (London, 1911); J. D. Symon, *The Press and Its Story* (London, 1914); J. Soames, *The English Press* (London, 1937); H. A. Innes, "The English Press in the Nineteenth Century," *University of Toronto Quarterly*, xv (1945), 37-53; *The History of "The Times"* (3v, London, 1935-47); W. H. Hindle, *"The Morning Post", 1772-1937* (London, 1937); W. H. Mills, *"The Manchester Guardian": A Century of*

History (London, 1921); W. Graham, *English Literary Periodicals* (New York, 1930); M. H. Spielmann, *The History of "Punch"* (London, 1895); *"The Edinburgh Review, 1802-1902," Edinburgh Review*, CXLV (1902). 275-318; "The Centenary of *The Quarterly Review," Quarterly Review*, CCX (1909). 731-84; CCXI (1909). 279-324; E. T. Cook, "The Jubilee of *The Cornhill," Cornhill Magazine*, CI (1910). 8-27; R. C. Lehmann, *Charles Dickens as Editor* (London, 1912); W. B. Thomas, *The Story of "The Spectator," 1828-1928* (London, 1928); M. M. Thrall, *Rebellious Fraser's* (New York, 1934); L. M. Littlewood, "A Victorian Magazine" [*Bentley's Miscellany*], *Contemporary Review*, CLI (1937). 331-39; E. M. Everett, *The Party of Humanity: "The Fortnightly Review" and Its Contributors, 1865-74* (Chapel Hill, 1940); M. M. Bevington, *"The Saturday Review," 1855-68* (New York, 1941); L. A. Marchand, *"The Athenaeum": A Mirror of Victorian Culture* (Chapel Hill, 1941).

POETRY

>>

I. TOPICS

The beginning of the Victorian period marks a definite
break in the continuity of English poetry, for the accidental reason that many of the major Romantic poets had died
comparatively young. It is hard to realize that Keats was
born in the same year as Carlyle, and might therefore have
lived to 1880, spanning practically the whole Victorian age.
The lives of Byron and Shelley could have lasted until the
seventies, those even of Scott and Coleridge to the fifties.
All these poets, however, died between 1821 and 1834, and
both Scott and Coleridge had ceased writing poetry many
years earlier.

Of the few Romantic poets who survived into the Victorian age, the literary significance was historical rather than
contemporary. Wordsworth, oldest of the original group,
lived until 1850 and held the distinction of the laureateship. It is now known that in the thirties and forties he
was doing significant work upon his great unfinished autobiographical poem; but by the Victorian public he was
respected merely as a living monument to the greatness of
Lyrical Ballads. Walter Savage Landor, who lived until
1864, had long before turned to the writing of prose, and his
exile in Italy was a further reason for his being ignored
among English poets. Other Romantic poets whose lives
lasted into Victorian times were Robert Southey (died
1843), Thomas Campbell (died 1844), and Thomas Moore
(died 1852); but they had long outworn their popularity,

and had contributed nothing noteworthy to poetry after about 1815.

Had Keats achieved full artistic maturity, he might have been the greatest author of the Victorian age, with Shelley, Byron, and other poets in their prime helping to dominate the scene. But the violent creative energy of the Romantic years seemed to have burned out the poets, either to actual death or to quiescence; and so the young generation which began writing about 1830 had an exceptionally clear field in which to seek distinction.

This did not mean, of course, that success would come easily to them. The reading public had become thoroughly addicted to the poetry of the preceding generation, and did not welcome change. Byron and Scott had been popular for twenty years, but Shelley and Keats were only beginning to be known and admired, even by the intelligentsia, in 1830. The successful younger poets of the time were now-forgotten people like Robert Montgomery and Letitia E. Landon, who produced glib imitations of Byron and Southey.

If the general public clung to the obvious exponents of poetical romanticism, some of the critical theorists went to the other extreme and proclaimed that all poetry was at an end. The new age, they asserted, was scientific in spirit, practical in outlook. Prose was much better suited for exposition of facts and discussion of theories; poetry, a survival from primitive and unsophisticated centuries, would rapidly become meaningless to those of the next generation.

There was a modicum of truth in the threat. In particular the vast increase in the influence of the novel after 1830 showed that the public had discovered a medium of literary entertainment that was easier to read than poetry, as well as being more topical in its application to ordinary experience.

In face of these difficulties the young poets began their work with a tendency to follow in the footsteps of the successful Romantics. Alfred Tennyson's first books of poetry, published in 1827, 1831, and 1833, were strongly reminiscent of Keats; Robert Browning's *Pauline*, in 1833, devoutly echoed Shelley; and Elizabeth Barrett's youthful volumes, in 1826 and 1833, completed the Romantic trilogy by revealing discipleship of Byron.

Poets of any real genius, however, are unwilling to remain imitators; and besides, the competition of prose fiction was becoming a menace. Ambitious for literary eminence, the young writers faced the alternative of turning to prose or of evolving new poetic themes and methods which could compete with the novel on its own ground. Both Tennyson and Browning provide autobiographical records of the arduous—even painful—struggle through which they realized that their poetry must turn from traditionally "beautiful" and "literary" topics and deal more directly with the concerns of human life. Tennyson symbolized his conversion in "The Palace of Art"; Browning inserted his confession in long digressions scattered through his difficult poem *Sordello*.

The major change was a shift from the subjective to the objective. Excepting Scott, the Romantic poets, in spite of their concern over "the common man" and "the welfare of humanity," were largely self-centered. Wordsworth wrote poetic autobiography; Coleridge explored his own imaginative processes of association; Byron dramatized himself in his heroes; Shelley created vast symbols for his emotional moods; Keats enthusiastically reported his discoveries of beauty. All of them could produce lyrics of supreme beauty and several of them were masters of the sonnet.

Tennyson and Browning began with considerable talent for lyrical expression, but they moved steadily away from so personal an utterance of feeling; and neither of them showed any aptitude for the sonnet, which is chiefly a vehicle for strong individual emotion.

Having made up his mind that it was the business of a modern poet to treat of the life of his own day and the problems which were growing insistent in current controversy, Tennyson spent the next few years in working out methods of dealing with them. As one type, he created poems of everyday life, modeled somewhat upon Wordsworth's. Some were fairly successful in presenting humble, unlettered people, though at the expense of a few prosy lines and occasional bathos. When he tried the same technique in delineating people of higher culture, as in "The Gardener's Daughter," "Audley Court," or "Edwin Morris," there was something almost ludicrous in the effort to reproduce familiar conversation in blank verse and to embellish commonplace activities with poetic imagery. In such poems as "The May Queen" and "The Miller's Daughter" Tennyson reached a wide area of the public which knew little of "literary" poetry but responded to the sentimental tales that he embodied in obvious metrical melodies.

A more ambitious attack upon a contemporary topic, not wholly successful as a work of art but all the more revealing of Tennyson's search for new media, was *The Princess*, in which he tried to use a synthetic medieval romance as a vehicle for a discussion of "women's rights" in general and college education for women in particular. This was a very new matter of controversy in 1847, and Tennyson had definite theories to contribute. Characteristically, he was suggesting a compromise between traditional customs and progressive experiment. The fictitious narrative, however, hampered his argument more than helping it.

He was more successful when he adapted existing literary material to serve as his vehicle. Admiring classical epic and medieval romance, he could find no justification for using

them as sources for merely artistic material, since the originals were more powerful than his reproductions could be;
but he felt that he could apply them to modern questions.
The literary connotations would give beauty and authority
while the contemporary inferences would supply value.
Therefore he borrowed Oenone, Ulysses, the Lotos Eaters,
Tithonus, and other classical figures to serve as spokesmen
for opinions on materialistic rationalism, or the scientific
spirit of inquiry, or the vice of passive self-indulgence as
contrasted with the virtues of "self-reverence, self-knowledge,
self-control." Tennyson's command of descriptive beauty
and classical dignity endowed these poems with unusual
appeal.

He treated the Arthurian legends in the same way, in-
tentionally making Arthur and his court into symbols for
ethical and social situations that belonged essentially to
Victorian England. None of the major Victorian poets
consciously undertook anything so pretentious or so outmoded as an "epic," but Tennyson's prolonged accumulation of these stories eventually became epic in length and
structure, though he concealed this under the title of
"idylls," which implied a group of short tales. And the
poem is to be regarded as an epic of Victoria's England,
just as *The Faerie Queene,* also using Arthurian themes, was
an epic of Elizabeth's England.

Other poems of Tennyson were more openly topical.
In "Locksley Hall" and *Maud* he used the monologue form
to display the mental confusion and emotional hysteria of
clever young men who were unbalanced by the conflicting
scientific and economic theories of the day. These matters
had been under discussion by Tennyson and his friends
from their university years onward. He was disturbed by
the unequal distribution of wealth and the handicaps
imposed on those who did not inherit rank or property,
and he was uncomfortable about the threat to individ-

ual liberty that he suspected in the embryonic labor unions (another very new problem a hundred years ago); but his most serious anxiety was directed toward the battle between religious faith and scientific rationalism.

From his boyhood he had been attracted to astronomy and other sciences, and he accepted the basic theory of physical evolution thirty years before Darwin published *The Origin of Species*. But he was also earnestly religious in training and temperament, and he discovered within himself the conflict between these two points of view which was also growing ever more violent in public debate. To Tennyson, the only solution, either for his own peace of mind or for that of the public in general, was to find some common understanding between the two opposed extremes. First sketched in "The Two Voices," this topic was fully debated in *In Memoriam,* with a frank use of the poet's own doubts and contradictions, which resulted in a more appealing, though less picturesque, poem than his monologues of fictitious characters. He offered man's intuitive "will to believe" as the basis for a religious faith independent of traditional creeds and compatible with scientific concepts.

In later poems he returned to these discussions, becoming all the more urgent in seeking to reconcile science and faith after the publication of Darwin's work had intensified the antagonism. Till the end of his life he was responsive to the trends of current interest: "Locksley Hall Sixty Years After," again a confusing mixture of involuntary self-portraiture and almost ironical psychological perception, shows the enthusiastic youth of the earlier poem grown into a querulous old man condemning vivisection and the novels of Zola.

Robert Browning took a different route in his approach to a kind of poetry that could compete with contemporary prose by depicting objective realities and by contributing to social and philosophical arguments. Persistent effort to write plays failed to achieve the necessary complete objectivity; but through these efforts Browning gained his distinctive technique of the dramatic monologue. Tennyson had also chosen this medium for some of his poems, apparently independently, but he was satisfied with the comparatively simple use of a fictitious or historical person as speaker, without much attention to the specific occasion, the listeners (if any), the motives for the speech, or the psychological complexities revealed. Browning, however, sometimes seemed able to condense into a few dozen lines the material of a whole play, novel, or historical treatise, by focusing it in a single well-selected moment in the life of a typical individual.

His earlier and most successful monologues were derived from an intimate knowledge of medieval and renaissance history; but he was not following the model of Scott and other Romantic writers. He did not turn to past centuries and foreign countries as a picturesque escape from the realities of everyday life; rather he tried to make historical conditions understandable in terms of human behavior.

Nor was Browning oblivious to the debates of his own day. Like Tennyson, he early recognized the significance of the evolutionary concept, which he included in *Paracelsus* (1835). In the same year as Tennyson's *In Memoriam*, Browning published a poem with the same central theme, *Christmas Eve and Easter Day*, in which the dramatic disguise was at a minimum in the presentation of current religious controversies. The "realistic" details in this strange poem have something in common with the novels of the time.

His interest in the psychology of religion produced a large group of poems which eventually covered almost the whole history of religious thought, from primitive superstition through Old Testament beliefs to the impact of Christ upon the cultures of His day, then various specimens of

Christian and Jewish ideas of medieval and renaissance centuries, and finally several recognizable portraits of living personalities ("Bishop Blougram" was based upon Cardinal Wiseman and "Mr. Sludge, the Medium," upon Daniel D. Home). In a comparable study of political ethics, Browning depicted Louis Napoleon as "Prince Hohenstiel-Schwangau." Thus Browning, like Tennyson, projected his poetry into the arena of his own time.

Although Browning was not so directly interested in the physical sciences as was Tennyson, his work followed one modern scientific trend—the study of psychology. In this respect Browning was far in advance of his rivals, the novelists. Whereas George Eliot, in the sixties, is regarded as the first author to write about the inner motivations of her characters instead of their external actions, Browning was attempting the same thing a quarter-century earlier.

As well as analyzing human character, however, Browning was conveying firm personal opinions. As he seldom spoke in his own person, it is unwise to attribute to him the views uttered by any particular dramatic character. But the cumulative evidence of many monologues reveals recurrent opinions and sympathies that can be accepted as his own.

One of these was his so-called "optimism"—a Platonic theory that imperfections and failures in earthly life give a basis for believing in some spiritual realm where the perfect fulfilment occurs. Man's efforts toward unobtainable objectives can persist only because those objectives exist on some ideal plane. This line of argument resembles Tennyson's reliance upon mankind's intuitive sense of immortality and of a divine being. Both poets were offering a creed which allowed for the new scientific concept of evolution.

Browning proclaimed also a strange ethical theory that every human being faces some supreme moment of decision, and that virtue consists in meeting this crisis positively, whereas the blackest sin is the cowardly and negative attitude of evading the issue. Here again Browning was trying to offer a code in line with the demands of his day, as a substitute for traditional dogmas. In common with the pragmatic and utilitarian concepts of the economists, this theory appealed to an age of ambition and decisive action.

Browning's third major tenet was that of tolerance—the right of every man to a hearing. This was the underlying principle of his dramatic monologues, many of which were uttered by perverts and rascals. Repeatedly Browning gave a voice to some historical figure whom he believed to be unfairly neglected or maligned. When he invented a character, this speaker served as a specimen of the baffling mixture of worthy and ignoble motives in every individual. Above all, Browning emphasized that no man is evil in his own eyes— everyone can find self-justification for behavior which actually is rooted in heredity, or upbringing, or current conditions. In this idea Browning definitely pointed the way to the modern outlook of the social sciences, which offer objective analysis of human actions instead of conventional labels of "good" and "bad," "hero" and "villain."

Just as Tennyson, without openly using the term *epic,* actually wrote one, so also did Browning. *The Ring and the Book,* even to its conventional twelve parts, is an epic of the dramatic monologue; and its controlling theme is this matter of the relativity of truth, the undependability of any single witness, and the slow emergence of acceptable hypothesis from accumulated testimony. As such, it might also be called an epic of the scientific method. Equally significant of the new literary era is the fact that it deals not with magnificent characters and the fate of nations, but with a sordid tale of crime. Essentially the story could have been taken from the current newspapers and court-reporters' notebooks of 1865 or any other year.

The poet whose popularity rivaled Tennyson's in the forties and fifties was Elizabeth Barrett. She too turned away from traditional and literary themes to deal with the world around her. In "Lady Geraldine's Courtship" and her novel in verse, *Aurora Leigh,* she followed Tennyson's example in writing melodramatic stories of her own time, which are marred by the inconsistency between the poetic manner and the commonplace details. In spite of her intellectual interests, Miss Barrett was better adapted to writing poetry of personal emotion than were her two male contemporaries. In contrast with Tennyson's long sequence of personal poems, *In Memoriam,* which may be termed the diary of his religious questionings, motivated by the grief of bereavement, Miss Barrett's sequence of poems was *Sonnets from the Portuguese,* the diary of her discovery of love.

Surprisingly, she also wrote poems of social and political protest more vigorous than any by the cautious and tolerant Tennyson and Browning. "The Cry of the Children," "A Curse for a Nation," and *Casa Guidi Windows* were eloquent attacks upon the evils of child labor, Negro slavery, and the denial of civil liberties in Italy. For comparable poems by men, we must turn to such minor authors as Ebenezer Elliott, "the Corn-Law Rhymer," and Thomas Hood, who had started as a disciple of Keats, turned to the fabrication of humor in order to make a living, and then startled his readers with the grim "Song of the Shirt" and "The Bridge of Sighs."

Although Tennyson and Browning had been able to evolve personal creeds of hopefulness which they considered compatible with the new scientific concepts and social complexities, several slightly younger poets were less positive. Matthew Arnold felt himself imprisoned in an intolerable dilemma. He could be happy only with a serene religious faith, and yet his knowledge of modern theories prevented him from adopting one. His poems are therefore a melancholy record of frustration and ineffectual protest against the pressures and complexities of modern civilization. The only affirmative spiritual force that he could accept was human stoicism and rectitude, the obstinate fortitude in misfortune and the impractical concept of "duty" which somehow survived all materialistic assaults.

Arnold sometimes turned to the past to find stories of tragedy more dignified and beautiful than in his own day, such as "Tristram and Iseult" and "Sohrab and Rustum." Being a literary critic as well as a poet, he wrote some of his most topical and personal poems about other authors— Lessing, Heine, Goethe, Wordsworth, and even so unfamiliar a writer as Senancour. Probably his finest poems, "The Scholar Gipsy" and "Thyrsis," dealt with his university days, enriched with unusual emotion through his love of the English countryside. "Thyrsis" was an elegy upon his friend from college days, Arthur Hugh Clough, who had become a far more embittered poet of disillusionment and skepticism than Arnold was. Clough's longer poems, *The Bothie of Tober-na-Vuolich* and "Mari Magno," were narratives of contemporary life after the Tennyson model, and a few of his short lyrics expressed fortitude and even hope, but his characteristic mood was shown in angry satires against the crassness and hypocrisy of the nineteenth century. Clough's unlucky career ended early, and by that time Arnold was turning away from poetry in favor of critical essays, more congenial to his analytical mind and restrained emotions.

For a while around the middle of the century it seemed as if every poet was using some ancient philosopher as a transparent screen for opinions upon current religious problems. Tennyson chose Lucretius as the voice of scientific materialism, with suicide as the only logical outcome, and "the Ancient Sage" as spokesman for his own more mystical faith. Arnold in "Empedocles on Etna" showed another ancient rationalist driven to suicide. In 1859 FitzGerald's adaptation of *The Rubáiyát of Omar Khayyám* proved the most effective of all; the more rebellious minds of the generation found their perfect representative in this Moslem cynic who proclaimed the insignificance of human life, the inadequacy of theology, and the resort to self-indulgence as the only way to make life endurable. Apparently in reply, Browning exhumed a forgotten contemporary of Omar's, Rabbi Ben Ezra, to preach a creed of courage and self-respect. Then came Swinburne with his "Hymn to Proserpine" in the mouth of an old Roman pagan assailing the austere ideals of Christianity.

Another work of didactic poetry popular during those years was *The Angel in the House,* in which Coventry Patmore carried the domestic idyls of Tennyson and Mrs. Browning to a sentimental extreme. Modern critics give higher praise to Patmore's later poems which were more mystical and symbolic.

The emphasis upon current controversies and the frequent portrayal of everyday life in the work of all these poets was responsible for the revolt of the Pre-Raphaelites, who announced that it was the duty of poetry, as of painting, to be a decorative art and to give purely aesthetic pleasure, rather than moralistic lectures. In effect this meant a return to the Romantic atmosphere of Coleridge and Keats. Rossetti, with his Catholic Italian ancestry, was a devoted medievalist. He wrote grimly powerful imitations of the old folk-ballads and symbolic poems that suggested fourteenth-century paintings. His sonnet sequence, *The House of Life,* ranks beside Mrs. Browning's as the record of a personal emotional experience, though more elaborate in imagery and more gloomy in mood. Rarely, as in "Jenny," Rossetti wrote realistically about his own time.

Rossetti's vigorous convictions drew other young poets into his circle. His sister, Christina, wrote lyrics of intense feeling and narrative poems of quaint fantasy. William Morris, Algernon Charles Swinburne, and George Meredith all fell for a while under the Rossetti fascination. In the early poems of Morris and Swinburne, Rossetti's pictorial and medieval emphasis is visible, and Morris retained and expanded this material for some years. His poetry can be appreciated only when read extensively, for his short poems are too artificial to arouse much emotional response. In his long narratives he captured something of the spaciousness, objectivity, and primitive strength of the Homeric epics and Norse sagas. As he became more concerned with socialist propaganda he wrote less poetry and more of his allegorical prose romances, which retained many poetic qualities of imagery and diction.

Swinburne, by contrast, from the start was full of such strong opinions that he could not long adhere to the Pre-Raphaelite injunction against didactic poetry. He turned from Rossetti to Shelley, Byron, and Victor Hugo as the models he preferred to follow. His love poetry, ecstatically chanting the physical and even the perverse aspects of sex, must be classified as propaganda poetry, since it was intended to shock the public and to discredit moral precepts that Swinburne regarded as hypocritical. With regard to religion, whereas some other poets, such as Arnold and Clough, finding themselves unable to believe the doctrines of Christianity, had regretfully resigned themselves to agnosticism, Swinburne went further and assailed the Christian church as an evil force. Nevertheless, he was anything but a scientific rationalist, and so he adopted remoter religious creeds, from ancient Greek and Scandinavian mythology to the new "religion of humanity" of Comte. All these poems horrified the public quite as much as Swinburne's political radicalism, with its attacks on royalty and every other form of organized government. Thus Swinburne, without recourse to writing realistically about actual human life, achieved the same result that the other poets had aimed at—a strong impact upon the public mind in competition with the novel and other widely-read forms of prose.

In the years after 1860 English poetry was less dominated by a few great figures than it had been in the preceding generation. A number of prolific poets, now forgotten, were successful in their day as disciples of Tennyson, such as Lewis Morris, Edwin Arnold, and Alfred Austin, who succeeded Tennyson as poet laureate. The Pre-Raphaelite romanticism, with its stress upon melancholy symbolism and frustrated passion, found its first disciples in Arthur O'Shaughnessy and Philip Marston. Later it influenced a group of young poets in the eighties and nineties, who also admired the French poets Baudelaire and Verlaine. Including James Thomson, Oscar Wilde, Lionel Johnson, Ernest Dowson, Francis Thompson, and John Davidson, this group reinforced the popular concept of the poet as an impractical dreamer who divided his time among drugs, liquor, and illicit love, and who died early from malnutrition.

Other poets turned their attention to the neat formalities of neo-classicism. Austin Dobson, Andrew Lang, and Edmund Gosse wrote precise ballades and rondeaux on literary and historical subjects, playful, graceful, and artificial. W. E. Henley was partly identified with this group, but his poetry had stronger elements, ranging from stark realism in his hospital sketches and "London Voluntaries" to a somewhat strident gospel of force and heroism—imperialism in "The Song of the Sword" and praise of modern machinery in "A Song of Speed."

Henley was a friend and admirer of Robert Louis Stevenson, whose poetry was attractive in its simplicity and its boyish love of the outdoors. Both Henley and Stevenson had something in common with Rudyard Kipling, who wrote ballads and descriptive poems about picturesque corners of the British Empire and about forceful characters —Indian bandits, Cockney infantrymen, ship's engineers.

Kipling's wide poetic range included graceful lyrics and evocative poems of English history, but his most obvious significance was in the energetic poems that appealed to readers (and listeners) who were not aware of the refinements of poetic art. He brought up to date, in the wider and speedier world of the newspaper, the railroad, the steamship, and the telegraph, the determination of Tennyson to write poems about the common interests of people in general.

The various contrasting or overlapping poetic types in the final decades of the nineteenth century might suggest a decline in poetic vigor, with superficial skill replacing the earnestness of the elder poets. Modern critics, however, find that the mood of major poetry survived in several writers who were not so fully recognized in their own day. The two greatest, George Meredith and Thomas Hardy, were better known to their contemporaries as novelists, but both of them began and ended their careers as poets and regarded themselves most seriously in that function. Although their thinking took very different courses, both undertook to work out a poetic philosophy of life that should be squarely consistent with the findings of modern science and particularly with the theory of evolution.

Both started from the concept of human destiny controlled wholly by the processes of nature; but Meredith emphasized the joy and encouragement that man may derive from the power of natural forces and the endless cycle of replacement, whereas Hardy saw the cruelty of the struggle for survival, with its apparently blind wastefulness and destruction. Meredith cited heredity as a new sort of "immortality" and a basis for a doctrine of unselfish service to the cause of humanity, whereas Hardy pointed out that the "Immanent Will" which holds the universe together is aimless and unconscious, and human purposes can have no effect upon it.

Both authors, of course, wrote many poems on other than philosophical subjects. Meredith's *Modern Love,* essentially a sonnet sequence though departing from one of the traditional rules, stands beside those of Mrs. Browning and Rossetti, if it does not surpass them by its psychological frankness and insight. Some of his later poems dealt with contemporary historical events, particularly in France, and thus continued a theme of international awareness which had been established by the Brownings and Swinburne. Hardy wrote characteristic narrative poems on the ironies and tragedies of English rural life, harking back to Wordsworth and Tennyson in the setting but not in the mood.

These two poets, Meredith and Hardy, and in a lesser degree their younger contemporaries, Robert Bridges, Gerard Manley Hopkins, and A. E. Housman, maintained past the end of the Victorian era its main poetic trait of serious discussion of the vast intellectual and spiritual problems that were besetting the modern world.

Apparently remote from all these trends, and yet strangely integrated with every one of them, was the Irish poetic renaissance that found its leader in W. B. Yeats. Starting with a revival of interest in the ancient Celtic folk-tales and the archaic Irish language, the movement progressed from translation of legends to creation of dreamy, mystical poetry. Like the "Aesthetes," Yeats was a disciple of the Pre-Raphaelites and the French symbolists; but he was also an adherent of Theosophy, and therefore his poetry mirrored the attempt to introduce Oriental mysticism as a new religion that might replace Christianity by being more amenable to scientific interpretation. These various elements were remarkably grafted by Yeats upon the simple stock of primitive Irish lore. The literary movement, chiefly as a result of his poems and essays and those of George Russell (AE), was translated into action by the political rebels who fought for Irish freedom; and Yeats's own later

poems acquired incisive force and philosophical independence as a reflection of that struggle. Thus Yeats became
the last and most extreme example of the phenomenon
that had shown itself throughout the Victorian era—the
writer who begins as a remote, impractical artist, and becomes drawn almost against his will into the vortex of
contemporary conflict.

Too much emphasis upon ideological controversies, however, would leave a false impression of the Victorian poets.
Not one of them was primarily a dogmatist. Each of them
told stories, portrayed personalities, gave voice to keen emotion in singing lyrics or brooding sonnets; and every one
of them showed his individual mastery of the techniques
of his craft.

II. TECHNIQUES

From the leading poets of the Romantic movement the
Victorian poets inherited the widest range of prosodic
forms that English literature had ever possessed. One major
objective of the Romantic revolt had been to break down
the predominance of the heroic couplet and give equal
status to all the verse patterns that had formerly existed
in English. Thus the strongly individualistic Romantic
poets were able to find whatever types of stanza and meter
best suited their diversified moods—ballad stanza, Spenserian
stanza, sonnet, tetrameter couplet, blank verse, and a vast
variety of lyrical stanza patterns. Even more important,
perhaps, was Coleridge's promulgation of the principle that
meter was determined by the occurrence of the stresses in
a line, and that considerable variation was possible in the
multiplication or omission of unaccented syllables. Thereby
English poetry was freed from the tyranny of syllable-
counting, and a fascinating range of musical effects was
revealed.

The Victorian poets maintained all these prosodic forms

and carried them to a further degree of conscious technical skill. Tennyson was a thorough student of the subject, and employed a very wide range of verse forms, carefully choosing each to suit his purpose. He was particularly attentive to the audible effects, in such matters as the exclusion of sibilants and the introduction of onomatopoeia. Some of his early poems were exercises in musical pattern almost to the exclusion of sense. From these exaggerated experiments he soon learned subtle control of his medium. He could give new effects to the familiar quatrain stanza by shortening the last line ("The Palace of Art," "A Dream of Fair Women") and by shifting the rhyme scheme *(In Memoriam)*. He made a popular success with "Locksley Hall" in a meter that had been regarded as unsuitable for English verse (8-stress trochaic). His facility in using heavily leaded rhythms and neatly emphatic rhymes, chosen purposely for poems aimed at the widest public, intensified the impression of obviousness and sentimentality produced by such poems as "Lady Clara Vere de Vere" and "The May Queen." On the other hand, when he was addressing himself to readers with more sophisticated literary taste he made good adaptations of classical meters and even attempted the long-forgotten Anglo-Saxon rhythm in his modernization of "The Battle of Brunanburh" and in "Merlin and the Gleam."

Another experiment of Tennyson was to break the monotony of a long poem by using different meters for different moods. Having first written *The Princess* entirely in blank verse, he later variegated it by the insertion of lyrics. And when he came to write his long psychological "monodrama" *Maud* he embodied each section of it in a metrical form appropriate to its emotional intention.

In the inevitable contrast with Tennyson, Browning has been termed careless of prosodic effects or deficient in musical ear. As a matter of fact, Browning was far more expert in music than was Tennyson, and the apparent roughness or grotesqueness of many of his poetic forms was a result of intentional experimentation or of his determination to give dynamic force to his poetry in lieu of Tennyson's static grace. In *Paracelsus* and *Pippa Passes* he anticipated Tennyson in the use of lyrical interludes to break up long poems. Like Tennyson, he used blank verse more extensively than any other form, for his long poems and his subtlest dramatic monologues; but he could also draw upon a wide range of patterns to suit his mood and topic. Sometimes the appropriateness is obvious—the galloping movement in "How They Brought the Good News from Ghent to Aix" or the labored mountain-climbing in "A Grammarian's Funeral." Other striking examples of planned selection are the flowing long lines of "Saul" and "Abt Vogler" to express inspired enthusiasm, the slow-moving stanzas of "Childe Roland to the Dark Tower Came," the comic irregularities and caricature rhymes of "The Pied Piper of Hamelin." Unlike Tennyson, Browning had no scruples against including conspicuously ugly sounds to produce special effects, such as the notorious line in "Rabbi Ben Ezra," "Irks care the crop-full bird? Frets doubt the maw-crammed beast?"

Browning's prosody was closely related with his extensive use of the dramatic monologue, a form that he practically created. For a majority of these poems he employed blank verse, as nearly approximating natural speech; but in order to suit the diversified characters who reveal themselves in the monologues he was ready to select special forms. The Duke of Ferrara was uttering a formal and studied speech, and so "My Last Duchess" is in decasyllabic couplets; but as he was a smooth and subtle diplomat, the couplets are run-on so that the reader is scarcely aware the poem is not blank verse. The Italian Person of Quality was excitable and loquacious; and so "Up at a Villa—Down in the City" gushes forth in long lines of mixed dactyls and trochees, with sometimes as many as six lines rhyming together. The Italian shepherd lad, on the other hand, was fumbling for words to express his simple philosophy, and so each couplet of "Love Among the Ruins" fades into silence with its short second line.

Browning's rhymes were often startling, especially multi-syllabic rhymes that sometimes involved a whole phrase. The extreme instances occur in his comic poems, as when he rhymed "ranunculus" with "Tommy-make-room-for-your-uncle-us." But in a perfectly serious poem he did not hesitate to rhyme "far gain" with "bargain," "loosened" with "dew send," "fabric" with "dab brick." These resulted from his desire to end his lines with one or two light syllables more often than the ordinary resources of English rhyme permitted. His poem "Christmas Eve" shows how much energy and colloquial flow were achieved by this device.

Elizabeth Barrett Browning was not an outstanding artist in prosody. Her melodic sense was exaggerated and facile, producing effects that were sentimentally over-sweet, as in "Lady Geraldine's Courtship" and to some extent even in "The Cry of the Children." Her rhymes, too, were frequently inaccurate, though there has recently been a tendency to defend them as foreshadowings of the modern preference for "oblique rhymes" or "assonances." Her best poetry was produced undoubtedly when she submitted to the discipline of a fixed form, the sonnet; and it is remarkable that she wrote the first important English sonnet-sequence since the Elizabethan period, whereas neither Tennyson nor Browning had any success in writing sonnets. The fixed form was too rigid for their prosodic sensitiveness but it was a wholesome restraint for Elizabeth Barrett's prosodic lushness.

In Matthew Arnold's prosody there are strange inconsistencies of skill. He could use over-stressed anapests, in

"A Modern Sappho," to be as syrupy as Mrs. Browning's "Lady Geraldine's Courtship" or Tennyson's "May Queen." He could be guilty of painfully ugly sound-effects: one of the clumsiest lines in English poetry is "Who prop, thou ask'st, in these bad days, my mind?" He sometimes had to fall back upon the use of italics for an important word instead of using position and metrical stress to produce the needed emphasis. On the other hand, "The Scholar Gipsy" and "Thyrsis" used a long, complex, Keatsian stanza with rich melody; he produced philosophical sonnets to stand beside those of his masters, Milton and Wordsworth; and he showed mastery of epic blank verse in "Sohrab and Rustum." Following the example of Tennyson, he broke up his "Tristram and Iseult" into sections with different metrical patterns to indicate emotional changes in the story.

His most significant contribution, however, was his adoption of irregular or "free" forms. Both Tennyson and Browning, in the tradition of the "irregular ode," had written some poems in which the lines varied in length with no fixed pattern of recurrence, the rhyme scheme was equally capricious, and the stanza units were unlike in length and even in basic meter. Examples are "Oenone" and "The Death of the Duke of Wellington," by Tennyson, and "The Flight of the Duchess" and "De Gustibus," by Browning. Arnold, however, who made similar use of varying line-lengths and unpatterned rhyme-sequences in "Dover Beach" and "The Buried Life," also took a further step in "Philomela" by discarding rhyme as well as consistent line-length.

The Victorian spirit of scientific experiment was often applied to metrics. In addition to Tennyson's exercises in classical prosody, several poets made more ambitious attempts to adapt the hexameter, the sapphic, and other ancient Greek meters, by seeking some sort of compromise between the quantitative principle of Greek poetry and the accentual principle of English. Examples in hexameter are Clough's *Bothie of Tober-na-Vuolich* and Kingsley's "Andromeda." Later in the century, the quantitative experiments were carried further by Robert Bridges.

When Edward FitzGerald began his translation of the *Rubáiyát* of Omar Khayyám, he borrowed the rhyme scheme of the original, *aaxa,* and by this slight shift gave a distinctive melody to his stanzas, which otherwise, as iambic pentameter quatrains, were in the same meter as Gray's *Elegy*.

By the middle of the century, it seemed as though the potentialities of English metrics had been fully exploited. The expert virtuosity of Tennyson, the eccentric vigor of Browning, and the skilled craftsmanship of many other poets had explored every stanza pattern and metrical device within the practical range of the language and its prosodic traditions. Then came Swinburne, with his apparently magical power to evoke new verbal melodies. Some of his techniques were easily distinguishable—alliteration, feminine rhymes, long lines, long stanzas, and especially a syncopated rhythm produced by freely shifting the position of unstressed syllables and increasing or decreasing the number. In this Swinburne brought to full maturity the principle initiated by Coleridge and thereby put an end to the old custom of classifying a poem by the standard types of "feet"—iambic, trochaic, anapestic, and dactyllic. In typical Swinburnian lines such as in "The Hounds of Spring" and "Hesperia" two or even three of these feet may be used in such equal proportions that no single one predominates. By such devices Swinburne could control the speed and stress with which his poems must be read, so as to give them individual musical patterns that can legitimately be called "tunes." His amazing ear for harmonies enabled his long lines to flow along swiftly and smoothly. For many readers, however, the extreme fluency and melodiousness produced a hypnotic effect that obscured the meaning of the poems and cast doubts upon their sincerity of emotion. Perhaps a more thoroughly effective example of the singing tune that resulted from alternation of more than one type of foot was George Meredith's "Love in the Valley."

Swinburne's metrical effects were so elaborately built of many elements and so strongly stamped with his individuality that any subsequent attempts to use them were bound to seem like crude parodies. Accordingly, the poets of the later quarter of the century veered rather in the direction of simplicity or of rigid form. Swinburne's friends the Pre-Raphaelites, as part of their medievalism, imitated the folk-ballad with its haunting use of refrain, as in D. G. Rossetti's "Sister Helen" and "Troy Town." Another offshoot of Pre-Raphaelism was the revival of the "fixed forms"—ballades, villanelles, rondeaux, triolets—which had been familiar to Chaucer but thereafter had faded out of literature. Although originating in the same general circumstances as the sonnet, they had proved too obviously artificial to satisfy poets wishing to utter serious emotions. Their decorative formality, however, was consistent with the artistic objectives of the Pre-Raphaelites; and the experiments of Rossetti and Swinburne in the forms were pleasing enough to encourage a group of minor poets to employ them further. Austin Dobson, Andrew Lang, W. E. Henley, and others became adept at using these complicated patterns. In addition to being dexterous examples of "light verse" these poems demonstrated the assured mastery over metrical difficulties that English prosody had now acquired.

Other types of light verse also contributed to the widening of techniques. From the graceful whimsies of W. M. Praed, at the beginning of the Victorian period, through the ballads and lyrics of W. S. Gilbert, to the parodies of

Lewis Carroll, C. S. Calverley, and J. K. Stephen, the wits discovered new devices for quick and easy fluency.

Formal perfection was threatening to resume the ascendancy that it had held a century earlier, and therefore the most important poets rebelled in the direction of simplicity. George Meredith in his later poetry used the plainest tetrameter couplets and quatrains, giving them distinction by his abrupt, allusive phrasing. Thomas Hardy, with an architect's interest in forms and patterns, composed his short poems in an immense variety of stanzas. A mathematical calculation might prove that he used more of the possible permutations of feet, line lengths, and rhyme schemes than any other English poet. Some of these prove pleasing to the ear, others sound wooden or positively ugly. As all are based upon traditional metrical principles and as each follows its particular pattern with conscientious fidelity, Hardy cannot be classed as an innovator or as a master of prosodic skill.

The trend to simplicity was reinforced by the poetry of Robert Louis Stevenson and of Robert Bridges. Both used the familiar old quatrains with pleasing naturalness, though Bridges also experimented with long lines and quantitative stresses. The early poems of Yeats, while using simple stanza forms, brought a new, melancholy music derived from his memories of Irish folksongs. W. E. Henley wrote a number of irregular, unrhymed poems in what later became known as *vers libre*. And Kipling, who in his schooldays assiduously studied and imitated Browning, Swinburne, and other Victorian masters, developed a style that retained something of Swinburne's rhythmic tunes but added a heavier emphasis which he may have borrowed from the melodramatic ballads recited in the popular music-halls.

Almost unrecognized in his own day, but now hailed as the most original prosodist of his generation, was Gerard

Manley Hopkins, who promulgated the theory of "sprung rhythm." Basically, this meant the dominant use of accent as the rhythmic determinant, with free variation of the unaccented syllables, and two strong accents often occurring together. Hopkins believed that his reversion to something like the Anglo-Saxon and Middle-English prosodic effects was more consistent with the nature of the English language than were the regular metrical feet, imported from France, that were made standard by Chaucer. Combined with much alliteration, compound phrases, transferred images, and other idiosyncracies, the new principle sounded so uncouth to his contemporaries that only a few friends realized what he was achieving, and the public had no chance to encounter his poetry until thirty years after his death.

Thus it may be seen that although the Victorian era had begun with an apparently boundless heritage of prosodic techniques, its poets added many fresh ones, and at the end of the century the seeds of radically new theories were germinating.

The Poets and the Poetry of the Century, ed. A. H. Miles (10v, London, 1891-97); H. B. Forman, *Our Living Poets* (London, 1871); J. A. Symonds, "A Comparison of Elizabethan and Victorian Poetry," in *Essays Speculative and Suggestive* (London, 1890); H. Walker, *The Greater Victorian Poets* (London, 1895); V. D. Scudder, *The Life of the Spirit in the Modern English Poets* (Boston, 1895); R. A. Armstrong, *Faith and Doubt in the Century's Poets* (London, 1898); W. Archer, *Poets of the Younger Generation* (London, 1902); A. Smith, *Main Tendencies of Victorian Poetry* (London, 1907); S. A. Brooke, *A Study of Clough, Arnold, Rossetti, and Morris* (London, 1908; Amer. ed. titled *Four Victorian Poets*); O. Elton, "Poetic Romancers After 1850," in *Proceedings of the British Academy,* VI (London, 1914); A. Waugh, "Some Movements in Victorian Poetry," in *Reticence in Literature* (London, 1915); L. Hearn, *Appreciations of Poetry* (New York, 1916); *Pre-Raphaelite and Other Poets* (New York, 1922); J. Drinkwater, *Victorian Poetry* (London, 1923); Sister M. Madeleva, "The Religious Poetry of the Nineteenth Century," in *Chaucer's Nuns and Other Essays* (New York, 1925); M. W. Mac-Callum, "The Dramatic Monologue in the Victorian Period," in *Proceedings of the British Academy*, XI (London, 1925); H. J. C. Grierson, *Lyrical Poetry from Blake to Hardy* (London, 1928); T. E. Welby, *The Victorian Romantics* (London, 1929); L. Stevenson, *Darwin Among the Poets* (Chicago, 1932); B. I. Evans, *English Poetry in the Later Nineteenth Century* (London, 1933); J. W. Beach, *The Concept of Nature in Nineteenth-Century English Poetry* (New York, 1936); C. Weygandt, *The Time of Tennyson: English Victorian Poetry As It Affected America* (New York, 1936); *The Time of Yeats* (New York, 1937); D. Bush, *Mythology and the Romantic Tradition in English Poetry* (Cambridge, Mass., 1937); F. L. Lucas, *Ten Victorian Poets* (Cambridge, 1940); I. B. Sessions, "The Dramatic Monologue," *Publications of the Modern Language Association*, LXII (1947). 503-516.

ALFRED TENNYSON (1809-1892)
>>

The one author who was accepted by the Victorian age as its poetic spokesman was Alfred Tennyson. Responsive to the main currents of thought in his day, he wrote in a wide range of poetic forms and perfected his style with elements reminiscent of all the major poets of the preceding Romantic generation.

The Tennyson family had lived for centuries in Lincolnshire, a flat, marshy county of northeast England, exposed to the storms of the North Sea. The poet's father was the son of a wealthy Member of Parliament, but had been disinherited in favor of a younger brother and had become a clergyman. As rector of the small village of Somersby he devoted himself to his extensive library and the upbringing of his twelve children. The rectory family in such a rural community was so separated by education and habits from the other inhabitants that they had to find their interests within their home. Fortunately the Tennysons could entertain one another to the full. There was a streak of genius in them that took the form of poetry in three of the brothers; and there was also a streak of morbidity that touched most of them in varying degrees.

Alfred, the fourth child of the family, was born on August 6, 1809. Between the ages of six and eleven he attended a grammar school at Louth, the nearest small town; but thereafter he stayed at home and studied under his father's tuition. He had been inventing rhymes from his earliest childhood; he wrote an epic of six thousand lines when he was twelve, and a blank-verse drama at fourteen. He was also interested in the study of science, particularly astronomy and geology.

In 1827 a volume entitled *Poems by Two Brothers,* chiefly by Charles and Alfred Tennyson, though with a few

ALFRED TENNYSON

contributions by their eldest brother, Frederick, a Cambridge undergraduate, was printed in the neighboring town and actually brought them twenty pounds. Early in the next year Charles and Alfred matriculated at Trinity College, Cambridge. The change from their isolated boyhood was so abrupt that for a while they were shy and friendless, but they were soon drawn into an informal club of brilliant undergraduates that had existed for several years and was nicknamed "the Apostles." Alfred Tennyson won high praise in this circle for his poetry. His closest friend and warmest admirer was Arthur Henry Hallam, whom the "Apostles" considered their most gifted member. In his second year Tennyson won the Chancellor's medal for his poem "Timbuctoo," and a year later he published a volume entitled *Poems, Chiefly Lyrical.* The poems showed his remarkable sense of the music of words and rhythms, but most of the subject-matter was artificial and sentimental.

Tennyson and Hallam went to Spain in the summer of 1830 with a romantic purpose of helping a rebel leader,

SOMERSBY RECTORY

General Torrijos. They stayed with his troops in the Pyrenees for some time, and Tennyson stored up vivid memories of the picturesque scenery, very different from his placid English countryside. In 1831 the death of his father caused Tennyson to leave the university without a degree, and he stayed quietly with his family at Somersby, writing poetry and enjoying outdoor sports. Hallam, who was now engaged to one of Tennyson's sisters, spent much time with them.

At the beginning of 1833 Tennyson published a volume

of *Poems,* containing "The Lady of Shalott," "The Lotos Eaters," "Oenone," "The Palace of Art," "A Dream of Fair Women," and many other poems that showed a great advance over his previous work. Hallam and other friends lauded the book in print so extravagantly that several important critics were roused to review it unfavorably, singling out the weakest poems for their notice. Tennyson, though hurt and disappointed, realized that there must be some basis for the objections and decided to study poetic technique more fully. In the autumn of 1833 Arthur Hallam died suddenly in Vienna during a foreign tour. Tennyson was so grieved that for a while he wrote nothing; but the bereavement turned his thoughts to the problems of religious faith and the immortality of the soul, causing him to write "The Two Voices" and to begin the series of short poems that grew into *In Memoriam.*

The family had to give up the home at Somersby in 1837, and went to live near London. They were low in funds, and though Tennyson had become engaged to Emily Sellwood he saw no prospect of marrying. Nevertheless he made no effort to earn money, but continued to work quietly on his poetry. He published in 1842 a two-volume collection which at once became popular. The poems that were retained from the volume of ten years before had been thoroughly revised and condensed, and the new material included such effective poems as "Morte d'Arthur," "Sir Galahad," "Ulysses," and "Locksley Hall." Hailed as the leading poet of the generation, Tennyson began to mingle with London literary people.

A glib promoter persuaded him to sell his small inherited property and to invest all his money—as well as some belonging to his brothers and sisters—in a company to exploit a patent process of wood-carving by machinery. The concern promptly failed and Tennyson suffered a nervous breakdown that threatened his reason and even his life.

After his recovery his friends persuaded the government to grant him a pension of two hundred pounds a year.

His next poem, *The Princess* (1847), annoyed some of his friends, though it appealed to the public. Having become seriously aware of the arguments over "women's rights," which many men ignored and others ridiculed, Tennyson tried to present the two sides of the case and to imply a solution. There was inconsistency between the romantic medievalism of his story and the modern application that it had to carry; and touches of comedy and satire obscured the serious purpose. Before the second edition Tennyson made revisions and interspersed a number of songs that are among his most graceful lyrics.

After seventeen years of intermittent work he finished the poem that had grown out of his grief for Hallam. According to his own statement, he had written the first sections merely to relieve his misery, with no thought of publication; but as the separate fragments were all in the same stanza form they gradually cohered, like a sonnet sequence, into a long poem that was also a series of short poems. When *In Memoriam* was published anonymously in 1850, most readers, unaware of the events underlying it, were puzzled. Gradually, however, people found in it a confession of the same spiritual conflicts that they were suffering, with suggestions of faith and hope that were all the more convincing because the poet offered them tentatively and did not adopt a self-confident air of superiority.

In June, 1850, after an engagement of thirteen years, Tennyson was married, and later in the same year became poet laureate in succession to Wordsworth. He was more fortunate than most holders of that office in the poems that he felt obliged to write upon public affairs: the "Ode on the Death of the Duke of Wellington" (1852) and "The Charge of the Light Brigade" (1854) were among his most successful poems.

He was soon able to afford a pretty, secluded home in the Isle of Wight, where his increasing fame began to attract sight-seers. Tall and broad-shouldered, with aquiline features and masses of dark hair, Tennyson fulfilled the popular idea of a poet, especially when he wore his black sombrero and flowing cape. He loved to read his poems aloud to his friends, but was shy of strangers and evaded the admirers who tried to break in upon his privacy.

In *Maud* (1855) he undertook to depict more intense passions than before, and to bring the story into close touch with contemporary life. As a result it was widely attacked as "crude," "ugly," "morbid," or "prosy." For the next four years he refrained from publication, busy with writing a series of poems on King Arthur and his knights. The subject had attracted him ever since the beginning of his career; when he published the fragmentary "Morte d'Arthur" in 1842 it was introduced by some half-humorous and very personal lines, "The Epic," in which he wistfully remarked that an epic on the subject would not appeal to modern readers. *Idylls of the King* was therefore presented not as a long narrative poem but as a series of short tales, as the title indicated. Nevertheless his use of blank verse and other traditional devices revealed the epic tendency; and when the first four *Idylls,* published in 1859, became his most popular book, he gradually added others, until by 1885 he brought the total to twelve—the classical epic length.

His later years were uneventful, marked only by visits from famous people—from abroad as well as from his own country—and quiet summer tours to enjoy beautiful scenery. In 1867 he removed from the Isle of Wight to Haslemere, in Surrey, where he was less exposed to intruders.

First introduced to Queen Victoria in 1862 when she was in the depths of grief for her husband's death, he won her friendship by his respectful tributes to herself and by his still stronger admiration for the late Prince Consort. By injudiciously suggesting that his portrait of King Arthur was modeled upon Prince Albert, Tennyson brought unmerited ridicule upon his poem in later generations when Albert was no longer revered.

The Prime Minister, W. E. Gladstone, also became a close friend of Tennyson, and together they paid a triumphal visit to Norway and Denmark in 1883. The next year Gladstone persuaded Tennyson to accept a peerage—the first English author to be raised to such high rank for literary distinction alone.

In these years he tried to write poetic drama in the Elizabethan tradition, intending a series of tragedies on great events of English history. He wrote seven plays in all, several of them being produced on the London stage, but all were unsuccessful. He continued to write poems with his usual skill and variety—ballads, lyrics, dramatic monologues. A reversion to themes of his early work was to be seen in "Locksley Hall Sixty Years After" and "The Death of Oenone." One of his last poems, "Merlin and the Gleam," used an Arthurian theme to convey a brief autobiography. Between this and his first Arthurian poem, "The Lady of Shalott," almost sixty years had elapsed.

Lord Tennyson died at Aldworth House, his home in Surrey, on the night of October 6, 1892, with a volume of Shakespeare in his hand. He was buried in the Poets' Corner of Westminster Abbey.

As the chosen poetic representative of Victorianism, Tennyson was doomed to suffer the full force of the disfavor that assailed Victorianism in the next generation. In the great bulk of his poetry it was possible to find some poems that were trivial or sentimental, and these were seized as evidence for the indictment against him, just as similar excerpts had been used by his first adversaries in 1833.

Even his detractors have been obliged to admit his technical mastery. In handling almost every type of English meter and stanza with perfect control, in selecting appropriate rhythms and correlating sound to meaning, in drawing vivid images in precisely chosen words, Tennyson was unsurpassed. Because he seldom startled or perplexed his readers, however, the subject-matter of his poetry seems over-obvious to some modern minds. After writing the decorative, musical, book-inspired poems of his college days, Tennyson definitely resolved to be a poet of the real life of his time. The resolution is announced in the explicit allegory of "The Palace of Art" (which contains a powerful and often-ignored picture of one of his attacks of neurotic despair) and is implied also in "The Lady of Shalott." Nor was his intention merely to deal with contemporary topics; he also felt an obligation to write the types of poetry that would reach as many people as possible. Ambition for fame or wealth was not the predominating reason; he genuinely wished to serve his fellow-men through what he could say for them in verse. This determination was the controlling force in all his work.

His stories of humble English life, such as "Dora" and "Enoch Arden," derived from Wordsworth's, and, like his, had an occasional prosy line. Some of Tennyson's other poems in this vein were appeals to easy tears. On the other hand, he displayed an unexpected power of earthy humor in his dialect pieces, such as "The Northern Farmer." In a dramatic monologue of that type, the objectiveness of the characterization is unmistakable; but some of his other dramatic monologues are often misinterpreted. Critics who would never make such an error with regard to Browning are apt to cite "Locksley Hall" or *Maud* or "Lady Clara Vere de Vere" as expressions of Tennyson's own views. In these poems, just as much as in "Ulysses" or "Tithonus," a fictitious character stood self-revealed. One should not miss the irony with which youthful egotism is displayed in "Locksley Hall." The lad boasts and scolds, and his imagination leaps from one self-glorifying dream to another. The poem is inconsistent from one stanza to the next because inconsistency is typical of such a mind in such a crisis. He grows naturally into the cranky, prejudiced old man of sixty years after. Here again is irony and psychological truth. Similarly the speaker in *Maud* is an overwrought, introspective dreamer, psychopathic from brooding over a childhood shock. And the young man in "Lady Clara Vere de Vere" expresses a naïve village boy's concept of the sophisticated aristocracy.

Another result of Tennyson's early resolve was his use of classical and medieval material with a modern application. He was not concerned with imitating Homer or Geoffrey of Monmouth; he chose Ulysses and Lucretius and Arthur and Lancelot in fulfilment of his belief that poetry ought to use beautiful and significant symbols as media of communication to the reader's mind, in relation to the reader's living interests. Modern critics have condemned the *Idylls of the King* for containing Victorian ideas, whereas some credit is due to Tennyson for his intention of making his readers think about the conflict of good and evil in the human soul, as symbolized picturesquely in this epic.

The same purpose was represented in another way in Tennyson's expressions of his own thinking, especially *In Memoriam*. The poem was effective because of its humility: Tennyson honestly recorded his gropings and his worries and his moods of black pessimism. As an enthusiastic amateur of science he could not ignore the new geology and astronomy and biology, and therefore he had to face their implications of the cruelty of nature and the mechanism of physical processes. On the other hand, as a son of the Church of England, with a large share of mysticism in him, he could not give up his intuitive belief in a benevolent

God and an immortal human soul. In reading *In Memoriam* one must trace the personal record of Tennyson's lamentation for his friend, marked by successive seasons and anniversaries, and his gradual consolation; and at the same time one follows the sequence of arguments on all angles of the conflict between reason and faith. Tennyson examined various forms of religious belief, such as spiritualism and reincarnation, and avoided presenting the specific dogmas of any particular creed. On the opposite side he gave full voice to the materialistic implications of science, emphasizing the concept of the struggle for survival a decade before Darwin promulgated his evolutionary hypothesis. Tennyson admitted the contradictions, and ended with a personal solution that he frankly admitted to be unprovable. By not setting himself up as knowing the answers, he won all the more sympathy from readers as muddled as himself. He is a truer exponent of both the Victorian and the modern feeling on these matters than either those who chose the way of faith, with Newman and Patmore, or those who accepted agnosticism.

In politics, as in religion, Tennyson chose compromise. He recommended humanitarian reforms and progress toward greater liberty, but distrusted precipitate utopianism. Such a point of view lacks emotional intensity. *In Memoriam* would be tedious if it were not redeemed by the personal feelings about Hallam; and the much briefer sequence of three untitled poems on politics ("You Ask Me Why," and so on), which were written at the time he was starting *In Memoriam,* and which appear to be the germ of a parallel discussion of social controversies, had none of the frenzy of Shelley or Swinburne.

A student of the Victorian period does well to begin with the work of Tennyson, for he touched upon the major concerns of his sixty years from a point of view that may be regarded as the norm, to which the other writers of the era can be correlated. In his avoidance of extremes, his anxiety to seek solutions for current problems, and his adaptation of all the techniques achieved by the un-controlled experimenters of the previous generation, Ten-nyson exemplified both the kinship and the difference between the Victorians and the great Romantics.

T. J. Wise, *A Bibliography of the Writings of Alfred, Lord Tennyson* (2v, London, 1908); A. E. Baker, *A Concordance to the Poetical and Dramatic Works* (London, 1914); *A Tennyson Dictionary* (London, 1916); M. Luce, *A Handbook to the Works of Alfred, Lord Tennyson* (London, 1908); *Works,* ed. Hallam, Lord Tennyson (6v, London, 1908); *Poetic and Dramatic Works,* ed. W. J. Rolfe (Boston, 1898; Cambridge edition); *Works,* ed. Hallam, Lord Tennyson (London, 1913); *Early Poems,* ed. J. C. Collins (London, 1900); *In Memoriam, The Princess, and Maud,* ed. J. C. Collins (London, 1902); *Unpublished Early Poems,* ed. C. Tennyson (London, 1931); *A Selection from the Poems,* ed. W. H. Auden (London, 1944); Hallam, Lord Tennyson, *Alfred, Lord Tennyson: A Memoir* (2v, London, 1897); *Tennyson and His Friends* (London, 1911); J. F. Genung, *Tennyson's "In Memoriam": Its Purpose and Its Structure* (Boston, 1884); J. C. Collins, *Illustrations of Tennyson* (London, 1891); M. W. MacCallum, *Tennyson's "Idylls of the King" and Arthurian Story from the Sixteenth Century* (Glasgow, 1894); R. Jones, *The Growth of "The Idylls of the King"* (Philadelphia, 1895); J. Royce, "Tennyson and Pessimism," in *Studies of Good and Evil* (New York, 1898); S. A. Brooke, *Tennyson: His Art and Relation to Modern Life* (London, 1900); E. H. Sneath, *The Mind of Tennyson* (New York, 1900); A. C. Bradley, *A Commentary on "In Memoriam"* (London, 1901); A. C. Lyall, *Tennyson* (London, 1902; English Men of Letters); A. C. Benson, *Alfred Tennyson* (London, 1904); W. P. Mustard, *Classical Echoes in Tennyson* (New York, 1904); W. C. Gordon, *The Social Ideas of Alfred Tennyson As Related to His Time* (Chicago, 1906); N. and W. L. Lockyer, *Tennyson As a Student and Poet of Nature* (London, 1910); T. R. Lounsbury, *The Life and Times of Tennyson* (New Haven, 1915); A. C. Bradley, *The Reaction Against Tennyson* (English Association Pamphlet XXXIX, 1917); T. P. Cross, "Alfred Tennyson As a Celticist," *Modern Philology,* XVIII (1921). 485-92; J. F. A. Pyre, *The Formation of Tennyson's Style* (Madison, Wisc., 1921); D. W. T.

Starnes, "The Influence of Carlyle upon Tennyson," *Texas Review*, VI (1921), 316-36; H. Van Dyke, *Studies in Tennyson* (New York, 1921); H. I'A. Fausset, *Tennyson: A Modern Portrait* (London, 1923); H. Nicolson, *Tennyson: Aspects of His Life, Character, and Poetry* (London, 1923); A. Noyes, "Tennyson and Some Recent Critics," in *Some Aspects of Modern Poetry* (London, 1924); L. Abercrombie, "Tennyson," in *Revaluations* (London, 1931); D. Bush, "The Personal Note in Tennyson's Classical Poems," *University of Toronto Quarterly*, IV (1934). 201-18; A. C. Howell, "Tennyson's 'Palace of Art'—An Interpretation," *Studies in Philology*, XXXIII (1936). 507-22; C. Tennyson, "Tennyson Papers," *Cornhill Magazine*, CLIII (1936). 283-305, 426-50, 534-58, 672-81; G. R. Potter, "Tennyson and the Biological Theory of Mutability," *Philological Quarterly*, XVI (1937). 321-43; W. D. Paden, *Tennyson in Egypt: A Study of the Imagery of His Earlier Work* (Lawrence, Kans., 1942); J. O. Eidson, *Tennyson in America: His Reputation and Influence, 1827-58* (Athens, Ga., 1943); E. F. Shannon, "Tennyson and the Reviewers," *Publications of the Modern Language Association*, LVIII (1943). 181-94; R. P. Basler, "Tennyson the Psychologist," *South Atlantic Quarterly*, XLIII (1944). 143-59; G. S. Haight, "Tennyson's Merlin," *Studies in Philology*, XLIV (1947). 549-66; P. F. Baum, *Tennyson Sixty Years After* (Chapel Hill, 1948).

ELIZABETH BARRETT BROWNING (1806-1861)

>>

In the eyes of her contemporaries, Elizabeth Barrett was one of the leading English poets. The eldest óf the eleven children of Edward Moulton Barrett, a wealthy owner of West Indian estates, she was born at Coxhoe Hall, Durham, on March 6, 1806, and spent her childhood chiefly at Hope End, in sight of the beautiful Malvern Hills. The beauty of her early home is reflected in the best of her country poems. From the age of eight she composed poetry, and her father printed her epic, *The Battle of Marathon,* when she was thirteen. Her enthusiasm for Pope's Homer led her to study Latin and Greek.

At the age of fifteen she strained her back while tightening the girths of her pony. The medical theory of the time recommended complete rest, and as a result she became a permanent invalid. Ten years later a hemorrhage indicated weak lungs. She seldom saw anyone outside of her family, and devoted all her time to study and writing. In 1832 she translated the *Prometheus Bound* of Aeschylus, and it was printed, with other poems, the next year.

ELIZABETH BARRETT
BROWNING

After 1835, London was the home of the Barretts. Except for occasional trips to health resorts, Elizabeth was practically a prisoner in the house in Wimpole Street. Deluding himself that he was devoted to his family's welfare, the autocratic Edward Barrett was determined to keep all his children about him, and violently opposed the marriage of any of his daughters. Elizabeth's frail health was his justification for secluding her from the world. Through R. H. Horne, one of her few acquaintances, she contributed poems and articles to the *New Monthly Magazine* and other literary journals. Her volume, *The Seraphim and Other Poems* (1838) was favorably reviewed, but not widely popular. She made the acquaintance of Wordsworth and Landor, and formed cordial friendships with Mary Russell Mitford and with her own distant cousin, John Kenyon.

In 1840 the accidental drowning of a brother was such a shock to her that for weeks she was believed to be dying, and thereafter she remained in her own darkened room as a hopeless invalid, almost incapable of walking. She plunged deeper into literary work, publishing *Chaucer Modernized* in 1841 (at Wordsworth's suggestion) and a series of essays on Greek and English poets in *The Athenaeum*. Her poem "The Cry of the Children" showed an awakened interest in the social problems of the contemporary world, and her long narrative, "Lady Geraldine's Courtship," told a romantic story of modern life in the style of some of Tennyson's poems. When these and other poems were collected in two volumes in 1844 they became very popular, and she was generally regarded as a rival of Tennyson.

Having been interested for some time in the much-neglected poetry of Robert Browning, she made a flattering reference to it in "Lady Geraldine's Courtship," and Browning wrote to her to express his gratitude. An active correspondence followed, and within a few months Browning persuaded Kenyon to bring him to call upon her. She was six years older than he, and in contrast with his vigorous health and strength she seemed more fragile and nervous than ever, with her head too large for her tiny body, and the heavy black ringlets almost concealing her face. Both came to realize that they were in love, but she made anxious efforts to repel him so that he should not be burdened with her illness. The full record of these months is preserved in their letters, which were later published, and also in her sonnets forming a poetical diary of her emotional experiences.

She was eager to escape from the London winter by going to Italy, and the doctors approved the idea, but her father would not consent. Browning thereupon decided that he must marry her and free her from such restraint. In the spring of 1846 she felt stronger than she had for many years, and agreed to the marriage, but insisted that it must be kept secret from all the family. On September 12 she slipped out of the house to marry him, and a week later he carried her off to the Continent.

In the confident belief that he was saving her life, Browning took a grave risk, for if he had been wrong he would have been held morally guilty of her death. When they settled in Italy, however, her health steadily improved, and for fifteen years she led an almost normal life. Her father never forgave them, and for this reason, as well as for her health, they seldom visited England.

Shortly after their arrival in Pisa, she showed Browning the sonnets that she had written during his courtship, and at his insistence she allowed them to be published under the deceptive title of *Sonnets from the Portuguese*.

They established their home in the Casa Guidi, Florence, where a son was born to them in 1849. About this time she was strongly recommended by many people for the poet laureateship, in succession to Wordsworth. Becoming intensely interested in the movements for Italian independence she wrote a number of poems which were published as *Casa Guidi Windows,* in the hope of arousing English sympathy for the cause. This book was followed in 1856 by her "novel in verse," *Aurora Leigh,* which was immensely popular and went through many editions. During these years the Browning casa was one of the centers of the brilliant literary and artistic Anglo-American colony in Florence. Mrs. Browning became interested in spiritualism, the only subject of disagreement that ever developed between her and her husband. In 1859 her strength began to wane, but she continued with preparations of her next volume of poetry, *Poems before Congress,* which aroused some anger in England among readers who mistook "A Curse for a Nation" for an attack upon her native country, whereas it was really one of her poems in favor of American abolitionism. She died in the arms of her husband on June 29, 1861.

Her poetry was fluent and copious, with emphatic rhythms. She was always motivated by generous enthusiasm: in her early work it was aroused chiefly by literary and historical subjects; later her husband's influence directed it toward contemporary events. Her narrative poems were inclined to slip into sentimentality, and her political poems were sometimes hysterically violent. Carried along by her flow of obvious rhythm, she often wrote too much, and was careless with the meaning of words and the accuracy of rhymes (though it has been suggested that in the latter respect she was a forerunner of Emily Dickinson and other users of assonance). The discipline of the sonnet was good for her, and artistically as well as emotionally the *Sonnets from the Portuguese* rank with her best work, whereas the diffuse *Aurora Leigh* is no longer read. She never learned to prune the over-luxuriant details from her poems, or to curb the intellectual restlessness that crowded her work with half-developed thoughts. Both the charm and the weakness of her poetry reside in the impulsive naïveté which originated in her bookish girlhood and was never subjected to the abrasions of everyday life.

T. J. Wise, *A Bibliography of the Writings in Prose and Verse of Elizabeth Barrett Browning* (London, 1918); *Complete Works,* ed. C. Porter and H. A. Clarke (6v, New York, 1900); *Poetical Works,* ed. F. G. Kenyon (London, 1897; Globe edition); *Hitherto Unpublished Poems and Stories* (2v, Boston, 1914); *Letters to R. H. Horne,* ed. S. R. T. Mayer (London, 1877); *Letters,* ed. F. G. Kenyon (2v, London, 1897); *Letters to Her Sister,* ed. L. Huxley (London, 1929); *Letters to B. R. Haydon, 1842-45,* ed. M. H. Shackford (London, 1939); L. Whiting, *A Study of Elizabeth Barrett Browning* (Boston, 1899); P. Lubbock, *Elizabeth Barrett Browning in Her Letters* (London, 1906); E. Hickey, "Elizabeth Barrett Browning, Woman and Poet," *Nineteenth Century,* LXXIV (1913). 164-84; K. E. Royds, *Elizabeth Barrett Browning and Her Poetry* (London, 1918); I. C. Willis, *Elizabeth Barrett Browning* (London, 1928); I. C. Clarke, *Elizabeth Barrett Browning* (London, 1929); D. Creston, *Andromeda in Wimpole Street* (London, 1929); J.

Marks, *The Family of the Barrett* (New York, 1938); F. M. Smith, "Mrs. Browning's Rhymes," *Publications of the Modern Language Association,* LIV (1939). 829-34.

ROBERT BROWNING (1812-1889)

>>

The son of a clerk in the Bank of England, Robert Browning was born in Camberwell, a suburb of London, on May 7, 1812. From his father, a man of artistic and literary tastes, he learned in his quiet childhood at Camber-

well to love all the arts—painting, sculpture, and music, as well as poetry. He received comparatively little formal education at a school in the neighborhood and at London University, where he attended a few lectures; but he learned a great deal from reading everything he could find in his father's library, which contained books on such unusual subjects as alchemy and medieval Italian history. Byron was his first poetic hero, until at the age of fourteen he discovered a more compelling ideal in Shelley.

ROBERT BROWNING

As he grew into manhood, Browning was urged to use his own discretion in selecting a career. His father had a comfortable income, and the family was happy and affectionate. Robert Browning had made few friends of his own age, and was restlessly ambitious for great achievements. Since he had shown promise in an unpublished volume of poetry, *Incondita*, written when he was twelve, his parents were sympathetic when he rejected an offer of a clerkship in the Bank of England and decided to become a poet.

His first published poem, at the age of twenty-one, was *Pauline*, showing clearly the influence of his idol, Shelley. It was planned as a vast psychological "confession" but after a few hundred lines he grew tired of it and printed the fragment anonymously. Partly because it revealed all too clearly his chaotic youthful visions, Browning later tried to suppress all evidence of its existence.

In 1833, spending the winter in St. Petersburg, he wrote his earliest dramatic lyrics, "Porphyria's Lover" and "Johannes Agricola in Meditation." A tour to Venice during the following year aroused his interest in Italian history and art. In 1835 he published *Paracelsus*, and was disappointed that it received little notice. A long and diffuse poem, it was ostensibly in dramatic form, but was almost entirely uttered by a single speaker and dealt with his philosophical development over thirty years. Browning chose a nearly forgotten figure of the early Renaissance and sought to vindicate him as a great scientist and humanist rather than the charlatan he was usually considered. The poem was also a study of what Browning regarded as the basis of all ethical questions—the conflict between Power and Love.

Browning was fascinated with the theater and aspired to be a dramatist. He had made the acquaintance of Macready, the leading tragedian of the day, who was trying to restore literary prestige to the English drama; and Macready was sufficiently impressed by *Paracelsus* to ask for a play. Browning's *Strafford* was accordingly produced at Covent Garden in May, 1837. During the next ten years he wrote six further plays, all in the Elizabethan poetic tradition, and several of them were performed with some success. Because of his preoccupation with psychological motives, however, Browning could never become an efficient dramatist; though some of his plays had good plots, they threw too much stress on moral crises and ethical problems, and failed to simplify characters enough for effectiveness on the stage.

Meanwhile, he had been working on a long narrative poem, which he had started soon after *Paracelsus,* carried unfinished to Italy in 1838, and finally published in 1840. This was *Sordello,* another study of the psychology of genius as revealed in an obscure historical character. In response to criticisms of the wordiness of *Paracelsus,* he strove for conciseness by omitting connective words and transitional phrases, with the result that the long, complex sentences are almost incomprehensible. Telling the history of thirteenth-century Italian city-states, he unwisely assumed that his readers would be familiar with the names and the complicated intrigues that he mentioned. As a further cause of difficulty, he repeatedly digressed from the story with subtle ethical and psychological analysis and with expositions of his personal artistic problems. When the poem was published it was ridiculed as unreadable, and for the rest of Browning's life he bore a reputation of obscurity. To anyone wishing a thorough understanding of Browning, however, *Sordello* is of primary importance as a detailed and sincere expression of ideas that controlled all his later work.

From 1841 to 1846 he published a series of eight cheaply-printed pamphlets, *Bells and Pomegranates,* containing his plays and many shorter poems. The first number contained *Pippa Passes,* in which at last he achieved an effective technique by retaining dramatic form but giving up the conventional plot-structure of stage plays. It is a series of four apparently separate episodes, each dramatically powerful, and united by implications which are skilfully conveyed to the reader and which increase the irony and suspense of the story. The interpolated lyrics are among his most charming short pieces.

In 1845, after a third visit to Italy, he read Elizabeth Barrett's compliment to his *Bells and Pomegranates,* and promptly opened a correspondence with her. His clandestine visits followed, and then their secret engagement. At the age of thirty-four he was faced with the first serious crisis in a life that had been comfortable and casual; by defying her father in marrying her and freeing her from enforced invalidism he incurred not only public disapproval but the gravest sort of responsibility. The experience strongly affected his poetry, not only with enriched emotional power but also with added emphasis upon his peculiar doctrine of the "crucial moment" which tests the strength of each human being's sincerity and self-reliance.

By this time he had developed his individual poetic method, the dramatic monologue. Among readers of his own day it increased his reputation for obscurity, for they were slow to learn that "I" in each poem did not mean the poet himself but an objectively created character. His fame was therefore of gradual growth, and his fifteen years in Italy kept him out of touch with the literary life of his own country. His poetic output during his marriage was comparatively small. *Christmas Eve and Easter Day,* published in 1850, was a puzzling discussion of current religious difficulties. It was on the same topic as *In Memoriam,* which appeared in the same year; but whereas Tennyson's poem appealed to a wide public who found their personal uncertainties sympathetically reproduced, Browning's baffled them with its mixture of satire and symbolism. Two volumes entitled *Men and Women* (1855) contained many of his best dramatic monologues and made a strong impression on some critics.

Holding their *salon* in Florence or traveling about Italy, studying its art and its political problems, the Brownings and their little boy were supremely happy. In 1856 John Kenyon left them a large legacy that made them financially secure.

Upon the death of his wife in 1861, Browning could not endure the associations of Florence and returned to England, bringing his twelve-year-old son to be educated. He sought solace in hard work upon his poetry, and in 1864 published another outstanding collection of monologues, *Dramatis Personae*. After a year or two of disconsolate seclusion, he made up his mind to shake off morbid self-pity. His witty conversation and his lack of literary pose soon made him a popular figure in London society.

For several years he worked on his most ambitious poem, *The Ring and the Book*, developing the *procès verbal* of a two-hundred-year-old Roman murder case, which he had picked up at a bookstall in Florence, into an epic of psychological analysis. Out of the sordid story of crime he created a panorama of seventeenth-century Italian life, and by his daring device of telling the story ten times he brought out his concept of the relativity of human knowledge and the personal bias that controls everyone's beliefs. Published in four volumes in 1868-69, the poem established his eminence as the most original and profound poet of his time. His work became a cult among readers with intellectual pretensions, and "Browning Societies" to study and expound his poetry were formed in England and America.

The Ring and the Book marked a turning-point in his poetic methods. Already the monologues in *Dramatis Personae* had tended to be longer than those in *Men and Women*, and thereafter he abandoned the condensation that had been a merit of his best monologues. The vast output of his later life, almost a volume a year, consisted mainly of long, abstruse poems. *Prince Hohenstiel-Schwangau* and *Fifine at the Fair* displayed complex, casuistical personalities, leaving the reader dizzy with the effort to separate truth from deceit in their monologues. *Red Cotton Nightcap Country* and *The Inn Album* told crime stories based on real occurrences. *La Saisiaz* was a rather mystical discussion of religious beliefs. Browning

PALAZZO REZZONICO, VENICE

gave a good deal of time to the study of Greek drama, and in several poems made an odd mixture of original work with adaptations of Aeschylus and Euripides. In *Parleyings with Certain People of Importance in Their Day* he reversed the technique of the dramatic monologue by talking to a series of eccentric historical characters instead of confining himself to their utterances.

For some years he spent his summers in France, and finally in 1878 he went to Italy for the first time since his wife's death. Thereafter he spent part of his time in Venice, but never revisited Florence. In 1887 he bought the Palazzo Rezzonico, in Venice, and died there on December 12, 1889. His last volume, *Asolando,* a collection of short poems, was published in London on the same day. He was buried in Westminster Abbey.

The distinctive quality of Browning's work arose from his curiosity about the workings of the human mind; his interest in painting, music, Italian history, and other scholarly subjects; his determination to expound a philosophy based upon the right of every person to a hearing for his self-justification, the supremacy of love over power, and the promise of fulfilment latent in imperfection or failure; and his indirect method of presenting his ideas through fictitious characters.

Although when he chose he could write melodious lyrics, his effort to give dynamic force to his lines and fresh impact to his diction often produced results that his contemporaries called harsh, distorted, or prosaic. In the first ten years of his career he painfully learned his limitations. The early poems were over-decorated with metaphor and inflated with abstract terms which he struggled ineffectually to define. Seeking escape from the vagueness of his philosophising, he wrote his group of plays, only to find himself hampered by the rigidity of stage technique. As he grew more and more unwilling to write introspectively of his personal emotions and beliefs, he evolved the subtle technique of the dramatic monologue. It retained the objectivity of the play or novel, but permitted concentration upon a single personality, through which philosophical implications could be conveyed.

Most of his characters were derived from history, either as real persons or as fictitious representatives of some specific time, place, and circumstances. His own classification of "dramatic lyrics," "dramatic romances," and "men and women" roughly indicates the main varieties of his work. In the first, mood and emotion predominate; in the second, the narrative is the chief interest; while the third is the fully articulated "dramatic monologue" which condenses a complex psychological study and a tense situation of conflict into a single climactic speech.

Though no single monologue can ever be regarded as Browning's personal expression, certain basic issues recur so frequently that his main assumptions become obvious. The opinions and motives of the characters toward whom he is unsympathetic can be contrasted with those of the characters depicted favorably. And by composing groups of monologues on certain topics he revealed his views through a series of facets.

Thus his concepts of music are built up in "A Toccata of Galuppi's," "Master Hugues of Saxe-Gotha," and "Abt Vogler." His interpretation of Italian Renaissance art and his general aesthetic principles run through "Pictor Ignotus," "Fra Lippo Lippi," and "Andrea Del Sarto," with a personal commentary added by "Old Pictures in Florence." These poems in turn become part of his great historical panorama of the Renaissance, including "A Grammarian's Funeral," "My Last Duchess," "The Bishop Orders his Tomb," and "The Statue and the Bust." His familiarity with modern Italian life produced "The Italian in England," "The Englishman in Italy," "Love Among the Ruins," "Up at a Villa—Down in the City." A growing curiosity about religion led to a sequence of monologues that sought its anthropological origin in the primitive mind ("Caliban upon Setebos"), touched upon the Old Testament ("Saul"), studied the impact of Christ upon the ancient world from three angles ("Cleon," "An Epistle of Karshish," "A Death in the Desert"), and came down to controversies of creeds in his own day ("Bishop Blougram's Apology," "Mr. Sludge, the Medium"). Probably his most personal revelation of faith is "Rabbi Ben Ezra," which reads like an intentional rebuttal of the melancholy hedonism of Omar Khayyám; but even this was put into the mouth of a medieval Jewish theologian.

All these monologues and many more can be shifted into other groupings. On the psychological side, there are the studies of hate, revenge, and murder, the studies of creative genius, and so on. On the philosophical side, there are Browning's persistent ethical principles.

Admitting the existence of evil and suffering, he believed that they were essential, since otherwise life would be perfect and no progress would be possible. All disappointments and failures in life implied the existence of some ideal or vision for which the individual was striving ("a man's reach should exceed his grasp"); the unfulfilment of an ambition was the best proof of its merit, and if the individual kept on toiling courageously, he would be rewarded in a future existence ("on earth the broken arc, in heaven the perfect round"). The Platonic element in this concept was a survival of Browning's early adoration of Shelley.

As growth was an essential of earthly existence, a person's worth was measured by his capacity for growth, which was tested by a crisis. If he proved weak and gave up his highest ideal under pressure of fear or greed or laziness, he committed the sin of "the unlit lamp and the ungirt loin." On the other hand, the person who proved equal to his ordeal, whether it were on a high or a low plane, demonstrated his fitness and would continue to develop. This situation was illustrated again and again in the monologues.

When these concepts of Browning's were gradually recognized as being in accord with other transcendental trends of the later half of the century, they were acclaimed as an "optimistic creed" that many people found comforting. In the last twenty years of his life, having come to be revered as a deep and inspiring thinker, he allowed himself to relax the economy of the monologue. His poems became long, abstractions and logical analyses invaded them, and his style grew more and more wilfully grotesque. Many of these later writings were closer to prose treatises than to genuine poetry. But until the end his work retained its energy, its wide human sympathy, and its tireless curiosity.

T. J. Wise, *A Complete Bibliography of the Writings in Prose and Verse of Robert Browning* (London, 1897); L. N. Broughton and B. F. Stelter, *A Concordance to the Poems* (2v, New York, 1924-25); Mrs. S. Orr, *A Handbook to the Works* (London, 1885); E. Berdoe, *The Browning Cyclopedia* (London, 1890); G. W. Cooke, *A Guide-Book to the Poetic and Dramatic Works* (Boston, 1891); W. C. DeVane, *A Browning Handbook* (New York, 1935); *Complete Works,* ed. C. Porter and H. A. Clarke (12v, New York, 1898); *Works,* ed. F. G. Kenyon (10v, London, 1912); *New Poems of Robert Browning and Elizabeth Barrett Browning,* ed. F. G. Kenyon (London, 1914); *Complete Poetic and Dramatic Works,* ed. H. E. Scudder (Boston, 1895; Cambridge edition); *Complete Poetical Works* (London, 1907); *Sordello,* ed. A. J. Whyte (London, 1913); *The Ring and the Book,* ed. E. Dowden and A. K. Cook (London, 1940); *The Letters of Robert Browning and Elizabeth Barrett Browning, 1845-46* (2v, London, 1899); *Robert Browning and Alfred Domett,* ed. F. G. Kenyon (London, 1906); *Letters of Robert Browning to Miss Isa Blagden,* ed. A. J. Armstrong (Baylor, Tex., 1923); *Letters of Robert Browning,* ed. T. L. Hood (New Haven, 1933); *From Robert and Elizabeth Browning,* ed. W. R. Benet (London, 1936); *Robert Browning and Julia Wedgwood,* ed. R. Curle (London, 1937); A. Symons, *An Introduction to the Study of Browning* (London, 1886; rev. ed., 1906); H. Corson, *An Introduction to the Study of Robert Browning's Poetry* (Boston, 1886); J. Fotheringham, *Studies in the Poetry of Robert Browning* (London, 1887); W. G. Kingsland, *Robert Browning, Chief Poet of the Age* (London, 1887); W. J. Alexander, *An Introduction to the Poetry of Robert Browning* (Boston, 1889); E. Berdoe, *Browning's Message to His Time* (London, 1890); T. J. Nettleship, *Robert Browning: Essays and Thoughts* (London, 1890); W. Sharp, *Life of Robert Browning* (London, 1890; Great

Writers); Mrs. S. Orr, *Life and Letters of Robert Browning* (London, 1891; rev. by F. G. Kenyon, 1908); H. Jones, *Browning as a Philosophical and Religious Teacher* (Glasgow, 1891); C. W. Hodell, *"The Ring and the Book": Its Moral Spirit and Motive* (Shelbyville, Ind., 1894); A. Beatty, *Browning's Verse-Form* (New York, 1897); G. Santayana, "The Poetry of Barbarism," in *Interpretations of Poetry and Religion* (New York, 1900); S. A. Brooke, *The Poetry of Robert Browning* (London, 1902); G. K. Chesterton, *Robert Browning* (London, 1903; English Men of Letters); E. Dowden, *Robert Browning* (London, 1904); C. H. Herford, *Robert Browning* (Edinburgh, 1905; Modern English Writers); P. E. More, "Why Is Browning Popular?," in *Shelburne Essays,* series III (New York, 1905); K. M. Loudon, *Browning's "Sordello"* (London, 1906); L. B. Campbell, *The Grotesque in the Poetry of Robert Browning* (Austin, Tex., 1907); H. A. Clarke, *Browning's Italy* (New York, 1907); *Browning's England* (New York, 1908); *Browning and His Century* (New York, 1912); J. W. Cunliffe, "Elizabeth Barrett's Influence on Browning's Poetry," *Publications of the Modern Language Association,* XXIV (1908). 169-83; *The Old Yellow Book,* ed. C. W. Hodell (Washington, 1908); W. H. Griffin and H. C. Minchin, *The Life of Robert Browning* (London, 1910; rev. ed., 1938); T. R. Lounsbury, *The Early Literary Career of Robert Browning* (New York, 1911); L. Whiting, *The Brownings: Their Life and Art* (New York, 1911); E. C. Mayne, *Browning's Heroines* (London, 1913); F. Treves, *The Country of "The Ring and the Book"* (London, 1913); H. James, "The Novel in *The Ring and the Book,"* in *Notes on Novelists* (New York, 1914); E. H. Thomson, *The Tragedy of a Troubadour* (London, 1914); A. K. Cook, *A Commentary upon Browning's "The Ring and the Book"* (London, 1920); F. A. Pottle, *Shelley and Browning: A Myth and Some Facts* (Chicago, 1923); C. N. Wenger, *The Aesthetics of Robert Browning* (Ann Arbor, 1924); R. M. Jones, *Mysticism in Robert Browning* (New York, 1924); J. M. Gest, *The Old Yellow Book* (Boston, 1925); W. C. DeVane, *Browning's "Parleyings"* (New Haven, 1927); F. T. Russell, *One Word More on Browning* (Stanford University, 1927); H. H. Hatcher, *The Versification of Robert Browning* (Columbus, 1928); O. Burdett, *The Brownings* (London, 1929); F. G. R. Duckworth, *Browning, Background and Conflict* (London, 1931); A. A. Brockington, *Browning and the Twentieth Century* (London, 1932); D. Kenmare, *Browning and Modern Thought* (London, 1939); W. O. Raymond, "Browning's Casuists," *Studies in Philology,* XXXVII

(1940). 641-66; C. W. Smith, *Browning's Star Imagery* (Princeton, 1941); S. W. Holmes, "Browning's Sordello and Jung," *Publications of the Modern Language Association*, LVI (1941). 758-96; "Browning: Semantic Stutterer," *Publications of the Modern Language Association*, LX (1945). 231-55.

MATTHEW ARNOLD (1822-1888)

>>

Prominent in the religious and educational life of the early nineteenth century was Dr. Thomas Arnold, a liberal theologian and earnest historian, who in 1827 became headmaster of Rugby School and undertook to reform the rigidity and oppression of the boarding-school system.

On Christmas Eve, 1822, his son Matthew was born at Laleham, on the Thames. All his life he was to be influenced by his father's teachings of tolerance, duty, and intellectual honesty; and because his family belonged to the academic rank of the upper middle class, he was always to feel that he had a cultural mission to perform.

At Rugby School he won a prize with his poem, "Alaric

MATTHEW ARNOLD

at Rome," and when he was at Balliol College, Oxford, he received the Newdigate poetry prize for his "Cromwell." To the disappointment of his family and friends, he graduated in 1844 with only second-class honors. Like A. H. Clough, who became his intimate friend, he accepted a fellowship at Oriel College, where he fell under the per-

sonal influence of Newman, although he did not subscribe
to Newman's doctrines.

In 1847 he left Oriel to become secretary to Lord Lansdowne. The ten years that followed were the period of his
greatest poetic activity. In 1849 *The Strayed Reveller and
Other Poems, by A.* was published. The second volume
"by A." was *Empedocles on Etna and Other Poems,* published in 1852 after he had become an Inspector of Schools
and had married. *Poems,* which appeared in the following
year and which included "The Scholar Gipsy" and "Sohrab
and Rustum," was the first volume to which Arnold signed
his full name. The preface to this collection contained the
poetic credo which earned for Arnold the title of "apostle
of the classical ideal of poetry." The narrative poem
"Balder Dead" appeared in a second series of *Poems* (1855),
which otherwise consisted almost wholly of reprintings from
his earlier books. Dealing with the issues of his age, Arnold's
poetry uttered a feeling of regret for the loss of the serene
faith and unhurried existence of the past, mingled with the
resolution that sees beyond disillusionment to endurance
and even to hope.

His work as an inspector of schools was heavy and responsible, for England had newly assumed governmental
charge of education, and a whole administration, curriculum, and so forth, had to be constructed. Arnold was a
member of several important commissions for the study of
educational methods in foreign countries, and his reports
were influential in the organizing of the English secondary
school system.

Not yet widely known to the reading public, he was
appointed in 1857 Professor of Poetry at Oxford University, and held the chair for ten years. As the position
entailed no academic duties beyond delivering a few lectures annually, it did not interrupt his professional career.
In compiling his lectures for publication, however, he

turned his attention to critical writing, and thereafter composed only a few poems in the last thirty years of his life. In 1861 and 1862 appeared two volumes of his lectures *On Translating Homer,* which contained significant views on various literary matters as well as the specific problems of translation. *On the Study of Celtic Literature,* regarded as one of the most charming of his prose works, was published from his lectures in 1867.

With the publication of *Essays in Criticism* (1865), a collection of literary articles previously contributed to periodicals, Arnold entered seriously into his analysis of culture. Convinced that it had a definite moral value, he thought of criticism first in terms of literature and life; poetry, therefore, was essentially a criticism of life. *Culture and Anarchy* (1869) expressed Arnold's social views. It was based upon the importance of culture, which he defined as "a disinterested endeavor to learn and propagate the best that is known and has been thought in the world." In his three works of religious criticism, *St. Paul and Protestantism, Literature and Dogma,* and *Last Essays on Church and Religion,* he pleaded for an admixture of "Hellenism" with the somber "Hebraism" of the Protestant creeds, and sought to define Christian beliefs in terms compatible with scientific thought.

Following a lecture tour in the United States, he published his *Discourses in America,* including a famous address on Emerson. In 1886 he retired from his inspectorship after thirty-five years of service, and on April 15, 1888, he died suddenly of a heart attack in Liverpool.

Arnold's poetry showed sincerity, restraint, and a classic austerity. Goethe, Wordsworth, Senancour, and the Greeks were his spiritual begetters. One of his most famous longer poems, "Sohrab and Rustum," has elevation of blank-verse style enriched by the use of the epic simile and quasi-Miltonic parade of sonorous proper names. "The Scholar

Gipsy" is unexpectedly reminiscent of Keats in its richly beautiful pictures of the natural scenery around Oxford. Its sequel, written thirteen years later but using the same stanzaic form and the same setting, is "Thyrsis," his elegy for Arthur Hugh Clough. Arnold was an excellent elegiac poet; some of his best poems were inspired by death, such as "Rugby Chapel" on the death of his father, "A Southern Night" on his brother and sister-in-law, "Thyrsis" on Clough, and "Westminster Abbey" on Dean Arthur Stanley. His affinity for the stoic or agnostic types of Greek philosophy is expressed in his lyrical drama "Empedocles on Etna," which is much superior to his formal imitation of Greek tragedy in "Merope." At all times Arnold chose to express intellectual rather than passionate emotion. Many of his best poems are discussions of other authors, and it is therefore not surprising that in the middle of his career he relinquished poetry in favor of critical prose.

One of his major objectives was to remove the insularity of English thought by making his fellow-countrymen familiar with the literature of other nations, and a number of his essays were on foreign authors, particularly French. Modeled after the *causeries* of Sainte-Beuve, his literary criticism aimed at the establishment of a classical purity in letters in place of romantic excesses. Renan was his model for social criticism. His own prose style was clear, graceful, and enhanced by great ability in coining phrases. When his social and religious theories involved him in controversy, his urbane irony was effective in making adversaries appear stupid. Though not infallible as a critic, he set up standards that influenced many successors. His poetry, not widely praised in his lifetime, slowly gained fame as the twentieth century came into sympathy with his disillusioned melancholy. By some admirers he is now rated among the greatest Victorian poets. He regarded his own "Empedocles on Etna" as too depressing to fulfil the

proper function of poetry, and withdrew it from circulation, being later persuaded by Browning to republish it.
The poem ranks with FitzGerald's translation of the
Rubáiyát as an early promulgation of the intellectual de-
featism that later flourished in Hardy, Housman, and many
others.

T. B. Smart, *The Bibliography of Matthew Arnold* (London,
1892); *Works* (15v, London, 1903-1904); *Complete Poetical Works*
(London, 1943; Oxford Standard Authors); *Selected Essays,* ed.
H. G. Rawlinson (London, 1924); *Letters, 1848-1888,* ed. G. W.
E. Russell (2v, London, 1895); *Unpublished Letters,* ed. A. Whit-
ridge (New Haven, 1923); *Letters to A. H. Clough,* ed. H. F.
Lowry (New York, 1932); J. Fitch, *Thomas and Matthew Arnold
and Their Influence on English Education* (New York, 1897);
Matthew Arnold and the Spirit of the Age, ed. G. White (New
York, 1898); G. Saintsbury, *Matthew Arnold* (Edinburgh, 1899;
Modern English Writers); H. W. Paul, *Matthew Arnold* (London,
1902; English Men of Letters); G. W. E. Russell, *Matthew Arnold*
(London, 1904; Literary Lives); W. H. Dawson, *Matthew Arnold
and His Relation to the Thought of Our Time* (New York, 1904);
A. P. Kelso, *Matthew Arnold on Continental Life and Literature*
(Oxford, 1914); R. E. C. Houghton, *The Influence of the Classics
on the Poetry of Matthew Arnold* (Oxford, 1923); J. B. Orrick,
Matthew Arnold and Goethe (London, 1928); G. R. Elliott, "The
Arnoldian Lyric Melancholy," in *The Cycle of Modern Poetry*
(Princeton, 1929); C. H. Harvey, *Matthew Arnold, a Critic of the
Victorian Period* (London, 1931); E. K. Brown, *Studies in the
Text of Matthew Arnold's Prose Works* (Paris, 1935); I. E. Sells,
Matthew Arnold and France: the Poet (London, 1935); A. Whit-
ridge, "Matthew Arnold and Sainte Beuve," *Publications of the
Modern Language Association,* LIII (1938). 303-13; F. Wickelgren,
"Matthew Arnold's Literary Relations With France," *Modern
Language Review,* XXXIII (1938). 200-14; L. Trilling, *Matthew
Arnold* (New York, 1939); C. B. Tinker and H. F. Lowry, *The
Poetry of Matthew Arnold* (New York, 1940); J. Hicks, "The
Stoicism of Matthew Arnold," in *University of Iowa Humanistic
Studies,* VI (1943); W. Blackburn, "The Background of Arnold's
Literature and Dogma," *Modern Philology,* XLIII (1945). 130-39;
E. K. Chambers, *Matthew Arnold: A Study* (London, 1947); E. K.
Brown, *Matthew Arnold: A Study in Conflict* (Chicago, 1948).

ARTHUR HUGH CLOUGH (1819-1861)
>>

A poet who never wholly fulfilled his promise of greatness, Arthur Hugh Clough was born at Liverpool on January 1, 1819, and spent most of his childhood in Charleston,
South Carolina, where his father established himself as a
cotton merchant in 1822. His family brought him to England in 1828 and left him at school in Chester, from which
he went the next year to Rugby. There under the super-
vision of Dr. Thomas Arnold he was happy and successful,
popular with the other boys and prominent in sports. He
won all possible scholastic honors and developed an intense religious feeling.

At Balliol College, Oxford, he was deeply admired by a
group of brilliant fellow-students, including Matthew
Arnold, but he was so disturbed by the conflicting religious
movements that he lost his spiritual security. When he received his degree, with only second-class honors, it was
with a troubled mind that he accepted a fellowship at
Oriel College, since this entailed a formal statement of
adherence to the Anglican faith. After spending six years
at Oriel as a tutor, his increasing religious doubts made
him feel obliged to resign in 1848. He then made a continental tour with Emerson, seeing Paris in the midst of
revolution.

He had been writing short poems since his undergraduate days, and in the autumn of 1848 he wrote his first
major work, *The Bothie of Tober-na-Vuolich*. Friends who
had expected a poem of disillusionment were surprised to
find a light-hearted story of an emancipated soul. Written
in Homeric hexameter, it was an idyll of a summer reading-
party he had enjoyed in the Scottish highlands. The colloquial mock-heroic style resembled some of Tennyson's

poems of about the same period, such as "Audley Court," "Edwin Morris," and the prologue to *The Princess*.

The following year Clough published a collection of his short poems, *Ambarvalia*, jointly with a friend, Thomas Burbidge. During a stay in Rome he wrote a second narrative poem in hexameters, *Amours de Voyage*, told as a series of letters. In October, 1849, he took up his duties as Principal of University Hall, a hostel for students at the University of London. Although he became friendly with the Carlyles, he was lonely and unhappy in London, finding the Unitarian doctrines of his colleagues as unsatisfactory as the Anglicanism of Oxford had been.

In 1850, during a vacation in Venice, he started his third long poem, *Dipsychus*, a series of dialogues on faith and doubt between a young man and a spirit, in Venetian settings. The style of the poem had much in common with Browning, particularly *Christmas Eve and Easter Day*, which had been published in that year. The poem was more bitter than Clough's previous ones in its satire of contemporary thought.

After two years at University Hall, Clough resigned and went to Cambridge, Massachusetts, where Emerson made him welcome and where he spent some months in lecturing and writing. Then the offer of an appointment as an examiner in the Education Office called him back to England. In 1854 he married Blanche Smith, a cousin of Florence Nightingale. As one of Miss Nightingale's so-called advisers, he worked with her for several years until his health began to fail. The insistence of her demands, in addition to his official duties and his work on a revised translation of Plutarch's *Lives*, left him little time for poetry. In 1860 he went abroad for his health, and he died in Florence on November 13, 1861.

Although his last seven years were reasonably happy, his friends grieved for his loss of ambition and courage. Matthew Arnold, his closest friend, who had faced some of the same problems of doubt with greater stamina, expressed this mixture of affection and condemnation in "Thyrsis."

Along with Arnold, Clough was the poetic spokesman of the spiritual crisis at the mid-century. His analytical mind and strict ethical standards brought him into conflict with popular ideals in conduct and religion. With a strong predilection for faith, he unwillingly became a sceptic, and the resultant melancholy and perplexity color his verse. *Dipsychus* in particular expressed his disillusionment. This and others of his satiric poems pain many readers by their harshness; but a few short poems such as "Qua Cursum Ventus," "Qui Laborat Orat," and "Say Not the Struggle Nought Availeth," achieve a dignity and stoic fortitude that give them permanent appeal.

Poems and Prose Remains, ed. B. Clough (2v, London, 1869); *Poems,* ed. H. Milford (London, 1910); S. Waddington, *Arthur Hugh Clough* (London, 1883); R. H. Hutton, "Arthur Hugh Clough," in *Literary Essays* (London, 1876); E. Guyot, *Essai sur la formation philosophique du poète A. H. Clough* (Paris, 1913); J. I. Osborne, *Arthur Hugh Clough* (London, 1920); A. M. Turner, "A Study of Clough's 'Mari Magno,'" *Publications of the Modern Language Association,* XLIV (1929). 569-89; H. W. Garrod, "Clough," in *Poetry and the Criticism of Life* (Cambridge, Mass., 1931); G. Levy, *Arthur Hugh Clough, 1819-1861* (London, 1938); F. W. Palmer, "Was Clough a Failure?" *Philological Quarterly,* XXII (1943). 58-68; "The Bearing of Science on the Thought of Clough," *Publications of the Modern Language Association,* LIX (1944). 212-25.

EDWARD FITZGERALD (1809-1883)
>>>

Only one English author had the distinction of gaining literary eminence through a single poem of only a few hundred lines—a poem, too, that was nominally a translation from a remote and forgotten author. The *Rubáiyát* of Omar Khayyám, a Persian poet of the twelfth century, became one of the most influential and significant poems of mid-Victorian England.

When Edward FitzGerald was born, on March 31, 1809, the name of his family was Purcell. Nine years later his father adopted the name and arms of his wife's family, the FitzGeralds. Both families were of Irish descent, but Mrs. Purcell's father, who was very wealthy, owned large estates in England also, and it was to inherit these that John Purcell changed his name.

Part of Edward FitzGerald's childhood was spent in France. He received his schooling, however, at Bury St. Edmunds, and in 1826 he became a student at Trinity College, Cambridge. A desultory student, he sought for no distinction in college, and among his many contemporaries there who later became famous, his closest friend was Thackeray, who was no more of a scholar than he. After his graduation he settled down to a quiet life in a small Suffolk town, to enjoy his hobbies of flowers, music, books, and languages. Although living almost the life of a recluse, he maintained and enlarged his circle of literary friends, becoming intimate with Tennyson, Carlyle, and many others.

In 1851 he published *Euphranor,* a prose dialogue modeled upon Plato's symposia, and dealing with recollections of his undergraduate days. This was followed the next year by *Polonius,* a collection of aphorisms, some original and others quoted. Both books were the productions of an amateur for his personal friends. An interest in Spanish led him to translate and publish *Six Dramas of Calderon.* He then began to study Oriental languages under a friend's guidance, and in 1856 translated *Salámán and Absál,* by Jámí. He next turned his attention to a manuscript of the quatrains ("rubá'i") of Omar Khayyám.

Famous as one of the greatest mathematicians and astronomers of Persia at a time when the Moslem world was eminent for scientific research, Omar enjoyed only a subordinate renown as a poet, and in the course of seven hundred years his verses became almost forgotten even in his own country. FitzGerald had no reason to think that modern readers would be interested in this poet of a distant culture, and when he sent part of his translation to *Fraser's Magazine* it was held for a year and then returned to him. In January, 1859, he printed 250 copies, presented a few to friends, and gave the rest to a London bookseller who was in need of money. Failing to sell them at five shillings, the bookseller reduced the price to a penny. A copy fell into the hands of Rossetti, who became enthusiastic and praised the poem to all his friends. Its fame grew gradually and nine years later a second edition was issued. FitzGerald had revised it extensively, rewriting many stanzas and adding thirty-five to the original seventy-five. He continued rewriting it throughout his lifetime, not always making improvements; the third and fourth editions (both containing 101 quatrains) differed widely from each other and from the first two.

His only later literary work was some further translations from Calderon and some from Greek dramatists. Growing more and more eccentric, he shifted frequently from one house to another, avoided his relations and old friends, and spent much time at sea on his yacht. He died on June 14, 1883.

In writing his version of the *Rubáiyát,* FitzGerald used much freedom in adapting the original material. The manuscript that he used contained 158 stanzas, which he cut and combined as he pleased. His justification was in the fact that other manuscripts had omitted some of these stanzas and included others; and as each quatrain was originally an independent poem, their sequence was never constant. By skilful development of certain symbols that recurred in many quatrains, FitzGerald was able to arrange them in an order that gave the effect of unity. Not one of his quatrains was identical with any one in the original, and yet only a very few of his lines were entirely without a prototype.

The poem appealed to English readers partly because its Oriental imagery was fresh to their imaginations and was rich in exotic color. The melody of the verse was also distinctive; FitzGerald gave the iambic pentameter quatrain a new effect by retaining the rhyme scheme of his Persian original *(aaxa)*.

The poem's wide appeal to readers not usually interested in poetry is chiefly due to its apparently joyous and sensual exaltation of love and wine. Such readers regard it as expressing a rebellion against conventional morality.

The philosophical significance of the poem, however, which was the reason for its particular success in the sixties, is entirely different. It is a bitter expression of intellectual disillusionment, a great scientist's lament that he can find no meaning in the traditional teachings of religion. Omar turned to self-indulgence in despair, rather than in delight, and the poem is full of the astronomer's sense of space and time, rendering all human concerns futile and ephemeral. What the Persian mathematician said about Moslem theology of the twelfth century was exactly applicable to what science was making some people think of Christian theology in the nineteenth. In fact, no English poet had as yet said it with such beautiful clarity and melancholy irony. Arnold and Clough, aware of the discrepancies between science and faith, were confused and depressed by their unwilling surrender of inherited moral and spiritual traditions. The Pre-Raphaelites were implying the same dilemma by expelling all philosophical discussion from their poetry and confining themselves to the cult of sensuous beauty. Omar's voice, aloof and logical, spoke from the past and supplied words for their anti-philosophical philosophy.

C. V. C. Wheeler, *A Bibliography of Edward FitzGerald* (3v, Washington, 1919); J. R. Tutin, *A Concordance to FitzGerald's Translation of the Rubáiyát* (London, 1900); *Variorum and Definitive Edition of the Poetical and Prose Writings,* ed. G. Bentham and E. Gosse (7v, New York, 1902-03); *Letters and Literary Remains,* ed. W. A. Wright (7v, London, 1902-03); *Some New Letters to Bernard Barton,* ed. F. R. Barton (London, 1923); *Letters to Bernard Quaritch,* ed. C. Q. Wrentmore (London, 1926); *A Fitz-Gerald Friendship,* ed. C. B. Johnson and N. C. Hannay (London, 1932); J. Glyde, *The Life of Edward FitzGerald* (London, 1900); T. Wright, *The Life of Edward FitzGerald* (2v, London, 1904); A. C. Benson, *Edward FitzGerald* (London, 1905; English Men of Letters); J. Blyth, *Edward FitzGerald and "Posh,"* (London, 1908); M: Adams, *Omar's Interpreter* (London, 1909); *In the Footsteps of Borrow and FitzGerald* (London, 1913); G. Bradford, "Edward FitzGerald," in *Bare Souls* (New York, 1924); A. M. Terhune, *The Life of Edward FitzGerald* (New Haven, 1947).

COVENTRY PATMORE (1823-1896)

>>

Coventry Kersey Dighton Patmore was born at Woodford in Essex on July 23, 1823. His father, a minor essayist who had been a member of the Lamb circle, was an erratic character and had gained disfavor by serving as a second in a notorious and fatal duel between two editors. The elder Patmore was inordinately proud of his son, and brought him up with little discipline or regular education. The boy grew up imaginative and impractical, with overweening self-confidence; to his father's delight he decided upon poetry as a profession. At the age of twenty-one he published a small volume of poems, which was so unfavorably reviewed that he recalled all the unsold copies and destroyed them.

The next year his father suddenly fled from England to evade his debts; and Coventry Patmore, who had never earned any money, was abandoned to his own resources. Trying to survive by hack writing, he came close to starvation, but various authors became interested in helping him, including Robert Browning, Elizabeth Barrett, and Alfred Tennyson. In 1846, on the recommendation of Monckton Milnes, Patmore was appointed an assistant librarian in the British Museum. He became intimate with the Pre-Raphaelite group, whom he and his first wife, Emily Andrews, entertained frequently in their home; one of his poems was contributed to Rossetti's magazine, *The Germ*.

COVENTRY PATMORE

His early poems, in their sentiment and their luscious melodies, had shown the influence of Elizabeth Barrett. In 1854 he published a volume which retained something of these traits but gave them a new emphasis—*The Angel in the House*. Its theme was marriage as the road to spiritual truth, and love as the mystical way to God. Mid-Victorian sentiment was deeply gratified with this mingling of erotic passion with domestic virtue. Three further installments of the poem were published during the next eight years. The last part, "The Victories of Love," was written after his wife's death, a loss that Patmore felt keenly. Shortly afterwards he became a convert to the Roman Catholic faith.

In 1865 he married Marianne Byles, whose wealth enabled him to resign his library position and buy a country estate. Displaying an unexpected business talent, he devoted himself to the management and improvement of his property. He decided not to continue *The Angel in the House*, though according to his original plan the story was to extend to six parts instead of the four that he completed. Instead, he turned to more mystical themes and to the irregular ode as his chosen form. He intended a great series that would assail the moral decadence of the modern world; but after writing nine odes he gave up the theme. Then in 1877 he suddenly began a series which was published as *The Unknown Eros*, and in the next year further odes were included in *Amelia*, which was his own favorite among his books.

His second wife, a gentle, anxious woman who had conscientiously brought up his six children, died in 1880, and in the next year he married for the third time, a friend of his eldest daughter. The birth of a son brought him consolation after the deaths of two of his grown-up children. In his last years he published two volumes of prose, and he died on November 26, 1896.

The great fame of *The Angel in the House* was followed by a reaction as readers became aware of the monotony of the verse and the tendency to bathos. His *Unknown Eros* came in the midst of this disfavor, and was at first little recognized. Then a group of younger Catholic poets began to admire him, and *The Unknown Eros* slowly gained reputation as a mystical work that sometimes came near to sublimity. Its theme is basically similar to that of *The Angel in the House*, but the treatment could not be more different—these poems are as profound in thought and as original in treatment as the previous ones were commonplace. Patmore's intermittent genius, by a sudden creative release in his fifty-fourth year, rescued him from mediocrity.

Works (5v, London, 1907); *Poems* (London, 1949; Oxford Standard Authors); A. De Vere, "Coventry Patmore's Poetry," in *Essays Chiefly Literary and Ethical* (London, 1889); B. Champneys, *Memoirs and Correspondence of Coventry Patmore* (2v, London, 1900); E. Gosse, *Coventry Patmore* (London, 1905; Literary Lives); F. Harris, "Coventry Patmore," in *Contemporary Portraits,* third series (New York, 1920); O. Burdett, *The Idea of Coventry Patmore* (London, 1921); J. Freeman, "Coventry Patmore," *North American Review,* ccxviii (1923). 221-32; F. Page, *Patmore: a Study in Poetry* (London, 1933); D. Patmore, *Portrait of My Family* (London, 1935).

DANTE GABRIEL ROSSETTI (1828-1882)
>>

In the years after Napoleon's defeat the separate states of Italy were disturbed by repeated revolutions. English liberals like Byron and Shelley supported the rebels, and when the outbreaks were suppressed the defeated leaders often found refuge in England. One such expatriate was Gabriele Rossetti, who fled from Italy after the Neapolitan insurrections of 1820 and 1821. A poet and artist, he had been librettist for the Naples Opera and curator of antiquities at the Naples Museum. In London he became Professor of Italian at King's College and wrote scholarly books

D. G. ROSSETTI IN 1847
(self-portrait)

on Dante. He married Frances Mary Lavinia Polidori, whose brother had been physician to Lord Byron. Their elder son was born on May 12, 1828, and was christened

Gabriel Charles Dante, a name which he later revised to Dante Gabriel.

The four Rossetti children, all of whom developed literary ability, were brought up with two cultural traditions. The English language and outlook that surrounded them was not more familiar than the Italian of their own home. The enthusiasm for art, music, and poetry, and the habit of free emotional expression, were part of their Latin heritage. Although the family had adopted the Episcopal faith, their Roman Catholic ancestry retained an effect upon them.

As early as the age of six, Dante Gabriel Rossetti had composed dramatic scenes in verse. At nine he was sent to King's College School, where he remained until he was thirteen. Since he showed great talent in drawing, he attended F. S. Cary's Art Academy for four years, after which he went to the Royal Academy School; but the methods of the Royal Academy did not satisfy him and after two years he left it to become a private pupil of Ford Madox Brown. Meanwhile, however, he and his friends, Holman Hunt and John Everett Millais, discovered a book of reproductions of frescoes by early Italian masters, in which they found proof of the greatness of the painters before Raphael. The three friends, with Rossetti's brother and three others, formed the Pre-Raphaelite Brotherhood. It was to work for individuality, freedom, and imagination in the arts, in contrast with the current sentimentality and matter-of-factness. To this freedom they added the elaborate detail and the mysticism typical of medieval art.

When the Brotherhood exhibited their first paintings in the new mode, they were condemned by most critics, but Rossetti and his friends were confident in their beliefs. To answer their adversaries and to extend their aesthetic theory into literature, they began in 1850 to publish a magazine, *The Germ*. Few people read it, and only four numbers were issued, but it printed the work of several authors who became famous, and Rossetti's first poems appeared in it.

He had been writing poetry from an early age; his grandfather had a poetic romance of his privately printed when he was fifteen. Stimulated by his reading of Shelley, Keats, and Browning, his poetry had a pictorial, symbolic quality that made it the verbal equivalent of his paintings. "The Blessed Damozel," written a year before the Brotherhood was founded, was a perfect representation in words of a Pre-Raphaelite scene. It was probably the most noteworthy of his twelve contributions to *The Germ.*

During the next few years he wrote several important poems, such as "Sister Helen" and "The Burden of Nineveh," but made little effort to get them published. Nor did he pursue his painting very ambitiously: he gave much of his time to water colors and book illustrations. About 1851 he became engaged to Elizabeth Eleanor Siddal, but poverty prevented their marriage. A milliner's apprentice, she had sat as a model for many paintings by Rossetti and his friends; but she was of meager education and her health was frail. It has been said that the pale and angular appearance so characteristic of the women in Pre-Raphaelite paintings is a record of Lizzy Siddal's tuberculosis.

John Ruskin, who had been the first notable critic to approve of the Pre-Raphaelite art, agreed to buy some of Rossetti's paintings. With the financial independence that resulted, he was able to take an active part in the art revival of William Morris; he helped Morris to paint the murals in the Oxford Union, and later was associated with Morris's production of decorative art for homes and churches. About this time he fell deeply in love with a woman who has not been identified by his biographers; but a feeling of obligation to his nine years' engagement caused him to marry Miss Siddal in 1860. For a time they seemed happy, but her illness became acute, and in less than two years she died from an overdose of laudanum which she had been taking to soothe pain. In the violence of his grief Rossetti entombed many of his manuscript poems in her coffin.

As a result of designing stained glass for Morris, he acquired stronger mastery of color and design, and his best paintings were produced during the sixties. His fame as a poet did not grow as fast as his fame as a painter. Although in 1861 he published *Early Italian Poets,* a collection of lyrics translated in the original meters, his original poetry was known to only a few admirers. He was becoming more and more eccentric: he shut himself up in his big house in Cheyne Walk, Chelsea (near the Carlyles), collected weird pet animals, and lost touch with most of his friends. A threat of blindness forced him to reduce the time he devoted to painting, and he regained his interest in poetry. In particular, he worked upon a sonnet sequence, *The House of Life.* His friends persuaded him in 1869 to apply for official sanction to open his wife's grave and recover his manuscripts. As a result, a volume of *Poems* was published in 1870 and won him an immediate reputation as one of the leading poets of the time.

The next year Robert Buchanan wrote an article (under a pseudonym) in *The Contemporary Review,* with the title "The Fleshly School of Poetry," stigmatizing some of Rossetti's sonnets as indecent. An angry controversy arose, and Rossetti defended himself hotly in *The Athenaeum,* but it was evident that he was deeply hurt. He had fallen into bad habits of over-indulgence in whiskey and was becoming an addict to chloral, which he had started to take to relieve neuralgia and insomnia. In 1872 he attempted suicide, and was saved only by quick action of friends. During the next decade he suffered from extreme depression and seldom went out of doors; he added a number of sonnets to *The House of Life* and with a sudden rekindling of poetical faculties in 1880 he wrote his narrative poems, "The White Ship" and "The King's Tragedy." A collection of *Ballads and Sonnets* was published in 1881, but by this time he was stricken with paralysis, and he died on April 9, 1882.

Rossetti was less important as a creative artist than as a stimulus to others. Both in painting and in poetry, the quantity and range of his work was more limited than that of others who received their first impetus from him. But in his younger days he radiated enthusiasm and confidence which inspired everyone who came near him. He was articulate enough to proclaim what his Anglo-Saxon friends were fumbling to discover.

Rather than depreciating him for not being preëminent in either of his two arts, one ought to give him credit for his unusual achievement of distinction in both of them. In poetry, as in painting, his work was marked by the strongest individuality. Totally indifferent to the political and religious issues of his age, he was a poet of imagery and passion. His intensity of feeling, his glowing and sumptuous diction, and his love of detail were in contradiction to the poetic standards of his day. The musical cadences of his verse also added much to the emotional effect, which was usually one of dreamy melancholy.

He worked hard upon the technique of his poems, repolishing every phrase. The poems are therefore too ornate to seem spontaneous in their feeling. "Sister Helen," for instance, used devices of repetition, dialogue, and refrain that he found in ancient folk ballads; but he added subtle modifications of phrase and suggestion that produced an effect very different from the primitive force of his originals. His sonnet sequence, *The House of Life,* was elaborated with difficult symbolism. Though it was largely, if not wholly, based upon his own love-experiences, he looked back upon them over several years and cloaked them in allusion and mystification so that the problem of interpreting the "story" underlying the cycle is second only to that of Shakespeare's.

Rossetti was the chief exponent of the "new medievalism." As his outlook was aesthetic rather than religious or philosophical, he freely mingled fairy-tale superstition, Catholic symbolism, and sensuous indulgence to create the unique mood of his work.

W. M. Rossetti, *Bibliography of the Works of Dante Gabriel Rossetti* (London, 1905); *Works,* ed. W. M. Rossetti (7v, London, 1900-01); (London, 1911); *The House of Life,* ed. P. F. Baum (Cambridge, Mass., 1928); *The Blessed Damozel,* ed. P. F. Baum (Chapel Hill, 1937); *Sister Helen,* ed. J. C. Troxell (New Haven, 1939); *Rossetti Papers, 1862-1870,* ed. W. M. Rossetti (London, 1902); *Family Letters,* ed. W. M. Rossetti (2v, London, 1895); *Letters to William Allingham,* ed. G. B. Hill (London, 1898); *Letters to His Publisher,* ed. O. Doughty (London, 1928); *Three Rossettis: Unpublished Letters,* ed. J. C. Troxell (Cambridge, Mass., 1937); *Letters to Fanny Cornworth,* ed. P. F. Baum (Baltimore, 1940); H. Caine, *Recollections of Dante Gabriel Rossetti* (London, 1882); W. Sharp, *Dante Gabriel Rossetti* (London, 1882); J. Knight, *Life of Dante Gabriel Rossetti* (London, 1887; Great Writers); W. M. Rossetti, *Dante Gabriel Rossetti as Designer and Writer* (London, 1889); W. Pater, "Dante Gabriel Rossetti," in *Appreciations* (London, 1889); E. Wood, *Dante Rossetti and the Pre-Raphaelite Movement* (London, 1894); H. C. Marillier, *Dante G. Rossetti* (London, 1899); E. L. Cary, *The Rossettis: Dante Gabriel and Christina* (New York, 1900); A. C. Benson, *Rossetti* (London, 1904; English Men of Letters); F. V. P. Rutter, *Dante Gabriel Rossetti, Painter and Man of Letters* (London, 1908); H. Shine, "The Influence of Keats upon Rossetti," *Englische Studien,* LXI (1927). 183-210; R. C. Wallerstein, "Personal Experience in Rossetti's 'House of Life,'" *Publications of the Modern Language Association,* XLII (1927). 492-504; R. L. Mégroz, *Dante Gabriel Rossetti* (London, 1928); E. Waugh, *Rossetti: His Life and Works* (London, 1928); A. Symons, "Dante Gabriel Rossetti," in *Studies in Strange Souls* (London, 1929); V. Hunt, *The Wife of Rossetti* (London, 1932); R. D. Waller, *The Rossetti Family,*

1824-1854 (Manchester, 1932); F. Winwar, *Poor Splendid Wings* (Boston, 1933); L. Wolff, *Dante Gabriel Rossetti* (Paris, 1934); E. R. Vincent, *Gabriele Rossetti in England* (Oxford, 1936); J. Masefield, *Thanks Before Going* (London, 1946).

CHRISTINA GEORGINA ROSSETTI (1830-1894)
≫≫

Christina Georgina Rossetti, the younger sister of Dante Gabriel Rossetti, became one of the leading women poets of the Victorian period. Although the range of her poetry was limited, she has seldom been excelled in the pure lyric.

She was born on December 5, 1830, into the artistic and Italianate home of the Rossettis in London. Educated entirely at home, she learned much from acquaintance with her father's clever and sometimes eccentric friends, and from the interests of her brothers and sister. Her first recorded verses were written when she was eleven, and five years later her grandfather, Gaetano Polidori, privately printed a small volume of her poems.

CHRISTINA ROSSETTI
AND MOTHER

Through her brothers she became associated with the Pre-Raphaelite movement, and sat for several paintings by its members. Under the pseudonym of Ellen Alleyne she wrote verses for *The Germ,* the official organ of the Brotherhood.

Her extremely religious temperament was heightened by the Oxford Movement. This return to pre-Reformation rituals and artistic embellishments of religion, which had much to do with the medievalism of the Pre-Raphaelite Brotherhood, led all the women of the Rossetti family to high Anglicanism. Therefore it was with religious misgivings that she became engaged to a painter, James Collinson. When she found herself unable to accept their difference in religious views she broke the engagement; and another proposal of marriage, from Charles B. Cayley, was later refused for the same reason. The poignant presentation of hopeless love in her verses resulted from these experiences.

When her father became disabled, she taught school for a time in London and later at Frome in Somerset. She was composing freely in both English and Italian, and in 1862 she published *Goblin Market and Other Poems,* with two illustrations by her brother. This became the first Pre-Raphaelite literary triumph. *The Prince's Progress, Sing-Song* (poems for children), and *A Pageant* were other volumes of her verse. In prose she published several volumes of short stories and of religious discussion.

From childhood Miss Rossetti had suffered from ill-health. A serious heart-ailment caused her a long illness in 1852. Then in 1871 she was attacked by Graves's disease, a thyroid affliction, which proved almost fatal and kept her an invalid for years, one of the effects being an abnormal protrusion of the eye-balls. She became almost a recluse, leaving her home only to attend church and other religious duties. Her elder sister had joined an Anglican sisterhood, and Christina might have done likewise had she not felt the responsibility of caring for her mother, whom she loved deeply. On December 29, 1894, she died of cancer and was buried beside her parents in the Highgate Cemetery.

Miss Rossetti was a fluent writer of lyric poetry, her "Dream Love," "A Birthday," and "An Apple Gathering" being examples of the perfect lyric. Like her brother, she had great skill in sonnet writing, and her simple, direct sonnets make an interesting contrast with his ornate ones. Her longer poem, "Goblin Market" is a unique combination of quaint fantasy with deep human feeling. Her songs and sonnets dealing with the themes of hopeless love, death, and the vanity of worldly desires are above criticism in their pure diction, haunting melody, and sincere emotion. In contrast, her poems for children are among the most charming of the era in their light-hearted simplicity.

Poetical Works, ed. W. M. Rossetti (London, 1903); *Family Letters,* ed. W. M. Rossetti (London, 1908); T. Watts-Dunton, "Reminiscences of Christina Rossetti," *Nineteenth Century,* XXXVII (1895). 355-66; A. C. Benson, "Christina Rossetti," in *Essays* (London, 1896); H. T. M. Bell, *Christina Rossetti: A Biographical and Critical Study* (London, 1898); W. de la Mare, "Christina Rossetti," *Essays by Divers Hands,* VI (1926); M. F. Sandars, *Life of Christina Rossetti* (London, 1930); D. M. Stuart, *Christina Rossetti* (London, 1930; English Men of Letters); F. L. Lucas, "Christina Rossetti," in *Eight Victorian Poets* (Cambridge, 1931); F. Shove, *Christina Rossetti: a Study* (London, 1931); E. W. Thomas, *Christina Georgina Rossetti* (New York, 1931); V. Woolf, "I Am Christina Rossetti," in *The Second Common Reader* (London, 1932); B. I. Evans, "The Sources of Christina Rossetti's 'Goblin Market,' " *Modern Language Review,* XXVIII (1933). 156-65.

WILLIAM MORRIS (1834-1896)
>>

William Morris, who was born in the London suburb of Walthamstow on March 24, 1834, was known in his day for three things: crafts, poetry, and socialism, probably in that order. The son of a wealthy business man, he spent a happy childhood reading the Waverley novels and riding about on his pony, making believe to be an Arthurian knight. Although he later became an exceptionally powerful man, he was delicate in childhood and did not go to school until he was nine. From 1848 to 1851 he attended Marlborough College, after which he entered Exeter College, Oxford.

At the university he and his intimate friend Edward Burne-Jones fell under the influence of the Anglo-Catholic movement. They were devoted to the poetry of Tennyson, and accepted the principles of Ruskin's essay on *The Nature of the Gothic.* Their travels on the Continent in 1854 and 1855 revealed to them the physical embodiment of their artistic ideals in the great French cathedrals. They abandoned all previous plans in favor of a career in art.

WILLIAM MORRIS

By 1856 Morris had become a member of a group of students who called themselves "The Brotherhood," their aim being to create more beauty in the arts and in religion. With Morris's financial aid, "The Brotherhood" published for twelve months a periodical called *The Oxford and Cambridge Magazine,* to which Dante Gabriel Rossetti became a contributor.

After receiving his degree in 1856 Morris went to work in an architect's office, but by the end of the year Rossetti persuaded him to give up this profession and devote himself to painting. A new building for the Oxford Union Society had just been erected, and Morris, with Rossetti and several other friends, undertook to decorate its hall with murals as a part of their program for the restoration of the fine arts to a place of importance. Since they painted directly upon the white-washed brick, on which the mortar had not yet hardened, the colors soon faded, so that only a few traces remained. The murals were based upon the Arthurian cycle, revealing a characteristic interest of the group.

Always interested in poetry and romance, Morris had surprised his Oxford friends by writing verse "by the mile." In 1858 he published his first book, *The Defense of Guenevere and Other Poems*, but it attracted little general notice. Meanwhile, when he and Burne-Jones had taken rooms together, they were unable to find furnishings to suit their tastes. Several years later, when Morris married beautiful Jane Burden and built "The Red House" at Upton, the same difficulty confronted him. He consequently undertook a study of the laws of ornament and their application to domestic art. As a result, he and six young friends formed a commercial company in 1861 to produce artistic wall-hangings, tiles, furniture, drapery, and carpets. The partnership continued until 1875, when Morris became the sole proprietor. The firm exerted a great influence in bringing about a renaissance of domestic crafts in England; in fact, the professions of interior decoration and industrial design may be regarded as originating in it. The restoration and decoration of English churches also provided Morris with much business, and his Gothic interests had full play in these ecclesiastical forms.

When the "dream house" at Upton proved to be cold and unhealthy, he moved into London and devoted himself to writing long poems. *The Life and Death of Jason* was well received in 1867; and between 1868 and 1870 he published in three installments his collection of poetic tales, *The Earthly Paradise*. As a result of visits to Iceland in 1871 and 1873 he became fascinated with the Norse sagas, and started to translate some of them.

He and Rossetti bought the manor house of Kelmscott, in the Thames valley. By this time the business was becoming large and profitable; but Morris with his tireless energy continued to take part in the actual handiwork, such as the mixing of dyes. His promotion of individual craftsmanship as a requisite for beautiful products led him to a concern with the social problems of his employees. The medievalists who had influenced him—Carlyle (in *Past and Present*) and Rossetti—had merely looked back to the pre-industrial days with envy; but Morris was making practical experiments. Like Ruskin, he came to the conclusion that good workmanship depended upon the happiness and self-respect of the worker. Always a radical in politics, he left the Liberal party in 1883 and joined a Socialist organization, the Democratic Federation, of which he was promptly elected treasurer. The next year he and some friends disagreed with the Federation's program and formed a new group, the Socialist League. Morris was its treasurer and an active leader for eight years, editing its magazine, writing much propaganda, and addressing open-air meetings (at which he was several times arrested).

One result was that he largely gave up poetry in favor of prose. *Sigurd the Volsung* (1876) was his last long poem. Among the striking prose works embodying his political doctrines were *The Dream of John Ball* (1888) and *News from Nowhere* (1890), the latter a forecast of life in England as a Socialist commonwealth.

A growing enthusiasm for weaving had led him into tapestry making, which was his main handicraft activity from 1881 to 1889; he then shifted his attention to the designing and printing of beautiful books. His Kelmscott Press brought out his own works and others, with typography, page lay-out, and illustrations all created by Morris himself. A great edition of Chaucer remains the most famous example of his work.

In 1890 an anarchist faction seized control of the Socialist League, and Morris withdrew from it. His writing now centered in fantastic prose romances on medieval themes, of which he wrote seven, with such fascinating titles as *The Roots of the Mountains, The Wood Beyond the World, The Well at the World's End,* and *The Water of the Wondrous Isles.* When his robust strength finally gave way under his ceaseless activities, he died on October 3, 1896.

As a poet Morris was at his best in long pieces; and since long poems are not popular with readers, few people are now well acquainted with his work. In his vigor, objectivity, and easy swing he genuinely approximated the feeling of the ancient epic—hence the success of his translations of the sagas. His versions of the *Aeneid* and the *Odyssey* are less distinguished. In his lyrics and ballads the elaborate reconstruction of medieval effects often seems artificial; the poems are less emotional than decorative.

His earliest volume of poetry was based largely on the romances of chivalry; his second, on the Greek legends. Then, in *The Earthly Paradise,* he achieved probably his most satisfactory work. Frankly imitating the device of *The Canterbury Tales,* he depicted a group of people who narrated to one another twenty-four stories, two for each month of the year. Twelve being told by the Hellenes of the Earthly Paradise and twelve by their Scandinavian guests, there was good contrast between the classic spirit of one group and the more primitive vigor of the other. To avoid monotony, Morris used different metrical patterns for the various tales.

The Story of Sigurd the Volsung and the Fall of the Niblungs, his other long poem, has genuine epic stature, with six-stress anapestic couplets giving the rush and sweep of a bard holding an audience entranced with his story. Following the example of the old minstrels, however, Morris did not worry about becoming wordy and diffuse, or about using clichés. Seldom does he seem to choose a word with precision; he prefers to keep to the small and well-worn stock of English words of Anglo-Saxon origin.

In view of this lack of self-discipline, it may be that his best literary artistry is to be found in the prose romances, where his imagination and rich medieval coloring have full expression without infringing the poetic canons of conciseness and verbal distinction. The rhythmic prose is excellently suited to the fairyland atmosphere.

In spite of the vast dimensions of his writings, Morris was apparently sincere in the modesty with which he deprecated himself as "the idle singer of an empty day." Like Walter Scott, he let his stories pour forth with little control. He seldom uttered any of his political doctrines in his poetry; nor did he record his personal emotional experiences. And in writing objectively about human beings he turned his back upon his own epoch. An idealist and a lover of beauty, he was influenced more by literature than by life; a painter before he was a poet, he made handsome pictures in words, and they remained two-dimensional.

Yet, paradoxically, he had a far more direct effect upon his own and later times than the writers who preached their creeds in the pages of their imaginative works.

T. Scott, *A Bibliography of the Works of William Morris* (London, 1897); H. B. Forman, *The Books of William Morris Described* (London, 1897); *Collected Works*, ed. M. Morris and S. Cockerell (24v, London, 1910-15); *Selected Writings*, ed. G. D. H. Cole (London, 1934); G. Saintsbury, "Mr. William Morris," in *Corrected Impressions* (London, 1895); A. Vallance, *William Morris: His Art, His Writings, and His Public Life* (London, 1897; rev. ed., 1909); J. W. Mackail, *The Life of William Morris* (2v, London, 1899); E. L. Cary, *William Morris, Poet, Craftsman, Socialist* (New York, 1902); W. B. Yeats, "The Happiest of the Poets," in *Ideas of Good and Evil* (London, 1903); G. K. Chesterton, "William Morris and His School," in *Varied Types* (London, 1903); J. W. Mackail, *William Morris and His Circle* (Oxford,

1907); A. Noyes, *William Morris* (London, 1908; English Men of Letters); H. Jackson, *William Morris, Craftsman-Socialist* (London, 1908; rev. ed., 1926); J. Drinkwater, *William Morris, A Critical Study* (London, 1912); A. Compton-Rickett, *William Morris: A Study in Personality* (London, 1913); A. Clutton-Brock, *William Morris, His Work and Influence* (London, 1914); G. Vidalenc, *William Morris* (Paris, 1920); J. B. Glasier, *William Morris and the Early Days of the Socialist Movement* (London, 1921); H. H. Sparling, *The Kelmscott Press and William Morris, Master Craftsman* (London, 1924); B. I. Evans, *William Morris and His Poetry* (London, 1925); A. von H. Phelan, *The Social Philosophy of William Morris* (Durham, N. C., 1927); G. H. Crow, *William Morris, Designer* (London, 1934); P. Bloomfield, *William Morris* (London, 1934); M. Morris, *William Morris, Artist, Writer, Socialist* (2v, Oxford, 1936); D. Hoare, *The Works of Morris and Yeats in Relation to Early Saga Literature* (Cambridge, 1937); L. W. Eshleman, *A Victorian Rebel* (New York, 1940); C. Short, "William Morris and Keats," *Publications of the Modern Language Association,* LIX (1944). 513-23; M. B. Grennan, *William Morris, Medievalist and Revolutionary* (New York, 1945).

ALGERNON CHARLES SWINBURNE (1837-1909)

>>

Algernon Charles Swinburne, who at his height was both hailed as the poet of a new age and condemned as a propagator of sin, was born in London on April 5, 1837, the eldest of six children of Admiral Charles Henry and Lady Jane Henrietta Swinburne. One of his grandfathers was a baronet, the other an earl. During a childhood spent in two of the most beautiful and contrasted parts of England, the placid Isle of Wight and the lonely hills of Northumberland, he developed a love for reading, the Bible and the works of French and Italian writers being his favorites. At Eton College he became interested in the Elizabethan dramatists and in Landor, Shelley, and Victor Hugo, whom he worshipped for their style and their spirit of republicanism. Meetings with Wordsworth and Samuel Rogers made him decide to become a poet.

At nineteen, when he went to Balliol College, Oxford, he made the acquaintance of Thomas Hill Green (later a famous philosopher), and Benjamin Jowett, who had just become Professor of Greek. He became involved in a dissipated group of students, however, and gave anxiety to the authorities, with the result that he was removed in the middle of his fourth year.

A. C. SWINBURNE

He had met Morris, Rossetti, and Burne-Jones when they were in Oxford painting their famous frescoes; and when he went down from the university to live in London he lived with Rossetti and George Meredith for a while in Cheyne Walk. In 1860 his first book, *The Queen Mother and Rosamund,* consisting of two poetic dramas in the Elizabethan manner, was published, but received little notice.

Swinburne was now an elfin-looking little man with a thatch of red hair, a shrill voice, and excited gestures. In 1862 he fell in love with the adopted daughter of Dr. John Simon, a friend of the Pre-Raphaelite circle; but upon declaring his love to her he was embarrassed and infuriated to find that she laughed at him. The critics' favorable reception of his Greek tragedy, *Atalanta in Calydon,* in 1865, heartened him somewhat. *Chastelard,* the first part of a trilogy of plays on Mary Stuart, was also published that year.

In the following year *Poems and Ballads* brought Swinburne both fame and notoriety. Since the poems were a direct challenge to the poetic authority of Tennyson, Browning, and Patmore, they were attacked by the conventional as heretical and immoral. With open disregard for reticence, Swinburne chanted the joys and agonies of passionate—and usually illicit—love. Many younger men, on the other hand, hailed it as a courageous revolt against prudery, and they were also fascinated by the rich melodies of his verse. Meredith and Ruskin were among his defenders.

Swinburne soon began to turn away from the purely decorative, medieval, and erotic themes of Pre-Raphaelitism to extol the political and religious rebellions of Mazzini and Hugo. In *Songs before Sunrise,* published in 1871, he proclaimed the violent republicanism with which he had been obsessed since his school days. His ferocious attacks on Christianity increased his reputation for vice. *Bothwell,* the second part of the Mary Stuart trilogy, was published in 1874, followed by *Songs of Two Nations,* on French and Italian themes, in 1875. The 1879 series of *Poems and Ballads,* which contained elegies on Baudelaire and Gautier, showed the influence of those writers upon Swinburne's form and melody.

Lacking all practical common sense, Swinburne had fallen into irregular habits and alcoholism, until at forty-two he was completely broken in health. A devoted friend, Theodore Watts-Dunton, took him to his own suburban home at Putney, and kept him there under firm though kind restraint for the rest of his life. Although his health improved so that he was able to write copiously for the next thirty years, his ideas became conventionalized, so that he turned his back upon some of the authors whom he had formerly worshipped as heroes. In addition to his poetry he published a number of volumes of literary criticism, and involved himself in several verbal wars with other critics, conducted with grotesque violence. With the exception of his romance, *Tristram of Lyonesse,* the poetry of his last thirty years added little to his reputation. He died on April 10, 1909.

Swinburne, like Byron and Shelley, was a rebellious genius born into a family of proudly aristocratic lineage. The traditions of behavior in their caste aroused these poets to particular violence in their flouting of established restraint. All three of them carried their defiance of convention into practice in their personal lives as well as proclaiming it in their poetry. Swinburne regarded all legal controls, civic or religious, as harmful shackles upon individual liberty. His approach to all opinions was so emotional that he was often inconsistent. He despised Christianity because it was part of the social organization of his time and because he interpreted it as repressing joy and beauty. Being innately religious in his love of nature and his idealized humanitarianism, he had to find some creed. Accordingly he turned to the ancient pagan mythologies with a sincerity of acceptance that no other modern writer has displayed. To him the gods of Ancient Greece were satisfactory symbols of the forces of nature that he revered. In two important later poems, "Hertha" and "Hymn of Man," he tried to create more adequate deities for himself. Under the influence of Darwin's science and Comte's positivism he proposed a worship of the Life Force and of the human race as its highest embodiment.

The poems that shocked his contemporaries by their sexual passion and sadism, such as "Faustine" and "Laus Veneris," have been so far exceeded by later writers that they seem artificial and self-conscious, as well as being too long. This squandering of his poetic force through too much wordage was Swinburne's besetting fault. Gifted with a prodigious fluency of words and melody of verse, which he could display with almost equal ease in five languages, he enjoyed his own eloquence too well to know when to stop. The more the reader enjoys the beautiful sound-effects the harder he finds it to keep his mind on what the poem means. Elaborate interweaving of stresses in his meter, frequent alliterations and assonances, long lines and complex stanza-forms all combined to give his verse its overwhelming flow and speed. His technical virtuosity showed itself also in the *Heptalogia,* a group of clever parodies of contemporary poets, including himself.

A hero-worshipper in literature and life, he wrote his best prose when voicing his delight in the Elizabethan dramas, the poetry of Blake, the novels of Dickens and Charlotte Brontë. His poems to Hugo, Mazzini, Landor, and others show the same enthusiasm. His love of the ocean is expressed in some of his most autobiographical poems, such as "Hesperia" and "Thalassius." The choruses in *Atalanta in Calydon* and a few other poems that avoided diffuseness are his best work.

T. J. Wise, *A Bibliography of the Writings in Prose and Verse of Algernon Charles Swinburne* (2v, London, 1919-20); *Complete Works,* ed. E. Gosse and T. J. Wise (20v, London, 1925-27); *Collected Poetical Works* (2v, London, 1924); *Letters,* ed. T. Hake and A. Compton-Rickett (London, 1918); *Letters,* ed. E. Gosse and T. J. Wise (2v, London, 1919); G. Saintsbury, "Mr. Swinburne," in *Corrected Impressions* (London, 1895); E. Thomas, *Algernon Charles Swinburne: A Critical Study* (London, 1912); O. Pound, "On the Application of the Principles of Greek Lyric Tragedy in the Classical Dramas of Swinburne," *University of Nebraska Studies,* XIII (1913). 341-60; T. E. Welby, *Swinburne: A Critical Study* (London, 1914; rev. ed., 1926); F. Harris, "Swinburne, the Poet of Youth and Revolt," in *Contemporary Portraits,* 1st ser. (New York, 1915); M. C. J. Leith, *The Boyhood of Algernon Charles Swinburne* (London, 1917); W. B. D. Henderson, *Swinburne and Landor* (London, 1918); C. Kernahan, *Swinburne As I Knew Him* (London, 1919); T. S. Eliot, "Swinburne As Critic," "Swinburne As Poet," in *The Sacred Wood* (London, 1920); M. Beerbohm, "No. 2, The Pines," in *And Even Now* (London, 1921); C. J. Watts-Dunton, *The Home Life of Swin-*

burne (London, 1922); P. de Reul, *L'oeuvre de Swinburne* (Brussels, 1922); H. Nicolson, *Swinburne* (London, 1926; English Men of Letters); G. Lafourcade, *La jeunesse de Swinburne* (2v, Oxford, 1928); S. C. Chew, *Swinburne* (Boston, 1929); W. R. Rutland, *Swinburne: A Nineteenth-Century Hellene* (Oxford, 1931); G. Lafourcade, *Swinburne: A Literary Biography* (London, 1932); C. K. Hyder, *Swinburne's Literary Career and Fame* (Durham, N. C., 1933); E. K. Brown, "Swinburne: A Centenary Estimate," *University of Toronto Quarterly,* VI (1937). 215-35; H. Hare, "Swinburne and 'le Vice Anglais,'" *Horizon,* XVI (1947). 268-89.

JAMES THOMSON (1834-1882)

>>

Son of a ship's officer, James Thomson was born at Port Glasgow, a dockyard town on the Firth of Clyde, on November 23, 1834. When he was seven years old his mother died and he was sent to an orphanage. As he showed scholarly ability he was eventually trained to be an army schoolmaster.

While serving in this capacity at a military station in Ireland he fell deeply in love with the pretty daughter of a sergeant in the garrison. Her affection for the first time brought happiness into his life; but within two years her death plunged him into incurable melancholy and actual physical illness.

One of the soldiers in the Irish garrison was Charles Bradlaugh, a militant atheist, who provided Thomson with much-needed literary and intellectual companionship. In 1853 Bradlaugh left the army, and later he established a radical paper, *The National Reformer,* to which Thomson sent some contributions, including the poem "To Our Ladies of Death," which foreshadowed the gloomy magnificence of his later work.

In 1862 he was one of a group of schoolmasters dismissed

from the army in a dispute over discipline. Turned loose upon the world without money and without a profession, Thomson made his way to London and sought out Brad-laugh, who took him into his home and found work for him in a legal office. When in a sociable mood, Thomson could be merry and gracious, attracting loyal friends; but his periods of black despair forced him to withdraw more and more from companionship. After leaving the Brad-laugh house in 1866 he lived alone in a single room and resorted immoderately to alcohol.

That he still could enjoy some normal human pleasures was indicated by his "middle-class idyls," entitled "Sun-day at Hampstead" and "Sunday Up the River," published in *Fraser's Magazine* in 1869. These gave a gay, half-ironic picture of the Londoners enjoying their week-end holiday out-of-doors. There was infectious enthusiasm in his lyric, "Give a Man a Horse He Can Ride."

In 1872 Thomson had a surprising adventure, when he was sent out to the western United States as investigator for the shareholders in a silver-mining company; he verified their suspicions that they had been cheated. The next year he went to Spain to write a series of special articles for the New York *World*. After these exciting travels his shabby room in London must have seemed doubly grim. He was running hopelessly into debt and suffering from insomnia that drove him to prowl the streets all night.

His most important poem, "The City of Dreadful Night," a long symbolic portrayal of morbid pessimism, was con-tributed to *The National Reformer* in 1874. He was also writing prose essays for this paper and for *The Secularist,* signing himself "B. V.," meaning "Bysshe Vanolis," as in-dication of his allegiance to two writers, Shelley and the German mystic poet Novalis. After a dispute with Brad-laugh in 1875 he contributed chiefly to an obscure paper named *Cope's Tobacco Plant*. In 1876 he found a new friend in Bertram Dobell, a bookseller, who aided him in many ways and arranged for the publication of a volume, *The City of Dreadful Night, and Other Poems,* in 1880. The success of this book led in rapid sequence to two others, *Vane's Story, Weddah and Om-el-Bouain, and other Poems* and *Essays and Phantasies.* Their contents, however, almost all dated back to earlier years. Cheered by success, he wrote a few happy poems in 1881, and enjoyed a visit with friends in the country. His melancholia was not conquered, however; on his return to London he drank more desperately than ever, roamed the slum streets in delirium, and died of exposure and neglect on June 3, 1882. Further volumes of his poems and essays were assembled later by the faithful Dobell.

The somber, musical dignity of Thomson's most characteristic poems and their dream-like symbolism recall the prose of De Quincey. The unqualified despair in these poems makes him the spokesman of the atheistic-pessimist movement of the seventies and eighties.

Poetical Works, ed. B. Dobell (2v, London, 1895); H. S. Salt, *The Life of James Thomson* (London, 1889, rev. ed., 1914); P. E. More, "James Thomson," *Shelburne Essays,* 5th ser. (New York, 1908); B. Dobell, *The Laureate of Pessimism* (London, 1910); J. E. Meeker, *The Life and Poetry of James Thomson* (New Haven, 1917); F. Harris, "James Thomson," in *Contemporary Portraits,* 2nd ser. (New York, 1919); J. Marks, "Disaster and Poetry; a Study of James Thomson," *North American Review,* CCXII (1920). 93-109; A. Symons, "James Thomson," in *Studies in Two Literatures* (London, 1924); R. Peyre, "Les sources du pessimisme de Thomson," *Revue Anglo-Americaine,* II (1924-25). 152-56, 217-31; N. H. Wallis, "James Thomson and His 'City of Dreadful Night,'" *Essays by Divers Hands,* XIV (1935); L. A. Cotten, "Leopardi and 'The City of Dreadful Night,'" *Studies in Philology,* XLII (1945). 675-89.

ROBERT BRIDGES (1844-1930)
>>

A poet who did not begin to publish his work until he was almost thirty, and whose fame thereafter was of gradual growth, Robert Seymour Bridges was born at Walmer, in northeastern Kent, on October 23, 1844. At Eton and at Corpus Christi College, Oxford, he was good in sports, particularly cricket and rowing, and his scholarly work was sufficient to gain him a degree with honors in 1867. He then traveled in the Near East, and studied medicine for eight months in Germany. As an interne at St. Bartholomew's Hospital he saw all the sordidness and suffering of London's crowded slums. Receiving his Bachelor of Medicine degree from Oxford in 1874, he also became a Fellow of the Royal College of Physicians.

In 1873 he published a small collection of lyrics, and three years later another slim volume, *Twenty-four Sonnets*. In subsequent editions many more sonnets were added, to make a sequence, *The Growth of Love*. It had been his intention to retire from medical practice at the age of forty; but an attack of pneumonia when he was thirty-seven brought his professional career to an end. For the rest of his long life he enjoyed a quiet rural existence, first at Yattendon Manor House in Berkshire, and after 1905 on Boar's Hill, outside Oxford.

Prometheus the Fire Giver (1883) was the first of a series of poems and poetic dramas on subjects from classical mythology and history. In 1890 a volume of *Shorter Poems* revealed the charm of his lyrical and descriptive pieces. Until the end of the century, most of his publications were small, limited editions, printed by the private presses that followed the lead of William Morris; and such a poem of Bridges as *Eros and Psyche* showed Morris's influence strongly in both rhyme-scheme and narrative method. In 1899 he reached the dignity of a collected edition, his *Poetical Works* being issued in two volumes.

In 1903 he began to publish his experiments in the adaptation of classical meters to English poetry. To help his readers with these unfamiliar rhythms, he invented special punctuation marks and variant spellings. His study of English rhythms had first shown itself in his important essay, *Milton's Prosody* (1887—later expanded), and had been intensified by his friendship with the daring innovator, Gerard Manley Hopkins. His increasing interest in questions of vocabulary and syntax led him to establish in 1913 the Society for Pure English, for which thereafter he wrote a number of pamphlets.

When he was appointed poet laureate in 1913, he was still so little known that much public discontent was expressed, and his refusal to write patriotic poems during the war aroused further attacks. Gradually, however, his personal integrity and the quiet beauty of his poems won general respect. In 1923 he visited the United States and spent an academic year on the University of Michigan faculty. His long and learned poem, *The Testament of Beauty,* published on his eighty-fifth birthday, was amazingly vigorous and original for a man of that age. In the same year he was awarded the Order of Merit. He died on April 21, 1930.

The poetry of Bridges fell into two types. One was his short lyrics, which were so simple in language and meter that readers scarcely recognized the artistic skill that controlled their easy grace. Some of them gave delightful pictures of the English countryside. His sonnet sequence was less successful, for the archaic diction seemed to lack spontaneity, and his rigorous restraint precluded passionate feeling. The other type of his work was learned and philosophical, showing his exceptional combination of classical and scientific knowledge. Beginning with his narrative and dramatic poems of ancient Greece and Rome, which had some symbolic reference to modern topics, he went on to discussions of modern philosophy and science written in a conversational style that contrasted with the quantitative classical hexameters he was experimenting with. A direct sequel to these was *The Testament of Beauty*, published twenty-five years later. A full statement of his views on poetry and life, the poem ranged over the whole of modern science—astronomy, chemistry, physics, embryology, eugenics, psycho-analysis. Accepting all the materialistic and mechanistic arguments, Bridges used them as a basis for a spiritual faith constructed out of human instinct, reason, and aesthetic enjoyment. *The Testament of Beauty* presented a modern interpretation of the same subject that Tennyson had surveyed in *In Memoriam* eighty years before.

G. L. McKay, *A Bibliography of Robert Bridges* (New York, 1933); *Poetical Works* (6v, London, 1929); (London, 1913); *Collected Essays, Papers, etc.* (10v, London, 1927-36); *Correspondence of Robert Bridges and Henry Bradley, 1900-27* (London, 1940); John Bailey, "The Poetry of Robert Bridges," *Quarterly Review*, CCXIX (1913). 231-55; F. E. B. Young, *Robert Bridges: A Critical Study* (London, 1914); T. Kelshall, *Robert Bridges* (London, 1924); A. Waugh, "Robert Bridges," *Fortnightly Review*, CXXXIII (1930). 832-43; L. P. Smith, "Robert Bridges: Recollections," and E. Daryush, "His Work on the English Language," *Society for Pure English Tract 35* (1931); N. C. Smith, *Notes on "The Testament of Beauty"* (London, 1931; rev. ed., 1940); M. L. V. Hughes, *Everyman's "Testament of Beauty"* (London, 1942); O. Elton, "Robert Bridges and *The Testament of Beauty*," *English Association Pamphlet 83* (1933); J. G. Eaker, "Robert Bridges' Concept of Nature," *Publications of the Modern Language Association*, LIV (1939). 1181-97; A. J. Guerard, *Robert Bridges: A Study of Traditionalism in Poetry* (Cambridge, Mass., 1942); E. Thompson, *Robert Bridges, 1844-1930* (London, 1945); G. S. Gordon, "Robert Bridges," in *The Discipline of Letters* (London, 1947).

GERARD MANLEY HOPKINS (1844-1889)

>>>

Having sought no public recognition as a poet, Gerard Manley Hopkins was unknown for thirty years after his death. When his poems were eventually published, in the year when the first World War ended, a new generation of poets was looking for new techniques, and Hopkins's peculiar idiom was ardently welcomed. He had more influence upon the English and American poets of the period between the wars than any other Victorian author.

Gerard Manley Hopkins was born in London on June 11, 1844, the eldest son of a prosperous business man. Brought up in the Church of England, he endured emotional crises of self-doubt in his boyhood, and when he entered Balliol College, Oxford, in 1863 he was soon attracted by the Anglo-Catholic group that was still active there, surviving from the days of Newman. Brilliant in his studies and popular with his fellows, talented in music and painting as well as in poetry, Hopkins was nicknamed "the star of Balliol."

In 1866 he announced his conversion to the Roman Catholic church, and soon became a novice of the Jesuit Society. As a part of the rigorous self-denial that he accepted, he burned the verses he had written, and for seven years abandoned poetry. In 1875, however, news of the drowning of five nuns in a shipwreck moved him so deeply that he wrote a long poem, "The Wreck of the *Deutschland*." Thereafter he composed poems that expressed both his love for natural beauty and his religious devotion. When editors of magazines rejected a few of his poems, he made no further effort to publish them, but fortunately sent copies to his friend and admirer, Robert Bridges. His conscience continued to trouble him as to whether poetry could be reconciled with his religious vocation.

When he was assigned to a slum parish in Liverpool the vice and poverty made him miserable, while the poetic imagery of his sermons puzzled or shocked his congregation. He was appointed to a fellowship in the University of Dublin in 1884, but his teaching methods were unorthodox and he was almost as unhappy there as in Liverpool. He died of typhoid fever on June 8, 1889.

As a student of poetic technique and its relation to music Hopkins worked out a theory of what he called "sprung rhythm," which he believed to be the true underlying principle of English verse. In so far as this meant scansion by stressed syllables only, it was a logical development of practices common to the Victorian poets; but by his addition of "counterpoint," his alliterations and internal rhymes, his run-on lines, invented words, harsh consonant-knots, inverted constructions, omitted connectives, repetitions, and other devices for emphasis, he baffled even the few friends who read his manuscripts. His imagery, too, was not only condensed but startlingly original. The long-delayed enthusiasm for his work was connected with a revival of interest in John Donne and the other "metaphysical" poets of the seventeenth century, to whom Hopkins had many resemblances. When Robert Bridges, who had familiarized his readers' ears with his own metrical experiments along somewhat similar (though less extreme) lines, edited a volume of Hopkins's poetry in 1918, this vigorous prosody and cryptic imagery supplied a fresh impetus that was being sought to displace the surviving techniques of the traditional Victorians. Not only his rhythm but also his frequent obscurity was admired and imitated.

Poems, ed. R. Bridges (London, 1918; rev. ed., 1930); ed. W. H. Gardner (London, 1948); *Letters,* ed. C. C. Abbott (2v, London

1934); *Further Letters,* ed. C. C. Abbott (London, 1937); *Note-Books,* ed. H. House (London, 1936); J. M. Murry, "Gerard Manley Hopkins," in *Aspects of Literature* (London, 1920); I. A. Richards, "Gerard Hopkins," *Dial,* LXXXI (1926). 195-203; G. F. Lahey, *The Life of Father Gerard Manley Hopkins* (London, 1930); E. E. Phare, *The Poetry of Gerard Manley Hopkins* (Cambridge, 1933); H. Read, "Gerard Manley Hopkins," in *In Defence of Shelley, and Other Essays* (London, 1936); J. Pick, *Gerard Manley Hopkins, Priest and Poet* (London, 1942); G. Lilly, "The Welsh Influence in the Poetry of Gerard Manley Hopkins," *Modern Language Review,* XXXVIII (1943). 192-205; W. H. Gardner, *Gerard Manley Hopkins (1844-1889)* (London, 1944); E. Ruggles, *Gerard Manley Hopkins: A Life* (New York, 1944); The Kenyon Critics, *Gerard Manley Hopkins* (New York, 1946); Sister M. M. Holloway, *The Prosodic Theory of Gerard Manley Hopkins* (Washington, 1947); S. J. Cohen, J. K. Matthison, "The Poetic Theory of Gerard Manley Hopkins," *Philological Quarterly,* XXVI (1947). 1-35; W. A. M. Peters, *Gerard Manley Hopkins* (London, 1948); K. R. S. Iyengar, *Gerard Manley Hopkins: The Man and the Poet* (London, 1949); *Immortal Diamond,* ed. N. Weyand (New York, 1949).

FRANCIS THOMPSON (1859-1907)

>>

Francis Thompson was born at Preston, Lancashire, on December 18, 1859. His father was a doctor and two of his uncles were writers. As the family had been converted to the Roman Catholic faith, Francis was brought up with the idea of becoming a priest, and studied for several years at Ushaw College, a Catholic seminary. When he was seventeen, his frail health and dreamy, unstable disposition were reasons for his being considered unsuitable for the priesthood. To satisfy his father he then took up medicine, and studied for six years at Owens College, Manchester, a severely practical institution where he was far from happy. After three failures to pass his examinations, he gave up the effort, quarreled with his father, and walked the two hundred miles to London.

He was already addicted to opium, having been first given it to relieve neuralgia. In London he spent three years of miserable poverty, sleeping on a park bench or in a church crypt. Such money as he earned by selling matches or holding horses went for narcotics and he was often close to starvation. Owning nothing in the world but two books—the plays of Aeschylus and the poems of Blake— he wrote poems in discarded account books begged from a shopkeeper who hired him for odd jobs.

In 1888 he sent two poems and a prose essay to *Merry England,* a Catholic magazine. They remained unopened for a month, and Thompson in despair decided to kill himself. After he had taken half of a lethal dose of laudanum a vision of Thomas Chatterton persuaded him to desist. Meanwhile the editor of the magazine, Wilfrid Meynell, on discovering the merits of the poems, managed with difficulty to trace the poet and make his acquaintance.

Meynell and his poet wife, Alice, promptly took charge of Thompson; he was sent to a hospital until he somewhat recovered his health, and thereafter for almost twenty years divided his time between the Meynells' home and various monasteries where he was well cared for. All his affection was centered upon Mr. and Mrs. Meynell and their little daughters. Spurred by their encouragement he published three slim volumes, *Poems* (1893), *Sister Songs* (1895), and *New Poems* (1897), as well as his essay on Shelley and other critical writings. His health remained very bad, however, and as he had not been entirely cured of his addiction to opium he could not be trusted with even the smallest sum of money. When he died of consumption on November 13, 1907, he weighed only seventy pounds.

Among the poets of the nineties who were in various ways influenced by the Pre-Raphaelite spirit, Thompson was one of those who adopted the mystical interpretation of beauty, as contrasted with the worldly group who chose sensuous indulgence. So utterly impractical that he retained a childlike innocence through all the horror and sin that surrounded him during his years of destitution, he lived in a realm of imagination and symbolism. "The Hound of Heaven," his great vision of God's goodness, has magnificent beauty and profound religious feeling. Some of his other odes are somewhat over-embroidered with rich imagery and sonorous words. On the other hand his short lyrics, such as "Daisy," "Little Jesus," "To a Snowflake," and "The Kingdom of God," have the perfect clarity and simplicity that link them with the songs of William Blake.

Works, ed. W. Meynell (3v, London, 1913); *Literary Criticisms,* ed. T. L. Connolly (New York, 1948); *Poems* (London, 1937; Oxford Standard Authors); ed. T. L. Connolly (New York, 1932; rev. ed., 1941); C. L. O'Donnel, *Francis Thompson* (Notre Dame, Ind., 1906); P. E. More, "Francis Thompson," in *Shelburne Essays,* 7th series (New York, 1910); J. F. X. O'Conor, *A Study of Francis Thompson's "Hound of Heaven"* (New York, 1912); E. Meynell, *The Life of Francis Thompson* (London, 1913); F. P. LeBuffe, *"The Hound of Heaven," An Interpretation* (New York, 1921); G. N. Schuster, "Francis Thompson the Master," in *The Catholic Spirit in Modern English Literature* (New York, 1922); A. Symons, "Francis Thompson," in *Dramatis Personae* (Indianapolis, 1923); J. Thomson, *Francis Thompson, Poet and Mystic* (London, 1923); Sister M. Madeleva, "The Prose of Francis Thompson," in *Chaucer's Nuns, and Other Essays* (New York, 1925); J. A. Hutton, *Guidance from Francis Thompson in Matters of Faith* (London, 1926); R. L. Mégroz, *Francis Thompson: The Poet of Earth in Heaven* (London, 1927); A. de la Gorce, *Francis Thompson et les poètes catholiques d'Angleterre* (Paris, 1932; Engl. trans., 1933); T. L. Connolly, *Francis Thompson: In His Paths* (Milwaukee, 1944).

RUDYARD KIPLING (1865-1936)
>>

Rudyard Kipling, poet and short-story writer, was born in Bombay, India, on December 30, 1865. His father, an able artist, was employed in the art school there, and later became curator of a museum at Lahore. At the age of five he was taken to England, where he lived under the severe discipline of a relative for seven years. In 1878 he began to attend the United Services College at Westward Ho, in Devonshire. Most of the pupils there were destined for the army, but defective eyesight made it advisable for Kipling to prepare for the Indian Civil Service. He edited the *College Chronicle* for two years and collected his earliest poems into a privately distributed volume called *School-Boy Lyrics*. These showed that he was teaching himself to write poetry by carefully and competently imitating the chief Victorian poets, especially Browning and Swinburne.

RUDYARD KIPLING

Upon returning to India in 1882 he joined the staff of the Lahore *Civil and Military Gazette,* and after five years he became assistant editor of the *Pioneer* at Allahabad. As early as 1886, when his collection of light verse, *Departmental Ditties,* was published at Lahore, he was becoming well known in India for the short stories and poems contributed to his newspaper. Two years later he published

Plain Tales from the Hills, satirical stories of the English military and administrative classes, in the same vein as the *Departmental Ditties.* With youthful impudence Kipling annoyed the complacent Anglo-Indians by ridiculing their pompous manners and shallow intrigues. Within the next two years six more collections of his short stories were brought out in the cheap, paper-covered volumes of "Wheeler's Railway Library." These revealed the wide range of his talent. *The Story of the Gadsbys* retained the mood of the *Plain Tales,* and so did *Under the Deodars,* though with a grimmer note. *Wee Willie Winkie* contained four stories about small boys. *The Phantom Rickshaw* was devoted to effective tales of horror, including the powerful story, "The Man Who Would Be King." *In Black and White* presented sympathetic pictures of native life. The most successful volume of the series, however, was *Soldiers Three,* with its uproarious episodes of army life as narrated by the gigantic Irishman, Private Mulvaney. In the seven volumes of stories Kipling ranged through the various strata of Indian life, both British and native, and tried every type of story from farce to tragedy.

In 1887 Kipling set out upon a tour of the world. One of his purposes was to find an American publisher for his works; his failure to secure one was reflected in the severe criticisms of America that he published in the *Pioneer.* These essays, along with those on China and Japan, later formed the book, *From Sea to Sea.* His journey ended in England, where he found his fame already established. He wrote another group of Indian stories, published as *Life's Handicap,* and a novel, *The Light That Failed* (1891). For W. E. Henley's paper, *The National Observer,* he wrote vigorous, slangy poems of army life, counterparts of the stories in *Soldiers Three.* When these *Barrack-Room Ballads* were collected in 1892 Kipling was hailed as a popular poet. The swinging rhythms made the poems suitable for recitation and for musical settings. In contrast with the artificial verses of the *Yellow Book* school, these poems of adventure and violence won the favor of non-literary readers. On the other hand, in reproducing the blunt speech and disrespectful opinions of the common soldier, Kipling offended the Queen and other high personages.

In 1892 he married an American girl and settled down at Brattleboro, Vermont, where in a rural New England environment he wrote some of his most notable work. *Many Inventions* (1893) included a short story of the Indian jungle, "In the Rukh," containing the character of Mowgli, a native boy brought up by the wolves. From this Kipling developed *The Jungle Book* (1894) and *The Second Jungle Book* (1895) which are among his most original and popular books.

Unfortunately Kipling became involved in a quarrel with a neighbor, and when he left Vermont after four years he carried away an opinion of the United States almost as unfavorable as his first impression eight years before. Having returned to England in time for the festivals celebrating the sixtieth anniversary of Queen Victoria's accession, he wrote "Recessional," a sober warning against too much imperialistic pride. His own imagination, however, was fired by the vastitude of the British dominions, and his new volume of poems, *The Seven Seas,* contained pieces that gloried in the Empire's greatness. He published in 1897 a novel of the North Atlantic fishing fleet, *Captains Courageous*. At this time trouble between the British and the Dutch was developing in South Africa, and Kipling paid a long visit to that region, remaining to serve as a correspondent during the Boer War.

In these years he published a variety of successful books, especially *The Day's Work* (1898), a diversified collection of short stories; *Stalky & Co.* (1899), stories of his school days, with an unflattering depiction of himself under the nickname of "Beetle"; and *Kim,* a picaresque novel of the swarming life of India.

After his return from Africa he bought a home in the quiet Sussex village of Burwash and settled down to a secluded life. A volume of poems in 1903, *The Five Nations,* contained the patriotic and imperialistic poems of the Boer War era, but thereafter he seldom wrote about the wide world he had known and loved. A book of quaint tales for young children, *Just So Stories* (1902), was followed by two for older boys and girls, *Puck of Pook's Hill* (1906) and *Rewards and Fairies* (1910), in which he used English fairy legends as a basis for stories illustrating historical episodes. Similar themes became predominant in his stories for adults and in his poems. He was now as devoted to the ancient traditions and quiet beauty of the English countryside as he had been to the vast spaces and violent adventures of the colonies. The supernatural, too, became a favorite subject of subtly evocative stories. *Traffics and Discoveries* (1904), *Actions and Reactions* (1910), and *A Diversity of Creatures* (1917) contained the best of his stories on these topics.

Although he received the Nobel Prize for literature in 1907, Kipling took but little part in the literary activities of his time. The death of a young daughter was a deep grief to him, and later his only son was killed in action during the war of 1914-18. Kipling wrote several prose works dealing with aspects of the war, and some poems that were grim and challenging rather than conventionally patriotic. He died in London on January 18, 1936.

Kipling achieved his earliest distinction in the short story. In fact, he was the first British author to become a master of its technique. With a wide range of themes and moods, he was able to produce his desired effect in each instance by condensation, selection, and suggestion. No matter what the setting of a story, he mastered enough of local color and technical jargon to give the impression that he was an expert, and the reader shares the illusion of insight. If a few of his earliest Anglo-Indian stories were youthfully arrogant, he wrote some stories even in his early twenties that gave the impression of maturity and sincerity. In his later manner, after the turn of the century, he was able to imply an incredible complexity of meaning in a few phrases.

His ability to create character was shown in the stories that were linked in series. The reader gets a sense of friendly recognition for Mulvaney, Ortheris, and Learoyd in *Soldiers Three,* for Corkran, McTurk, "Beetle," and various masters in *Stalky & Co.,* even for the bear and the black panther in *The Jungle Books.* In writing a long, sustained narrative, Kipling was less successful. *The Light That Failed,* his only novel of a conventional type, was rather artificial. *Captains Courageous* is usually regarded as a book for boys. *Kim,* though a masterpiece, can be described as a series of episodes rather than a unified novel.

Kipling's poetry had much in common with his short stories. The same power of concise narrative gave effectiveness to his stirring ballads. His earlier books of poetry paralleled the short-story collections—*Departmental Ditties* and *Plain Tales from the Hills, Barrack-Room Ballads* and *Soldiers Three, The Seven Seas* and the nautical tales in *The Day's Work* and *Traffics and Discoveries.* Gradually he formed the habit of publishing stories and poems alternately in the same volume, with a close relationship of theme that was later obscured when the poems were brought together in a collected edition.

Because Kipling was the most widely popular poet of his era, pedantic critics assumed that he must be a cheap and obvious rhymester. Because some of his poems dealt with the British army, the British navy, and the British colonists overseas, ideological radicals assumed that he must be an imperialistic "jingo." Neither opinion is supported by an unbiased reading of his work. Like all authors he was occasionally controlled by the emotions of his nation in a time of crisis. Not pretending to be a profound philosopher, he was sometimes inconsistent in his ideas. To him, intellectual sophistication was less significant than loyalty, self-sacrifice, and courage. These virtues he often found in the soldier, the seaman, the engineer. But he was equally capable of writing stories and poems that had delicate artistry, elusive grace, and almost feminine intuition.

F. V. Livingston, *Bibliography of the Works of Rudyard Kipling* (New York, 1927; supplement, 1938); *Works* (28v, London, 1941, Burwash edition); *Verse, 1885-1936* (London, 1941); *A Choice of Kipling's Verse*, ed. T. S. Eliot (London, 1941); R. Le Gallienne, *Rudyard Kipling: A Criticism* (London, 1900); G. K. Chesterton, "On Mr. Kipling and Making the World Small," in *Heretics* (London, 1905); C. Falls, *Rudyard Kipling: A Modern Study* (London, 1915); J. L. Palmer, *Rudyard Kipling* (London, 1915; Writers of the Day); R. T. Hopkins, *Rudyard Kipling* (London, 1916); W. M. Hart, *Kipling, the Story-Writer* (Berkeley, 1918); J. D. Ferguson, "Rudyard Kipling's Revisions of His Published Work," *Journal of English and Germanic Philology*, XXII (1923). 114-24; R. T. Hopkins, *Rudyard Kipling's World* (London, 1925); L. Stevenson, "The Ideas in Kipling's Poetry," *University of Toronto Quarterly*, I (1932). 467-89; Sir G. F. MacMunn, *Kipling's Women* (London, 1933); G. C. Beresford, *Schooldays With Kipling* (London, 1936); A. Chevrillon, *Rudyard Kipling* (Paris, 1936); Sir G. F. MacMunn, *Rudyard Kipling: Craftsman* (London, 1937); F. Van de Water, *Rudyard Kipling's Vermont Feud* (New York, 1937); A. M. Weygandt, *Kipling's Reading and Its Influence on His Poetry* (Philadelphia, 1939); E. Shanks, *Rudyard Kipling: A Study in Literature and Political Ideas* (London, 1940); E. Wilson, "The Kipling That Nobody Read," in *The Wound and the Bow* (Cambridge, Mass., 1941); H. Brown, *Rudyard Kipling: A New Appreciation* (London, 1945); R. Croft-Cooke, *Rudyard Kipling* (London, 1948).

WILLIAM BUTLER YEATS (1865-1939)
>>>

To represent the various facets of the "Celtic Revival" in the last two decades of the nineteenth century the most significant figure is William Butler Yeats, poet, playwright, and essayist. Born at Sandymount, near Dublin, on June 13, 1865, he was the son of a painter of Anglo-Irish descent. As a child he often stayed with his mother's parents in Sligo, on the western coast, where he learned much old folk-lore. He went to live with his parents in London at the age of nine, and was sent to the Godolphin School in Hammersmith. Studying proved hard for him, as his mind was always apt to stray. At fifteen he was back in Dublin at the Erasmus Smith School, after which he studied painting at the Metropolitan School of Art. Here he made friends with a fellow-student, George Russell, later to be known as the mystical poet "AE."

Through Russell and other young enthusiasts Yeats became interested in psychical research and Theosophical occultism, which he linked symbolically with the ancient Irish legends. About the age of twenty he started to contribute poems and articles to the *Dublin University Review* and the *Irish Monthly*. A long dramatic poem was privately printed the next year, and was soon followed by a volume of fairy stories. He went back to London with his parents in 1887, and during the next few years wrote newspaper columns and edited anthologies for a living. As a contributor to the *National Observer* he came under the influence of W. E. Henley. He also attended Morris's Socialist meetings and allied himself with Ernest Dowson, Lionel Johnson, and Arthur Symons to form the Rhymers' Club, dedicated to the cause of "art for art's sake." To

The Yellow Book, the organ of the Club, Yeats contributed a number of poems.

In 1889 he published a volume of poems based upon Irish legends, *The Wanderings of Oisin.* Two years later he helped to found the Irish Literary Society in London, and in 1892, after his return to Dublin, he organized the National Literary Society there. Long interested in the "Young Ireland" movement, he had become a friend of an old Fenian agitator, John O'Leary, who roused him to enthusiasm for the ideal of Irish freedom. In Yeats's opinion a necessary preliminary was an Irish literature written in clear and beautiful English. Thus, like earlier disciples of Pre-Raphaelitism and "art for art's sake," he found himself giving up his concept of the supremacy of beauty and its isolation from the problems of the human world. With the publication of his poetic drama, *The Countess Cathleen,* in 1892, Yeats became known as a great Irish nationalist poet. It was the performance of this play in Dublin in 1899 that started the dramatic movement culminating in the Irish National Theater. Yeats became a director of this organization, which promoted the plays of J. M. Synge, Lady Gregory, and others. Yeats himself wrote several further plays for it, including *The Land of Heart's Desire, Cathleen ni Houlihan,* and *The Shadowy Waters.*

Besides several collections of legends, Yeats published *The Celtic Twilight* (1893), a group of essays discussing the same material. In 1903 his literary essays were collected under the title, *Ideas of Good and Evil.* In his successive volumes of lyric poetry a great change in style and outlook occurred. His earlier poems were romantic and musical, more notable for sensuous languor than for depth of thought. Reflecting the influence of Blake and the French symbolists, he used vague images that were supposed to stimulate the reader's imagination. After the end of the century he turned to a clearer and more concentrated style, and chose subjects related to the intellect and the actual world. Although he continued to use symbols he devised a new set to express new ideas. The change began to show itself in *The Wind Among the Reeds* (1899); by the time he published *Responsibilities,* in 1914, he was writing rather bitter poems of protest; and in *The Wild Swans at Coole* (1919) he revealed his "later style" of stripped, philosophical allusiveness. During the same years he continued to publish volumes of prose, especially *Discoveries* (1907) and three books of his early recollections, later republished together as *Autobiographies* in 1927.

When the Irish Free State government was set up in 1922 he became a senator, and remained in office until 1928. The Nobel Prize for literature was awarded to him in 1923. He died on January 28, 1939.

Yeats was always a student of literary theories and techniques, as expressed in his prose criticisms and embodied in his poetry. He not only proceeded from one type of poetry to another, but persistently revised his earlier work, not always advantageously. The melancholy cadences and dreamy imagery of his first period, partly derived from various English and French poets, acquired a distinctive tone from ancient Irish lore and folk tunes. His experience in writing plays and in administering the practical affairs of the Abbey Theater taught him a more direct and colloquial style, full of abrupt emphasis. Although much of his later poetry was rooted in the political situation in Ireland, it expressed also a stoic personal philosophy that appealed to English and American readers.

A. J. A. Symons, *A Bibliography of William Butler Yeats* (London, 1924); *Collected Works* (8v, London, 1908); *Essays* (London, 1924); *Collected Poems* (London, 1933); *Collected Plays* (London, 1934); *Last Poems and Plays* (London, 1940); *Letters on Poetry to Dorothy Wellesley* (London, 1940); H. S. Krans, *W. B. Yeats and the Irish Literary Revival* (New York, 1904);

G. W. Russell, "The Poet of Shadows," in *Some Irish Essays* (Dublin, 1906); J. G. Huneker, "A Poet of Visions," in *The Pathos of Distance* (New York, 1913); F. Reid, *W. B. Yeats: A Critical Study* (London, 1915); J. M. Hone, *William Butler Yeats* (Dublin, 1916); C. L. Wrenn, *W. B. Yeats: A Literary Study* (London, 1920); N. J. O'Conor, "Yeats and His Vision," in *Changing Ireland* (Cambridge, Mass., 1924); J. Eglinton, "Yeats and His Story," *Dial*, LXXX (1926). 357-67; E. Wilson, "William Butler Yeats," in *Axel's Castle* (New York, 1931); J. H. Pollock, *William Butler Yeats* (London, 1935); *Scattering Branches,* ed. S. Gwynn (London, 1940); L. MacNeice, *The Poetry of W. B. Yeats* (London, 1941); J. Masefield, *Some Memories of W. B. Yeats* (London, 1941); J. M. Hone, *W. B. Yeats, 1865-1939* (London, 1942); *Southern Review,* William Butler Yeats Memorial Issue, VII (1942); V. K. N. Menon, *The Development of W. B. Yeats* (Edinburgh, 1943); D. S. Savage, "The Aestheticism of W. B. Yeats," *Kenyon Review,* VII (1945). 118-34; P. Ure, *Towards a Mythology: Studies in the Poetry of W. B. Yeats* (London, 1947); R. Ellmann, *Yeats: The Man and the Masks* (New York, 1948).

MINOR POETS

▸▸▸

William Allingham (1824-1889). A customs official in a remote corner of Ireland, Allingham published a volume of poems in 1850 and followed it with others which won him the friendship of Tennyson, Browning, Carlyle, and Rossetti. *Laurence Bloomfield in Ireland* (1864) was an attempt at a novel in verse. In 1870 he settled in London, where he became editor of *Fraser's Magazine.*

William Allingham: a Diary, ed. H. Allingham and D. Radford (London, 1907).

Edwin Arnold (1832-1904). While in India as principal of a government college, Arnold studied Asiatic religions and published a translation of the Sanskrit *Book of Good Counsels.* Upon his return to England in 1861 he joined the staff of the *Daily Telegraph* and became an outstanding London journalist. His epic of the teachings of Buddha, *The Light of Asia* (1879), was vastly successful and did much to spread interest in Buddhism. He attempted a similar poetic biography of Jesus in *The Light of the World* (1891). He published many other volumes of poetry, history, and travel, was knighted in 1888, and spent some of his final years in Japan.

Alfred Austin (1835-1913). A London lawyer and journalist, Austin published numerous volumes of undistinguished verse, and was appointed poet laureate in 1896 chiefly because the more notable poets, such as Swinburne, were disqualified on political or moral grounds. Austin wrote some competent satire, and his nature poems have mild charm.

Autobiography (2v, London, 1911).

Philip James Bailey (1816-1902). At the age of twenty-three Bailey published *Festus*, an epic of 20,000 lines, using the Faust legend for a philosophical allegory. Passages of Shelleyan imagination were scattered through its confused length. His later volumes, *The Angel World* (1850), *The Mystic* (1855), *The Universal Hymn* (1867), were less successful, and so Bailey kept inserting passages from them into *Festus,* until the eleventh edition, in 1889, was twice the original length.

J. Ward, *Philip James Bailey, Personal Recollections* (London, 1905); E. Goldschmidt, "Die Gedankenwelt von Baileys Festus," *Englische Studien,* LXVII (1932). 228-37; G. Black, "P. J. Bailey's Debt to Goethe's *Faust* in his *Festus,*" *Modern Language Review,* XXVIII (1933). 166-75.

William Barnes (1800-1886). Son of a Dorsetshire farmer, Barnes became a clergyman of the Church of England and spent his long life as a country schoolmaster and vicar. A learned philologist, he published volumes on comparative philology, Anglo-Saxon, and English dialects, insisting on the literary value of the Anglo-Saxon element in English. His books of poetry in the Dorset dialect have lyrical beauty, once the reader overcomes the unfamiliarity of diction. Thomas Hardy admired his work.

L. E. Baxter, *The Life of William Barnes, Poet and Philologist* (London, 1887).

Thomas Lovell Beddoes (1803-1849). Son of a noted medical scientist, and nephew of Maria Edgeworth, the Irish novelist, Beddoes began to publish poetic drama while an Oxford undergraduate. *The Bride's Tragedy* (1822) was a powerful imitation of Jacobean tragedy. In 1825, the year of his graduation, he began to write *Death's Jest Book, or The Fool's Tragedy*, a weirdly imaginative play, and went to Germany to study medicine, which he then practiced in Zurich for some years. He indulged in fantastic theatrical experiments and continued to revise *Death's Jest Book* until his suicide by poison. His lyrics show the influence of Shelley.

Complete Poetical Works, ed. H. W. Donner (London, 1935); H. W. Donner, *Thomas Lovell Beddoes: The Making of a Poet* (Oxford, 1935); *The Browning Box, or the Life and Works of Thomas Lovell Beddoes* (London, 1935).

Wilfrid Scawen Blunt (1840-1922). An English diplomat, who married a granddaughter of Byron, Blunt inherited a country estate where he bred Arab horses. He traveled widely in the Near East and North Africa, and became so violent an opponent of British policies in Africa, India, and Ireland that he was once imprisoned for two months. His *Love Sonnets of Proteus* (1880) is a sonnet sequence of unusual emotional intensity.

E. Finch, *Wilfrid Scawen Blunt, 1840-1922* (London, 1938); Sister M. J. Reinehr, *The Writings of Wilfrid Scawen Blunt* (Milwaukee, 1941).

Thomas Edward Brown (1830-1897). For many years a master in a boys' school, loved and laughed at for his oddities, Brown was a native of the Isle of Man. Most of his poems dealt with the local customs of that island, and were written in the Manx dialect.

The Letters of Thomas Edward Brown, with memoir by S. T. Irwin (2v, London, 1900); S. G. Simpson, *Thomas Edward Brown, the Manx Poet* (London, 1907).

Robert Williams Buchanan (1841-1901). Educated in Glasgow, Buchanan became a London journalist, novelist, and playwright, but regarded himself chiefly as a poet, with *Undertones* (1863), *London Poems* (1866), *The Book of Orm* (1870), *The City of Dream* (1888), *The Wandering Jew* (1893), and other volumes, ambitiously attempting epic and mystical themes as well as satire and realism. He is best remembered for his injudicious attack on Rossetti, "The Fleshly School of Poetry," which he later retracted.

A. Stoddart-Walker, *Robert Buchanan, the Poet of Modern Revolt* (London, 1901); H. Jay, *Robert Buchanan, Some Account of His Life* (London, 1903).

Thomas Cooper (1805-1892). The son of a dyer, Cooper was first a shoemaker, later a schoolmaster, Methodist preacher, and radical journalist. For his Chartist activities he was imprisoned for two years, during which he wrote a political epic, *The Purgatory of Suicides* (1845). A later poem was *The Paradise of Martyrs,* and he also wrote an effective autobiography.

William Johnson Cory (1823-92). After twenty-six years as a schoolmaster at Eton, William Johnson inherited an estate and assumed the name of Cory. His poems, chiefly lyrics of classical precision and clarity, were published in *Ionica* (1858).

Extracts from the Letters and Journals of William Johnson Cory, ed. F. W. Cornish (London, 1897).

John Davidson (1857-1909). Son of a Scottish minister, Davidson taught school in Scotland until 1890, when he went to London to make his living as a journalist. He was a prolific writer of plays, satires, and so forth, as well as of a series of powerful and often bitter volumes of poetry—*Fleet Street Eclogues, Ballads and Songs, New Ballads, The Last Ballad.* After 1900 he devoted himself to a series of "Testaments" expounding a "new cosmogony" based on Nietzsche. He lived in Cornwall in his later years on a small government pension, and died by drowning.

H. Fineman, *John Davidson: A Study of the Relation of His Ideas to His Poetry* (Philadelphia, 1916); G. von Petzold, *John Davidson und Sein Geistiges Werden unter dem Einfluss Nietzsches* (Leipzig, 1928).

J. B. Leicester Warren, Lord de Tabley (1835-1895). A friend of Tennyson and a dabbler in varied intellectual hobbies, Warren (who inherited the title of Baron de Tabley in 1887) published several books of poetry which showed command of Miltonic dignity and richness of style.

Aubrey Thomas de Vere (1814-1902). A prolific Irish poet and a devout Catholic, de Vere wrote poems on traditional Irish themes which did much to prepare the ground for the "Celtic Revival." He also published poetic dramas and several volumes of sound critical essays.

Collected Works (11v, London, 1897); W. P. Ward, *Aubrey de Vere: A Memoir* (London, 1904).

Richard Watson Dixon (1833-1900). As a college friend of Morris and Burne-Jones, Dixon was early influenced by Pre-Raphaelitism. Later he was a devoted friend of Gerard Manley Hopkins and Robert Bridges. A canon of the Church of England and a scholarly ecclesiastical historian, he published several volumes of idealistic poetry.

Collected Poems, ed. R. Bridges (London, 1909).

Sydney Thomas Dobell (1824-1874). Mid-Victorian critics made fun of the "spasmodic school" of poetry, in which Dobell was prominent, along with P. J. Bailey, Alexander Smith, and Gerald Massey. An agitator for Italian freedom and political reform, he wrote pretentious and confused but sincere poems, expressing skepticism and discontent.

E. Jolly, *The Life and Letters of Sydney Dobell* (2v, London, 1878).

Henry Austin Dobson (1840-1921). During a long career in the English civil service, Dobson published many volumes of graceful verse, chiefly on topics of eighteenth-century France, and usually in the restricted French verse forms, which he helped to popularize in England. He wrote extensively in prose also, critical and biographical studies of eighteenth-century literature.

Alban Dobson, *Austin Dobson, Some Notes* (London, 1928).

Ernest Dowson (1867-1900). A representative of the "fin de siècle" esthetes, Dowson left Oxford without a degree and spent the remainder of his short life dissolutely in London and Paris, writing sensuous, melancholy poetry in the intervals of alcoholism and disease. His psychological break-down was intensified when he was jilted by an inn-keeper's daughter whom he passionately loved. Shortly before his death he joined the Roman Catholic Church.

M. Longaker, *Ernest Dowson* (Philadelphia, 1944).

Ebenezer Elliott (1781-1849). A self-educated Yorkshire iron-worker, Elliott became involved in the anti-corn-law agitation and the Chartist movement. His *Corn-Law Rhymes* (1831) were vigorous propaganda verse, and his later poems contained some realistic portrayals of humble life, though written in a formal, old-fashioned style.

Samuel Ferguson (1810-1886). An Irish lawyer and antiquarian, knighted in 1878, Ferguson published *Lays of the*

Western Gael (1865), *Congal,* an epic (1872), and other vigorous narrative poems that shared with de Vere's in awakening interest in the heroic age of Irish history.

M. C. Ferguson, *Sir Samuel Ferguson in the Ireland of His Day* (2v, Edinburgh, 1896).

Robert Stephen Hawker (1803-1875). An eccentric clergyman and historian of Cornwall, Hawker wrote vigorous ballads on local traditional subjects. Shortly before his death he provoked controversy through his conversion to Roman Catholicism.

S. Baring-Gould, *The Vicar of Morwenstow* (London, 1876); C. E. Byles, *The Life and Letters of Robert Stephen Hawker* (London, 1905).

William Ernest Henley (1849-1903). *The National Observer,* under Henley's editorship, was the medium for the "virile" poets of the nineties—Kipling, Stevenson, *et al*—and Henley in such poems as "The Song of the Sword" and "A Song of Speed" was the most virile of them all; but he could also write dainty lyrics in the restricted French forms and realistic free-verse poems like his "Hospital" sequence, depicting his experiences when a foot was amputated. He wrote influential criticism, and collaborated with his friend Stevenson in three plays.

J. H. Buckley, *William Ernest Henley* (Princeton, 1945).

Richard Henry ("Hengist") Horne (1803-1884). A picturesque adventurer, who fought in the Mexican navy and later pioneered in Australia, Horne published several poetical tragedies and a pretentious epic, *Orion* (1843), which he issued at the price of one farthing (one-half cent) a copy. His collection of essays on contemporary writers, *A New Spirit of the Age* (1844), included contributions by Elizabeth Barrett.

Richard Monckton Milnes, Lord Houghton (1809-1885). At Cambridge the rich young Milnes was a member of the "Apostles" with Tennyson and other future celebrities. In addition to his four volumes of pleasant lyric and reflective poetry, and his important biography of Keats (1848), he was noteworthy for his witty conversation, his sponsoring of struggling authors, and his promotion of copyright legislation. After twenty-six years in Parliament, he received a peerage for his political services.

T. W. Reid, *The Life, Letters, and Friendships of Richard Monckton Milnes, First Lord Houghton* (2v, London, 1890).

Alfred Edward Housman (1859-1936). Although Housman's poetic reputation was very limited until after 1920, he must be mentioned in a survey of Victorian poetry because his first (and best) book, *A Shropshire Lad,* appeared in 1896. A shy professor of Latin at London and Cambridge Universities, he later published two further slender volumes of his brief and gloomy lyrics.

T. G. Ehrsam, *A Bibliography of A. E. Housman* (Boston, 1941); C. K. Hyder, *A Concordance to the Poems* (Lawrence, Kan., 1940); A. S. F. Gow, *A. E. Housman* (Cambridge, 1936); L. Housman, *A. E. H.: Some Poems, Some Letters, and a Personal Memoir* (London, 1937); G. Richards, *Housman, 1897-1936* (London, 1942); P. Withers, *A Buried Life* (London, 1940).

Jean Ingelow (1820-1897). The fluent and somewhat sentimental poems of Miss Ingelow were typical of the popular poetry in the mid-Victorian years, but were better than the average, sometimes achieving genuine pathos and drama. She wrote several novels and meritorious books for children.

Lionel Pigot Johnson (1867-1902). Like his exact contemporary, Dowson, Johnson attended Oxford, wrote for the papers in London, ruined his health with liquor, joined the Roman Catholic Church, and died in his early thirties.

A less decadent character than Dowson, however, he gained scholastic distinction at college, turned to religion soon enough to reflect its austerity in his writings, and showed more intellect than passion in most of his poems. He published a good critical study on *The Art of Thomas Hardy*.

John Keble (1792-1866). Though Keble was a decade older than most other early Victorian authors, and his chief book of poetry, *The Christian Year,* appeared as early as 1827, his association with the Oxford Movement insures his inclusion in a survey of Victorian poetry, and his gentle, spiritual verse had a wide influence on devout Anglicans throughout the century. His book of verse for children, *Lyra Innocentium,* came in 1846. After serving as Professor of Poetry at Oxford, he spent his final thirty years as a country vicar.

J. T. Coleridge, *A Memoir of the Rev. John Keble* (2v, Oxford, 1869); W. Lock, *John Keble, a Biography* (London, 1892); E. F. L. Wood, *John Keble* (London, 1909).

Frederick Locker-Lampson (1821-1895). A noted book-collector, witty conversationalist, and lavish host, Frederick Locker (who added the name of his second wife, Lampson, in 1885) wrote *vers de société* that forms the link between Praed's and Dobson's. His *London Lyrics* was first published in 1857, and ten years later he edited a good anthology of light verse, *Lyra Elegantiarum*.

My Confidences, ed. A. Birrell (London, 1896); A. Birrell, *Frederick Locker-Lampson* (London, 1920).

James Clarence Mangan (1803-1849). Suffering from poverty, illness, hallucinations, and addiction to opium, Mangan wrote abundant poetry in many styles, from nonsense verse to translations (sometimes spurious) from Irish, German, and Oriental sources. His best poems have morbid intensity and Irish patriotic fire.

D. J. O'Donoghue, *The Life and Writings of James Clarence Mangan* (Edinburgh, 1897); H. E. Cain, *James Clarence Mangan and the Poe-Mangan Question* (Washington, 1929).

Philip Bourke Marston (1850-1887). Through his father, a writer of poetical drama, Marston in his childhood knew most of the leading writers of the period, particularly the Pre-Raphaelites, who admired his precocious verse and pitied his blindness. His three volumes of poetry had dreamlike beauty and deep melancholy.

Collected Poems, with memoir by L. C. Moulton (London, 1892).

Gerald Massey (1828-1907). One of the self-educated "proletarian" poets, Massey began as a child-laborer, became active in the Christian Socialist movement, edited a radical paper, and published copious poetry which was earnest and energetic though often sentimental and trite. Later he became an exponent of spiritualism.

Alice Meynell (1847-1922). In 1877 Alice Christiana Thompson married Wilfrid Meynell, editor and critic, and they became friends of most of the late-Victorian poets, particularly their fellow Catholics, but also freethinkers like Meredith. Several of their eight children later became writers. A fragile, shy person, Mrs. Meynell wrote prose essays as well as lyrical poetry on themes of both love and religion, which was fastidiously intelligent and sensitive.

A. K. Tuell, *Mrs. Meynell and Her Literary Generation* (New York, 1925); V. Meynell, *Alice Meynell: A Memoir* (London, 1929).

Lewis Morris (1833-1907). Welsh by birth, Morris won distinctions at Oxford and practiced law for twenty years. His many volumes of fluent and ambitious, but commonplace, verse included *Songs of Two Worlds* (1872) and *The Epic of Hades* (1876-77). He was knighted in 1896.

Arthur William Edgar O'Shaughnessy (1844-1881). Spending all his short career in the British Museum, where he became an expert on fish, O'Shaughnessy wrote several volumes of ethereal, melodious poetry in the Pre-Raphaelite tradition—*An Epic of Women* (1870), *Lays of France* (1872), *Music and Moonlight* (1874), *Songs of a Worker* (1881).

L. C. Moulton, *Arthur O'Shaughnessy, His Life and His Work* (Chicago, 1894); O. Brönner, *Das Leben Arthur O'Shaughnessys* (Heidelberg, 1933).

Winthrop Mackworth Praed (1802-1839). A brilliant Cambridge graduate, Praed embarked on a political career, but died at thirty-six. His witty, good-humored *vers de société* set the pattern for later writers throughout the century.

D. Hudson, *A Poet in Parliament: The Life of W. M. Praed* (London, 1939).

Adelaide Anne Procter (1825-1864). A popular sentimental poet of the mid-Victorian years, Miss Procter was a daughter of another minor poet, "Barry Cornwall," a friend of Byron and Lamb. Her *Legends and Lyrics* (1858) went through nine editions in seven years. Her best-known poem is "The Lost Chord."

Alexander Smith (1830-1867). A Scottish factory-worker, Smith published *A Life Drama* in 1853 and *City Poems* in 1857, and came to be classified among the "spasmodic poets" with Dobell and Bailey. Later he wrote an agreeable volume of prose essays, *Dreamthorpe*.

Frederick Tennyson (1807-1898). An older brother of Alfred Tennyson, Frederick preceded him at Cambridge, and spent much of his later life in Italy. He developed an interest in Swedenborgian mysticism. He published a book of poems, *Days and Hours* in 1854, and three more in the last decade of his life.

Charles Tennyson Turner (1808-1879). Another older brother of Alfred Tennyson, Charles collaborated with him in *Poems by Two Brothers* and attended the university with him, later becoming vicar of Grasby and taking the name Turner with an inheritance. Between 1830 and 1873 he published four volumes of sonnets, which were reissued in a collected volume in 1880.

Martin Farquhar Tupper (1810-1889). The literary embodiment of Victorian middle-class smugness, Tupper was an Oxford graduate who in 1838 published *Proverbial Philosophy*, a sequence of moral platitudes in prosy hexameters. The book was so successful that he added three further series at intervals until 1876.

My Life As an Author (London, 1886); R. Buchmann, *Martin F. Tupper and the Victorian Middle-Class Mind* (Bern, 1942); D. Hudson, *Martin Tupper: His Rise and Fall* (London, 1949).

PROSE FICTION

>>

One of the most notable instances of the strength with which the Romantic movement obliterated realism and satire from English literature was an almost total interruption in the history of the novel. As established in the middle of the eighteenth century and still practiced at the present day, the novel may be defined as a long fictitious prose narrative, having unified structure and individualized characterization, with illusion of reality as a principal objective. The Gothic romances, however, departed so far from these traits and were written so feebly that prose fiction lost its prestige in the eyes of serious writers. Jane Austen, sole survivor of the satiric realists, could not even find a publisher. Most of the Romantic writers may have lacked the power of objective observation of character which is necessary for a good novelist, but they did not even make an attempt.

When Walter Scott was driven by economic necessity to write novels, he was so doubtful of success and so ashamed of the degradation from his status as a poet that he kept his identity strictly a secret. Under the influence of the Gothic romance he chose settings in the past and plots of conventional love and adventure; but his inherent talents of accurate detail, lifelike characterization, and familiar humor enabled him almost unintentionally to restore the main features of the novel of the preceding century.

The vast financial success of Scott led young and ambitious writers to follow his example; but only gradually did they achieve a technical mastery equal to his. His type of historical romance had won such a popular following that throughout the nineteenth century and until the present day it remained a favorite form of the novel. Some secondary authors, such as G. P. R. James and W. Harrison Ainsworth, produced numerous books after the Scott model; Bulwer-Lytton and Charles Kingsley did some of their outstanding work in it; but more remarkable is the fact that almost all the major novelists of the Victorian era were tempted to try their hand. Dickens wrote *Barnaby Rudge* and *A Tale of Two Cities;* Thackeray, *Barry Lyndon, Henry Esmond,* and *The Virginians;* George Eliot, *Romola;* Charles Reade, *The Cloister and the Hearth;* Trollope several rather unsuccessful stories. Toward the end of the century Robert Louis Stevenson, Arthur Conan Doyle and others gave it new vigor. There was naturally a wide divergence of treatment among the various writers, reflecting their personalities and artistic tastes: some of the books were almost in the category of adventure stories for boys, others were subtle studies of character or scholarly interpretations of historical forces; but all basically followed the pattern that Scott had set.

Meanwhile, during the years 1825-30 other writers were awkwardly and almost accidentally discovering that they could write prose fiction about their own day. What was known as the "silver fork" school of novelists, dealing with aristocratic manners and political intrigues, with recognizable portraits of contemporary celebrities, was started by Robert Plumer Ward and other now-forgotten writers, and was promptly seized upon by two brilliant young men who were eager to use authorship as a step to self-advertisement, wealth, and a political career. Benjamin Disraeli published *Vivian Grey* in 1826, and Edward Lytton Bulwer published *Pelham* two years later. Both books were episodic and digressive, more noteworthy for epigrams and philosophical disquisitions than for either plot or characterization. Their immediate ancestor was Byron's *Don Juan* rather than any work of prose fiction. But they proved to their authors that novel-writing could command cash and public attention.

Depicting an opposite extreme of the social scale, the "Newgate Calendar" school of fiction dealt with the underworld of poverty and crime, and was accused of being immoral by making heroes of criminals. The authors retorted that on the contrary they were showing crime in its most disgusting colors. At any rate, they brought new elements into the novel both through the thrills of violent action and through the picturesquely "realistic" portrayal of scenes outside of the reader's own experiences. A development of the historical romance, the crime novel substituted "social distance" for the perspective of time. Outstanding examples were Ainsworth's *Rookwood* and *Jack Sheppard* and Bulwer's *Paul Clifford* and *Eugene Aram*.

A fresh and vigorous though crude force was supplied by Captain Frederick Marryat, a naval veteran of the Napoleonic wars, who turned to fiction writing for a living when he retired from active service. Using his own experiences as a basis, he is reminiscent of Defoe in his matter-of-fact reporting of danger and horror; but the more immediate model for his coarse humor and gruesome excitement was Smollett. Marryat's series of successful stories included *Peter Simple, Jacob Faithful, Japhet in Search of a Father,* and *Mr. Midshipman Easy*. In spite of exaggeration, he extended the scope of the Victorian novel by giving realistic pictures of the rough, masculine side of life, and some of his comic characters had unforgettable vitality.

A similar type of rugged comedy was provided by the fox-hunting stories of Robert Smith Surtees, which had little grace of style or skill in plot construction, but plentiful action and farce. His chief character, John Jorrocks, a grocer who takes to fox-hunting, appeared in several novels and gained wide popularity.

Also in the category of "masculine" fiction of the thirties and forties may be mentioned Charles Lever, an Irish writer whose first novels, *Harry Lorrequer* and *Charles O'Malley,* also episodic in structure, combined army adventures of the Napoleonic wars with broad Irish comedy.

New methods of reaching the public were largely responsible for the emergence of these and other fiction writers. The popular magazine has just come into existence and authors who began to contribute character sketches, reminiscent anecdotes, and other disjointed material soon found it convenient to invent characters who could be carried along from one issue to the next; and eventually some sort of coherent plot was tardily introduced. Because most of their stories were thus serialized either in the popular magazines or in the separate "monthly parts," neither authors nor readers immediately recognized how close was the kinship of this sort of narration with the expansive four-volume or six-volume novels of Fielding, Richardson, or Scott. As most of the writers thus started composing novels without intending to do so, and therefore without any preliminary study of techniques, they had to teach themselves the art as they went along. Lever, for instance, used far more carefully planned plots in his later novels, changed his tone from comic to serious, and attempted analytical studies of psychological types and social conditions both in Ireland and on the Continent. Surtees, too, developed his characterization from sheer burlesque to maturer portraiture. Marryat, on the other hand, unable to keep pace with the growth of complexity, turned eventually to writing books for children.

Charles Dickens is the most outstanding example of the accidental beginning and the rapid reorganization. As an ambitious young journalist, he published in magazines and newspapers his "Sketches by Boz," a miscellaneous assortment, of which some were realistic word-pictures of what he saw every day in the London streets, others were what would now be called "short stories." Hired by a publisher to provide some sort of continuity for a monthly series of comic pictures, he adopted the artist's characters, brought them to life, and then gradually gave them some complexity of personality and some sequence of experience. By the time he had finished *The Pickwick Papers,* Dickens knew that he was a novelist and that he could thus win wealth and fame.

For his next book, *Oliver Twist,* he consciously imitated one of the most successful current types—the "Newgate" crime story—but he added his own qualities of humor and pathos, and a distinct crusading attitude that soon became his chief characteristic. In his next four or five novels, however, Dickens remained very episodic. He depended upon his control over laughter and tears, his melodramatic scenes, his special knowledge of low life in England, and his inexhaustible fecundity in creating distinctive characters. As long as these gifts sufficed, he did not have to concern himself with questions of construction, plausibility, psychological depth, or consistency of purpose.

William M. Thackeray, about the same age as Dickens, took much longer to discover how to write novels. Ten years of professional authorship, including various types of fictitious character sketches and short stories, as well as several unsuccessful short novels, preceded the writing of *Vanity Fair.* Although descended in some respects from the "silver fork" novels, and with distinct reminiscences of the eighteenth-century authors whom Thackeray admired, *Vanity Fair* introduced new qualities of urbane satire and intimate delineation of upper-class English and continental society. Thackeray, nevertheless, remained always something of the amateur in fiction, in contrast with the professional "mass production" habits of Dickens, Trollope, and others. He wrote only five important novels, and for only one of them—

his historical *Henry Esmond*—did he undertake careful fore-thought or technical experimentation.

At this time (1846-50) Dickens was at the height of his power and fame with *David Copperfield,* which had greater unity and reality than his earlier books because it was based more directly on the author's own experiences and was brought to a focus by the first-personal point of view. Thackeray believed that its less lush style and more realistic outlook showed that Dickens had been influenced by *Vanity Fair.*

Dickens's example of using the wide popular appeal of the novel as a vehicle for propaganda against social abuses was being imitated. Even in *The Pickwick Papers* Dickens had attacked the system of imprisonment for debt, and he followed with campaigns on the poorhouses and orphan-ages *(Oliver Twist),* the Yorkshire boarding schools *(Nicholas Nickleby),* and others. Between 1844 and 1847 Disraeli gained new stature both as novelist and as politician with his trilogy, *Coningsby, Sybil,* and *Tancred,* in which he set forth a proposed platform for the Conservative party which eventually made him Prime Minister. In *Sybil,* particularly, he attacked the problem which was giving more and more concern to novelists as well as to social and political thinkers—industrialism. Along the same line, Mrs. Elizabeth Gaskell published her studies of life in one of the big new midland cities, *Mary Barton* and *North and South.* Charles Kingsley, too, just at the same time, gave his interpretation of the economic unrest and the rise of new radical theories in *Yeast, Alton Locke,* and *Two Years Ago.* All these novels differed from the previous works of Dickens in that the propaganda theme was fundamental to the whole concept of the story, instead of being introduced in isolated epi-sodes. Influenced by such books, Bulwer-Lytton also attempted more realistic stories of contemporary life, be-ginning with *The Caxtons* (1849)

Completely different from any of these was the somber, subjective type of novel produced between 1847 and 1853 by the Brontë sisters. Using their own emotional and imaginative intensity to compensate for their very restricted experience, they gave a sort of spiritual realism in *Wuthering Heights* and *Jane Eyre* to material which actually was almost as melodramatic and improbable as the Gothic romances. As nowhere else in a survey of the Victorian novel, it is possible here to apply such terms as "lyrical beauty," "tragic exaltation," and "unity of impression."

Thus by 1850 the novel had expanded in only twenty years from comparative obscurity to unrivaled eminence, alike in popularity, in influence, and in the wide range of effects contributed by many authors of diverse gifts. The process is comparable to that of the evolution of Elizabethan drama from 1575 to 1595. As at that time, the lure of profit and the stimulus of competition spurred authors to active experiment. Whenever any one of them made a successful innovation, the others almost unconsciously adapted it.

The very speed and extent of the development, however, had prevented the authors and the critics from taking stock of the new product, defining its objectives, or analyzing its technical problems. Each writer had simply made the exciting discovery that he possessed the miraculous power of originating characters who became real in his imagination, taking on so much life that they often "ran away with the story." Next in importance to this vitality of characterization was the lavish use of "local color"—the detailed presentation of landscapes, streets, houses, costume, dialect. Dickens, particularly, made his scenes so vivid that the reader saw each chapter like a stage setting. The positive delight of the authors in their "atmospheric" descriptions prevented these passages from being dull and static.

As compared with characters and setting, action was incompetently handled. "Plot" was certainly present—usually violent and unconvincing plot borrowed from the exaggerated drama of the day. Often several separate plots were loosely linked, but for many chapters at a time the story might not seem to progress at all. Most of the novels retained the biographical or autobiographical pretense that had originated with Richardson and Fielding, a structure that tended to cover many years of the central character's life and many scores of persons whom he encountered.

It was actually this lack of logical integration, however, that gave the mid-Victorian novel its distinctive value. At last a literary form had emerged adequate for delineating the confused, crowded panorama of modern life. The expansion of cities, of transportation and communication and all the mechanical facilities, had made human experience more varied and interdependent than ever before. A play, a biography, or an epic seemed too simple and concise to be a truthful record of observation. Hence the long, non-selective novel, with its mixture of farce and pathos, its jostling throng of characters who sometimes scarcely met one another, gave an unsurpassed illusion of reality; and as such it could carry the messages of reform, of satire, of personal theory, which many of the writers were cramming into it.

In the next ten years two strong new forces came into play. One was Anthony Trollope, who can be called the first truly professional novelist. Undeluded by any crusading mission or any self-esteem as a creative genius, he adopted novel-writing frankly to make a living, and turned out a vast total of solidly constructed books. For each one he planned the main action in advance, and then efficiently wrote his daily quota of words. Not one book stands out as a masterpiece, no "big scenes" of emotion startle the reader; he depicts ordinary people in commonplace settings of contemporary village, town, or city, with common sense, sincerity, and unobtrusive humor as his chief merits. His success proved that the public could enjoy a novel solely for the pleasure of recognizing what was already familiar in real life.

A more important innovator was George Eliot, whose logical mind and philosophical training obliged her to ponder the basic difficulties and potentialities of the novel before she began to write in this form. In subject-matter, too, she contributed something different, by using English rural settings for her principal books. She planned each novel as a consistent whole, limited to a comparatively small group of characters who were revealed with more emphasis upon their inner motivations than upon their outer adventures. Paradoxically, her characters seem less vivid in the reader's memory than those of previous novelists, precisely because we are more intimately acquainted with their subtleties. While many preceding novelists had filled their books with opinions and propaganda, nevertheless they had catered to the public taste with a liberal admixture of sensational excitement and other elementary forms of entertainment. As with the motion pictures of the present day, an adolescent or irresponsible audience was aimed at. George Eliot assumed that the novel had reached a point where it could appeal to mature minds. Each of her novels was constructed around a serious ethical problem. She was the first to recognize that the novel had truly become the most important existing form of literature and that therefore the novelist should have self-respect and a sense of responsibility.

What George Eliot was doing about 1860 for the theme of the novel, Wilkie Collins was doing for the plot. While regarding himself as a disciple of Dickens, Collins originated the technique of the mystery story, with elaborate clues and a surprise ending. For this effect, every detail of the situation had to be planned from the beginning.

The hit-or-miss progression of the old serial novels was doomed.

Another able and successful follower of Dickens, Charles Reade, expanded the "sensational" novel in another direction, using violent scenes of strikes, shipwrecks, legal trials, and so on, all closely drawn from actual newspaper reports, to reinforce the belligerent crusading that inspired most of his books. Reade thus made the novel more topical and controversial than ever before.

One of Dickens's strongest traits (which he shared with Shakespeare) was his ability to change the mood and technique of his work in conformity to shifts of public interest. In the 1850's his novels became more somber and introspective in tone and more realistic in action, with few caricature characters and with a much closer integration between the social criticism and the narrative structure. In the 1860's he responded to the success of Collins by using elaborate mystery plots for his last two novels. At the time of his death, therefore, the hold of Dickens upon the public was as strong as ever, and his type of novel was continued till nearly the end of the century by such best-sellers as James Payn and Walter Besant.

The other major mid-Victorian novelists also had their successors in the eighties and nineties. Thackeray's irony and Bohemianism appeared in the three novels of George Du Maurier, with an unexpected admixture of occultism; Collins and Reade were followed as "sensation novelists" by a group of women writers—Mary E. Braddon, Rhoda Broughton, Mrs. Henry Wood; along another line of development, Collins fathered the "Sherlock Holmes" of Arthur Conan Doyle, and many other detectives. George Eliot's serious intellectualism was imitated by Mrs. Humphry Ward, Joseph Henry Shorthouse, and Mark Rutherford.

The influence of George Eliot may also have been partly

responsible for the "local color" novels, dealing with rural life in various corners of the British Isles, such as Devonshire (R. D. Blackmore) and Scotland (beginning with George MacDonald and developing into the "Kailyard School" of Barrie, Crockett, and Maclaren). Another forerunner of this type of fiction was the Irish peasant stories of the Banim brothers, Griffin, and Carleton, earlier in the century.

The most significant result, however, of George Eliot's impact upon later nineteenth-century fiction was an essential demarcation between the "popular" and the "intellectual" novel. Publishers, critics, and authors realized that a novel as a work of art and an expression of serious individual thinking might be of lasting literary importance even though it had little appeal for the mass of fiction readers.

This trend was intensified by the sudden expansion of the biological sciences. The appearance of Darwin's *Origin of Species* in 1859 made people aware that scientific theories were being applied to human behavior. Until this date, novelists had automatically accepted traditional ethical standards. Characters were classified as "good" or "bad," actions as "virtuous" or "wicked," and the happy ending of a story required the rewarding of virtue and punishment of vice. The new, objective attitude, however, tried to understand actions rather than to assert their moral values. The science of psychology was emerging, though it had not yet acquired a terminology. As the study of human character and behavior was the particular function of novelists, the more thoughtful of them could not escape the new analytical approach.

One consequence was an attack by some segments of the public, who declared that the novel was becoming immoral. A century before, puritanical people had condemned all fiction as being "lies" and as presenting worldly actions and emotions in a favorable light. Now the charge was renewed upon a fresh basis: the novel was assailed for describing sexual and other passions without either evasion or moral condemnation.

The first of the "intellectual" novelists, who was beginning his career just when Darwin's book was published, was George Meredith. He slowly emerged into public notice with a reputation for baffling obscurity. His ironic portrayal of fashionable society had some kinship with Thackeray's; but he added an allusive style, an independent philosophy of fiction, and an attention to the inner psychology of his characters, with consequent slow motion and infrequent crises.

His chief contemporary, Thomas Hardy, used a prose style almost as individual and leisurely, though much less intricate. His intimate knowledge of rural Wessex was a background for displaying the depths of human motivation and the interplay of character with environment. The development of action in Hardy's stories was controlled by a distinct philosophic concept, which led to a tragic outcome in his major books. The conflict between the public desire for cheerful entertainment and the intellectual novelist's obstinate adherence to his own theories is illustrated by the uproar over *Jude the Obscure;* when this book was censured for its grim emphasis upon frustration and perversion, Hardy refused to write any more novels.

Modern criticism inclines to place Samuel Butler alongside of these two novelists; but his one novel, *The Way of All Flesh,* though first written in the seventies, did not appear in print till after the end of the century, and did not gain renown until even later. Butler, however, like Meredith and Hardy, exemplifies the change in the novel as a vehicle for ideas. Dickens and his contemporaries had used their stories to attack specific social abuses or to propose specific reforms; the later novelists transmitted to the public the fundamental speculations of the scientists with regard to human character and social relations.

Foreign influences were also increasing. From Stendhal and Balzac onward, French writers had been more concerned with the artistic significance of the novel than their English brethren had been; and after the middle of the century a group of Russians wrote powerful books which emphasized analysis of emotions and frank portrayal of psychopathic behavior. The English public regarded such books with suspicion as "degenerate" or "vicious," and in the eighties there was a furore when translations of Zola's novels were banned by censorship. The controversy made the public acquainted with the "naturalistic" school of fiction which assumed to interpret all human behavior in terms of primitive impulses. This new force had some effect upon the novels of George Moore and George Gissing. The drab sordidness of such books, as well as the disillusionments that they implied, widened the chasm between readers for entertainment and devotees of the intellect. The former turned with enthusiasm to the stories of stirring adventure, usually picturesquely remote in place or time, of Robert Louis Stevenson, Rudyard Kipling, Rider Haggard, and Anthony Hope.

A word must be said about the short story, which was strangely slow in developing in England. Although popular magazines were numerous from the beginning of the Victorian period, there was no English equivalent of Poe, Hawthorne, or Maupassant. Most of the novelists occasionally wrote a brief piece of fiction: Dickens included several in *Sketches by Boz* and Thackeray in *The Yellowplush Papers* and elsewhere. The "Christmas books" which were successful in the middle years of the century might be regarded as long "short stories," and so might the three tales in George Eliot's *Scenes of Clerical Life*. None of these writers, however, gave much thought to any special

techniques of the short-story form, and all of them graduated happily into novel-writing.

Good novelists are seldom equally skilful in the short
story, and vice versa. The two greatest English short-story
writers after 1880, Robert Louis Stevenson and Rudyard
Kipling, each produced several book-length stories; but
they lacked the firmness of structure and the psychological
subtlety that had come to be considered as essential for
first-class novels. *Kidnapped* and *Kim* are now regarded as
stories for boys rather than as mature novels; and *The
Light That Failed* is melodramatic and unconvincing. Their
short stories, on the other hand, were masterpieces of conciseness and unity of impression.

In seventy years English fiction had gone through a
whole process of evolution and had developed many new
moods and effects. In so doing it had established itself
solidly as the most widely read, the most influential, and
the most representative literary form of its era.

E. A. Baker, *History of the English Novel,* vii-x (London,
1936-39); E. Wagenknecht, *Cavalcade of the English Novel* (New
York, 1943); H. Williams, *Two Centuries of the English Novel*
(London, 1911); C. Weygandt, *A Century of the English Novel*
(New York, 1925); W. S. Lilly, *Four English Humourists of the
Nineteenth Century* (London, 1895); L. Cazamian, *Le roman
social en Angleterre, 1830-50* (Paris, 1903; new ed., 2v, 1935);
L. Melville, *Victorian Novelists* (London, 1906); W. C. Phillips,
Dickens, Reade, and Collins, Sensation Novelists (New York,
1919); F. T. Russell, *Satire in the Victorian Novel* (New York,
1920); M. E. Speare, *The Political Novel* (New York, 1921); L.
Villard, *La femme anglaise au XIXe siècle et son évolution d'après
le roman anglais contemporain* (Paris, 1921); M. L. Cazamian,
Le roman et les idées en Angleterre, i, *L'influence de la science,
1860-90* (Strasbourg, 1923), ii, *L'anti-intellectualisme et l'esthé-
ticisme, 1880-1900* (Paris, 1935); M. Bald, *Women Writers of the
Nineteenth Century* (Cambridge, 1923); W. C. Frierson, *L'influence du naturalisme français sur les romanciers anglais, 1885-
1900* (Paris, 1925); A. T. Quiller-Couch, *Charles Dickens and*

Other Victorians (Cambridge, 1925); S. M. Ellis, *Mainly Victorian* (London, 1925); *Wilkie Collins, LeFanu, and Others* (London, 1931); J. E. Baker, *The Novel and the Oxford Movement* (Princeton, 1932); M. Elwin, *Victorian Wallflowers* (London, 1934); Lord D. Cecil, *Early Victorian Novelists* (London, 1935); M. W. Rosa, *The Silver-Fork School: Novels of Fashion Preceding "Vanity Fair"* (New York, 1936); A. Shepperson, *The Novel in Motley: A History of the Burlesque Novel* (Cambridge, Mass., 1936); E. M. Delafield, *Ladies and Gentlemen in Victorian Fiction* (London, 1937); L. J. Henkin, *Darwinism in the English Novel* (Brooklyn, 1940); "Problems and Digressions in the Victorian Novel, 1860-1900," *Bulletin of Bibliography*, XVIII (1936), XIX (1937), *passim;* L. P. Stebbins, *A Victorian Album: Some Lady Novelists of the Period* (New York, 1946).

BENJAMIN DISRAELI (1804-1881)

>>

Descended from noted Italian, Spanish, and Portuguese Jewish families, Benjamin Disraeli was the namesake of a grandfather who had migrated from Venice to England in 1748. The latter's son, Isaac D'Israeli, was a prosperous amateur scholar and author. Benjamin Disraeli was born in London on December 21, 1804, and thirteen years later was baptized into the Church of England, his father having quarreled with the Jewish congregation to which he had formerly belonged.

Young Disraeli attended several small private schools, but obtained most of his wide, though rather superficial, knowledge of books from reading in his father's library. He also learned much through conversation with the literary men who were his father's friends. At the age of seventeen he was apprenticed to a firm of attorneys, but found the work uncongenial and gave it up after three years. Full of ambition and self-confidence, he gambled on the stock market and incurred heavy debts, after which he made a bold but unsuccessful attempt to found a daily newspaper. The failure of this scheme brought him into disfavor with a number of influential writers and publishers. Undeterred, he courted public notice as a wit and a dandy, affecting paradoxical opinions and flamboyant clothes.

In 1826 he published *Vivian Grey,* a "fashionable novel" which was incoherent in structure and improbable in plot, but which attracted notice by its startling comments and by the thinly disguised portraits of contemporary celebrities. In the midst of its juvenile cynicism and impudent egotism, Disraeli revealed the serious political ambitions that already controlled him.

His second novel in the same style, *The Young Duke,* brought him five hundred pounds, with which he made a three-year Byronic tour of the Near East, where he was fascinated by the Oriental atmosphere and garbed himself in gorgeous robes. His impressions provided material for his next two books, *Alroy,* a tale of a twelfth-century Jewish national leader, and *Contarini Fleming,* a "psychological romance" which garishly dramatized his aspirations.

In 1832 he contested a parliamentary election as a Radical, but a year later changed his allegiance to the Tory party. To defend himself from charges of opportunism he wrote clever pamphlets. Two further novels appeared in 1836 and 1837, *Henrietta Temple* and *Venetia* (notable for having fictional portraits of Byron and Shelley among the characters). In 1837 he became a Member of Parliament, after four failures. Two years later he married Mrs. Wyndham Lewis, twelve years older than he and the widow of a political colleague. The marriage proved ideally happy.

As his novels had served their purpose of gaining publicity for him, he devoted the next seven years to his parliamentary advancement. By 1844 he had become conspicuous in the "Young England" faction which was seeking to revitalize the Tory party by making it a champion of the working class, in opposition to the industrialists. In order to bring his political doctrines before the public he wrote a trilogy of novels that constitute his most important work. *Coningsby* (1844) presented his views of party politics, with the personal leadership of gifted men as the basis of government. *Sybil, or The Two Nations* (1845) dealt with the problems of industrialism; he showed the division of the country into two classes, the rich and the poor, between whom there was no intercourse or sympathy. He suggested that a generous aristocracy, exercising a kindly rule, would remedy the misery of the workers. In *Tancred, or The New Crusade* (1847) he intended to handle the current crisis in religion, offering "theocratic equality" as the solution for the quest for faith; but his personal bias made him throw excessive emphasis upon the Asiatic heritage of Christianity as the true source of inspiration.

Following out the policies outlined in these three "political novels," Disraeli rose steadily until he became one of the most influential statesmen in English history. He was Prime Minister for a brief term in 1868; and in 1870, during a political lull, he wrote *Lothair*. His first novel in a quarter of a century, it was an investigation of the Roman Catholic Church's rôle in contemporary European affairs.

From 1874 to 1880 he was again Prime Minister and vitally affected the development of British imperialism. In 1876 he was created Earl of Beaconsfield. After his loss of office in 1880 he completed *Endymion,* a novel that had been interrupted at an earlier date. It was a witty retrospective picture of social and political life at the time he was beginning his career. He died on April 19, 1881.

Disraeli's epigrams are often dated, his style is self-conscious, and he had an over-lavish taste in magnificent settings. His novels are too closely related to the issues of his own day to be easy for the modern reader. On the other hand, anyone wishing to become familiar with the main forces in Victorian political life can find penetrating analysis in Disraeli's works. The intuitions which provided his political strategy are equally effective in his fiction. And nowhere else is there a stronger instance of the influence of literature upon history. Not only did Disraeli's novels serve as propaganda for his doctrines; they also were put into practical effect. Because Byron had gone to Greece and Turkey and had written *Childe Harold's Pilgrimage,* Disraeli made a similar tour and wrote *Contarini Fleming* and *Alroy.* The eventual result was that Queen Victoria became Empress of India and England financed the Suez Canal.

Works (11v, London, 1881; Hughenden edition; 12v, London, 1926-27; Bradenham edition); *Lord Beaconsfield's Letters, 1830-52,* ed. R. Disraeli (London, 1887); *Letters of Disraeli to Lady Bradford and Lady Chesterfield,* ed. Marquess of Zetland (London, 1929); *Letters to Frances Anne, Marchioness of Londonderry,* ed. Marchioness of Londonderry (London, 1938); C. Brown, *An Appreciative Life of the Earl of Beaconsfield* (2v, London, 1882); W. Meynell, *Benjamin Disraeli, an Unconventional Biography* (London, 1903; rev. ed., 1927); W. F. Monypenny and G. E. Buckle, *The Life of Benjamin Disraeli* (10v, London, 1910-20; rev. ed., 2v, 1929); A. Maurois, *La vie de Disraeli* (Paris, 1927; Eng. trans., 1928); L. Stephen, "Disraeli's Novels," in *Hours in a Library,* 2nd ser. (London, 1876); G. Brandes, *Lord Beaconsfield: A Study* (London, 1880); W. E. Henley, "Disraeli," in *Views and Reviews* (London, 1890); R. Garnett, "Shelley and Lord Beaconsfield," in *Essays of an Ex-Librarian* (London, 1901); R. W. Howes, *A Key to the Characters in Disraeli's Novels* (New York, 1907); J. R. Lowell, "Disraeli As a Novelist," in *The Round Table* (Boston, 1913); E. Gosse, "The Novels of Benjamin Disraeli," *Transactions of the Royal Society of Literature,* xxxvi (1918). 61-90; F. Swinnerton, "Disraeli As a Novelist," *Yale Review,* xvii (1927). 283-300; C. L. Cline, "Disraeli and Thackeray," *Review of English Studies,* xix (1943). 404-08.

EDWARD BULWER-LYTTON (1803-1873)

>>

Descended from aristocratic lines through both parents, Edward George Earle Lytton Bulwer was born in London on May 25, 1803. From his father, a general, he inherited a turbulent spirit, and from his mother, a wealthy heiress, he derived a love of letters. His father died when he was four, and his strong-willed mother supervised his education. He spent most of his boyhood days in his grandfather's library, reading and writing Byronic verses which he published before he was seventeen. With similar precocity he went through an unhappy love affair, paid court to Byron's one-time mistress, Lady Caroline Lamb, and spent some time with a gipsy tribe. After attending various private schools he entered Trinity College, Cambridge, in 1822, but soon migrated to Trinity Hall to avoid the necessity of attending lectures. During his college days he won the Chancellor's medal for poetry, sketched two novels, read history, and published more Byronic verse. Before he received his degree, in 1826, he had fallen in love with Rosina Wheeler, a beautiful and clever girl of violent temper.

He spent a few months in Paris, establishing a reputation as a dandy. His distinguished appearance, witty conversation, and exaggerated fashionable dress, combined with a reputation for flirtation, won him a place in London society. His marriage to Miss Wheeler was opposed by his mother, who withdrew his allowance and left the young couple without means of support.

Bulwer adopted the profession of authorship with two purposes—to earn money and to gain public notice as a basis for a political career. His first novel, *Falkland*, was a feeble piece of romanticism imitative of Rousseau's *Nouvelle Héloïse;* but his next, *Pelham,* published in 1828, created a sensation. Following the example of Disraeli's *Vivian Grey,* which came out two years earlier, it was a digressive book exploiting the impudent wit and affected worldliness of the current dandyism. Most of the characters were obviously modeled upon well-known people of the day, and the hero was presumably a self-portrait.

Bulwer followed his success with a novel every year, in varied styles: *Devereux,* a historical romance; *Paul Clifford* and *Eugene Aram,* sordid stories of crime; and *Godolphin,* another "fashionable novel." The crime stories were accused of sentimentalizing criminals, though Bulwer claimed that they had a moral purpose of displaying the social causes of crime and the possibilities of reform. In fact, all these novels showed definitely didactic intentions.

For a while he edited the *New Monthly Magazine,* and in 1831 he was elected to Parliament as a Liberal. He made immense success with his historical novels, *The Last Days of Pompeii* (1834) and *Rienzi* (1835). His personal life, however, was embittered by the failure of his marriage; he was legally separated from his wife in 1836 and she devoted herself to a fanatical campaign of slander against him. Among his fellow authors he was unpopular for his affected manners and attitude of lordly patronage.

In 1836 he turned his attention to drama and wrote five highly successful plays, the most famous being *The Lady of Lyons* and *Richelieu.* He also produced poetic satires, an epic on King Arthur, translations, and so forth. His parliamentary prestige increased, and he was created a baronet in 1838. On the death of his mother in 1843 he inherited her estate of Knebworth and added "Lytton" to his name. Novels of his different types continued to appear: *Ernest Maltravers* and *Alice* (fashionable), *The Last of the Barons* and *Harold* (historical), *Night and Morning* and *Lucretia* (crime). His growing interest in the supernatural showed itself in *Zanoni* (1842) which he considered his most original work. In 1849 he attempted a new style of "domestic comedy" in *The Caxtons,* modeled somewhat upon *Tristram Shandy* and bringing him into closer conformity with Dickens and other contemporaries. Published anonymously, this story was successful enough to be followed by *My Novel* and *What Will He Do With It,* in the same style.

After ten years' absence from Parliament, he was re-elected in 1852, this time as a Conservative; in 1858-59 he was Secretary of State for the Colonies, his main achievement in office being the foundation of the colony of British Columbia. Raised to the peerage as Baron Lytton of Knebworth in 1866, he was prevented by his increasing deafness from taking much further part in public affairs.

His later novels included *A Strange Story* (supernatural), *The Coming Race* (a utopian romance), and *Kenelm Chillingly* (a realistic picture of English society in the mid-Victorian era). He dabbled more and more in astrology and other occult studies, and as a result of his over-strained years of activity he suffered physical breakdown that led to his death on January 18, 1873. He was buried in Westminster Abbey.

Bulwer-Lytton possessed versatile talent and an uncanny ability to know exactly what the public wanted. No other novelist ever achieved success in so many different types of story, and he could exploit each to the full. His brilliant abilities, however, were marred by affectation, pedantry, and lapses of taste. His historical novels were burdened with documentation, and his style in them was rhetorical to the extreme. His fantastic stories, while they have skilful suspense and lavish horror, do not carry full conviction. His diction was artificial and prolix, his sentiment often became mawkish, and his characterization was seldom plausible. He could always tell an effective story, however, and in all his books may be found flashes of insight. It is

to his credit that his later novels became less pretentious
and more realistic.

Works (29v, London, 1895-98; New Knebworth edition); First
Earl of Lytton, *The Life, Letters, and Literary Remains of Edward Bulwer, Lord Lytton* [to 1832 only] (2v, London, 1883);
W. F. Lord, "Lord Lytton," in *The Mirror of the Century* (London, 1906); T. H. S. Escott, *Edward Bulwer, First Baron Lytton
of Knebworth* (London, 1910); Second Earl of Lytton, *The Life
of Edward Bulwer, First Lord Lytton* (2v, London, 1913); E. Gosse,
"The Life of Edward Bulwer," in *Fortnightly Review*, c (1913).
1033-46; E. G. Bell, *Introductions to the Prose Romances, Plays,
and Comedies of Edward Bulwer, Lord Lytton* (Chicago, 1914);
E. B. Burgum, *The Literary Career of Edward Bulwer, Lord
Lytton* (Urbana, 1924); C. N. Stewart, *Bulwer-Lytton As an
Occultist* (London, 1927); M. Sadleir, *Bulwer, A Panorama: I,
Edward and Rosina* (London, 1931); H. H. Watts, "Lytton's
Theories of Prose Fiction," *Publications of the Modern Lan-
guage Association*, L (1935). 274-89.

CHARLES DICKENS (1812-1870)
>>>

The best-loved novelist of the Victorian age, Charles
Dickens was born on February 7, 1812, at Landport, a
suburb of Portsmouth, the naval station on the English
Channel. He was the second of eight children of a clerk
in the navy pay office. From 1816 to 1821 the family lived
at Chatham, a drab dockyard town, where the little boy
received some elementary schooling and read voraciously
in the works of the earlier novelists, notably Fielding,
Smollett, Cervantes, and LeSage.

Both parents were impractical; and in London, where
they settled in 1821, the father got into financial troubles,
lost his government position, and was eventually imprisoned
for debt. Charles was put to work pasting labels on bottles
of shoe-polish in a dingy factory. The humiliation of these

circumstances, as well as the actual discomforts of long working hours and poor food, left indelible impressions upon the proud, sensitive child. He acquired not only a determination to rise above all danger of poverty, but also a sympathy for the poor and underprivileged, especially children.

When relatives finally came to the family's aid, John Dickens was released from the Marshalsea Prison, and

CHARLES DICKENS

Charles attended Wellington House Academy, a cheap school. When he was fifteen he began to earn his own living as a lawyer's clerk. In his spare time he taught himself shorthand, and in 1832 he became a parliamentary reporter. Meanwhile he had fallen in love with a vivacious girl, Maria Beadnell, only to be deeply hurt when he found that her family considered him socially unacceptable and that she had been merely flirting with him.

In 1834 he became a regular reporter on an important Whig newspaper, the *Morning Chronicle.* As he went about London and its environs in search of news, he learned to observe and describe graphically the peculiarities of the people he saw. Sketches based upon these observations were contributed to the *Monthly Magazine,* the *Evening Chronicle,* and other periodicals. In 1836 he married Catherine Hogarth, a daughter of the owner of the *Evening Chronicle,* and in the same year his essays and short stories were collected and published as *Sketches by Boz.*

A new publishing firm, Chapman & Hall, was planning

to bring out a series of humorous engravings of sporting events by a popular illustrator, Robert Seymour, and asked Dickens to write short comic episodes to appear in monthly pamphlets accompanying the pictures. Shortly after the project began, in April, 1836, Seymour died, leaving Dickens free to develop the serial as he would. The characters soon grew in depth and plausibility beyond the range of caricature, and some continuity of plot was introduced. As *The Posthumous Papers of the Pickwick Club* the story became immensely popular, especially after Sam Weller was added to the characters.

Having almost accidentally discovered his ability as a novelist, Dickens devoted himself vigorously to his literary career. For a while he was editor of a new magazine, *Bentley's Miscellany,* in which his *Oliver Twist* appeared serially. This was really his first novel, in the sense of being written with a conscious plan or technique, and it was modeled somewhat upon the sensational underworld stories of Ainsworth and Bulwer. *The Pickwick Papers* had been loved for the uproarious humor, but *Oliver Twist* showed Dickens's mastery of melodrama and horror. Even in *Pickwick* he had begun to insert some of his propaganda against social abuses, and *Oliver Twist* was openly committed to the purpose of reform, by displaying the iniquitous administration of the poor-laws.

His next novel, *Nicholas Nickleby* (1838-39) showed the full development of his characteristics: the loose, episodic plot; the contrasts of broad comedy and unrestrained pathos; the multitude of strongly marked characters, depicted by the method of "humors" that had descended through Smollett from Ben Jonson; and always the philanthropic mission—this time to expose the cruelty of the cheap boarding schools for unwanted boys.

Not yet thirty, Dickens was unquestionably the most popular author in England. He was making a great deal

"A CHARITY DINNER," BY CRUIKSHANK
(*L.* to *R.*: Chapman, Dickens, Hall, Cruikshank)

of money, and had become a familiar figure in literary and social circles. Somewhat over-dressed and over-dramatic in appearance, he possessed enough energy and enthusiasm to overcome all obstacles.

GAD'S HILL PLACE, HOME
OF DICKENS IN KENT

In 1840 came *The Old Curiosity Shop,* his most idyllic and pathetic novel. Little Nell, the personification of the innocence of childhood that he had treated in both his previous novels, was suggested by his wife's youngest sister, who had recently died. Although often condemned for improbability and sentimentalism, the story is imaginatively and emotionally potent as a sort of allegory of the contrast of good and evil. As in *Oliver Twist,* the atmosphere of crime is conveyed with grisly vividness.

Barnaby Rudge, published in the next year, was Dickens's first historical novel. The Gordon Riots of 1784 were strikingly depicted, but in spite of an elaborate plot and skilful use of terror, the story was uneven, the fictitious action being poorly articulated with the historical setting.

Dickens and his wife spent nearly five months of 1842 in the United States and Canada. Although welcomed in the United States enthusiastically, Dickens was not favorably impressed. Like other English radicals he had idealized the American democracy, and was disappointed by the prevalence of greed, graft, assertiveness, and other defects. Besides, he was annoyed that the lack of international copyright laws enabled American publishers to profit from his books without paying anything to him. On his return to England he expressed his opinions in *American Notes,* which aroused bitter anger among his recent hosts. As a matter of fact, he had already been just as outspoken in condemning the faults of his own country; but Americans had been delighted with that feature of his work and had accepted even its wildest exaggeration as a true picture of English life. They were not so willing to believe that he was an honest reporter of conditions in the U.S.A.

He repeated some of his criticisms in his next novel, *Martin Chuzzlewit,* changing the plot in order to bring a couple of his characters from England to a raw frontier settlement. The English part of the story contained some of his best specimens of comic characterization, such as Mr. Pecksniff and Mrs. Gamp.

In December, 1843, Dickens published *A Christmas Carol,* which was taken to the heart of the English and American public, and permanently influenced the customs of celebrating Christmas in both countries. He followed its success with an annual series of similar little "Christmas books."

During the next few years he spent part of his time in Italy and France. In 1846 he helped to found a new Radical paper, the *Daily News,* and edited it for a few weeks. His next novel, *Dombey and Son,* which began to appear serially in October of that year, marked the beginning of a new manner, with less exuberance and exaggeration, and particularly a more realistic handling of the upper social levels.

From his early years Dickens had been fascinated by the stage and had dreamed of becoming an actor. At the beginning of his career he wrote several feeble farces and operettas. The stage undoubtedly had a strong effect upon his novels. His lavish use of dialogue, his attention to the settings and to the attitudes and costumes of his characters, and above all, his over-simplified characterization and his dramatic situations, can all be traced to the techniques of the theater. These traits give his novels their lasting hold on the reader's imagination and memory.

In 1847 he organized an amateur theatrical company, which during the next five years put on performances for charity in various towns, Dickens himself serving as manager and playing important rôles. In March, 1850, he started a monthly periodical, *Household Words,* which was intended to be an inexpensive and wholesome magazine for popular reading. In spite of these activities, however, Dickens continued his writing of novels without a break.

David Copperfield, generally considered his masterpiece, was published between May, 1849, and November, 1850. His genius was at its height, and the autobiographical element in the story gave it sincerity and restraint. In previous novels he had used a few of his friends and relatives as models for characters (always with very free adaptation), but in *David Copperfield* the whole story closely followed his own career. Dickens regarded it as his best work.

In the fifties appeared three novels in which social reform was an integral part of the concept, rather than a subject of separate episodes, as in his earlier works. *Bleak House* attacked the delays and inequities of the legal system,

DICKENS READING *THE CHIMES*

especially the Court of Chancery. *Hard Times,* revealing the influence of Carlyle, condemned the industrial system and the Utilitarian economic theories. *Little Dorrit* satirized governmental bureaucracy, and also recalled Dickens's unhappy boyhood by depicting the miseries of imprisonment for debt. All three of these novels were predominantly gloomy in mood, with very little of Dickens's usual humor. He was paying unusual attention to the construction of plot, *Bleak House* having a specially ingenious structure which has gained it the title of "the first detective novel." The greater unity and intellectualism of novels by some of his younger contemporaries led Dickens to experiment with these qualities. While he was successful in achieving the effects he sought, many readers regretted the decline of the high spirits and spontaneity of his earlier works. The feeling of strain and sadness in these three "dark" novels was partly due to private miseries. Dickens and his wife had gradually become incompatible, and now that all his children were past their infancy he decided upon a separation.

With insatiable energy he began in 1858 to give dramatic readings from his books, which brought him added popularity and immense profits. After performing repeatedly all over Great Britain, he made a triumphant reading tour of the United States in 1867-68. During all these years he continued his editorial work, for when *Household Words* stopped publication in 1859 it was immediately followed by a similar journal, *All the Year Round.*

His second historical novel, *A Tale of Two Cities,* was written in 1859, based largely upon Carlyle's *French Revolution.* Shorter than many of Dickens's novels, it has less digression and a more tragic atmosphere and climax. It was followed by *Great Expectations,* also short, which was his nearest approach to a subtle psychological study. In contrast, *Our Mutual Friend* (1864-65) reverted to the old length and complexity, with much of the old humor. The mystery element in the plot was unconvincing, but some admirers rate the novel among Dickens's best.

Ignoring warnings that his health was being over-strained, he persisted with all his activities. He was unable to relax, and the applause of audiences had become the very breath of life to him. During his American tour he almost collapsed after every reading, but in 1870 he was again performing in various English towns. In that year also he started a new novel, the first in five years, *The Mystery of Edwin Drood*. As with all his novels, he wrote concurrently with the serial publication from month to month, not even making an outline of the future chapters. On June 8, 1870, after completing the sixth installment, he suffered a stroke of apoplexy, and died the next evening. The secret of the novel's plot died with him.

On technical grounds Dickens's novels were widely defective. Before the end of his career, new standards of realism and psychological analysis had entered the novel, making his external method of approach obsolete. His style was rhetorical, his plots were either disjointed or too elaborately neat, his characters were grotesquely exaggerated. Nevertheless, he had the mysterious creative genius that linked him with Chaucer and Shakespeare—the power of inventing people who come to life in the reader's mind. Literally hundreds of his characters assume this illusion of reality—many of them minor performers occupying only a page.

The secret of his emotional vitality was his personal participation in the story as he wrote it. He laughed and wept with his characters. As a result, he can still affect readers of every type, from childhood to old age, from the semi-literate to the scholarly. The inescapable intensity with which he depicted injustice and corruption impressed itself upon countless people who would otherwise have ignored the social wrongs of his day; and the improvement of many of those conditions can be attributed largely to his influence. With the reporter's eye for minute details and odd twists of behavior, the dramatist's feeling for dialogue and suspense, the moralist's knack of embodying a single attribute in a typical figure, Dickens can fascinate readers so that they forget the customary challenges of consistency or psychological truth.

J. C. Eckel, *A Bibliography of the First Editions of Charles Dickens* (London, 1913; rev. ed., 1932); T. Hatton and A. H. Cleaver, *A Bibliography of the Periodical Works of Charles Dickens* (London, 1934); W. Miller, *The Dickens Student and Collector: A List of Writings Relating to Dickens and His Works, 1836-1945* (Cambridge, Mass., 1946); C. A. Pierce and W. A. Wheeler, *The Dickens Dictionary* (Boston, 1878); A. J. Philip and W. L. Gadd, *A Dickens Dictionary* (London, 1928); *Works* [including Letters, ed. W. Dexter] (23v, London, 1937-38; Nonesuch edition); J. Forster, *Life of Charles Dickens* (3v, London, 1871-74; revised by J. W. T. Ley, London, 1928); A. W. Ward, *Dickens* (London, 1882; English Men of Letters); R. Langton, *The Childhood and Youth of Dickens* (London, 1883; rev. ed., 1891); F. T. Marzials, *The Life of Charles Dickens* (London, 1887; Great Writers); G. Gissing, *Charles Dickens* (London, 1898); *Critical Studies of the Works of Charles Dickens* (New York, 1924); F. G. Kitton, *Charles Dickens* (London, 1902); P. Fitzgerald, *Life of Charles Dickens* (2v, London, 1905); G. K. Chesterton, *Charles Dickens* (London, 1906); *Appreciations and Criticisms of the Works of Charles Dickens* (London, 1911); A. S. G. Canning, *Dickens Studied in Six Novels* (London, 1912); A. C. Swinburne, *Charles Dickens* (London, 1913); G. Santayana, "Dickens," in *Soliloquies in England* (London, 1922); R. Straus, *Charles Dickens: A Portrait in Pencil* (London, 1928); E. Wagenknecht, *The Man Charles Dickens* (Boston, 1929); S. Leacock, *Charles Dickens: His Life and Work* (New York, 1933); A. Maurois, *Dickens* (London, 1934); T. Wright, *The Life of Charles Dickens* (London, 1935); L. Clendening, *A Handbook to the Pickwick Papers* (New York, 1936); W. Dexter and J. W. T. Ley, *The Origin of Pickwick* (London, 1936); T. A. Jackson, *Charles Dickens: The Progress of a Radical* (London, 1937); H. House, *The Dickens World* (London, 1940); E. Wilson, "Dickens: The Two Scrooges," in *The*

Wound and the Bow (Boston, 1941); U. Pope-Hennessy, *Charles Dickens, 1812-70* (London, 1945). See also *The Dickensian* (quarterly, 1905-).

WILLIAM MAKEPEACE THACKERAY (1811-1863)

>>>

Although sharing with Dickens the reputation of "chief Victorian novelist," William Makepeace Thackeray was much slower in mastering the art of the novel; a large proportion of his work was in other literary forms, and he produced only five major novels, in contrast with Dickens's fourteen.

WILLIAM MAKEPEACE
THACKERAY

Born in Calcutta on July 18, 1811, only son of a successful official of the British administration in India, he was left fatherless at five and was sent to England the next year for his education. His school days were rather lonely and unhappy; Charterhouse School, which he entered at the age of eleven, was overcrowded and rowdy, and he was permanently disfigured by a broken nose received in a fight. Too short-sighted for games, he was also too indolent for hard study, and was often humiliated by the sarcasms of the headmaster; but he gradually grew popular with the boys for his ability to tell stories and draw funny pictures.

In 1829 he went to Trinity College, Cambridge, where he engaged in college journalism. A particularly brilliant group of students were at the university, most of them in his own college, and he made friends with the Tennysons, FitzGerald, and others. After incurring heavy debts through a fondness for gambling, he left in his second year.

He spent the winter of 1830 in Weimar, where he was introduced to Goethe. Upon his return to England he studied law in the Middle Temple, but as soon as he came of age and inherited his fortune he bought a weekly literary journal and went to Paris as its correspondent. His chief interest at this time, however, was art study, and he spent the next two or three years chiefly in the studios of the Latin Quarter. When the failure of his paper, and other bad speculations, reduced his funds, he joined the staff of *The Constitutional*, a new daily newspaper in which his stepfather was a heavy shareholder. In 1836 he married Isabella Shawe, a young Irish girl. The next year the last of the family's funds were lost when the newspaper collapsed, and Thackeray was left entirely without support.

Only after several attempts to find employment as an illustrator did he fall back upon authorship as a way to earn a living. He became a book reviewer for *The Times* and a contributor to *Fraser's Magazine*. This was the year of *The Pickwick Papers,* which suddenly raised Dickens from obscure poverty to fame. The situation of Thackeray was the exact reverse: from wealth and social distinction he had suddenly been reduced to hardship and he was struggling as a hack writer with no thought of literary art or fame. His sketches were signed with various absurd pseudonyms that prevented the public from even knowing that the same man was writing the varied material.

His earliest notable contribution to *Fraser's* was "The Yellowplush Correspondence," 1837-38, sharp satire on contemporary literature and fashion, supposedly written by a footman. It was followed in 1840 by a novelette, *Catherine,* ridiculing the current idealization of the criminal in the novels of Bulwer, Ainsworth, and others. It was so little noticed that it was not reissued in volume form until thirty years later. During 1840 Thackeray brought out his first book, *The Paris Sketch Book,* a collection of short stories and essays. He also began a serial for *Fraser's* that might have grown into a novel had it not been interrupted when Thackeray's family life was shattered by his wife's mental illness. She had to be committed to an institution, leaving Thackeray with two baby daughters, whom he entrusted to his mother's charge.

When he painfully resumed literary work he became a staff contributor to the new humorous weekly, *Punch.* In 1842 he was sent to Ireland by the publishing firm of Chapman & Hall to observe conditions, and as a result published *The Irish Sketch Book.* A similar trip to the Near East two years later produced *Notes on a Journey from Cornhill to Grand Cairo.* His first work that could be called a novel was *The Luck of Barry Lyndon,* a picaresque story of an eighteenth-century Irish rascal. Published serially in *Fraser's* in 1844, it attracted little notice.

His work was appearing chiefly with the pseudonym of Michael Angelo Titmarsh, but a few people were becoming aware of his identity. His best source of income continued to be his weekly skits and drawings for *Punch.* A long series on "The Snobs of England" became particularly famous, and was reissued as a volume called *The Book of Snobs.* Another clever series was "Prize Novelists," burlesquing the popular authors of the day. The satire in these two series was bitter enough to make Thackeray unpopular in some quarters.

After six years of a lonely life in lodgings and clubs he was able to afford a house in London in 1846 and brought his little daughters to live with him. At this time he finally found himself as a novelist with *Vanity Fair,* which began to appear in monthly parts on January 1, 1847. By the time it was completed, nineteen months later, many readers were comparing him favorably with Dickens. As a portrayer of upper-class English life, he counterbalanced Dickens's pictures of poverty and slums; and his elegant irony was the antithesis of Dickens's emotionalism.

Thackeray became a popular figure in London society, where his quaint wit, huge height, and good-natured ugliness made him distinctive. Belated success, however, could not cure him of a certain bitterness acquired during his years of neglect, and life still held secret tragedies for him. The permanent illness of his wife deprived him of normal domestic companionship, and when he fell in love it was with Mrs. Brookfield, whose husband had been his closest friend ever since their college days. For several years Mrs. Brookfield was his most helpful adviser, but when they

FIRST EDITION
TITLE-PAGE

finally realized the seriousness of their mutual feelings they decided to break off the friendship. Meanwhile, in 1849 Thackeray had a severe illness that warned him of an incurable malady.

His second long novel, *Pendennis*, was completed in 1850; it was the most autobiographical of his works, with particularly vivid pictures of the journalists and hack-writers among whom Thackeray had labored for so long. After his resignation from the staff of *Punch* in 1851, he delivered a series of lectures on the eighteenth-century humorists.

When these proved successful in London, he repeated them in other parts of England, and in 1852 he made a profitable lecture-tour in the United States. At this time he published *Henry Esmond,* the most artistic and unified of all his novels. Dealing with the times of Queen Anne and written with a fine balance of romance and realism, this novel displayed Thackeray's love for the eighteenth century. The next novel, *The Newcomes,* was a story of domestic life, in which Thackeray's stepfather was the model for the principal character.

On a second tour of America in 1855 he lectured on "The Four Georges." Never wholly satisfied with the profession of literature, he had unsuccessfully applied for positions in the civil service and the diplomatic service, and for appointment as a magistrate in the London courts. In 1857 he was a candidate for Parliament, but was not elected. His last important novel, *The Virginians,* in monthly parts from 1857 to 1859, dealt with English and American life a hundred years before, introducing such historical characters as George Washington and Dr. Samuel Johnson. It was to some extent a sequel to *Henry Esmond.*

In 1860, when the firm of Smith and Elder started the *Cornhill Magazine,* Thackeray became editor at a large salary. He wrote for it a series of monthly essays, "The Roundabout Papers," which were the best familiar essays of the mid-Victorian period. In contrast, the two short novels that he contributed as serials were far below his best work. He resigned from the editorship in April, 1862, because of declining health, but continued to contribute. A new historical novel, *Denis Duval,* was to appear in the magazine, but after writing the first few chapters he died on December 24, 1863.

Thackeray's qualities as a novelist arose largely from the amateur attitude that he maintained. The effort of writing a long novel was always painful to him, and he relieved himself in digressions of informal gossip with his readers. His style, with its easy colloquial flow that was unobtrusively precise, showed the poise and polish of good society. His use of pseudonyms for the first ten years of his authorship was only partly the result of diffidence; he was also influenced by the idea that authorship was not quite a respectable occupation for a gentleman. Even when his novels brought him wealth and fame he tried to use this prestige to obtain for himself some more dignified post in public affairs.

His natural affinity for the eighteenth century made him a good essayist in the tradition of Addison and Steele; both in his *Punch* contributions and in his later *Roundabout Papers* he enjoyed himself to the full. Throughout his novels he digressed frequently into similar essay material. The eighteenth century, however, also gave him the models for his novels, and he was strongly influenced by Fielding. His power of lifelike characterization, as shown in Becky Sharp, Major Pendennis, Colonel Newcome, and scores of others, contrasted with the more exaggerated method of Dickens. His plots were seldom well managed, as the spasmodic writing of monthly installments prevented good integration. In *The Virginians* he became so interested in his reconstruction of Georgian life that he gave up what was originally intended to be the main element of the plot.

Thackeray put a great deal of his own experience into all his novels, even the historical ones. *Vanity Fair* in one sense must be regarded as historical, since the events belonged to the time of Thackeray's birth; and the picture of the Waterloo campaign is a famous specimen of historical fiction. Yet the novel is full of details from Thackeray's life and environment. *Henry Esmond* derives much of its emotional sincerity from its parallelism with Thackeray's own love for Mrs. Brookfield. Being the only one of his novels that he completed before publication, *Esmond* was the most consistent of his major works; even in style it brilliantly gave the illusion of being an actual memoir of the Augustan Age. But this very unity and perfection make it more artificial and less lifelike than the disorganized novels, *Pendennis* and *The Newcomes,* that are full of Thackeray himself and all his kinsfolk.

Aware of his own lack of inventiveness, he was convinced some years before his death that he had exhausted all his material. His novels, however, take their place in the large, varied fabric of his work, all contributing to his distinctive place in literature. As a social satirist he warred endlessly upon the pretensions and the selfishness of society. To establish a rational attitude in opposition to the melodrama and the emotional extremes of his contemporaries in fiction, he emphasized the commonplace details of life and the admixture of petty motives in even the finest personalities. In *Vanity Fair* one cannot help liking Becky Sharp for her courage and resourcefulness, in spite of her dishonesty; nor can one help somewhat despising Amelia Sedley, because all her sweetness and purity are combined not only with stupidity but with selfishness. In that novel he gave a panorama of the lives of people whose virtues and vices were neither heroic nor great.

Unlike many of his contemporaries, he assailed no specific abuses and crusaded for no reforms. He mirrored for his readers the aspects of society that seemed to him false and shabby, but implied that these were inherent in the inadequacy of human nature. Because of his detached and critical point of view, he was a master of the comedy of manners. As a moralist, he praised such virtues as generosity, honesty, and chivalry, but he never preached the doctrine of the reward of virtue.

For that reason superficial readers often accuse him of cynicism. He went out of his way to sneer at many popular ideals and sentiments, and to suggest doubts that disquiet shallow optimism. But this element was intermingled with tender-hearted sympathies and unexpected moral affirmations. The key to the paradoxes of his novels is to be found in his life. A gentle, good-natured boy, he was forced by the hardships of his schooldays to assume a defiant hardness; and throughout his career he was a victim of persistent misfortunes. He learned to look upon the world with tolerant laughter and wry pity. Under his playful manner lurked implications of pathos and disillusionment that disturb the reader's complacency. His satire was without cruelty or anger because in ridiculing the worldliness and egotism and frustration of society he knew with ironic clearness that he was himself a part of it.

H. S. Van Duzer, *A Thackeray Library* (New York, 1919); I. G. Mudge and M. E. Sears, *A Thackeray Dictionary* (New York, 1910); *Works,* ed. A. T. Ritchie (13v, London, 1897-99; Biographical edition); ed. G. Saintsbury (17v, London, 1908; Oxford edition); *Letters and Private Papers,* ed. G. N. Ray (4v, Cambridge, Mass., 1945-46); A. Trollope, *Thackeray* (London, 1879; English Men of Letters); H. Merivale and F. T. Marzials, *Life of William Makepeace Thackeray* (London, 1891; Great Writers); W. D. Howells, "Thackeray," in *My Literary Passions* (New York, 1895); L. Melville, *The Life of William Makepeace Thackeray* (2v, London, 1899; rev. ed., 1v, 1928); C. Whibley, *William Makepeace Thackeray* (Edinburgh, 1903; Modern English Writers); J. G. Wilson, *Thackeray in the United States* (2v, New York, 1904); E. B. Chancellor, *The London of Thackeray* (London, 1923); C. W. Wells, "Thackeray and the Victorian Compromise," *University of California Publications in English,* I (1929). 179-99; M. Elwin, *Thackeray: A Personality* (London, 1932); R. Las Vergnas, *William Makepeace Thackeray: l'homme, le penseur, le romancier* (Paris, 1932); H. S. Gulliver, *Thackeray's Literary Apprenticeship* (Valdosta, Ga., 1934); H. N. Wethered, *On the Art of Thackeray* (London, 1938); J. W. Dodds, *Thackeray: A Critical Portrait* (New York, 1941); L. Stevenson, *The Showman of Vanity Fair* (New York, 1947).

THE BRONTË SISTERS: CHARLOTTE (1816-1855), EMILY (1818-1848), ANNE (1820-1849)

>>>

Charlotte, Emily, and Anne Brontë, the most remarkable family of geniuses in literary history, were rather insignificant to those who did not know them well, but, in Charlotte's words, "genuinely good and truly great" in their way. Their father, the son of an Irish peasant farmer

HAWORTH RECTORY

named Brunty or Prunty, by great economy and determination managed to come to England, take a degree at Cambridge University, and become a clergyman of the Church of England. As part of this ambitious proceeding he changed the spelling of his name, borrowing that of the Italian town which was conferred as a dukedom upon Lord Nelson.

His poverty and lack of influence obliged him to accept

poor and uncomfortable appointments. In 1812 he married Maria Branwell, a Cornish woman; and in 1820, when he was made perpetual curate at Haworth, there were six children: Maria, Elizabeth, Charlotte (born on April 21, 1816), Patrick Branwell, Emily Jane (born on July 30, 1818), and Anne (born on January 17, 1820). The children grew up in Haworth, a lonely little village of gray stone houses on the wild, bleak Yorkshire moors. After the death of Mrs. Brontë in 1821, an unmarried and sedate sister came to look after the household. Patrick Brontë, a brilliant but eccentric man, had taught his children at home, but in 1824 he sent the daughters to a poor boarding school at Cowan Bridge, where, according to Charlotte, they received bad food and unkind treatment. The two oldest girls died, supposedly of consumption, soon after.

During the six years that followed, the remaining children stayed at Haworth. Their father paid little attention to them, and much of their time was spent in reading and in rambling over the moors. The literary talent which all of them had inherited from both their parents showed itself in the "original compositions" that they wrote in a "spidery and microscopic" hand and sewed into books. They invented complete imaginary countries with all details of history and geography, as the settings for fantastic romances in which they identified themselves with the principal characters.

In 1831, when Charlotte was fifteen, she was sent to a school kept by Margaret Wooler at Roe Head, where in spite of her shyness she made a few friends and was fairly happy. In 1835 she returned to Roe Head as a teacher for several months, while Emily and Anne spent a short while there as pupils. At the beginning of the next year, Charlotte and Anne went out to various villages as governesses, while Emily remained at Haworth with her father. Between 1835 and 1842 Charlotte rejected two offers of marriage.

Charlotte

Emily

Ann

THE BRONTË
SISTERS

In 1842, to prepare themselves for setting up a school of their own, Charlotte and Emily went to Brussels to study French and German at the Pension Héger. Within a year both returned home, but Charlotte later went back to Brussels as a teacher of English. She seems to have fallen somewhat in love with M. Héger, the principal of the school, and to have incurred his wife's jealousy. These circumstances combined with her loneliness and her ill success in teaching to make her very unhappy.

Back at Haworth the three sisters wrote poetry and worked on novels. In 1846 under the pseudonyms Currer, Ellis, and Acton Bell they published a volume of poems which received no recognition. Emily's was the only poetry in the collection that had strength and individuality. Meanwhile, Charlotte's first attempt at novel writing, *The Professor,* had been repeatedly rejected; but in October, 1847, her next novel, *Jane Eyre,* was published and caused a sensation. Two months later Emily's novel, *Wuthering Heights,* and Anne's, *Agnes Grey,* came out together in one volume.

Anne's second novel, *The Tenant of Wildfell Hall,* was published in 1848, but that year was filled with tragedy for the Brontës. Their brother Branwell, who had shown promise of ability as a painter, had been a great disappointment; after being dismissed from a post with a railway company he lived for several years on his sisters' earnings, dissipating his energies in drink; and in September, 1848, he died after several attacks of delirium tremens. In December Emily sickened and died, leaving many unpublished poems, including her "last lines," which Matthew Arnold later considered to rival Byron's poems for passionate and vehement expression. When Anne became ill soon after, she was taken to Scarborough near the sea, where she died on May 28, 1849. She, too, left some "last lines," which showed a more subdued tone than Emily's.

Following these tragedies, Charlotte and her father remained in the loneliness of Haworth. Her two later novels, *Shirley* and *Villette,* appeared in 1849 and 1853 respectively. During one of her short trips she made the acquaintance of Mrs. Elizabeth Gaskell, the novelist of reform, at Westmoreland, in 1850. She was eventually persuaded to reveal her identity as author of *Jane Eyre* and to pay a few brief visits to London, where public curiosity had been intense, and where literary people had difficulty in believing that the drab little woman with the blunt, awkward manner was really the author of such an emotionally intense novel.

The last years of her life were happy, and following a courtship of several years she married the Rev. Arthur Bell Nicholls, her father's assistant. After a visit to her husband's home in Ireland she returned to Haworth to die in childbirth on March 31, 1855. She was buried in the village church by the side of Emily and Branwell. Her first novel, *The Professor,* was published posthumously with a note by Nicholls. In 1857 Mrs. Gaskell brought out her biography, presenting a sympathetic and vivid—though occasionally inaccurate—picture of the household. Thackeray, whom Charlotte had long admired, paid tribute to her when he published the fragment of her last story, *Emma,* with a "Last Sketch" in the *Cornhill Magazine* for April, 1860.

All the Brontës had original talent and Emily had the emotional intensity and the love of independence that mark a genius. Of the three sisters, Anne possessed the least fire. Her first novel, *Agnes Grey,* based on her experiences as a governess, is full of biographical details concerning her strange family. *The Tenant of Wildfell Hall* has been called "as interesting a novel as was ever written without any element of greatness;" and there is a fairy-tale quality in its intrigues, although it has touches of strength and even of revolt.

Charlotte's novels have the element of humanity which Emily's work lacks. *Jane Eyre* is a mixture of events from her own life and of wildly melodramatic imagination dating back to the tales of "Angria" that she invented in her childhood. Jane's school life at Lowood is a counterpart of Charlotte's at Cowan Bridge School. But the mystery and horror in the later episodes belong to the Gothic tradition, and the hero, Rochester, is reminiscent of Byronism. Another romantic tendency is the use of nature as a background, sometimes symbolic, for the action. The incoherent plot and unconventional characters have been attacked, but the sense of reality derived from the autobiographic portions is strong enough to sustain the whole story.

In her second novel, *Shirley*, many of the characters could be identified in her family. The heroine, Shirley Keeldar, depicted Emily Brontë; Caroline Helstone, her foil, is Charlotte herself; the Rev. Mr. Helstone is their father. In this novel Charlotte tried to assume the detached manner of Jane Austen, but with little success. She also dragged in some traces of the industrial troubles of the day. *Villette*, her last completed novel, and in some ways her masterpiece, reveals the story of her own experiences and yearnings while at Brussels, though here again the identification of Paul Emanuel with Constantin Héger is confused with melodramatic survivals from her girlhood "make-believe." The psychological study of mental and spiritual perversions is more profound than in her previous novels, and produces memorable scenes and characters, though the plot is still improbable and badly organized.

More than in the work of either of her sisters, the Yorkshire moors find their way into Emily Brontë's one novel, *Wuthering Heights*. It is a mysterious and diabolical story, with the peculiarities of the characters emphasized to the verge of madness. The few normal characters seem insipid and weak by comparison with Heathcliff and Catherine.

The passionate utterances of these two, the supernatural influence of Catherine's spirit, the satanic cruelty and vengefulness of Heathcliff, carry the novel outside of all realism, and only the peace which comes at the end holds it to the human level. The indirect method of narration adds to the strangeness. The book has come to be recognized as a great poetic tragedy rather than what is conventionally regarded as a novel. Its truth is in its symbolism of ultimate human issues, of conflicts "beyond good and evil." As well as being the best poet of the three, Emily was something of a mystic, living in a world of her own. Charlotte, therefore, has a greater significance in the novel, not only because she wrote four novels but also because, in spite of their inconsistencies, their Gothic melodrama, their mid-Victorian prejudices, they dug revealingly into the elemental forces controlling the psychology of passion.

T. J. Wise, *A Bibliography of the Writings in Prose and Verse of the Brontë Family* (London, 1917); *Works,* ed. T. J. Wise and J. A. Symington (15v, Oxford, 1932-38; Shakespeare Head edition); *Legends of Angria,* ed. F. E. Ratchford and W. C. DeVane (New Haven, 1933); *The Complete Poems of Emily Brontë,* ed. C. W. Hatfield (New York, 1941); E. C. Gaskell, *Life of Charlotte Brontë* (London, 1857); T. W. Reid, *Charlotte Brontë, A Monograph* (London, 1877); A. M. F. Robinson, *Emily Brontë* (London, 1883); F. A. Leyland, *The Brontë Family, with Special Reference to Patrick Branwell Brontë* (2v, London, 1886); A. Birrell, *Charlotte Brontë* (London, 1887; Great Writers); W. Wright, *The Brontës in Ireland* (London, 1893); C. K. Shorter, *The Brontës and Their Circle* (London, 1896); *The Brontës: Life and Letters* (2v, London, 1908); E. Dimnet, *Les soeurs Brontë* (Paris, 1910; trans. 1927); M. Sinclair, *The Three Brontës* (London, 1912; rev. ed., 1914); F. Masson, *The Brontës* (London, 1912); K. A. R. Sugden, *A Short History of the Brontës* (Oxford, 1929); C. Simpson, *Emily Brontë* (London, 1929); W. T. Hale, *Anne Brontë, Her Life and Writings* (Bloomington, 1929); R. Langbridge, *Charlotte Brontë, A Psychological Study* (London, 1929); E. and G. Romieu, *La vie des soeurs Brontë* (Paris, 1930; trans. 1931); T. J. Wise and J. A. Symington, *The Brontës: Their Lives,*

Friendships, and Correspondence (4v, Oxford, 1932); E. F. Benson, *Charlotte Brontë* (London, 1932); E. S. Haldane, "The Brontës and Their Biographers," *Nineteenth Century,* CXII (1932). 752-64; E. M. Delafield, *The Brontës: Their Lives Recorded by Their Contemporaries* (London, 1935); I. C. Willis, *The Authorship of "Wuthering Heights,"* (London, 1936); F. Gary, "Charlotte Brontë and George Henry Lewes," *Publications of the Modern Language Association,* LI (1936). 518-42; G. E. Harrison, *Haworth Parsonage: A Study of Wesley and the Brontës* (London, 1937); W. B. White, *The Miracle of Haworth* (London, 1937); E. Kinsley, *Pattern For Genius* (New York, 1939); F. E. Ratchford, *The Brontës' Web of Childhood* (New York, 1941); L. L. Hinkley, *Charlotte and Emily: The Brontës* (New York, 1945); P. Bentley, *The Brontës* (London, 1947).

ELIZABETH CLEGHORN GASKELL (1810-1865)

>>>

Elizabeth Cleghorn Stevenson was born at Chelsea on September 29, 1810, daughter of a government official who had previously been a Unitarian minister and who was a writer of some ability. When the child was a month old her mother died and she was adopted by an aunt living at Knutsford in Cheshire. After spending her girlhood in that quiet little town, Elizabeth Stevenson in 1832 married the Rev. William Gaskell, a Unitarian clergyman and scholar, and went to live in Manchester, where he had his church. In her home she entertained an intellectual circle of friends, but her deepest interest was in caring for the poor and the workers in the Manchester factories.

Having attempted the writing of fiction at her husband's suggestion, Mrs. Gaskell in 1848 published her first novel, *Mary Barton, a Tale of Manchester Life.* Basing the story upon conditions which she had seen in the industrial district during the troubled years from 1837 to 1842, she presented the life of Mary Barton and Jem Wilson with sympathy for those who endured poverty and injustice. The novel offered the ideal of mutual understanding between social and economic classes as the basis for reform.

Mary Barton made so strong an impression upon Dickens that he invited Mrs. Gaskell to be one of the first contributors to his magazine, *Household Words*. In it and

ELIZABETH CLEGHORN GASKELL

its successor, *All the Year Round,* many of her writings were published. In 1853 she brought out her second novel, *Ruth,* which aimed such a blow at the narrow moral judgments of society that it became the object of much controversy. Treating the theme of forgiveness for sin and atonement through the Victorian virtue of renunciation, the story told about an unfortunate milliner's apprentice and her struggle to gain a respectable place in society. In the same year Mrs. Gaskell published the most distinctive of her novels, *Cranford,* a story of a sequestered village of old maids and widows of limited means. Using memories of her childhood home, Knutsford, she combined pathos and tenderness with humor.

Mrs. Gaskell's next novel, *North and South* (1855), was a companion piece to *Mary Barton*. It dealt with similar problems of a society based upon industrialism and labor. In its presentation of both sides of the question and in its development of sympathy, this novel was superior to its predecessor.

Having been a friend of Charlotte Brontë during the final years of Miss Brontë's life, Mrs. Gaskell undertook to write her biography, which appeared in 1857. Both its merits and its defects arose from its being written with the vivid descriptions and emotional energy of a novelist. Some of its information was later proved wrong, but it unforgettably portrayed the tragic Brontë household.

In 1863 she published *Sylvia's Lovers*, a story with more of history and adventure than her previous ones. The next year she collected a volume of shorter tales, and then began work on a long novel of quiet country life, *Wives and Daughters*. When she had only a few more pages of it to write, she died suddenly on November 12, 1865.

Mrs. Gaskell's novels fall evenly into two groups. In one of them, containing *Mary Barton, North and South,* and *Ruth,* were the earnest studies of social problems that her conscience obliged her to write in order to make the public aware of such desperate conditions as she saw in her husband's big-city parish. The other three novels, lacking any purpose of propaganda, were gentle pictures of rural life, with kindly humor and subtle characterization. Her style was the most lucid and natural of all the Victorian novelists.

Works, ed. A. W. Ward (8v, London, 1906; Knutsford edition); *Letters of Mrs. Gaskell and Charles Eliot Norton, 1855-65,* ed. J. Whitehill (London, 1932); E. A. Chadwick, *Mrs. Gaskell, Haunts, Homes, and Stories* (London, 1910); L. Melville, "The Centenary of Mrs. Gaskell," *Nineteenth Century,* LXVIII (1910). 467-82; K. L. Montgomery, "Mrs. Gaskell," *Fortnightly Review,* XCIV (1910). 450-63; A. K. Tuell, "Mrs. Gaskell," *Contemporary Review,* C (1911). 681-92; G. D. Sanders, *Elizabeth Gaskell* (New Haven, 1929); A. S. Whitfield, *Mrs. Gaskell, Her Life and Work* (London, 1929); G. A. Payne, *Mrs. Gaskell, a Brief Biography* (Manchester, 1929); E. Haldane, *Mrs. Gaskell and Her Friends* (London, 1931).

CHARLES KINGSLEY (1819-1875)

>>

Convincing proof of the respectability and influence that the novel attained in the mid-Victorian period was its adoption as a medium of expression by prominent churchmen. Most noteworthy of these was Charles Kingsley, who was born at Holne Vicarage near Dartmouth in Devon-

CHARLES KINGSLEY

shire on June 12, 1819. As the son of a country clergyman, he was destined for the same profession, and was educated at King's College, London, and Magdalene College, Cambridge. In 1842, after his graduation from Cambridge with high honors, he took orders in the Church of England and became rector of Eversley in Hampshire.

As a clergyman he was one of the initiators of the Broad Church Movement; and in advocating "muscular Christianity" he emphasized the value of athletics and physical energy as an element in moral living. In 1854, with F. D. Maurice, Julius Hare, and John Ruskin, he established the Workingmen's College in London. He shared with these men the idea that they called "Christian Socialism," namely, that the duty of the Church was to improve the conditions of the working classes not only by giving them Christian ideals but by bettering their material comfort as well. To gain attention for these views Kingsley preached sermons and printed pamphlets (using the pen-name "Parson Lot") that aroused angry controversy. A high-spirited enthusiast, he had adopted his ideals by emotional rather than rational processes, and was not well equipped to defend himself in the arguments that ensued. He was a sincere believer in the traditions of English patriotism, English Protestantism, and the code of the English gentleman.

From 1860 to 1869 he was Professor of Modern History at Cambridge, but his scholarly qualifications proved rather inadequate. Being a firm opponent of the High Church Movement, he made an injudicious statement about Newman in a magazine article which resulted in Newman's writing of the *Apologia Pro Vita Sua*. Ill-health and the loss of his bold self-confidence made Kingsley withdraw gradually from public affairs. At the time of his death on January 23, 1875, he was still rector at Eversley and held a canonry in the chapter of Westminster.

Kingsley had a versatile literary talent. His first book was a collection of poems, and in 1858 he published another containing "Andromeda," his remarkably successful poem in hexameters. Several of his lyrics retain their popularity.

When he began to write pamphlets he was strongly under the influence of Carlyle, both in style and thought, and more than any other author he echoed Carlyle's peculiar mannerisms. These survived in a quaint and playful form in Kingsley's allegorical fairy-tale, *The Water Babies* (1863). His other works for children were *The Heroes* (a retelling of Greek legends) and two books intended to teach elementary science, *Glaucus* and *Madam How and Lady Why*. These popularizations were praised by Darwin and Huxley.

In the writing of fiction Kingsley strangely paralleled Mrs. Gaskell, whose novels were synchronous with his between 1848 and 1866. Each wrote six novels that consisted of three propaganda stories on social problems and three on other subjects. Kingsley's first was *Yeast* (1848) a story reflecting the diverse attitudes of youth toward questions of religion and social organization. The plan of the novel has been likened to that of a medieval morality, with the characters representing various aspects of the times; Lancelot Smith, for example, who is the author's spokesman, typified religious doubt. Kingsley expressed his distrust of the Neo-Catholic movement through a caricature of Newman in the person of a newly-converted Catholic. The book also dwelt upon the miserable plight of agricultural laborers following upon the recent repeal of the corn laws. After appearing serially in *Fraser's Magazine,* the novel was not republished in volume form until 1851.

Alton Locke, Tailor and Poet, published in 1850, was another novel of purpose, an attack upon the terrible conditions of the sweated industries. The action centered in the Chartist crisis of 1848. Combining the vivid description of Dickens with some of the philosophy of Carlyle, Kingsley produced a novel of indubitable power. These two books, together with his pamphlets and sermons, gained him a reputation as a dangerous radical who was regarded as a disgrace to his religious calling.

In 1857 he published his third social novel, *Two Years Ago,* a study of conditions during the Crimean War. In its emphasis upon public health and sanitation it reflected the work of Florence Nightingale, and American abolitionism was also introduced. As usual, the High Church party and the dissenters appeared as objects of attack.

Kingsley's three other novels are classified as historical, although they often echo his contemporary prejudices. *Hypatia* (1853), which insisted upon this fact by its subtitle, "New Foes with an Old Face," showed his hatred of Catholicism. Dealing with the conflict of paganism and Christianity in fifth-century Alexandria, it included an attack on powerful politician-churchmen, resembling such figures as Manning in his own day. *Westward Ho!* (1855)

glorified the nobility of the English in their struggles against Spain in the days of Elizabeth, the victory of England symbolizing the triumph of Protestantism. For its exciting action and its pictures of the ocean and the Caribbean area, as well as its presentation of the spirit of the English Renaissance, it is not excelled.

Kingsley's final novel was *Hereward the Wake, "Last of the English,"* the story of an outlaw of the fen country who resented the conquests of William the Conqueror. A symptom of revived interest in the pre-Norman period, it was rather successful in imitating the Anglo-Saxon diction and style.

Since Kingsley was occupied with his duties as a clergyman and as an instructor, his novels were often hastily written. The general tone of his work was serious; in fact, it approached fanaticism, especially in matters of religion and of social injustice. His ideas were sometimes inconsistent. In his ability to present striking situations lay his primary claim as a literary artist. The intensity of personal bias in his books, while it diminishes their greatness, is a revelation of some main currents of conflict in mid-Victorian thought.

M. L. Parrish and B. K. Maun, *Charles Kingsley and Thomas Hughes: First Editions at Dormy House, N. J.* (London, 1936); *Works* (29v, London, 1888-90); F. E. Kingsley, *Charles Kingsley: His Letters and Memories of His Life* (2v, London, 1877); M. Kaufman, *Charles Kingsley, Christian Socialist and Social Reformer* (London, 1892); C. W. Stubbs, *Charles Kingsley and the Christian Socialist Movement* (London, 1899); W. F. Lord, "The Kingsleys," in *The Mirror of the Century* (London, 1906); S. T. Williams, "*Yeast*: A Victorian Heresy," *North American Review*, CCXII (1920). 697-704; W. H. Brown, *Charles Kingsley: The Work and Influence of Parson Lot* (London, 1924); S. E. Baldwin, *Charles Kingsley* (Ithaca, 1934); M. F. Thorp, *Charles Kingsley, 1819-75* (Princeton, 1937); M. W. Hanawalt, "Charles Kingsley and Science," *Studies in Philology*, XXXIV (1937). 589-611; G. Kendall, *Charles Kingsley and His Ideas* (London, 1947).

CHARLES READE (1814-1884)

>>

One of the most sensational of Victorian novelists, Charles Reade combined a strong sense of drama with a preference for controversial subject-matter. Through his powers of description and his documented presentation of social problems, he played an important part in the reform program. Born at Ipsden House, in Oxfordshire, on June 8, 1814, he was the son of a country squire of strong Tory views. He received his degree from Magdalen College, Oxford, in 1835, and was appointed a fellow of the college. He later read law in London, being called to the Bar in 1843. Finding literature more attractive than law, however, he never practiced his legal profession. Although he spent much of his time in London, he became Dean of Arts and Vice-president of his Oxford college. Somewhat to the surprise of his friends, he retained his fellowship until the end of his life, even though this prevented him from contracting a legal marriage.

Reade first became known as a dramatist, writing numerous plays alone or in collaboration. His earliest success was a comedy, *Masks and Faces* (1852), written with Tom Taylor. At the suggestion of Mrs. Seymour, an actress who was his constant companion, he made the play into a short novel, *Peg Woffington*. The central character was a famous actress of the eighteenth century. In 1853 another short novel, *Christie Johnstone,* depicted the life of Scottish fisher folk.

The stage being his primary interest, his strong feeling for drama inevitably influenced his novels. Like Dickens, he believed that dramatic situations and sensational events were the proper material for fiction and he was convinced that unusual occurrences in real life were suitable sources.

In preparation for prison scenes in his first novel of purpose—and his first popular success—*It Is Never Too Late to Mend,* he visited the jails at Durham, Oxford, and Reading. A topical element was added to the plot by exciting episodes in the Australian gold-fields, partly adapted from one of Reade's recent plays. When the novel appeared in 1856 it not only established Reade's reputation but also eventually brought about a reform in English prison discipline.

During the next five years he published five minor novels, full of details that showed a journalistic flair. He had developed a method of composing his fiction with the aid of immense files of clippings from current newspapers. His intention was to give realism to his stories, but actually the items that attracted his notice were so exceptional that they were seldom plausible when incorporated into his plots. He also adopted a variety of extreme devices for vividness and emphasis—one-sentence paragraphs, whole passages in capital letters, italics, or tiny type, even diagrams interspersed in his text.

Abruptly turning his attention away from the contemporary scene, he wrote a long historical novel that has come to be considered his masterpiece. Published in 1861, *The Cloister and the Hearth* told the story of Gerard and Margaret, the parents of Erasmus, and presented a panorama of the changes wrought by the new learning of the Renaissance all over Europe. It has been classified with George Eliot's *Romola,* both novels being based upon research in the same period; but Reade's book has much less psychological analysis and much more action and color. Reade succeeded in making his novel live with the spirit of the age—its learning, its innovations, and its gusto.

Reade did not agree with the high estimation that was accorded *The Cloister and the Hearth.* Instead of going on with historical fiction, he returned with new vigor to the novel of social purpose. In 1863 appeared *Hard Cash,* an attack upon the abuse of power by the Commissioners of Lunacy, who could put into an asylum anyone declared insane by interested parties. Like his previous reform novel, this one was based upon investigation of real conditions. *Foul Play,* which came out in 1869, attacked the practice of over-loading and over-insuring ships. *Put Yourself In His Place,* published in the following year, was based upon sensational scenes of labor outbreaks described in the newspapers. In his concern over the labor problem, Reade joined Dickens, Kingsley, and Mrs. Gaskell, but his point of view was different from theirs. In the experiences of his hero, a worker who insisted upon being union-free, Reade showed the fate of an independent laborer at the hands of union leaders. Attacking the autocracy and cruelty of organized labor, he recommended more forceful legislation to control its activities. In its dramatic conflict and its creation of violent sympathies, this story was probably the greatest of his novels of purpose.

His own favorite among his novels was *Griffith Gaunt* (1866), a psychological study with a plot involving bigamy. This and *A Terrible Temptation* (1877) shocked many contemporaries by the outspokenness with which sex and doubtful moral situations were discussed. As well as these and other novels, he continued to write numerous plays, and to spend his own money in producing them when professional managers refused to do so. At last in 1879 he achieved a stage success with *Drink,* a sensational play based on Zola's novel *L'Assommoir.*

An opinionated and quarrelsome man, Reade not only conducted his private life unconventionally but also became involved in disputes and lawsuits, in which his behavior was more courageous than wise. After spending his last years in loneliness and ill-health, he died in London on April 11, 1884.

With fullest use of conflict and suspense Reade was always able to hold a reader's attention and to arouse strong sympathy through his stories. He made his ideas convincing by his methodical arrangement of significant details, a trait derived from his legal training. He was always ready and eager to produce the actual evidence underlying his fictitious episodes. Through the series of his novels he came vigorously to grips with many grievances of the contemporary social system—prison administration, factory conditions, labor unions, private insane asylums, dangerous shipping conditions. His picture of the disregard for the lives of sailors, as given in *Foul Play,* stirred up the public feeling that enabled Samuel Plimsoll to push his Merchant Shipping Act through Parliament six years later. Reade turned his attention to feminism in *A Woman Hater* (1877), in which a woman physician was a prominent character. Even *The Cloister and the Hearth* had an indirect purpose of propaganda: in condemning the celibacy of the clergy it revealed Reade's own unhappiness under the rule of celibacy that was still enforced in Oxford fellowships.

His conscientious research was not successful in making his novels realistic for the modern reader because he overcrowded them with violent excitement. In spite of his attacks on specific abuses he was so enthusiastic about the power and drama of the age in which he lived that he struggled breathlessly to cram it between the covers of his books.

Works (17v, London, 1895; uniform library edition); C. L. and C. Reade, *Charles Reade: Dramatist, Novelist, Journalist* (2v, London, 1887); J. Coleman, *Charles Reade As I Knew Him* (London, 1903); E. G. Sutcliffe, "Charles Reade's Notebooks," *Studies in Philology,* xxvii (1930). 64-109; M. Elwin, *Charles Reade, A Biography* (London, 1931); A. M. Turner, *The Making of "The Cloister and the Hearth,"* (Chicago, 1938); L. Rives, *Charles Reade: sa vie, ses romans* (Toulouse, 1940); E. G. Sutcliffe, "Psychological Presentation in Reade's Novels," *Studies in Phil-*

ology, XXXVIII (1941). 521-42; "Fact, Realism, and Morality in Reade's Fiction," *Studies in Philology,* XLI (1944). 582-98; L. F. Haines, "Reade, Mill, and Zola," *Studies in Philology,* XL (1943). 463-80; W. Burns, "More Reade Notebooks," *Studies in Philology,* XLII (1945). 824-42.

WILKIE COLLINS (1824-1889)
>>>

William Wilkie Collins, the son of a famous landscape painter, was born in London on January 8, 1824. He was educated at a private school and lived in Italy with his parents between the ages of twelve and fifteen. Although he became a skilful painter he never regarded this as more than a hobby, and for a career in life he first worked for a time in a tea-importing firm and then studied law and was called to the bar. Like many other authors of his century, however, he immediately gave up the law in order to become an author.

His first book was a biography of his father, and in 1850 he brought out an historical novel which was obviously modeled upon those of Bulwer-Lytton. In 1854 he became a friend of Dickens and began to contribute to *Household Words,* in which several of his novels appeared as serials. Beginning with *After Dark* (1856) he wrote a group of novels that became immensely popular and served as the model for the "mystery novels" that are numerous at the present time. The best known of Collins's novels were *The Dead Secret* (1857), *The Woman in White* (1860), *No Name* (1862), *Armadale* (1866), and *The Moonstone* (1868). During the remaining twenty years of his life his novels deteriorated, partly because he tried to introduce social problems, in the manner of Dickens and Reade, and was not successful in combining this element with his own particular brand of melodrama.

Collins lived an irregular and unconventional life, which narrowed his circle of friends. Seeking relief from a painful eye malady, he became addicted to laudanum, which probably contributed the weird and Poe-like quality in his imagination. In 1873 he toured the United States, giving readings from his works. His death occurred in London on September 23, 1889.

Collins was the first novelist who gave primary importance to ingenious plot structure. By complex clues and powerful suspense he held the reader's attention from the first page to the last. In his best stories he aroused the feeling of excitement not so much by violent action as by imaginative suggestion, especially in the use of terrifying atmosphere. Although an element of the supernatural was occasionally introduced, he produced most of his shudders by the interplay of crime and evil characters. To increase the plausibility of his stories he made good use of the "documentary" method, fitting together a series of statements by various people connected with the case.

His novels had an immediate effect upon those of Dickens, who borrowed some of Collins's devices for his later works. On the other hand, Collins was a follower of Dickens in his methods of characterization and created a number of vivid personalities, especially Count Fosco, the fat, courtly villain of *The Woman in White*.

In Collins's own opinion, *The Woman in White* was his best work. It contained memorable characters, and the suspense and horror were admirably sustained. Its rival in popular fame is *The Moonstone*, from which have been derived many later stories of a mysterious jewel stolen from an Oriental temple and pursued by sinister natives.

By his attention to the structural aspect of the novel, Collins introduced the mechanical or "formula" method that has made the modern mystery story a kind of intellectual contest between author and reader.

E. Von Wolzogen, *Wilkie Collins: ein biographisch-kritischer Versuch* (Leipzig, 1885); T. S. Eliot, "Wilkie Collins and Dickens," in *Selected Essays, 1917-32* (London, 1932); W. de la Mare, "The Early Novels of Wilkie Collins," in *The Eighteen-Sixties* (Cambridge, 1932); C. K. Hyder, "Wilkie Collins and *The Woman in White*," *Publications of the Modern Language Association*, LIV (1939). 297-303.

ANTHONY TROLLOPE (1815-1882)

>>

Anthony Trollope's fame as a novelist has in recent years emerged strongly from an eclipse that obscured it during the decades following his death. Because he gave a precise and almost impersonal picture of his time, he appeals to some modern readers more than the writers who used their novels as vehicles for their personal opinions or their social crusades.

ANTHONY TROLLOPE

Born in London on April 24, 1815, he suffered in his boyhood from the vagaries of his clever but eccentric parents. His father, an unsuccessful lawyer and amateur author, sent his wife and three of their children to the United States in 1828 to establish a fashionable shop in the frontier city of Cincinnati. Mr. Trollope followed later with another son, but Anthony was left at school in England. When the venture failed, and the family returned penniless from America, Mrs. Trollope at the age of fifty undertook their support by authorship, and during the remaining years of her life she was a prolific and successful novelist.

Anthony had been sent to good schools, but the family difficulties caused him to be shifted back and forth between Winchester and Harrow, where as a shabbily-dressed day-boy he was ridiculed by masters and pupils alike. In 1834 he became a clerk in the general post-office in London, where he served for seven years, awkward, self-conscious, and unhappy. He was always short of money, he involved himself in foolish love-affairs, and he felt overshadowed by his mother's literary fame. When he was transferred in 1841 to a remote assignment in Ireland, a larger income and greater responsibility suddenly developed the latent resources of his character. He became a good fox-hunter and a popular member of the community, and in 1844 he married.

He was past thirty before he made any effort to become a writer. Between 1847 and 1850 he published three novels, two of them being rather grim pictures of Irish life and the third a French historical romance. As all three were unsuccessful, he waited for some time before his next attempt. In 1851 he was appointed to supervise a reform of the letter-carrier system in southwestern England, and during his visit to Salisbury he was struck with the idea of writing a novel about a cathedral town. *The Warden*, published in 1855, was successful enough to encourage him to continue, and he carried the same characters into his next book, *Barchester Towers*, which became famous. Having created his imaginary city of Barchester and county of Barsetshire with careful attention to geographical detail, he retained the same setting through several further novels—*Doctor Thorne* (1858), *Framley Parsonage* (1861), *The Small House at Allington* (1864), and *The Last Chronicle of Barset* (1867). His characterization grew with each novel of the series, as he showed how the characters mellowed or hardened with the passing of the years. It was his custom to draw characters of ordinary types and introduce them to the reader in such a manner that the acquaintance grows as naturally as it would in real life.

He had developed systematic methods of work that enabled him to maintain a vast output of fiction while continuing to handle his increasingly important official duties. During the period of the Barsetshire series he also wrote a number of other novels. *The Three Clerks* (1858) and *Orley Farm* (1862) contained some recollections of his depressed youth. Another novel of this period, *Can You Forgive Her?* (1864), marked the beginning of a political series that carried its group of characters through five further novels in the next sixteen years: *Phineas Finn, The Irish Member* (1869), *The Eustace Diamonds* (1873), *Phineas Redux* (1874), *The Prime Minister* (1876), and *The Duke's Children* (1880). The character of Plantagenet Palliser, as developed through this series, is perhaps the greatest example of Trollope's steady, convincing method of creating personality.

Although his headquarters remained in Ireland until 1859, when he was transferred to London, he was sent on several important official tours, which resulted in travel books. In 1858 he went to Egypt to make a postal treaty with the Pasha, and upon his return he was sent to inspect the postal system in the West Indies. A nine months' visit to the United States was described in *North America,* published in 1862. He also wrote an account of his travels to Australia and South Africa after his retirement from the postal service in 1866.

Concurrently with the political novels he wrote several dealing with the life of the country gentleman, including *He Knew He Was Right, The Belton Estate, The Claverings, The Vicar of Bulhampton, The Way We Live Now,* and *Is He Popenjoy?* In all, in thirty-five years he published forty-seven novels, four volumes of short stories, and a number of travel books, biographies, and so on. During more than half this time, he held his responsible government position. Yet he always had time for fox-hunting, whist-playing, and social engagements. A large, blunt, loud-voiced man, he regarded his authorship as a business and made no pretensions to artistic temperament. With customary honesty and common sense he wrote an autobiography that presented his own character and career as impartially as he depicted the characters in his novels. After his death, which occurred on December 6, 1882, the publication of this book was a heavy blow to his reputation. The statistics on his speed of production, his number of words per hour and hours per day, and the exact totals of his profits on every book, made people feel that he was an uninspired journeyman of letters. More recently, however, the *Autobiography* itself has taken its place as one of his finest works.

The appeal of Trollope's novels resides in their complete naturalness. Apparently without any literary artifice the lives of ordinary people are revealed with slow accumulation of humor and pathos. Although Trollope does not seem to attempt psychological analysis, the characters become familiar and comprehensible. As a social historian of the upper and middle classes, with a peculiar ability to make the commonplace interesting, he gives a more complete and dependable picture of Victorian England than any other author.

M. Sadleir, *Trollope: A Bibliography* (London, 1928); *Works,* ed. M. Sadleir (14v, Oxford, 1929; Shakespeare Head edition [Barsetshire series only]); (?v, London, 1948- ; Oxford Illustrated edition); *Autobiography,* ed. B. A. Booth (Berkeley, 1947); *Correspondence,* ed. B. A. Booth (London, 1949); H. James, "Anthony Trollope," in *Partial Portraits* (London, 1888); L. Stephen, "Anthony Trollope," in *Studies of a Biographer,* IV (London, 1902); J. Bryce, "Anthony Trollope," in *Studies in Contemporary*

Biography (London, 1903); T. H. S. Escott, *Anthony Trollope: His Work, Associates, and Literary Originals* (London, 1913); A. E. Newton, "A Great Victorian," in *Amenities of Book Collecting* (New York, 1918); G. Saintsbury, "Trollope Revisited," *Essays and Studies by Members of the English Association,* VI (1920); S. V. Nichols, *The Significance of Trollope* (New York, 1925); G. Bradford, "Anthony Trollope," in *A Naturalist of Souls* (New York, 1926); H. Walpole, *Anthony Trollope* (London, 1928; English Men of Letters); A. Waugh, "Trollope After Sixty Years," *Fortnightly Review,* CXXXII (1932). 712-24; M. Sadleir, *Trollope: A Commentary* (London, 1927; rev. ed., 1945); J. H. Wildman, *Anthony Trollope's England* (Providence, 1940); R. W. Chapman, "The Text of Trollope's Novels," *Review of English Studies,* XVII (1941). 322-31; L. P. and R. P. Stebbins, *The Trollopes: The Chronicle of a Writing Family* (New York, 1945); C. B. Tinker, "Trollope," *Yale Review,* XXXVI (1947). 424-34. See also *The Trollopian* (quarterly, 1945-   ).

GEORGE ELIOT (MARY ANN EVANS) (1819-1880)

>>>

The most distinguished woman novelist of the Victorian age published all her fiction under a masculine pseudonym. Mary Ann Evans was born at Arbury Farm near Nuneaton in Warwickshire on November 22, 1819. Her father was an estate-agent for a rich landowner, and by going with him on his business drives the little girl became familiar with the beautiful countryside and the quaint rural characters. The family was earnestly Methodist, and when Mary Ann was at a boarding school in Nuneaton she first became personally conscious of religious zeal, a feeling which was deepened when she was sent at thirteen to a school in Coventry.

After the death of her mother in 1836 and of her sister soon after, Mary Ann assumed the full management of the household. In spite of her many duties, she took lessons in Italian, German, Latin, and Greek, as well as reading omnivorously, mostly in history and philosophy. She also became a good pianist.

When her father retired, turning his position over to his son, he and Mary Ann moved to Coventry. Her ardent belief in evangelical religion was rapidly weakened through new friendships with liberal intellectuals. In 1842 she resolved to cease church attendance and to quit the religion of her girlhood. A brief period of breach between her and her father resulted, but in his recurrent illnesses she attended him until his death in 1849.

GEORGE ELIOT

She applied herself for two years to a translation from the German of David Strauss's *Life of Jesus,* a rationalistic work that was causing violent argument; and some of her friends financed its publication in 1846. After her father's death friends took her abroad to recuperate from the strain of nursing him; she spent eight months at Geneva, chiefly in studying physics. Upon returning to England she became sub-editor of the *Westminster Review,* and made the acquaintance of such prominent writers as Carlyle, Mill, Froude, Spencer, and Harriet Martineau. In 1853 she brought out a translation of Feuerbach's *Essence of Christianity,* which defined God as a projection of humanity's inner hopes and desires. This was the only book that she published under her own name.

In mid-Victorian England it required exceptional courage for a young woman to be a professional writer and to live alone on her own resources; still more to be a free-thinker uttering advanced rationalistic views. Miss Evans was plain in appearance and often ill; but her determination never weakened, and people who made her acquaintance became deeply attached to her.

Among the radical writers whom she met in London was George Henry Lewes, a man no handsomer than she was, whose wife had deserted him in circumstances that precluded divorce. Finding that their tastes were congenial, Miss Evans agreed to live with him and bring up his three sons. Lewes proved to be a great help to her as a critic, encourager, and business manager. For a short time they lived in Germany, where Lewes was writing an important biography of Goethe, but in 1855 they settled in London.

Ostracised by conventional society, Miss Evans worked on a translation of Spinoza's *Ethics* and wrote reviews for periodicals. In 1857 she contributed a story, "The Sad Fortunes of the Reverend Amos Barton," to *Blackwood's Magazine*. It was followed by two others, and the three were published in 1858 as a volume entitled *Scenes From Clerical Life,* by George Eliot.

Her talent had matured slowly; she was already forty before her career in fiction began. Emily Brontë, only sixteen months her senior, had been dead for ten years. She went on to write a long novel, *Adam Bede* (1859), based on a story that had been told her by her aunt, a Methodist preacher. Several family portraits were included. The next year it was followed by *The Mill on the Floss,* of which a great deal of the charm lay in the autobiographical account of the childhood of Maggie and Tom Tulliver, the counterparts of Mary Ann Evans herself and her brother Isaac. The disaster at the end was not so satisfactory. *Silas Marner,* a shorter and more idyllic novel, was published in 1861.

In these books she depicted the Warwickshire life that

she knew well. Though a serious person herself, she included a pleasant vein of rustic humor. As the identity of "George Eliot" gradually became known, however, she determined to depart from familiar settings and reminiscent material. The summer of 1860 was spent in Italy to obtain realistic background for an historical novel of the Renaissance. *Romola,* a story of Florence in the time of Savonarola, brought her the unheard-of sum of seven thousand pounds. Thorough in its historical data and powerful in its psychological study, it lacked the naturalness of her previous books.

In *Felix Holt, the Radical* (1866) she turned to politics and dealt with the turbulent Reform election of 1832. Unlike her usual plots, which grew out of the characters, this one was rather artificially constructed. *Middlemarch* (1872), a very long novel, was a complex narrative of several interwoven lives. Described as "A Study of Provincial Life," it was an attempt to depict the conditions of a whole community, such as she had observed in her girlhood in Coventry. While lacking the humor and the emotion of her early novels, it was her greatest work so far as intellectual power was concerned. Her last novel was *Daniel Deronda,* a sympathetic study of the Jewish problem and a rather melodramatic view of gambling.

In November, 1878, she was prostrated with grief by the death of Lewes. So completely had she depended upon him that she had to find someone to take his place; a year and a half later she married a man young enough to be her son, John Walter Cross, a banker from New York. He adored her as sincerely as Lewes had done, but her health was failing. That winter she caught a chill at a concert, and died on December 22, 1880.

As a novelist, George Eliot has been called a moralist first and an artist second. Influenced by the two greatest events of her life, her forsaking of formal Christianity and her union with Lewes, she was determined to become a "moral scientist," one who would trace laws and principles that could be applied to a person's moral life just as formulae can be applied in an exact science. Particularly in her later novels, she taught through individual cases: Tito Melema's deterioration in *Romola,* Lydgate's failure to fulfil his own potentialities in *Middlemarch,* Gwendolyn Harleth's repentance in *Daniel Deronda.* She proclaimed a creed of duty before joy.

As to the technique of the novel, she introduced basic innovations. Her predecessors had written novels either to entertain, or to propagate their personal views, or both. George Eliot's purpose was to offer a serious interpretation of life. She approached fiction in the spirit of the scientist, using it as a procedure for analysis and understanding. Depicting the action of her characters as arising out of their personalities, she persistently probed their motives. Like Browning, she wanted to strip off the conventional labels of "virtue" and "vice" and arrive at the inner truth of each individual.

P. H. Muir, "A Bibliography of the First Editions of Books by George Eliot," *Bookman's Journal,* ser. 3, xv, xvi supps. (1927-28); *Works* (12v, Edinburgh, 1901-03; Warwick edition); I. G. Mudge and M. E. Sears, *A George Eliot Dictionary* (New York, 1924); J. W. Cross, *George Eliot's Life, As Related in her Letters and Journals* (3v, London, 1885); *Letters of George Eliot to Elma Stuart, 1872-80,* ed. R. Stuart (London, 1909); A. Paterson, *George Eliot's Family Life and Letters* (London, 1928); G. W. Cooke, *George Eliot: A Critical Study* (Boston, 1883); M. Blind, *George Eliot* (London, 1883; rev. ed., 1904); O. Browning, *George Eliot* (London, 1890; Great Writers); L. Stephen, *George Eliot* (London, 1902; English Men of Letters); W. Mottram, *The Story of George Eliot in Relation to "Adam Bede"* (London, 1906); C. S. Olcott, *George Eliot: Scenes and People in Her Novels* (New York, 1910); C. Gardner, *The Inner Life of George Eliot* (London, 1912); M. H. Deakin, *The Early Life of George Eliot* (Manchester, 1913); E. A. Parry, "The Humour of George Eliot," *Fortnightly Review,*

CXII (1919). 883-95; E. S. Haldane, *George Eliot and Her Times* (London, 1927); J. L. May, *George Eliot: A Study* (London, 1930); J. Macy, "George Eliot, Victorian Queen," *Bookman*, LXXV (1932). 16-25; P. Bourl'honne, *George Eliot: essai de biographie intellectuelle et morale* (Paris, 1933); A. T. Kitchel, *George Lewes and George Eliot* (New York, 1933); M. Parlett, "The Influence of Contemporary Criticism on George Eliot," *Studies in Philology*, XXX (1933). 103-32; B. C. Williams, *George Eliot, A Biography* (New York, 1936); G. S. Haight, *George Eliot and John Chapman* (New Haven, 1940); W. F. Wright, "George Eliot As Industrial Reformer," *Publications of the Modern Language Association*, LVI (1941). 1107-15; G. Bullitt, *George Eliot* (London, 1947); F. R. Leavis, "George Eliot," in *The Great Tradition* (London, 1948).

GEORGE MEREDITH (1828-1909)

>>

George Meredith, poet and novelist, was born at Portsmouth on February 12, 1828. Being somewhat embarrassed by the fact that his father and grandfather had been tailors and that the once-prosperous business had ended in bankruptcy, Meredith never supplied much information about his family, except to emphasize that both his parents were of Celtic descent. His mother died when he was three, and he became a ward in chancery. At fourteen he was sent to a Moravian school at Neuwied on the Rhine, where he stayed for more than a year and absorbed the German influence chiefly through poetry and music. After returning to London, he worked for a while in a solicitor's office, but soon turned to literature for a living. He contributed poems to magazines and worked on the staff of various newspapers. Handsome, red-headed, and athletic, he gained a reputation for ironic wit. He became intimate with the family of the satirical novelist, Thomas Love Peacock, whose daughter, a widow nine years older than himself, he married when he was twenty-one.

A small volume of his poems was published in 1851, and was favorably reviewed by Charles Kingsley. One of the poems, "Love in the Valley," was warmly praised by Tennyson. Four years later came his first prose work, *The Shaving of Shagpat*. By this time he was a leading figure in a group of young radicals and positivists that included John Morley and Frederic Harrison; and he was also an intimate friend of Rossetti and Swinburne at the height of their Pre-Raphaelite activities, sharing a house with them for a brief while.

GEORGE MEREDITH

In 1858 Meredith was deserted by his wife, who died three years later, and in 1864 he married Marie Vulliamy. Although he had become a reader for the publishing house of Chapman & Hall in 1860, he found time to write a dozen novels in the next thirty-five years, as well as four volumes of poetry. During the Austro-Italian War he acted as a special correspondent for the *Morning Post*, obtaining material which he used in several novels. His fiction never became widely popular, being too allusive in style and intellectual in attitude, but he gradually gained a reputation even among people who did not read his work. One of his later novels, *Diana of the Crossways*, attracted notice not so much for its literary qualities as for the rumor that it reproduced a famous political scandal. After the death of his second wife in 1885 (subject of his poem "A Faith on Trial") he lived quietly at Flint Cottage, in Surrey, afflicted with growing deafness and later with paralysis. He received the Order of Merit in 1905 and died on May 18, 1909.

Meredith is now recognized as sharing with Hardy the preëminent place in English fiction in the seventies and eighties; and like Hardy he has a secure second fame as a poet of philosophical depth. His first two works of fiction were fantasies—*The Shaving of Shagpat,* in the style of *The Arabian Nights,* and *Farina,* a medieval German legend. Then in 1859 (a year of many famous books) he published his first novel, which is still probably his best-known one, *The Ordeal of Richard Feverel.* A story of the conflict between the desires of a wilful young man and the rigid educational system of his strict father, it was the first of Meredith's studies of human temperament and individual adjustment. The emotional crises of young love, told with lavish poetic feeling, prevailed so strongly that many years later Meredith revised the novel and eliminated some of the comic elements as inappropriate.

In three other novels he showed the struggle of gifted youth to gain maturity: *Evan Harrington* (1861), which revealed his unhappiness over his shopkeeping parentage and his grudge against the prosperous aunts who had failed to help him in his boyhood; *Emilia in England* (1864), later re-named *Sandra Belloni;* and a later work, *The Adventures of Harry Richmond* (1871), a more adventurous and romantic story. *Vittoria* (1866) had the same heroine as *Emilia in England,* an unaffected Italian opera singer, and told of her experiences in Italy during the revolution of 1848. Unlike his previous novels, *Rhoda Fleming* dealt with a humbler stratum of society in depicting a girl's seduction.

Contemporary politics figured largely in *Beauchamp's Career* (1876), the story of a young man who in the eyes of a conventional world makes a failure of his life because of his earnestness. *The Egoist,* perhaps the most skilfully written of Meredith's works, revealed with unsparing detail the inner selfishness and conceit of a distinguished gentleman. The real life story of Ferdinand Lassalle, a brilliant German Socialist, provided the material for *The Tragic Comedians* (1880).

Meredith's last four novels were all chiefly concerned with the defence of women: *Diana of the Crossways, One of Our Conquerors, Lord Ormont and His Aminta,* and *The Amazing Marriage.* Throughout these stories he depicted the women as being on an equal intellectual plane with men—sometimes apparently superior; and when the heroines were compromised, it was through the pride and selfishness of masculine despotism.

Meredith has been regarded as "eccentric." His isolation came from his extreme intellectualism and detached psychological analysis. He was not primarily concerned with plot, but with his characters as types of temperament. In his important essay, *On the Idea of Comedy and the Uses of the Comic Spirit,* he explained that his novels represent the Comic Spirit or pure intelligence in conflict with prejudice, sham, and stupidity. His attacks upon sentimentalism and his tribute to women are examples of this intelligence in action.

Much of the difficulty of reading Meredith's novels is due to the lack of formal plot-structure, for his method was not to outline a novel but to let himself be led by his group of characters and their states of mind in a given situation. Confining himself almost wholly to the most cultivated and sophisticated level of modern society, he sought to reproduce the subtle shades of their thinking and the complexities of their behavior. The emotional reactions of such people, controlled by inherited standards of etiquette, are at the opposite extreme from the directness of action and feeling in the characters of such a novelist as Hardy. Another source of difficulty lay in Meredith's epigrammatic style and his habit of condensing the narrative so that the reader must read between the lines. In his later work the habit of implication became so strong that he seemed incapable of using ordinary words; even the most trivial or commonplace statement had to be disguised in allusive symbols.

Much of Meredith's poetry is as abstruse as his prose. His early work included the limpidly beautiful "Love in the Valley"—the poetic counterpart of the love scenes in *Richard Feverel;* and he wrote a few quaint dramatic monologues of humble characters. But in most of his poems the meaning is not easy to follow, because of the effort to convey intellectual ideas concisely and with originality. His most powerful long poem is *Modern Love,* a psychological study reflecting his own unhappy marriage. Were the component units not sixteen lines in length it would be described as a sonnet sequence, being a diary of emotional experiences linked into an implied narrative—a tragic equivalent for Elizabeth Barrett's *Sonnets from the Portuguese.*

The most characteristic of Meredith's poems, however, were those in which he embodied his philosophy of man's relationship with nature. His ideas were based upon those of both Wordsworth and Shelley, but profoundly modified by the findings of modern science and particularly the evolutionary theory. As early as 1851 he set the pattern for these poems in "South-West Wind in the Woodland," and the later examples included "Ode to the Spirit of Earth in Autumn," "The Lark Ascending," "The Woods of Westermain," "Earth and Man," and "The Thrush in February." His last volume of verse, *A Reading of Life* (1901), still expressed the ideas that he had indicated fifty years earlier.

Although he rejected the belief in personal immortality as firmly as Hardy did, the creed which Meredith derived from his acceptance of the modern scientific universe was the antithesis of Hardy's gloom. While Hardy regarded nature as blindly destructive and wantonly cruel, Meredith saw in the rightness and wholeness and serenity of nature a source of healing and joy for any human being who would accept it trustfully instead of wilfully fighting against it. These philosophical ideas were presented against a background of the seasons and the woods and fields and birds that Meredith loved in his English countryside. Once certain recurrent symbols are recognized, and his concentrated method of suggestion is mastered, these poems yield their full value in both beauty and stimulation.

M. B. Forman, *A Bibliography of the Writings in Prose and Verse of George Meredith* (London, 1922); *Meredithiana* (London, 1924); *Works* (27v, London, 1909-11; Memorial edition); *Poetical Works,* ed. G. M. Trevelyan (London, 1912); *Letters,* ed. W. M. Meredith (2v, London, 1912); R. Le Gallienne, *George Meredith: Some Characteristics* (London, 1890); H. Lynch, *George Meredith* (London, 1891); G. M. Trevelyan, *The Poetry and Philosophy of George Meredith* (London, 1906); M. S. Henderson, *George Meredith, Novelist, Poet, Reformer* (London, 1907); R. H. P. Curle, *Aspects of George Meredith* (London, 1908); J. A. Hammerton, *George Meredith: His Life and Art in Anecdote and Criticism* (London, 1909); J. Moffatt, *George Meredith: A Primer to the Novels* (London, 1909); C. Photiadès, *George Meredith: sa vie, son imagination, son art, sa doctrine* (Paris, 1910; trans. 1913); J. W. Beach, *The Comic Spirit in George Meredith* (New York, 1911); Lady Butcher, *Memories of George Meredith* (London, 1919); S. M. Ellis, *George Meredith: His Life and Friends in Relation to His Work* (London, 1919; rev. ed., 1920); J. B. Priestley, *George Meredith* (London, 1926; English Men of Letters); R. E. Sencourt, *The Life of George Meredith* (London, 1929); R. Peel, *The Creed of a Victorian Pagan* (Cambridge, 1931); A. H. Able, *George Meredith and Thomas Love Peacock* (Philadelphia, 1933); M. E. Mackay, *Meredith et la France* (Paris, 1937); E. A. Robinson, "Meredith's Literary Theory and Science," *Publications of the Modern Language Association,* LIII (1938). 857-68; S. Sassoon, *Meredith* (London, 1948).

THOMAS HARDY (1840-1928)

>>

In a long lifetime Thomas Hardy had two separate literary careers, first as a novelist, then as a poet. He was born at Upper Bockhampton, near Dorchester, in Dorsetshire, on June 2, 1840. Educated in local schools, he learned to know the people and the ways of the countryside of Dorsetshire, which he depicted under the name of Wessex in his novels. At sixteen he was articled to an ecclesiastical architect in Dorchester and worked for several years making plans for church restorations. In 1862 he moved to London as assistant to a famous architect, Arthur Blomfield. The next year he won the prize of the Architectural Association for design and the medal of the Institute of British Architects for an essay on "Colored Brick and Terra-Cotta Architecture." At the same time he was studying Greek and Roman classics and the New Testament.

THOMAS HARDY

In spite of his professional successes, his dislike of city life made him leave London and try to be a writer of fiction. His first attempt at a novel was a work of social purpose, *The Poor Man and the Lady,* which George Meredith advised him not to publish because of its inadequate plot. Consequently his first published novel was *Desperate Remedies,* a melodrama in the Wilkie Collins vein, which appeared anonymously in 1871. In the next year came *Under the Greenwood Tree,* an idyl in which rustic characters were presented with charm and humor. *A Pair of Blue Eyes* was published in 1873; but it was his fourth novel, *Far From the Madding Crowd,* which determined Hardy's career as a writer. When serialized unsigned in the *Cornhill Magazine,* it was attributed by some to George Eliot, and consequently Hardy was brought out of his anonymity.

HARDY'S BIRTHPLACE

During the next twenty years Hardy published many novels, the most important being *The Return of the Native* (1878), usually considered his most powerful and typical work; *The Mayor of Casterbridge* (1886), an impressive tragedy that Stevenson wished to dramatize; and *The Woodlanders* (1887). There were also three volumes of short stories, *Wessex Tales, Life's Little Ironies,* and *A Group of Noble Dames.*

In 1891 *Tess of the D'Urbervilles,* the story of a laborer's daughter brought to ruin by her own trustful innocence, stirred readers into conflicting opinions about Victorian conventions. Some passages were accused of impropriety, and the climax of the story, in which Tess murders her seducer and is executed, gave wide offence. The outcry, however, was much more violent when *Jude the Obscure* was published in 1895. In this novel Jude Fawley, a boy of fine intellectual ambitions, is destroyed by the inner conflict of his two natures; and as his relations with the crude Arabella and the more refined Sue bring him to ruin, the reader is made to feel that the only result of the conflict against a society based on conventions can be defeat for the rebellious individual. Readers were further shocked by the sexual frankness of the story, the free-thinking opinions expressed by the main characters, and a gruesome episode in which two children were murdered by their little half-brother, who then committed suicide. The general horror aroused by the book was a tribute to the success with which it embodied a philosophy of gloomy determinism.

Hardy used this one theme with variations in all his major novels. Individuals struggle hopelessly against the blind powers that control the world. In *The Return of the Native* nature, as represented by Egdon Heath, is shown as passively hostile to those who do not conform to its laws. *Tess* shows how man-made conventions can bring disaster into a life which could have been a happy one. *Jude* goes even further in depicting the natural forces as actively hostile to man, when the lower nature of Jude drags down his higher nature, until the very act of struggle is disastrous. Even the glory of having fought is lost to man. As Hardy's concept of the scheme of things allowed no importance to human beings, his philosophy seemed to be one of dark and hopeless futility.

In the opinion of many readers, he overworked the device of coincidence and accident in order to bring catastrophe upon his characters; but this was an illustration of his idea that it is not a malignant fate that controls human lives, but an almost ludicrously meaningless caprice. He asserted that he did not present his stories as typical of all human experience. Many people, he admitted, live happily and successfully enough; but such themes did not arouse his creative interest.

Apart from his philosophy, Hardy's novels were distinguished by his use of nature as an integral part of the story (in which he was anticipated by *Wuthering Heights* and to some degree by *The Mill on the Floss*). With haunting poetic imagery he made the heath set the keynote for *The Return of the Native,* and the forest for *The Woodlanders.* His depiction of rustic life showed his close intimacy and sympathy with a people whose language and beliefs were little changed since Anglo-Saxon—even since pre-Christian— times. An outstanding trait of his peasants is their stolid impassivity to misfortune. The Wessex dialect that he used with much skill is earthy and primitive, and yet it is effective in expressing both the pathos and the humor of the countryside.

In response to the public protests against *Jude the Obscure,* Hardy promptly gave up the writing of fiction. Apparently he felt that he had carried the theme of his novels to its ultimate limitation, and he had nothing further to say in this form. During his early years he had written some poems, but they were too far from the accepted poetic standards of the sixties to be published. At the age of fifty-five he resumed this interest, producing numerous poems in the same simple and rather harsh technique that he had used thirty years before. *Wessex Poems* came out in 1898 and *Poems of the Past and Present* in 1901. He then turned his attention to writing a vast epic-drama called *The Dynasts,* which appeared in three parts between 1904 and 1908. In nineteen acts and a hundred and thirty scenes, *The Dynasts* presented a poetic interpretation of the period of Napoleon. Choruses of spiritual beings were used for philosophical commentary between the historical episodes. At first received with ridicule, *The Dynasts* has gradually come to be recognized as one of the greatest works of modern literature.

In the remaining twenty years of his life, Hardy brought out six further volumes of poems—a remarkable record of sustained production for a man in his seventies and eighties. He had perfected a style that was well suited to his needs— blunt, expository, ranging from colloquial phrases to technical words and literary clichés, and yet incisive. He practiced an amazing range of verse patterns, some proving stiff and mechanical, while others danced with the lilt of folk songs. Many of the poems were symbolic presentations of his philosophy, others were narratives so condensed that the bitter "satires of circumstance" (as he called one collection) occasionally became unintentional burlesques.

Again and again he depicted the same ideas that underlay his novels—the irony of chance, the blind mindless force that controls the universe—showing more specifically now the source of this belief to be in the mechanistic concepts of modern science. Yet the poems gradually took on a mood that was less depressing. *The Dynasts* had contained hints of some other power that might conceivably arise to oppose the unguided fumblings of the "Immanent Will"— the term that Hardy came to use for the "life force" that governs all existence. In the preface to a later volume he disclaimed the term *pessimism* and described himself as an "evolutionary meliorist." If the cruel aimlessness of life can ever be mastered, it must be by the determined effort of all rational beings. Therefore, he implied, his writings might serve a purpose by forcing his readers to recognize the adversary in its extremest form.

In all the later years of his life Hardy lived quietly in an unpretentious country home near Dorchester. Widely

revered not only as the last great Victorian but also as
the most sincere and potent philosophical poet of the early
twentieth century, he received high honors but remained
a shy, almost inarticulate little man of simple tastes and

MAX GATE, DORCHESTER

pleasures. When he died on January 11, 1928, his ashes
were buried in Westminster Abbey, but his heart was laid
in his parish churchyard in Wessex, the region that his
novels and poems had made familiar to all the world.

A. P. Webb, *A Bibliography of the Works of Thomas Hardy,
1865-1915* (London, 1916); C. J. Weber, *The First Hundred Years
of Thomas Hardy, 1840-1940* (Waterville, Me., 1942); F. O. Saxelby,
A Thomas Hardy Dictionary (London, 1911); *Works* (23v, London, 1912-14; Wessex edition); (37v, London, 1919-20; Mellstock
edition); A. Macdonnell, *Thomas Hardy* (London, 1894); L. Johnson, *The Art of Thomas Hardy* (London, 1894; rev. ed., 1923);
B. C. A. Windle, *The Wessex of Thomas Hardy* (London, 1902);
C. G. Harper, *The Hardy Country* (London, 1904); F. A. Hedg-
cock, *Thomas Hardy, penseur et artiste* (Paris, 1910); L. Abercrombie, *Thomas Hardy: A Critical Study* (London, 1912); H. C.

Duffin, *Thomas Hardy: A Study of the Wessex Novels* (Manchester, 1916); L. W. Berle, *George Eliot and Thomas Hardy* (New York, 1917); J. M. Murry, "The Poetry of Thomas Hardy," in *Aspects of Literature* (London, 1920); S. C. Chew, *Thomas Hardy, Poet and Novelist* (New York, 1921; rev. ed., 1928); A. S. Whitfield, *Thomas Hardy: The Artist, the Man, and the Disciple of Destiny* (London, 1921); R. T. Hopkins, *Thomas Hardy's Dorset* (London, 1922); J. W. Beach, *The Technique of Thomas Hardy* (Chicago, 1922); J. G. Fletcher, "The Spirit of Thomas Hardy," *Yale Review*, XIII (1924). 322-33; R. M. Smith, "Philosophy in Thomas Hardy's Poetry," *North American Review*, CCXX (1924). 330-40; R. Williams, *The Wessex Novels* (London, 1924); E. Brennecke, *Thomas Hardy's Universe* (Boston, 1924); *The Life of Thomas Hardy* (New York, 1925); H. B. Grimsditch, *Character and Environment in the Novels of Thomas Hardy* (London, 1925); J. L. Lowes, "Two Readings of Earth," *Yale Review*, XV (1926). 515-39; M. E. Chase, *Thomas Hardy from Serial to Novel* (Minneapolis, 1927); A. Symons, *A Study of Thomas Hardy* (London, 1927); P. d'Exideuil, *Le couple humain dans l'oeuvre de Thomas Hardy* (Paris, 1928; Eng. trans., 1930); F. E. Hardy, *The Early Life of Thomas Hardy, The Later Years of Thomas Hardy* (London, 1928-30); A. S. McDowall, *Thomas Hardy: A Critical Study* (London, 1931); R. A. Firor, *Folkways in Thomas Hardy* (Philadelphia, 1931); E. C. Hickson, *The Versification of Thomas Hardy* (Philadelphia, 1931); A. P. Elliott, *Fatalism in the Works of Thomas Hardy* (Philadelphia, 1935); A. C. Chakravarti, *"The Dynasts" and the Post-war Age in Poetry* (London, 1938); W. R. Rutland, *Thomas Hardy: A Study of His Writings and Their Background* (Oxford, 1938); P. Bentley, "Thomas Hardy As a Regional Novelist," *Fortnightly Review*, CLIII (1940). 647-52; C. J. Weber, *Hardy of Wessex* (New York, 1940); *Southern Review*, Thomas Hardy Centennial Issue, VI (1940); E. Blunden, *Thomas Hardy* (London, 1942; English Men of Letters); D. Cecil, *Hardy the Novelist* (London, 1943); J. G. Southworth, *The Poetry of Thomas Hardy* (New York, 1947); H. C. Webster, *On a Darkling Plain: The Art and Thought of Thomas Hardy* (Chicago, 1947).

SAMUEL BUTLER (1835-1902)

>>>

Although a prolific writer, Samuel Butler achieved literary success during his lifetime with only one book, and then in the twentieth century became celebrated for another of an entirely different type, which had remained unpublished for twenty years.

SAMUEL BUTLER

Born into a family of distinguished churchmen, on December 4, 1835, he was educated at Shrewsbury School, of which his grandfather had formerly been headmaster, and at St. John's College, Cambridge. He was intended for the church, and after graduation did parish work for a few years among the poor of London, but on the grounds of religious doubt he refused to be ordained. His family discouraged his desire to be a painter, and in 1859 his father advanced the money for him to emigrate to New Zealand and establish a sheep ranch. As this was unexpectedly successful, he was able to return to England in five years with his capital doubled, and to take rooms in Clifford's Inn, London, where he remained for the rest of his life, cultivating his many hobbies, including scientific research, classical scholarship, painting pictures, and composing music. With Henry Festing Jones he composed a cantata, an oratorio, and many shorter pieces—gavottes, minuets, fugues, and so forth. For a number of years he exhibited his paintings regularly at the Royal Academy.

A fellow-artist, Eliza Savage, was devotedly in love with him, but as she was crippled and unbeautiful, he preferred his bachelor existence. He wrote copiously on all the subjects that interested him, and one of his early books,

15 CLIFFORD'S INN

Erewhon, a utopian satire, attracted attention, but thereafter most of his works were so eccentric in their opinions that he had to pay to have them printed. Although he was a friend of Charles Darwin he disputed Darwin's hypothesis of evolution by "natural selection," insisting instead upon a principle of "unconscious memory." His books on this subject—*Life and Habit, Evolution Old and New, Unconscious Memory,* and *Luck or Cunning*—have been seriously considered by some modern scientists. On the religious theme he wrote *The Fair Haven,* an ironic "defence" of the miraculous element in Christianity, which some reviewers took seriously when it was published under a pseudonym. His musical writings were devoted to exalting Handel as the greatest of all composers; and his extensive studies of the Homeric poems were colored by his theory that the *Odyssey* was the work of a woman. He also wrote several travel books, and a biography of his grandfather.

Butler died on June 18, 1902, and his only novel, *The Way of All Flesh*, on which he had worked from 1872 to 1884, was published in 1903. Nine years later his many manuscript notebooks were gathered and printed.

Of all his works, only *Erewhon, or Over the Range* (1872) won fame in his lifetime. The title was an anagram of "nowhere," and the setting was derived from Butler's experiences in New Zealand. As a picture of an ideal culture, it ranks with the great utopian books, and it has something in common with *Gulliver's Travels* in its satire upon existing conditions in Europe. Several of its most startling ideas, such as the tyranny of the machines over human behavior and the medical treatment of criminals, were amazingly prophetic of modern developments. A sequel, *Erewhon Revisited* (1901), which was more effective as narrative, contained some clever satire upon religion.

With the posthumous publication of *The Way of All Flesh* Butler gained an entirely new reputation. It was an iconoclastic attack upon the cherished Victorian institution of the family. Traditional subservience to religion, money, and other *bourgeois* standards was also ridiculed. Butler's avoidance of publishing it was undoubtedly due to the fact that his own parents and early environment were plainly and unfavorably depicted. The novel's common-sense contempt for cant, ritual, and pretension was strengthened by the scientific detachment with which the weakling hero, Ernest Pontifex, was revealed as a victim of both heredity and environment.

The fictional technique was not skilful, the plot being improbable and ill-proportioned, with long digressive comments; but Butler's blunt directness of style and his cynical wit gave the book great power. Appearing just at a time when a new generation was in revolt against Victorian orthodoxy, it elicited immense praise from George Bernard Shaw, and in various ways influenced most of the subsequent English novelists—Bennett, Wells, Galsworthy, Maugham, and D. H. Lawrence.

A. J. Hoppé, *A Bibliography of the Writings of Samuel Butler* (New York, 1925); *Works,* ed. H. F. Jones and A. T. Bartholomew (20v, London, 1923-26; Shrewsbury edition); *Letters Between Samuel Butler and Miss E. M. A. Savage* (London, 1935); H. F. Jones, *Charles Darwin and Samuel Butler* (London, 1911); G. Cannan, *Samuel Butler: A Critical Study* (London, 1915); J. F. Harris, *Samuel Butler, Author of "Erewhon"* (London, 1916); H. F. Jones, *Samuel Butler: A Memoir* (2v, London, 1919); C. E. M. Joad, *Samuel Butler* (London, 1926); M. Garnett, *Samuel Butler and His Family Relations* (London, 1926); *Life and Letters,* Samuel Butler Issue, VII (1931). C. G. Stillman, *Samuel Butler: A Mid-Victorian Modern* (New York, 1932); J. B. Fort, *Samuel Butler* (2v, Bordeaux, 1935); R. F. Rattray, *Samuel Butler* (London, 1935); M. Muggeridge, *The Earnest Atheist* (London, 1936); E. Wilson, "The Satire of Samuel Butler," in *The Triple Thinkers* (New York, 1938); C. T. Bissell, "A Study of *The Way of All Flesh,*" in *Nineteenth-Century Studies,* ed. H. J. Davis, W. C. DeVane, and R. C. Bald (Ithaca, 1940); N. Dilworth, "The Second Passing of Samuel Butler," *South Atlantic Quarterly,* XL (1941). 37-45; G. D. H. Cole, *Samuel Butler and "The Way of All Flesh"* (London, 1947).

ROBERT LOUIS STEVENSON (1850-1894)

>>

Robert Louis Stevenson is one of the authors who generally receive inadequate recognition in literary history because of being too versatile. He cannot be accurately classified as novelist, poet, or essayist, because his work was equally distributed in the three forms. Besides, in all of them he went counter to the trend of his period, and so he cannot be included in generalizations about the "realistic" novel or the "aesthetic" poetry of the eighties and nineties.

Robert Lewis Balfour Stevenson, as he was christened,

was born in Edinburgh on November 13, 1850. The only child of an eminent engineer who specialized in lighthouses, he was a playful, imaginative boy. His childhood, as a result of illness, was rather lonely, and school work was taken lightly. He read a great deal and began composing by dictation when he was six. Later in his walks into the country he would take along his copybook, in which he recorded his impressions of people and places in cadences imitative of some favorite author.

ROBERT LOUIS STEVENSON

Stevenson entered Edinburgh University in 1867 with a view to following the family profession of engineering. He caused his parents and friends much grief at this time by his radical religious views and his flouting of social codes. He claimed to be a Socialist and a free-thinker, wore his hair long, and dressed carelessly. In the austere atmosphere of Edinburgh such bohemianism was particularly rebellious. A growing disinclination for engineering led him to the study of law, and he was called to the Scottish Bar in 1875. At once, however, he abandoned the legal profession in favor of literature. He joined the Savile

Club in London, made friends with such prominent literary men as George Meredith, Leslie Stephen, Edmund Gosse, William Ernest Henley, and Sidney Colvin, and became noted for the brilliance and ardor of his talk.

In 1873 his health had obliged him to winter in Southern France, and thereafter he spent as much time as possible in the open, making long walking tours. In 1876, in company with a friend, he took a canoe trip through the canals and rivers from Antwerp to Grez, his account of which appeared in 1878 as *An Inland Voyage*. This book was followed the next year by *Travels with a Donkey*, the narrative of a tramping tour in the southern French mountains. The two works revealed his mastery of an easy, humorous style. Beginning in 1876 he contributed serial stories and tales to *The Cornhill* and other magazines. He also wrote critical essays, which were later published as a collection called *Familiar Studies of Men and Books*, and the essays on life and youth that were collected as *Virginibus Puerisque*.

Stevenson's meeting with Mrs. Fanny Osbourne, an American who was studying art in France, led to his falling in love with her, though she was ten years older than he was, and had a daughter and son in their teens. They first met in 1876, and two years later she went home to California to obtain a divorce. In the summer of 1879, against his parents' wishes, he followed her, crossing the ocean in steerage and traversing the width of the United States in an immigrant train. His experiences were recounted in *The Amateur Emigrant* and *Across the Plains*. In San Francisco, where he tried to live on one meal a day, he became dangerously ill and was nursed back to health by Mrs. Osbourne. Upon their marriage in 1880 they went to live in a deserted mining camp that he described in *Silverado Squatters*.

When Stevenson brought his wife to England she was warmly received by his family and friends. During the early eighties he spent his summers in Scotland and his winters in Switzerland. At Davos Platz he completed his adventure story, *Treasure Island,* which made him famous. During the next few years he brought out *A Child's Garden of Verses* (1885), *Dr. Jekyll and Mr. Hyde* (1886), *Kidnapped* (1886), the volume of verse called *Underwoods* (1887), and a number of other books. This large and varied output was maintained in spite of long spells of severe illness. After the death of his father in 1887 severed the ties that held Stevenson to his homeland, he sailed for America with his wife and his mother. He lived for a few months at a health resort in the Adirondacks, contributing essays to *Scribner's Magazine.* In the hope that a long sea voyage would be curative he chartered the schooner *Casco* and took his family to San Francisco to board it. For two years they cruised through the South Seas, with long pauses at various islands; *The Master of Ballantrae* and *The Wrong Box* were written during six months in Honolulu. Finally in 1890 he bought a property at Vailima in the Samoan Islands. Loved by the natives, who called him "Tusitala," The Teller of Tales, Stevenson took an active part in local affairs, defending the rights and welfare of the natives against exploitation. He wrote *The Wrecker* and *The Ebb Tide,* both in collaboration with his stepson, Lloyd Osbourne; also a sequel to *Kidnapped,* which he named *Catriona,* but which is known in its American edition as *David Balfour;* a collection of South Seas tales, *Island Nights' Entertainments;* and several others. On December 3, 1894, he died suddenly of a cerebral hemorrhage. The natives carried his body to the summit of Vaea Mountain for burial.

There has been an unfortunate tendency to regard Stevenson as primarily a writer for children. That he was so successful in pleasing young people with *Treasure Island* and *A Child's Garden of Verses* is indeed one example of his genius; but most of his work was of a very different nature, extending to such masterpieces of horror as *Dr. Jekyll and Mr. Hyde* and "Markheim." He chose to write imaginative, adventurous fiction at a time when most of the leading authors were grim and gloomy realists. In such essays as "A Gossip on Romance" and "The Lantern Bearers" he explained his reasons for this choice. His earlier novels were not very firm in plot or subtle in characterization, but *The Master of Ballantrae, Catriona,* and the unfinished *Weir of Hermiston* showed progress in those respects. It is noteworthy that he was the first English writer to produce short stories with a skill to rival the mastery already acquired by authors in France and the United States. He restored the familiar essay to a plane that it had not held since the time of Lamb. As a poet he gave his ballads and lyrics a fresh directness that charmed countless readers and influenced a whole generation of English and American poets.

Most of his work, and especially the essays and the poems, displayed the courageous personal philosophy of the man. His love of life, which often drove him beyond his meager strength, gave vitality to his writing in spite of his carefully studied techniques.

J. H. Slater, *Robert Louis Stevenson: A Bibliography of His Complete Works* (London, 1914); W. F. Prideaux, *A Bibliography of the Works* (London, 1917); *Works* (26v, London, 1922-23; Vailima edition); (35v, London, 1923-24, Tusitala edition); *Letters,* ed. S. Colvin (4v, London, 1912); H. James, "Robert Louis Stevenson," in *Partial Portraits* (London, 1888); J. M. Barrie, "Robert Louis Stevenson," in *An Edinburgh Eleven* (London, 1888); W. Raleigh, *Robert Louis Stevenson* (London, 1895); E. B. Simpson, *Robert Louis Stevenson's Edinburgh Days* (London, 1898); L. C. Cornford, *Robert Louis Stevenson* (Edinburgh, 1899; Modern English Writers); G. Balfour, *The Life of Robert Louis*

Stevenson (2v, London, 1901); J. A. Hammerton, *Stevensoniana* (Edinburgh, 1903; rev. ed., 1910); I. Strong and L. Osbourne, *Memories of Vailima* (New York, 1903); K. D. Osbourne, *Robert Louis Stevenson in California* (Chicago, 1911); F. Swinnerton, *Robert Louis Stevenson: A Critical Study* (London, 1914; rev. ed., 1923); C. M. Hamilton, *On the Trail of Stevenson* (New York, 1915); G. E. Brown, *A Book of R. L. S.* (London, 1919); R. O. Masson, *The Life of Robert Louis Stevenson* (London, 1923); *I Can Remember Robert Louis Stevenson,* ed. R. O. Masson (Edinburgh, 1923); L. Osbourne, *An Intimate Portrait of R. L. S.* (New York, 1924); G. S. Hellman, *The True Stevenson* (Boston, 1925); E. F. Benson, "The Myth of Robert Louis Stevenson," *London Mercury,* XII (1925). 268-83, 372-84; J. A. Steuart, *Robert Louis Stevenson, Man and Writer* (2v, London, 1926); G. K. Chesterton, *Stevenson* (London, 1927); J. M. Carré, *La vie de Robert Louis Stevenson* (Paris, 1929; Eng. trans., 1931); S. Gwynn, *Robert Louis Stevenson* (London, 1939; English Men of Letters); D. Daiches, *Robert Louis Stevenson* (New York, 1947).

MINOR NOVELISTS

>>

William Harrison Ainsworth (1805-1882). The most successful writer of historical romance after Scott, Ainsworth edited magazines and was a hospitable friend of Dickens and other authors. His forty-two novels, including *The Tower of London, Old St. Paul's, Windsor Castle,* and *The Lancashire Witches,* have much of the old Gothic terrors and bombast. In *Rookwood* and *Jack Sheppard* he helped to originate the "Newgate Calendar" type of underworld romance which affected Dickens's *Oliver Twist* and several early novels of Bulwer-Lytton.

S. M. Ellis, *William Harrison Ainsworth and His Friends* (2v, London, 1911).

Walter Besant (1836-1901). The first twelve novels of Besant were written in collaboration with James Rice (1843-

1882), and during the subsequent twenty years he wrote many more. *Ready-Money Mortiboy* and *The Golden Butterfly* were sensational novels of business; *All Sorts and Conditions of Men* and *Children of Gibeon* depicted the poverty of London's East End. He was knighted in 1895.

Autobiography (London, 1902).

William Black (1841-1898). A Scottish journalist, Black was a business-like producer of pleasant romantic stories with picturesque outdoor settings. Best known were *Kilmeny, A Daughter of Heth, The Strange Adventures of a Phaeton, A Princess of Thule,* and *Macleod of Dare.*

T. W. Reid, *William Black, Novelist* (London, 1902).

Richard Doddridge Blackmore (1825-1900). Trained in the law, Blackmore tried poetry and then turned to fiction, making a huge success with *Lorna Doone,* a charming romance of the Devonshire countryside where he had gone to school. Published in 1869, it marked the beginning of a revived vogue for romance. The best of his later novels were *The Maid of Sker, Alice Lorraine,* and *Springhaven.* His style had poetic qualities of rhythm and imagery.

Q. G. Burris, *Richard Doddridge Blackmore, His Life and Novels* (Urbana, 1930).

George Henry Borrow (1803-1881). An eccentric character with an almost pathological gift of languages, Borrow tried to make a literary career in London as a translator, then wandered the English roads as a vagabond, impelled by his interest in the gypsies. As a representative of the Bible Society he traveled in Russia, Spain, and Morocco, and made his first literary success with *The Bible in Spain* (1843). His only novels, if they can be so called, are *Lavengro* and its sequel, *The Romany Rye,* which are largely autobiographical accounts of his experiences with the gypsies, and his opinions on sundry subjects, embroidered with elements of picaresque fiction.

T. J. Wise, *A Bibliography of the Writings of George Borrow* (London, 1912); W. I. Knapp, *The Life, Writings, and Letters of George Borrow* (2v, London, 1899); H. Jenkins, *The Life of George Borrow* (London, 1912); C. K. Shorter, *George Borrow and His Circle* (London, 1913); S. Dearden, *The Gypsy Gentleman, A Study of George Borrow* (London, 1939).

Mary Elizabeth Braddon (1837-1915). Beginning with *Lady Audley's Secret* in 1862, Miss Braddon (later Mrs. Maxwell) wrote more than eighty books. Most of them were serialized in magazines and all were thrilling stories which nevertheless depicted contemporary life perceptively and with a touch of satire. A disciple of Bulwer-Lytton and Collins, she was for some years editor of *Belgravia,* a popular magazine.

Rhoda Broughton (1840-1920). In popularity and fecundity Miss Broughton was a rival of Miss Braddon, with the additional quality of outspoken rebellion against conventional decorum, which brought charges of immorality against her early novels, *Not Wisely But Too Well, Cometh Up as a Flower, Red As a Rose Is She,* and *Belinda.* Her work had considerable realism and humor.

William Carleton (1794-1869). Son of a poor Irish farmer, Carleton picked up an education in the hope of entering the priesthood, but settled in Dublin as a writer. His *Traits and Stories of the Irish Peasantry* (1830) was the first of a series of books presenting Irish life realistically, sympathetically, and humorously, though occasionally with exaggerated grimness and didacticism. His short stories are superior to his novels, which are weak in structure.

D. J. O'Donoghue, *The Life of William Carleton* (Dublin, 1896); R. McHugh, "William Carleton: a Portrait of the Artist As Propagandist," *Studies,* xxvii (1938). 47-62; B. Kiely, *Poor Scholar* (New York, 1948).

Dinah Maria Mulock Craik (1826-1887). Under her unmarried name, Miss Mulock gained immense success with *John Halifax, Gentleman* (1856), a novel which expressed the ideas of the evangelical movement and therefore won approval from earnest religious people who ordinarily disapproved of fiction. *A Life for a Life* was a propaganda novel attacking capital punishment. She wrote several much-loved books for children. In 1864 she married **G. L. Craik**, a publisher.

L. Parr, *The Author of John Halifax, Gentleman* (London, 1898).

George L. P. B. Du Maurier (1834-1896). Born and partly educated in Paris, Du Maurier studied painting there and in the Low Countries, until eye trouble forced him to turn to black-and-white sketching. For years he was a leading member of the staff of *Punch*, with drawings that gently satirized fashionable English society. At the age of fifty-eight he published his first novel, *Peter Ibbetson*, an attractive mixture of social comedy and romantic fantasy. This was followed by his immensely successful *Trilby*, based on recollections of his youth in the Latin Quarter, and by *The Martian*, which used the theme of reincarnation.

T. M. Wood, *George Du Maurier* (London, 1913); D. Du Maurier, *The Du Mauriers* (London, 1937).

George Gissing (1857-1903). Gissing's early years were darkened by a term in prison for stealing money from fellow-students at college in Manchester. Trying to start a new life in the United States, he taught school in Massachusetts and wrote for the Chicago *Tribune* before returning to England. Foolish marriages brought further unhappiness. A shy man of scholarly interests and frail health, he set out to write uncompromisingly realistic novels about the poor white-collar workers of London. *Workers in the Dawn* (1880) was followed by *The Unclassed, Demos,*

Thyrza, The Nether World, and others. His books are depressing because they indicate no hope of improvement in the drab conditions he depicts. An admirer of Dickens, he used the old-fashioned melodramatic type of plot though in other respects he shows the influence of the Russian and French realists.

Letters of George Gissing to Members of His Family, ed. A. and E. Gissing (London, 1927); F. Swinnerton, *George Gissing, A Critical Study* (London, 1912; rev. ed., 1923); M. Yates, *George Gissing, An Appreciation* (Manchester, 1922); A. Weber, *George Gissing und die soziale Frage* (Munich, 1932); S. V. Gapp, *George Gissing, Classicist* (Philadelphia, 1936).

Catherine G. F. Gore (1799-1861). A leading representative of the "silver fork" school of society novelists, Mrs. Gore (née Moody) was parodied by Thackeray; but in a few of her books, particularly *Mothers and Daughters* (1831) and *Cecil, Adventures of a Coxcomb* (1841), she wrote skilful social satire.

Theodore Edward Hook (1788-1841). A transitional figure between the regency and the Victorian period, Hook was a fashionable wit and man-about-town, famous for his hoaxes. His short stories, collected in *Sayings and Doings* (1824-28), were followed by melodramatic novels, *Maxwell* and *The Parson's Daughter,* and picaresque stories in the Smollett vein, *Gilbert Gurney, Jack Brag,* and *Peregrine Bunce.* Like Pierce Egan, he gave a vivid, if exaggerated, picture of London life, and had some influence on Dickens.

M. F. Brightfield, *Theodore Hook and His Novels* (Cambridge, Mass., 1928).

Thomas Hughes (1822-1896). After an education at Rugby School and Oxford, Hughes became a lawyer and later a judge and Member of Parliament. Associated with the Christian Socialist movement, he served as principal of its Workingmen's College. His *Tom Brown's School Days*

(1857), an idealized picture of his Rugby years, set the pattern for school novels. *Tom Brown at Oxford* was less successful.

George Payne Rainsford James (1799-1860). The chief rival of Ainsworth in historical romance, James wrote dozens of books with a monotonous formula and pompous style, but undeniable picturesqueness. In later life he was a British consul in Virginia and Italy.

S. M. Ellis, *The Solitary Horseman* (London, 1927).

Henry Kingsley (1830-1876). A younger brother of Charles Kingsley, Henry had literary gifts but unstable character. He left Oxford to spend five years at the Australian gold fields and later was a war correspondent in the Franco-Prussian war. Like his brother, he sought to inculcate noble ideals in his novels, which have likable characters and open-air freshness. The best are *Geoffrey Hamlyn, Ravenshoe, Austin Elliott,* and *The Hillyars and the Burtons.* Illness and poverty caused deterioration in his later books.

S. M. Ellis, *Henry Kingsley, 1830-1876—Towards a Vindication* (London, 1931).

George Alfred Lawrence (1827-1876). Trained by Dr. Arnold at Rugby, Lawrence became an exponent of the same "muscular Christianity" as the Kingsley brothers and Hughes. His most popular novels, published anonymously, were *Guy Livingstone, or Thorough* (1857), *Sword and Gown,* and *Barren Honour.* His heroes are all paragons of physical strength, military courage, and aristocratic ideals.

Joseph Sheridan Le Fanu (1814-1873). An Irish magazine editor, Le Fanu was a student of occultism and a master of uncanny tales of terror, both short stories and novels, such as *The House by the Churchyard, Wylder's Hand, Uncle Silas,* and *The Wyvern Mystery.*

Charles Lever (1806-1872). Trained in medicine at Trinity College, Dublin, and in Germany, Lever left his native Ireland to practice as a physician in Brussels, returned to edit the *Dublin University Magazine,* and then settled permanently on the Continent as a vice-consul in Italy. His *Confessions of Harry Lorrequer* (1837-40), started in a magazine as a series of comic episodes based largely on his escapades and those of his college friends, grew into a picaresque novel, and was followed by *Charles O'Malley,* an adventurous story of the Napoleonic war. In his many later novels the element of high-spirited humor diminished as he tried with varying success to master realism and psychological truth. By their very irresponsibility the earlier novels give a good picture of the Protestant "ascendancy" era in Ireland.

E. Downey, *Charles Lever, His Life in His Letters* (2v, Edinburgh, 1906); L. Stevenson, *Doctor Quicksilver* (London, 1939).

Samuel Lover (1797-1868). A portrait painter by profession, and a writer of Irish songs in the tradition of Moore, Lover published slipshod farcical novels—*Rory O'More* (1837) and *Handy Andy* (1842)—which did much to establish the popular concept of the Irish people as humorous and impractical.

W. B. Bernard, *Life of Samuel Lover* (London, 1874).

George MacDonald (1824-1905). Forerunner of the "Kailyard School" of Scottish local-color fiction, MacDonald was a Congregational minister who became interested in the mysticism of Novalis and wrote several remarkable books of occult symbolism, notably *Phantastes* and *Lilith.* His idealistic novels of rural life include *David Elginbrod* (1862), *Alec Forbes of Howglen, Annals of a Quiet Neighborhood, Robert Falconer, The Marquis of Lossie,* and *Sir Gibbie.* He also wrote charming fairy-tales for children.

Greville MacDonald, *George MacDonald and His Wife* (London, 1924); *George MacDonald, an Anthology,* ed. C. S. Lewis (London, 1947).

William Hurrell Mallock (1849-1923). A writer of controversial books attacking rationalism and socialism, Mallock wrote nine satirical novels in the tradition of Peacock, debating current problems in dialogue and portraying such prominent contemporaries as Arnold in fictional disguise. His chief novels are *The New Republic* (1877), *The New Paul and Virginia, A Romance of the Nineteenth Century* and *The Old Order Changes.*

A. B. Adams, *The Novels of W. H. Mallock* (Orono, 1934).

Frederick Marryat (1792-1848). After distinguishing himself as a naval officer in the Napoleonic wars, Marryat retired with the rank of Captain in 1830 and began to use his varied experiences as a basis for picaresque novels, obviously modeled upon Smollett's and rich in farcical humor, masculine excitement, and some crude sadism. His first novels, *Frank Mildmay* and *The King's Own,* were amateurish in technique; but he gained greater mastery in *Peter Simple, Jacob Faithful, Mr. Midshipman Easy,* and *Snarley-yow, or the Dog Fiend.* Later he applied himself to writing books for boys.

Florence Marryat, *The Life and Letters of Captain Marryat* (2v, London, 1872); C. Lloyd, *Captain Marryat and the Old Navy* (London, 1939).

Harriet Martineau (1802-1876). Though Miss Martineau is usually remembered as a writer on economics and other social subjects, her most influential books were cast in the form of fiction. Didactic stories were collected under the titles *Illustrations of Political Economy* (1832-34) and *Poor Laws and Paupers Illustrated* (1833). Her novels are *Deerbrook* (1839) and *The Hour and the Man* (1841). Some of her stories for children, such as *Feats on the Fjord,* are still read.

T. Bosanquet, *Harriet Martineau* (London, 1927); N. Rivenburg, *Harriet Martineau, an Example of Victorian Conflict* (Philadelphia, 1932); J. C. Nevill, *Harriet Martineau* (London, 1943).

George Moore (1852-1933). The first exponent of French naturalism in English fiction, Moore was the son of a wealthy Irish landowner. At eighteen he went to Paris to study painting, and also tried his hand at poetry, meanwhile becoming enthusiastic over the new French fiction. Determined to defy the conventional taboos of English literature, he published *A Modern Lover* (1883) and *A Mummer's Wife* (1885), which aroused bitter controversy and subjected his publishers to legal action. After writing five more novels he moved into a "second phase" in which he produced his three major works, *Esther Waters, Evelyn Innes,* and its sequel, *Sister Theresa,* novels in which the sordidness of his previous books is modified by greater sympathy and humanity. After the turn of the century he went back to live in Ireland and resumed also an interest in religion. His later books were chiefly autobiographical, but he wrote three imaginative novels, *The Lake, The Brook Kerith,* and *Heloïse and Abelard.* Until the end he was experimenting with technical matters of style.

J. Freeman, *A Portrait of George Moore* (London, 1922); C. Morgan, *Epitaph on George Moore* (London, 1935); J. Hone, *The Life of George Moore* (1936).

Margaret O. Wilson Oliphant (1828-1897). A gifted woman who wrote too much (over 120 books), being burdened with the support of dependents, Mrs. Oliphant began with novels of Scottish life, and then wrote a series dealing with English clerical characters—*Salem Chapel, The Perpetual Curate, Miss Marjoribanks,* and so on—which were grouped under the title of *The Chronicles of Carlingford,* and which have some resemblance to Trollope's Barsetshire series. She also wrote several remarkable series of the supernatural—*A Beleaguered City, A Little Pilgrim of the Unseen, The Land of Darkness.*

Autobiography and Letters, ed. A. L. Coghill (London, 1899).

Ouida (Marie Louise de la Ramée) (1839-1908). Strongly eccentric, and determined to make her own life as melodramatic as her novels, Miss Ramée (who later gave her name a more aristocratic form) shocked the mid-Victorian public by the unconventional behavior of her characters and the violence of her plots. The reputation of wickedness brought valuable publicity to her works, and she had a good deal of influence in undermining the hypocritical prudery of the time. Her most notable novels were *Strathmore* (1865), *Under Two Flags,* and *Moths.*

E. Lee, *Ouida, a Memoir* (London, 1914); G. ffrench, *Ouida, a Study in Ostentation* (London, 1938).

Anne Thackeray Ritchie (1837-1919). The last years of W. M. Thackeray's life were cheered by the fact that his elder daughter was making a name for herself as an author. After his death she married her cousin, Richmond Ritchie, who received a knighthood for his work in the government service. Her gently melancholy novels have charm of style and atmosphere, the best being *The Story of Elizabeth* (1863) and *The Village on the Cliff* (1867). She also wrote essays and reminiscences.

The Letters of Anne Thackeray Ritchie, ed. H. Ritchie (London, 1924).

Mark Rutherford (William Hale White) (1831-1913). More an autobiographer than a novelist, W. H. White adopted the name of the hero of his first book as his penname; but he used the form and some of the embellishments of fiction for his two most significant books, *The Autobiography of Mark Rutherford* (1881) and *Mark Rutherford's Deliverance* (1885), the record of his struggle to escape from the narrow-minded dogmas of his early environment. He also wrote three less personal novels.

Joseph Henry Shorthouse (1834-1903). A Birmingham business man, brought up a Quaker, Shorthouse was converted to the Church of England and developed a special interest in its mystical tradition. His one outstanding novel, *John Inglesant* (1880), was a lyrical and sensitive picture of the Anglican Platonists of the seventeenth century and Nicholas Ferrar's religious community at Little Gidding. Shorthouse wrote several other novels with the same sacramental earnestness, derived from the Oxford movement.

Life, Letters, and Literary Remains of J. Henry Shorthouse, ed. by His Wife (2v, London, 1905).

Robert Smith Surtees (1803-1864). A country squire in Northumberland, Surtees found time in the midst of his local duties to write a series of amusing stories which nearly all dealt with fox-hunting. To the *New Sporting Magazine,* of which he was the editor, he started to contribute in 1832 a sequence of comic sketches, later collected as *The Jaunts and Jollities of . . . Mr. John Jorrocks.* Jorrocks reappeared as a character in two later and more unified novels, *Handley Cross* and *Hillingdon Hall;* and four other novels were in the same general vein. With a slangy, amateur style and a strong touch of caricature, Surtees created a group of characters which in illustrated editions remained popular with admirers of English life and sport, and which had some influence on the early writings of Dickens.

E. D. Cuming, *Robert Smith Surtees, Creator of Jorrocks* (London, 1924); A. Steel, *Jorrocks's England* (London, 1932); F. Watson, *Robert Smith Surtees, a Critical Study* (London, 1933).

Frances Milton Trollope (1780-1863). After an unfortunate business venture in frontier Cincinnati, which produced her vigorous book, *Domestic Manners of the Americans,* Mrs. Trollope settled down, when past fifty, to writing novels to support her family (including two sons who became famous authors in their turn). Her numerous books had good observation of character and touches of satire. Some of them, such as *The Vicar of Wrexhill* (1837), *Michael Armstrong, the Factory Boy* (1840), and *Jessie Phillips* (1843), dealt with current problems.

F. E. Trollope, *Frances Trollope* (2v, London, 1895); L. P. and R. P. Stebbins, *The Trollopes* (New York, 1945).

Mrs. Humphry Ward (1851-1920). Mary Augusta Arnold, a niece of Matthew Arnold, and kinswoman of several other grave Victorian thinkers, was brought up in the midst of Oxford dons, and in 1872 married one of them, Thomas Humphry Ward. After several scholarly publications she turned to fiction, and her novel *Robert Elsmere* (1888), a study of a conscientious clergyman's surrender to modern rational ideas, was immensely successful. Gladstone praised it, and Mrs. Ward was regarded as George Eliot's successor as a serious novelist of ideas. *David Grieve, Helbeck of Bannisdale, The Marriage of William Ashe, The Case of Richard Meynell,* and others, dealt similarly with controversial problems, religious or political. Some of her characters were recognizably suggested by real celebrities.

J. S. Walters, *Mrs. Humphry Ward, Her Work and Influence* (London, 1912); S. Gwynne, *Mrs. Humphry Ward* (London, 1917); J. P. Trevelyan, *The Life of Mrs. Humphry Ward* (London, 1923).

George James Whyte-Melville (1821-1878). A novelist of action in the same school as G. A. Lawrence and Henry Kingsley, Whyte-Melville wrote stories about fox-hunting and army life, and several historical novels, notably *The Gladiators* (1863). Grandson of a duke, he was educated at

Eton and served as a captain in the aristocratic Coldstream Guards, facts which helped to secure his popularity among the English country gentry.

Mrs. Henry Wood (1814-1887). Among the women who took advantage of the new magazines to become prolific authors of fiction, Ellen (Price) Wood was a rival of Miss Braddon and Miss Yonge, standing midway between the sensationalism of the one and the saintliness of the other. She first wrote stories to relieve the tedium of ill-health, until her husband's bankruptcy made it necessary for her to earn a living. Beginning with *Danesbury House* (1860), a temperance propaganda novel, she next wrote *East Lynne*, which became a best-seller and was equally popular when dramatized. *The Channings* was a more placid domestic tale. In 1867 she became proprietor and editor of *The Argosy*, in which her later novels were serialized.

C. W. Wood, *Memorials of Mrs. Henry Wood* (London, 1894).

Charlotte Mary Yonge (1823-1901). A devout high-church Anglican, Miss Yonge led a secluded life in a Hampshire village, and devoted all her literary earnings to charity. Publishing her first novel at twenty-one, she produced about 150 books. *The Heir of Redclyffe* (1853) had a vast success, as had *The Daisy Chain* (1856). Of her historical romances, the best was *The Dove in the Eagle's Nest*. She wrote many juvenile books and for forty years edited a magazine for girls, *The Monthly Packet*. Reflecting the spiritual earnestness of the Oxford movement, her earlier novels were admired by Morris, Rossetti, Kingsley, and other men of distinction.

C. Coleridge, *Charlotte M. Yonge, Her Life and Letters* (London, 1903); E. Romanes, *Charlotte M. Yonge: an Appreciation* (London, 1908); G. Battiscombe, *Charlotte M. Yonge, the Story of an Uneventful Life* (London, 1943).

DRAMA AND THE THEATER
>>>

The drama differs from other kinds of literature in that its fortunes are identified with those of the physical medium through which it reaches its consumer. The types of plays that are written, their intellectual level and literary artistry, are controlled by such forces as the structure of theater buildings, the technique of actors, and the social class of the audience.

At all times, to be sure, there are "closet dramas" written in conformity with literary traditions, but very few of them reach greatness even by literary criteria, apart from their lack of theatrical effectiveness. As the justification for the use of the dramatic form must be the successful performance of the play before an audience, first-rate drama can exist only when those conditions are favorable.

Through much of the Victorian period, the professional English drama was miserably bad. Its inferiority was partly due to the "licensing" system, which permitted only two theaters, Covent Garden and Drury Lane, to hold the royal warrant for the production of plays. This system was interwoven with the government censorship: an official in the office of the Lord Chamberlain had to approve every play before it was performed, and his moral and political tenets were so narrow that dramatists were discouraged from expressing unpopular ideas or depicting life realistically.

The growth of London in the late eighteenth century, and the increasing prosperity, literacy, and leisure of the middle classes, enlarged the audiences vastly. In order to reap the full profits from this expansion and to combat any demand for the granting of patents to other theaters, the two "theaters royal" were rebuilt with such huge proportions that all subtleties of acting were lost to the audience. As the actors thus necessarily developed a bombastic style, the type of play that could be performed became exaggerated in the direction of melodrama or farce.

Even when enlarged, the two patent theaters could accommodate only a fraction of the entertainment-seeking public. Therefore many subterfuges were developed to cover the presentation of drama in unlicensed playhouses. Chiefly this was achieved by the pretense of musical performance—either by interspersing plays among concert numbers or by introducing songs and dances illogically into the very texture of the play. When "melodrama" was introduced from France by Holcroft in 1802, it was so named because an actual orchestral obbligato accompanied the reciting of the lines.

Probably the strangest, and yet most characteristic, expression of these nineteenth-century theatrical conditions in England was the "Christmas Pantomime," which is incapable of reproduction in printed form—a mixture of fairy-tale, musical comedy, and circus, supposedly for the entertainment of children, but enjoyed by people of all ages during the weeks of Christmas vacation. Still performed throughout England, almost unchanged for one hundred and fifty years, these extravaganzas have never been acknowledged as a branch of dramatic literature.

Early-Victorian audiences liked their money's worth, and therefore even at the patent theaters it was customary for an evening's program to include two plays, several monologues, and other variety turns. Most of the unlicensed theaters were small, makeshift affairs, with little financial stability. In this respect they might have fostered an intimate and subtle style of acting; but unfortunately the audiences were of the poorer and less cultivated class, and the actors were ill-trained. Besides, the actors tried to model themselves upon the popular stars at the two big play-houses. Hence the ranting manner which had a certain effectiveness on the huge stage of Drury Lane became ludicrous when crudely imitated in a little back-street show-house.

The provincial towns of England had theaters and enthusiastic audiences; but few of the towns were large enough to support permanent companies, and the traveling companies were usually those that were incapable of succeeding in London in even the smaller theaters. Vivid glimpses of the stupidity and futility of the actors and their plays are given by Dickens with only slight exaggeration for comic effect: he depicts a provincial strolling company in *Nicholas Nickleby* and a small London theater in chapters 31 and 47 of *Great Expectations*.

The unhealthy state of the theater was investigated by a committee of Parliament as early as 1832, and in 1843 the restriction in number of licensed theaters was abolished by the Theater Regulation Act, which authorized the Lord Chamberlain to license other theaters in proportion to public demand. Thereafter the Adelphi, the Haymarket, the Prince of Wales's, and others became favorites with the upper-class audiences; but theaters are slow to build and taste is slow to change, so that many years elapsed before there was a marked development in the fashions of plays or of acting.

The quantity of theatrical performance throughout the Victorian era was immense, but for the reasons stated above the quality was mediocre. Few authors of merit were willing to write plays of the type that was in demand, especially as the managers had an inexhaustible supply of such material in French, requiring only the services of a cheap translator, and therefore the payment offered for original plays was pitifully small. Any writer who wanted to deal with life realistically and intelligently could produce novels and thus appeal directly to readers of similar taste—and with some prospect of earning good profits. Dickens, for instance, wrote four farces and burlettas before deciding that his talent was better suited to fiction.

The great plays of earlier centuries were not neglected. Shakespeare was played regularly, as were many other standard works, such as Otway's *Venice Preserved* and Lillo's *George Barnwell*. But in the patent theaters Shakespeare was made the vehicle of spectacular scenic effects and exaggerated acting, and in the smaller houses his plays were sometimes transformed into operettas. These revivals of older plays were a further discouragement to the contemporary author.

In the opinion of the public, the art of acting had never been higher. The succession of famous players throughout the period included Charles Kemble and his daughter Fanny, William C. Macready, Charles Mathews the Younger and his wife Madame Vestris, Charles Kean and his wife Ellen Tree, Helena Faucit, Samuel Phelps, Edward A. Sothern, Henry Irving, William H. Kendal and his wife Madge Robertson, Squire Bancroft and his wife Marie Wilton, and John Hare. Customarily the star was also manager of the company and made sure that his own rôle predominated in each play, a further detriment to good playwriting.

For all the foregoing reasons, most of the professional playwrights were frankly journeymen who ground out countless melodramas, farces, and extravaganzas, most of which were brazenly "borrowed" from France. If printed at all, they were issued only in cheap and flimsy "acting editions" that never reached library shelves. The few that are still available to read are dull, implausible, and unoriginal; the jokes are flat and the emotional scenes are insincere and sentimental. It must be remembered, however, that the glamour of the stage can work wonders. These mediocre plays, when performed by popular actors for sympathetic audiences, gave delight not only to the uncritical masses but also to men and women of cultivated taste.

Partly out of respect for the Elizabethan tradition and partly in hopes of being accepted by some actor famous in Shakespearian rôles, a number of the Victorian poets tried to write verse tragedy, undeterred by the fact that their immediate predecessors—Wordsworth, Coleridge, Scott, Byron, Shelley, and Keats—had met failure in the same effort.

Robert Browning was particularly ambitious for a dramatist's career. Between 1837 and 1847 he wrote seven plays, mostly historical tragedies, several of which were produced at leading theaters with slight success. Browning also used a semi-dramatic form for *Paracelsus* and *Pippa Passes*. He gradually realized, however, that his interest in psychological complexities could not be effectively embodied upon the stage, and so he evolved the dramatic monologue as a poetic form which retained certain traces of the play.

In respect of playwriting, the career of Tennyson was the converse of Browning's. Tennyson did not attempt a play until he was sixty-five, and then he too wrote seven poetical dramas. His *Queen Mary* was acted by Irving, just as Browning's *Strafford* forty years before had been acted by Macready, but even the popularity of the star did not suffice in either case to bring success to the play.

Matthew Arnold's *Merope,* a faithful imitation of classical Greek tragedy, was presumably not intended for stage presentation, nor was Swinburne's *Atalanta in Calydon;* but Swinburne also wrote a number of historical plays in the style of his favorite Jacobean dramatists. Their florid eloquence and subtle complexities would have been a fatal handicap to production in the theater. His huge *Bothwell* was really an epic in dramatic scenes, and it was only the middle play of a trilogy on Mary of Scotland.

Several other writers gained a measure of fame with poetic dramas and did not make any mark in other forms of poetry. Henry Taylor was always known as the author of *Philip van Artevelde* and T. N. Talfourd as the author of *Ion*. John Westland Marston also received attention for plays in verse.

Although some of the above-mentioned plays were acted in good London theaters and received critics' praise, they were essentially closet dramas, full of verbose speeches and deficient in clear-cut characterization and vigorous action. At the beginning of the Victorian period there were two dramatists who combined genuine stage effectiveness with adequate literacy and dignity. James Sheridan Knowles had already established his reputation before 1830, but he wrote *The Hunchback* and *The Love Chase* during the thirties and continued with plays until 1842, when he entered the Baptist ministry. Edward Bulwer-Lytton, in the course of his fervent pursuit of fame and fortune through his pen, turned briefly from novels to plays, and produced five between 1836 and 1840—*The Duchess de la Vallière* and *Richelieu* (historical tragedies), *The Lady of Lyons* and *The Sea-Captain* (melodramas), and *Money* (a comedy). All except the first were highly successful. The modern reader finds them grandiloquent, sensational, and full of coincidence, but they were more restrained in these respects than most works of his contemporaries, and they had unquestionable power over an audience.

Among early-Victorian playwrights of less literary pretension the most prominent was Douglas Jerrold, whose chief plays were *Black-ey'd Susan* (1829), "a nautical and domestic drama," and *The Rent Day* (1832). He continued until 1854 with a total of nearly seventy plays, mostly farces and melodramas. Other writers of farces and burlesques were Mark Lemon, Gilbert Abbott à Beckett, and his son Gilbert Arthur à Beckett. These three, like Jerrold, were on the staff of *Punch,* as were Tom Taylor and F. C. Burnand, later burlesque-writers. It has been suggested that this "*Punch* school" of burlesque was partly responsible for keeping the drama in a trivial and puerile status and delaying its acceptance as a serious vehicle for intelligent ideas.

The slow improvement in the quality of popular drama after the end of the licensing system can be seen in the work of Dion Boucicault. Boasting that he had written four hundred plays, he made no claim to artistic distinction, but there was a measure of originality and vigor in *The Corsican Brothers, The Octoroon,* and his Irish dramas, *The Colleen Bawn* and *The Shaughraun.* He also wrote comedies of manners, such as *London Assurance,* in the tradition that came down from the Restoration *via* Goldsmith and Sheridan. The defect in his plays is extreme dependence upon situation, at the expense of characterization. His insistence upon realistic stage sets and genuine "properties" did much to improve the illusion of reality behind the footlights. He also made a strong and eventually successful fight, in both England and the United States, to establish the claim of authors for "royalties" on their plays, in place of a single payment, and thus he helped to give playwrights prosperity and self-respect.

Another better-than-average dramatist of the middle years of the century was Tom Taylor, a Cambridge graduate who was a Professor of English at London University before becoming a lawyer and public official. After writing numerous burlesques for the stage, he collaborated with Charles Reade, the novelist, in a successful play, *Masks and Faces.* Taylor was famous for two comedies, *Still Waters Run Deep* (1855) and *Our American Cousin* (1858), and a melodrama of crime, *The Ticket-of-Leave*

Man (1863). In all, he wrote over a hundred dramatic pieces, including several historical plays in verse. His exaggerated but effective methods of characterization were proved by the wide fame of two of his characters, "Lord Dundreary" and "Hawkshaw the Detective."

The turning-point in English dramatic writing, away from exaggeration and rhetoric and in the direction of naturalness, came with the work of Thomas William Robertson. With theatrical ancestry for several generations, he spent his early years acting with provincial companies and in London, after which he became a hack-playwright, selling his translations and skits at three pounds each. Even his first successful play, *David Garrick,* was adapted from a French original. After this historical comedy he turned to contemporary subjects and wrote plays which seemed startlingly original because he depicted familiar types of people and imitated the speech of real life. His outstanding plays, nicknamed "cup-and-saucer comedies," between 1865 and 1870, were *Society, Ours, Caste, Play, School, Home,* and *M.P.* At last the new small theaters had discovered the possibility of subtle acting that made characterization and dialogue more important than violent action. Another of Robertson's innovations was the inclusion of working-class characters depicted as human beings and not as comic clowns or depraved criminals.

Equally symptomatic of the change were the comic operas of William S. Gilbert, who had previously been a writer of dramatic travesties in the old *Punch* school. Though his operas were an outgrowth of the long-popular burlettas and even of the Christmas pantomimes, their mixture of wit, fantasy, and satire, with ingenious plots and brilliant phrasing, combined with the distinctive tunes of Arthur Sullivan, gave to English musical comedy a new sophistication and literary respectability.

Through these influences, the London theater by 1880

was ready for the production of plays which depicted human behavior with some degree of naturalness, and which held a certain intellectual content, whether as satire or as serious presentation of ethical and social problems. The audiences in the better theaters no longer demanded thrills and uproar, and the actors had learned to moderate their declamation.

A contributing influence from abroad was the fame of Henrik Ibsen, whose *Doll's House,* first performed in Norway in 1879, was quickly a topic of discussion throughout Europe. Edmund Gosse and William Archer (a leading dramatic critic) were tireless in introducing Ibsen in England, Archer's translation of *The Pillars of Society* being acted in London in 1880. Another foreign influence was that of Victorien Sardou's "well-made play," with emphasis upon structure and technical precision.

The two dramatists whose work fully represented the "new drama" were Henry Arthur Jones and Arthur Wing Pinero, both of whom wrote their first significant plays in 1880. They achieved much of their early success with farces and melodramas, such as *The Magistrate,* by Pinero, and *The Silver King,* by Jones; but they were fully conscious of the new opportunities of "naturalism," and from time to time both staged plays of serious import. Jones also in a series of essays and prefaces expounded his theories of how the theater could improve its intellectual level. His principal plays were *Saints and Sinners* (1884), *The Middleman* (1889), *Judah* (1890), *The Masqueraders* (1894), *The Case of Rebellious Susan* (1894), *Michael and His Lost Angel* (1896), *The Liars* (1897), and *Mrs. Dane's Defense* (1900). In fulfilling his sense of the dramatist's responsibility, Jones sometimes loaded his plays somewhat too obviously with moral earnestness.

Pinero's first serious play was *The Squire* (1881). His other "problem plays," notably *The Profligate* (1889), *The*

Second Mrs. Tanqueray (1893), and *The Notorious Mrs. Ebbsmith* (1895), were interspersed with highly profitable farces and with sentimental comedies like *Sweet Lavender* (1888).

The competent, intelligent, and somewhat wooden plays of Jones and Pinero stand in contrast with the satirical comedies of the two dramatists who were their contemporaries. Oscar Wilde had already made a reputation as a poet, an essayist, a wit, and a poseur, the extreme exponent of the "aesthetic" cult, before he won success in the theater with *Lady Windermere's Fan* (1892), followed by his three other comedies in rapid succession. His brilliant dialogue, studded with paradox, and the impudence with which the characters flouted conventional ideas, were far from realistic, since every speaker was a mouthpiece for Wilde's wit; but the plots were contrived well enough to hold the attention of the audience, and the baffling mixture of irony and seriousness tantalized and delighted them.

Three months older than Wilde, but slower in gaining literary fame, George Bernard Shaw had written five novels and quantities of dramatic and musical criticism before his first play, *Widowers' Houses,* which appeared in the same year as Wilde's first comedy. Like Wilde, Shaw fascinated and annoyed the public with startling phrases and challenging opinions. Unlike Wilde, however, he let his social theories dominate his plays with a didactic flavor. Shaw was a devotee of Ibsen, but he realized that he could gain more influence over his audience by amusing them than by preaching at them. Accordingly the controversial attitude of his earlier plays gave place to paradox and epigram. In all his plays there are long passages of discussion which are really essays cast in dialogue; but Shaw learned how to use suspense and surprise effectively enough to make his dramas acceptable to even the most frivolous theater-goers. When published in well-printed volumes, with challenging prefaces by the author, these plays did much to restore drama to a high standing as literature.

During the closing years of the century other dramatists, notably James M. Barrie, learned the secret of combining literary value with theatrical skill. The whole world of the theater had moved forward in seventy years to a state of prosperity and prestige. Actors and managers were receiving knighthoods as distinguished citizens, audiences appreciated subtle wit and bold ideas on the stage, plays were technically expert and artistically distinctive, and dramatists figured among the most influential authors of the generation.

T. Purnell, *Dramatists of the Present Day* (London, 1871); P. Fitzgerald, *The Romance of the English Stage* (2v, London, 1874); D. Cook, *Hours with the Players* (2v, London, 1881); *Nights at the Play* (2v, London, 1883); W. Archer, *English Dramatists of Today* (London, 1882); *About the Theatre* (London, 1886); J. Coleman, *Players and Playwrights I Have Known* (London, 1888); J. W. Marston, *Recollections of Our Recent Actors* (London, 1888); H. A. Jones, *The Renascence of the English Drama* (London, 1895); A. Filon, *Le théâtre anglais: hier, aujourd'hui, demain* (Paris, 1896; trans. F. Whyte, as *The English Stage: Being an Account of the Victorian Drama*, London, 1897); C. W. Scott, *The Drama of Yesterday and Today* (2v, London, 1899); J. Knight, *History of the Stage During the Victorian Era* (London, 1901); H. B. Baker, *The History of the London Stage* (London, 1904); H. S. Wyndham, *The Annals of Covent Garden Theatre* (2v, London, 1906); A. Darbyshire, *The Art of the Victorian Stage* (London, 1907); M. Borsa, *The English Stage Today* (trans. S. Brinton, London, 1908); R. F. Sharp, *A Short History of the English Stage* (London, 1909); C. Weygandt, *Irish Plays and Playwrights* (Boston, 1913); E. L. Stahl, *Das englische Theater im 19 Jahrhundert* (Leipzig, 1914); T. H. Dickinson, *The Contemporary Drama of England* (Boston, 1917); E. A. Boyd, *The Contemporary Drama of Ireland* (Boston, 1917); W. Archer, *The Old Drama and the New* (London, 1923); A. E. Morgan, *Tendencies of Modern English Drama* (London, 1924); E. B. Watson, *Sheridan to Robertson* (London, 1926); J. W. Cunliffe, *Modern English Playwrights* (New York, 1927); A. Nicoll, *A History of Early Nineteenth-*

Century Drama (2v, London, 1930); *A History of Late Nineteenth-Century Drama* (2v, London, 1946); N. W. Sawyer, *The Comedy of Manners from Sheridan to Maugham* (Philadelphia, 1931); E. Reynolds, *Early Victorian Drama: 1830-1870* (Cambridge, 1936); E. J. West, "The London Stage, 1870-1890," *University of Colorado Studies,* series B, II (1943). 31-84; W. Klemm, *Die englische Farce im 19 Jahrhundert* (Bern, 1946).

OSCAR WILDE (1856-1900)

>>

Oscar Fingal O'Flahertie Wills Wilde, whose life was a focus for public suspicion as to the morality and decency of the "aesthetic" cult of beauty and sensation, was born in Dublin on October 15, 1856. His father, an ear and eye specialist who was knighted in 1864, aroused some scandal by his foolish love affairs. Oscar's mother had written fervid poems on Irish nationalism in her youth, with the pen-name of "Speranza." Their two sons, of whom Oscar was the younger, went on excursions with their father to collect folk-lore, and took a precocious part in the conversations of their mother's *salon.*

As a boy, Oscar was brilliant and lazy, winning prizes by his literary talent but not willing to work hard at mathematics and science, in which he had no interest. At Trinity College, Dublin, he won a gold medal for Greek. In 1874 he gained a scholarship at Magdalen College, Oxford, where he soon attracted unfavorable attention by his contempt for athletics, his affected dress and manners, and the bizarre decorations of his rooms. Walter Pater was gaining the attention of some undergraduates by his doctrine of beauty as the supreme pleasure of life, and Wilde became his disciple, by both word and action. After a trip to Greece and Rome with his great friend and former tutor, J. P. Mahaffy, he settled definitely upon the classic life of Greece as his ideal. In spite of his pose as an idle pleasure-seeker, he won the Newdigate Prize in 1878 with his poem "Ravenna," and in the same year received his degree with first-class honors in Classics. Even before leaving Oxford he had begun to publish poems and essays, in all of which he praised pagan Greek beauty.

Having taken rooms in London, he began to widen his Oxford reputation as a wit and a rebel. He wore his hair long, and dressed in velvet breeches. His sarcastic and often insolent comments were widely quoted, as he attacked the accepted reputations of his more dignified contemporaries and ridiculed the approved conventions. When he published a book of poems in 1881 it quickly went through five editions. Gilbert and Sullivan lampooned his aesthetic cult in their comic opera *Patience,* and *Punch* started a campaign of caricature at his expense.

The next year he made a lecture tour of the United States, where he was received warmly by the "cultured" and roughly by the press. He crossed the Atlantic again in 1883 to see his first play, *Vera,* produced in New York. He now seemed to achieve more stability; his finances were better, his essays and stories appeared in leading magazines, and he married a lovely young woman with an adequate fortune. For two years he edited a women's magazine, in which he printed his articles on art and interior decoration.

Wilde wrote in many mediums. He was influenced by a school of *fin de siècle* French writers who enjoyed exotic depiction of sin, crime, decadence, and perversion, with a sophisticated assumption that virtue was an outmoded superstition. "The Sphinx," a long and elaborate poem, showed this influence strongly. So also did Wilde's novel, *The Picture of Dorian Gray* (1891), a "horror story" in which a beautiful young man's degeneration is told with all the embellishments of epigram and worldly poise. On the other hand, Wilde's charming stories for children, such as "The Happy Prince," had only a faint touch of satire and no taint of perversion.

With the success of his work as a dramatist Wilde rose to the heights of fame, fortune, and arrogance. His first two plays were not notable; but in 1892 came *Lady Windermere's Fan,* followed by *A Woman of No Importance* (1893), *Salome* (1894), *An Ideal Husband* (1895), and *The Importance of Being Earnest* (1895). Of these, *Salome* is apart from the others. Written in French, it was intended for Sarah Bernhardt, though even she hesitated before producing it, on account of its strange symbolism, its unhidden passion, and its emphasis on evil. It was printed, however, both in French and English, with illustrations by Aubrey Beardsley. Confined to one act, it showed the influence of Maeterlinck in its use of repetitions and of a very restricted vocabulary.

Lady Windermere's Fan, A Woman of No Importance, and *An Ideal Husband* are alike in being witty examples of the well-made play, but basically they are theatrical rather than dramatic; their problems are not treated with sincerity. This did not prevent their being highly successful. *The Importance of Being Earnest* was his masterpiece. A comedy of manners, admittedly artificial, it achieved in this genre a success scarcely second to that of the best work of Sheridan. It did nothing new, but its wit and paradox were brilliantly sustained.

Just at the peak of his success, in 1895, Wilde met with disaster. The father of a young friend made accusations of moral perversion against him, which he felt he must take to court. Wilde lost his libel action and was then brought to trial for the crime of which he had been accused. Although he had been urged by his friends to escape to the Continent rather than submit to disgrace, Wilde insisted on remaining, and was convicted and sentenced to two years in Reading Gaol at hard labor. During the first part of his term he was treated with extreme severity, and upon his release he found himself a bankrupt and a pariah. He went abroad, lived in France under the name of "Sebastian Melmoth," and never returned to England.

His last works, *The Ballad of Reading Gaol* and *De Profundis,* were written at least partly in prison. Both showed a new sincerity in his attitude, and have been regarded as his greatest work. Thereafter, however, he seemed to be written out, and his disintegration was rapid. He died on November 30, 1900, in Paris, shortly after his conversion to Catholicism. *De Profundis,* which had been written as an apology for his life, was published in 1905 by his executors.

Wilde's great ability in three literary types, poetry, essay, and drama, was often weakened by self-conscious mannerisms and dilettantism. He seldom forgot his purpose of shocking conventional minds. To be consistent with his praises of free sensual indulgence, which he uttered in his writings and for which he claimed the precedent of the ancient Greeks, he behaved in defiance of accepted moral laws with a sort of logical obstinacy. At the same time, in *The Picture of Dorian Gray* and elsewhere, he sometimes revealed grimly the ugly side of such excesses.

As he had been a subject of public controversy and newspaper diatribes in both Britain and the United States for a dozen years, his trial received the widest notoriety. It provided a sensational climax to the record of drinking, drug-addiction, and other aberrations of half-a-dozen recent poets of hedonism. Accordingly the whole "aesthetic" movement suffered such general censure that it quickly faded from sight. Many years were to elapse before Wilde's writings could be evaluated upon their intrinsic qualities as art, free of prejudices aroused by his personal conduct.

S. Mason [C. S. Millard], *Bibliography of Oscar Wilde* (London, 1914); *Works* (14v, London, 1907-09); *Complete Works,* ed. R. Ross (10v, New York, 1921); *After Reading: Letters to Robert Ross* (London, 1921); *After Berneval: Letters to Robert Ross* (London, 1922); *Some Letters to Alfred Douglas,* ed. A. C. Dennison and H. Post (San Francisco, 1924); *Sixteen Letters,* ed. J. Rothenstein (London, 1930); R. H. Sherard, *Oscar Wilde: The Story of an Unhappy Friendship* (London, 1902); *The Life of Oscar Wilde* (London, 1906); A. Symons, "An Artist in Attitudes," in *Studies in Prose and Verse* (London, 1904); A. Gide, *Oscar Wilde: A Study,* ed. S. Mason (Oxford, 1905); L. C. Ingleby, *Oscar Wilde* (London, 1907); A. Esdaile, "The New Hellenism," *Fortnightly Review,* XCIV (1910). 706-22; R. T. Hopkins, *Oscar Wilde: A Study of the Man and His Work* (London, 1912); S. Mason, *Oscar Wilde: Art and Morality* (London, 1912); A. Ransome, *Oscar Wilde: A Critical Study* (London, 1912); Lord A. Douglas, *Oscar Wilde and Myself* (London, 1914); R. H. Sherard, *The Real Oscar Wilde* (London, 1915); F. Harris, *Oscar Wilde: His Life and Confessions* (2v, New York, 1916; rev. ed., 1930); A. Symons, *A Study of Oscar Wilde* (London, 1930); A. H. Cooper-Pritchard, *Conversations with Oscar Wilde* (London, 1931); J. P. Raymond [C. Ricketts], *Oscar Wilde: Recollections* (London, 1932); G. J. Renier, *Oscar Wilde* (London, 1933); L. Lewis and H. J. Smith, *Oscar Wilde Discovers America* (New York, 1936); V. O'Sullivan, *Aspects of Wilde* (London, 1936); R. H. Sherard, *Bernard Shaw, Frank Harris, and Oscar Wilde* (London, 1937); B. L. Brasol, *Oscar Wilde: The Man, the Artist, the Martyr* (London, 1938); F. Winwar, *Oscar Wilde and the Yellow Nineties* (New York, 1940); Lord A. Douglas, *Oscar Wilde: A Summing-Up* (London, 1940); A. H. Nethercot, "Oscar Wilde and the Devil's Advocate," *Publications of the Modern Language Association,* LIX (1944). 833-50; H. Pearson, *The Life of Oscar Wilde* (London, 1946).

GEORGE BERNARD SHAW (1856-   )

>>

Mr. George Bernard Shaw, as he himself would be first to suggest, was the most important single figure in the revival of English drama in the closing decade of the nineteenth century. Although he was born in Ireland, his parents were of chiefly English and Scottish descent. He classifies himself as "a genuine typical Irishman of the Danish, Norman, Cromwellian, and (of course) Scottish invasions."

Born in Dublin on July 26, 1856, Shaw first received private tuition from an uncle, a clergyman; and later, when sent to school, he was "generally near or at the bottom of his classes." He felt that the masters knew nothing that he wanted to know; but he read widely, with a natural good taste that prevented his wasting time on unimportant books. At the age of fifteen he escaped from classes to take a minor clerical position in a Dublin land office. The money he earned, though it was not much, was useful to the family, for the Shaws, in spite of being well connected, were impecunious. The father was not successful financially as a corn merchant, and drank more than was necessary. Mrs. Shaw had a fine voice, and her son learned to understand music and to love it through her and her teacher. As Mrs. Shaw took part in amateur productions of opera, George Bernard became familiar with the backstage of the theater. By the time he was twenty, his mother was establishing herself in London as a music teacher.

Shaw could see little opportunity in his office position. He was not enough of a musician to follow his mother's profession, and some study of art convinced him of his inadequacy for a career as a painter. Although he had not particularly considered authorship, that way of expression was easy for him; he had a pungent style of utterance and had already contributed a few startling letters to newspapers. Therefore he made up his mind to seek his fortune as a writer in London. This involved his becoming a charge on his family again. "I did not throw myself into the battle of life," he confessed with characteristic candor; "I threw my mother into it." He felt later that the knowledge that he was one of the coming men of literature should have repaid his parents for any inconvenience his long dependence might have occasioned them.

His years in the land agent's office had given him a clear handwriting and steady habits of work. In 1879 he set himself to write a novel a year, at the rate of five pages a day. The first, entitled *Immaturity,* was rejected by numerous publishers (George Meredith, in his capacity of publisher's reader, was one who declined it). The novels that followed, *The Irrational Knot* (1880), *Love Among the Artists* (1881), *Cashel Byron's Profession* (1882), and *An Unsocial Socialist* (1883), also remained unpublished until a later date. All of them suffered from lack of plot and from Shaw's inability to draw sympathetic characters. Annoyed with a society that would appreciate neither him nor his works, he made his heroines weak or stultified and his heroes caddish in an effort to show that he disapproved of it as much as it neglected him. In general style the novels resembled those of the eighteenth century, with the characters indulging in long lectures that were supposed to represent conversation.

After writing *Cashel Byron's Profession,* a story of the prize ring, Shaw heard a lecture by Henry George and decided to espouse the cause of the Single Tax. This study soon led him to read Karl Marx, who converted him to socialism. In his enthusiasm he began a new work that was to be a gigantic panorama of capitalistic society. After finishing two chapters he stopped, with enough material for his fifth novel, *An Unsocial Socialist.*

Already in his Dublin days he had become bitterly contemptuous of pretension and authority and injustice and social barriers. Socialism gave him a specific channel into which to direct these opinions. He attended William Morris's meetings, and soon joined the newly-organized Fabian Society, in which he became a leader, along with a group of other brilliant and unorthodox writers and talkers. He wrote copiously for the short-lived propaganda magazines of the movement, in which four of his novels appeared as serials.

Though Shaw was too individualistic and egotistic to accept all the rigid principles of the Socialist party, he remained active in the Fabian Society for many years. Until 1895 he lectured several times a week, ranging from the platform of a scholarly association to a soap-box on a slum street-corner. As his addresses provoked violent argument and heckling, he had to master the arts of debate and emphasis. In preparation for them he studied widely in economics and political science.

His propaganda writings were contributed free to the cause, but about the age of thirty he began to earn his living in journalism, as a critic of books, pictures, and music for various newspapers and then as dramatic critic for the *Saturday Review*. Gradually the initials G. B. S. became familiar when signed to reviews that were independent in thought and caustic in expression. He persistently championed the realistic, intellectual type of drama represented by Ibsen, whose plays were generally regarded as dangerously immoral. Shaw was equally positive in defending Wagner's operas against charges of musical anarchism. His essays on these topics were collected in *The Quintessence of Ibsenism* (1891) and *The Perfect Wagnerite* (1898). Some of his other important critical writings were issued as *Dramatic Opinions and Essays* (1907).

His praise of Ibsen led him to assert the inferiority of Shakespeare. Although uttered with his usual iconoclasm, his opinion was useful in challenging the conventional Shakespeare-worship of the time. There was more ample justification for his consistent diatribes against the inane mechanical type of play that held the London stage.

As early as 1885 he had tried to write a comedy with another drama critic, William Archer, but they disagreed so totally that it was abandoned. Seven years later Shaw was begged to provide a play for the Independent Theater, an experimental organization that was struggling to survive. He transformed the old effort into a serious Ibsen-like attack on rapacious slum-landlords, *Widowers' Houses,* which was performed a few times in December, 1892. His former collaborator, Archer, reviewed it unfavorably, saying that Shaw revealed no ability in playwriting. Shaw next wrote *The Philanderer,* a satire on pseudo-Ibsenism and the war of the sexes. This was rejected by the Independent Theater, and when Shaw followed it with *Mrs. Warren's Profession,* condemning the hypocrisy of certain laws against immorality, the censor refused to sanction its performance. These three plays resembled Shaw's novels in being stiff and wordy, with little wit and few effective characters. They were too obviously didactic in their handling of current problems.

His next play, *Arms and the Man,* concealing its social purpose under gay comedy, enjoyed a London run of four months in 1894 and was also successful in New York; but its successor, *Candida,* was refused by London producers, though it was well received in Germany. *You Never Can Tell* got as far as rehearsal in 1897 but did not reach the stage.

At this time an illness forced Shaw to give up his journalistic work and his political speaking. In 1898 he married a wealthy woman. In the same year he published his dramatic works in two volumes, entitled *Plays Pleasant and Unpleasant,* adding to each play a long preface in which he provocatively argued the play's social and literary values. The originality of his ideas, the paradoxical wit of the dialogue, even the amusing stage-directions, made the plays very readable, and Shaw gained wide public attention. *The Devil's Disciple,* a play of the American Revolution, was produced in New York in 1897 and in London in 1900, a year that also witnessed a London production of *Captain Brassbound's Conversion.* These were published in the same year in *Three Plays for Puritans,* the third being his historical satire, *Caesar and Cleopatra,* a sort of comic inversion of Shakespeare's tragedy.

His first real success on the London stage was *John Bull's Other Island,* a study of the causes of trouble in Ireland, produced in 1903. In this year he published *Man and Superman,* which aroused much discussion both in book form and when staged two years later. Thus Shaw was nearing fifty before he was recognized as a major dramatist rather than a conceited mountebank and outrageous rebel who insisted on trying to write plays. First by his essays and later by his prefaces, as much as by the plays themselves, he had slowly trained a public to appreciate the dramatic presentation of controversial ideas.

From that time onward, his career was a sequence of successes. *Major Barbara* (1905) was concerned with public charity and the responsibilities of wealth. *The Doctor's Dilemma* (1906) satirized various types of physicians. In *Getting Married* (1908) Shaw offered a treatise in brilliant dialogue, almost without plot. *Fanny's First Play* (1911) included a satire upon dramatic critics, one of whom was his old friend Archer. *Androcles and the Lion* (1912), apparently farcical in its portrayal of the Christian martyrs, implied some serious ideas about religious faith. One of his most successful comedies, *Pygmalion* (1913), scandalized the public by using a slang word that English usage considered vulgar. *Heartbreak House* (1917), another experiment in plotless debate, had somewhat the somber tone of Chekov's *Cherry Orchard.* In 1922 came his most amazing work, *Back to Methuselah,* a group of five plays requiring three evenings for complete performance, and summarizing Shaw's views on life in general and biology in particular, from an opening episode in the Garden of

Eden to a conclusion thirty-two thousand years hence. This work was taken to indicate that Shaw had at last defied all traditions of dramatic technique, but the next year came *Saint Joan,* one of his greatest plays and (except for its ironic epilogue) his nearest approach to a conventional tragedy. Later plays that showed only slight waning of his power were *The Apple Cart* and *Too True to Be Good.*

In 1926 Shaw was awarded the Nobel Prize for literature. By that time he had become a world-famous personality whose acid comments on even the most trivial matters were accorded newspaper headlines. Shaw belongs to the tradition of the great satirists, who stimulated people to think by annoying them. With assertions that were often exaggerated and yet contained an uncomfortable amount of logic, he calmly contradicted the most sacrosanct assumptions of his country and his era. Relentlessly he waged war on shallow sentimentality and exalted the value of common sense. His egotistical manner, which supplied his adversaries with easy grounds of attack, was carefully cultivated as a device of publicity. With sufficient skill in characterization to enable him to embody his heterodox ideas in entertaining dramatic dialogue, he created plays brilliant enough to attract audiences and readers who often violently opposed his views.

It is not possible to determine exactly to what extent Shaw's works contributed to the eventual acceptance of many of his opinions; but certainly his influence upon English and American thought was strong. Realizing that the theater reached only a small segment of the public, he used his considerable business ability in the promotion of his writings in book form, and the general habit of reading modern plays was largely the result of his efforts. Beyond a doubt he gave new vitality to the English drama by proving that it could be a vehicle for the expression of independent and stimulating ideas.

L. C. and V. M. Broad, *Dictionary to the Plays and Novels of Bernard Shaw, with a Bibliography* (London, 1929); *Collected Works* (30v, London, 1930- ; Ayot St. Lawrence edition); *Complete Plays* (London, 1931); A. B. Walkley, "Mr. Bernard Shaw's Plays," in *Frames of Mind* (London, 1899); H. Jackson, *Bernard Shaw* (London, 1907); G. K. Chesterton, *George Bernard Shaw* (London, 1909); J. Bab, *Bernard Shaw* (Berlin, 1910); R. Deacon, *Bernard Shaw As Artist Philosopher* (London, 1910); A. Henderson, *George Bernard Shaw: His Life and Works* (Cincinnati, 1911); G. Norwood, *Euripides and Shaw* (London, 1913); F. Hamon, *The Technique of Bernard Shaw's Plays* (London, 1912); *The Twentieth-Century Molière* (London, 1915); J. McCabe, *George Bernard Shaw: A Study* (London, 1914); P. P. Howe, *Bernard Shaw: A Critical Study* (London, 1915); R. Burton, *Bernard Shaw: The Man and the Mask* (New York, 1916); H. Skimpole, *Bernard Shaw: The Man and His Work* (London, 1918); H. C. Duffin, *The Quintessence of Shaw* (London, 1920); E. Shanks, *Bernard Shaw* (London, 1924); J. S. Collis, *Bernard Shaw* (London, 1925); E. Wagenknecht, *A Guide to Bernard Shaw* (New York, 1929); F. Harris, *Bernard Shaw: An Unauthorized Biography* (London, 1931); A. Henderson: *Bernard Shaw, Playboy and Prophet* (New York, 1932); R. F. Rattray, *Bernard Shaw: A Chronicle and an Introduction* (London, 1934); H. Pearson, *G. B. S.: A Full-length Portrait* (London, 1942); *G. B. S. at Ninety*, ed. S. Winsten (London, 1946); E. Bentley, *Bernard Shaw* (New York, 1947); S. Winsten, *Days With Bernard Shaw* (London, 1948).

MINOR DRAMATISTS

▷▷▷

Dionysius Lardner Boucicault (1822-1890). Half French and half Irish, Dion Boucicault was born in Dublin, and made a success with his first play, *London Assurance,* before he was twenty. He followed with *Old Heads and Young Hearts* and *The Corsican Brothers.* After being in the United States from 1853 to 1859 he returned to England and produced *The Colleen Bawn,* based on Gerald Griffin's Irish novel, *The Collegians.* His other Irish plays were

Arrah na Pogue (1865) and *The Shaughraun* (1875). Of his several hundred plays, many were unsuccessful. *The Poor of New York, The Octoroon,* and *After Dark* were among his best melodramas. He acted in many of his own plays, and lost most of his profits in managerial ventures.

T. Walsh, *The Career of Dion Boucicault* (New York, 1915).

Henry James Byron (1834-1884). After experience as actor, dramatic manager, and editor of comic papers, Byron became a playwright, with his chief success in burlesques, extravaganzas, and farces. *Our Boys* established a record by running for four years (1875-1879).

Henry Arthur Jones (1851-1929). Following the success of his melodrama, *The Silver King,* in 1882, Jones turned to the writing of serious plays about contemporary life, the first being *Saints and Sinners* (1884). Later plays included *The Crusaders, The Tempter, The Masqueraders, The Case of Rebellious Susan, The Liars, The Physician, Carnac Sahib, Mrs. Dane's Defense.* His book on *The Renascence of the English Drama* (1895) was important in defining the new trend under the influence of Ibsen.

D. A. Jones, *Taking the Curtain Call: The Life and Letters of Henry Arthur Jones* (London, 1930).

James Sheridan Knowles (1784-1862). A native of Cork, and a cousin of Richard Brinsley Sheridan, Knowles came to London in childhood and became a friend of Hazlitt, Coleridge, and Lamb. After serving in the army and studying medicine, he became an actor, and thereafter wrote a number of poetic dramas, the most famous being *Virginius* (1820). Only his last three came after 1830. He ended as a popular Baptist preacher.

R. B. Knowles, *Life of James Sheridan Knowles* (London, 1872); L. H. Meeks, *Sheridan Knowles and the Theatre of His Time* (Bloomington, 1933).

John Maddison Morton (1811-1891). The son of a successful playwright, Morton was typical of the hack writers who translated and adapted French plays. Of his forty-five plays, most of which were farces, the best known is *Box and Cox* (1847).

Arthur Wing Pinero (1855-1934). Descended from a Portuguese Jewish family long settled in England, Pinero was trained for the law, but at nineteen became an actor, and wrote a successful play, *The Money Spinner*, at the age of twenty-five. *The Squire* (1881) was a serious play of contemporary life, but thereafter he devoted himself for eight years to farces *(The Magistrate, The Schoolmistress, Dandy Dick, The Cabinet Minister, The Amazons)* and to sentimental comedies *(Sweet Lavender, The Weaker Sex)*. In 1889 he returned to serious plays with *The Profligate,* and four years later attracted great attention with *The Second Mrs. Tanqueray,* which was regarded as a daring treatment of a moral problem. Later successes were *The Notorious Mrs. Ebbsmith, Trelawney of the Wells, The Gay Lord Quex, Iris, Letty, The Thunderbolt, His House in Order.* He received a knighthood for his achievements.

H. H. Fyfe, *Arthur Wing Pinero* (London, 1902); W. D. Dunkel, *Sir Arthur Pinero: A Critical Biography* (Chicago, 1941).

Thomas William Robertson (1829-1871). After some years as an actor and journalist in provincial towns, Tom Robertson settled in London in 1860, and made his first dramatic success with *David Garrick* in 1864. This was followed by his sequence of domestic "cup and saucer" comedies at the Prince of Wales's Theatre—*Society* (1865), *Ours* (1866), *Caste* (1867), *Play* (1868), *School* (1869), *M. P.* (1870).

T. E. Pemberton, *The Life and Writings of T. W. Robertson* (London, 1893).

Thomas Noon Talfourd (1795-1854). In a successful legal and political career, Talfourd was a friend of many authors, from Lamb to Dickens, led the parliamentary fight for an international copyright law, and received a knighthood. His tragedy, *Ion,* was successful at Covent Garden Theater in 1836, and was followed by *The Athenian Captive, Glencoe,* and *The Castilian.*

Henry Taylor (1800-1886). A civil servant in the Colonial Office for almost fifty years, Taylor was knighted for his services in 1869. His drama, *Philip van Artevelde* (1834), in rhetorical blank verse, was widely acclaimed. Other plays were *Edwin the Fair* (1842) and *St. Clement's Eve* (1862).

Autobiography (2v, London, 1885); *Correspondence,* ed. E. Dowden (London, 1888).

Tom Taylor (1817-1880). Beginning his career as a Fellow of Trinity College, Cambridge, and a Professor of English Literature at University College, London, Taylor turned to the law and then entered the government service, where he rose to responsible office while giving much time to journalism and drama. Long a member of the staff of *Punch,* he became editor in 1874. His dramatic work began with burlesques in 1844. He collaborated with Charles Reade in *Masks and Faces* in 1852. Among his hundred or more plays were historical tragedies *(Joan of Arc,* 1871, *Anne Boleyn,* 1875), social comedies *(Still Waters Run Deep,* 1855, *Our American Cousin,* 1858), and dramas of contemporary life *(The Contested Election,* 1859, *The Ticket-of-Leave Man,* 1863, *Arkwright's Wife,* 1873).

W. Tolles, *Tom Taylor and the Victorian Drama* (New York, 1940).

EXPOSITORY PROSE
>>>

The Victorian age was so strongly excited over opinions, ideas, theories, and even the acquiring of new information, that many books of expository prose attained not only the wide influence but also the qualities of originality and emotional force which put them into the class of literature. Philosophy, religion, physical science, political theory, economics, and history all contributed books which were written with distinguished style and originality.

One trait was shared by practically all of these books: they were long. Accordingly, the modern reader has little opportunity of becoming familiar with them. Sample excerpts are incapable of giving a true impression of the chief writings of Carlyle or Ruskin, Darwin or Spencer, Mill or Macaulay. Writing in a day when fewer competing interests distracted a reader's attention, they assumed that their subject-matter was important enough to deserve full development. The various main types of expository prose will here be discussed separately, though some authors were equally prominent in more than one category, and sometimes a single book is hard to assign because it ranges from one category into another.

The oldest of all the Victorians, and the most positive of the many strong personalities that expressed themselves in literature, was Thomas Carlyle. Owing to his slow struggle to gain an education and a start in his literary career, he was publishing his first books alongside men ten or twelve years younger. In his long lifetime he wrote in many of the different fields of prose.

It is impossible to separate Carlyle's writings on "philosophy" from those on economic and social subjects. His various doctrines of work, duty, and leadership, an ethical system derived largely from the Calvinism of his Scottish background, were spread through the lectures *On Heroes and Hero Worship,* the semi-historical theorizing in *Past and Present,* and elsewhere. His impressive style and confident (though often inconsistent) opinions strongly stimulated many younger writers. In philosophy he attacked the rationalism and empiricism of a scientific and industrial epoch and pioneered for the German "idealism" of Kant and Hegel, with its emphasis on the human mind and spirit as the creating and controlling force in our existence.

The school of thought which Carlyle opposed had been set up in England by Jeremy Bentham and James Mill, and was led by the latter's son, John Stuart Mill, whose *Logic* was a landmark of 1843. Its influence reached into practically every branch of thinking. In political theory it was known as "Utilitarianism," based on the concept that the advisability of any procedure should be determined by the general welfare ("the greatest happiness of the greatest number") rather than by abstract principles. This doctrine obviously carried implications of grave significance to the whole realm of ethics.

In philosophy, the equivalent system was "Positivism," which insisted that the only acceptable material for consideration is provided by experience, without regard to metaphysical theories and deductive reasoning. Religion fell under this ban, and accordingly most of the utilitarians and positivists were "free-thinkers," though few of them took the outright stand of skepticism or atheism. About 1870 Thomas Henry Huxley proposed the word *agnostic* to describe their point of view, indicating that they regarded the immaterial concepts of the existence of God and the immortality of the human soul as being beyond any possible power of proof, either negative or affirmative.

The change in attitude toward the human soul was partly due to the newly emerging science of psychology. Its basis was the "Associationist" theory which originated in the seventeenth century with Hobbes and was formalized in the eighteenth by David Hartley. Analogous to the atomic theory of matter, it postulated a small group of basic units of consciousness which are constantly rearranged into different groupings.

The whole texture of rationalistic ideas had a chilly, inhuman quality that appealed but little to the average reader; but the Mills, father and son, expounded it with a grim lucidity that could not be lightly ignored. The growing scientific hypotheses had given impetus to this line of thought as early as the thirties, in the writings of William Whewell; and it provided the basis for the vast and influential series of books by Herbert Spencer which he grouped under the title of *Synthetic Philosophy*.

These writers depended on the inductive method as adequate to solve all problems and to explain all phenomena. Their work was therefore closely connected with the growth of rationalism in reference to religion. A characteristic figure was George Henry Lewes, who was notorious as a "free-thinker." His *Biographical History of Philosophy* was strongly positivist; and his last work, *The Problems of Life and Mind,* was a psychological study that impinged upon both biology and metaphysics. The opposite point of view, based on Spinoza (by James Martineau), and on Kant and Hegel (by Edward Caird and Thomas Hill Green), gradually gained ground, and in the later part of the century was strengthened by the books of F. H. Bradley and Bernard Bosanquet.

Various offshoots of these conflicting doctrines expanded throughout the second half of the Victorian period. The positivist view, which had been presented as a general principle by the Mills, became affiliated with the "religion of humanity" which had been proposed in France by Auguste Comte as a substitute for creeds based on divine revelation. The Positivist Society, which conducted church services with a regular ritual, was led by a group of able dialecticians and writers, the best known of whom were Frederic Harrison and John Morley. They adopted the *Fortnightly Review* as the vehicle of their opinions.

Attempting to bridge the growing gap between scientific and religious thinking, an architect named James Knowles combined with his friend Tennyson in 1869 to found the Metaphysical Society, at which many of the most brilliant leaders of both camps met to debate their ideas. Knowles edited the *Contemporary Review* from 1870 to 1877 and the *Nineteenth Century* thereafter, and the discussions of the Metaphysical Society were transmitted to a wider public through their pages.

Another hopeful seeker for compromise, Francis William Newman, who shared some measure of the literary skill of his elder brother, the great Cardinal, wrote articles and books such as *Phases of Faith,* his spiritual autobiography, which argued for a non-sectarian theism that did not depend on supernatural revelation. Another persistent adversary of orthodox traditions was Leslie Stephen, who made a wide impression with his *Essays on Free Thinking and Plain Speaking, Science and Ethics, An Agnostic's Apology,* and other books.

George John Romanes, a biologist by profession and a friend of Darwin, published in 1878 *A Candid Examination of Theism* which asserted that no adherent of science could consistently believe in a beneficent and omnipotent God. William K. Clifford, a brilliant young mathematician, also plunged into the philosophical conflict, and in *Body and Mind* (1874) declared that research into the automatic functioning of living creatures might produce actual scientific disproof of the existence of God. Other books written by Clifford during his short career were *Seeing and Thinking* and *The Common Sense of the Exact Sciences*. He contributed to the philosophical vocabulary the phrases "mind-stuff" and "the tribal self."

A versatile biologist, Grant Allen, who wrote verse and many sensational novels as well as both scholarly and popular books on science, was an exponent of the evolutionary philosophy of Spencer, in such books as *Physiological Aesthetics* (1877) and *The Evolution of the Idea of God* (1897).

William Winwood Reade, a nephew of the novelist, was a venturesome African explorer who plunged into the philosophical arguments with *The Veil of Isis* (1861), a study of comparative religion, and followed in 1872 with a more violently controversial book, *The Martyrdom of Man,* which carried the positivist "religion of humanity" to the degree of militant atheism. On the other hand, Arthur James Balfour, a future Prime Minister of England, offered a restrained and even witty manifesto of free speculation in *A Defence of Philosophic Doubt* (1879).

Another significant attitude was that of Frederic W. H. Myers, a poet and critic of distinct merit, who tried to apply scientific methods to the investigation of hypnotism, spiritualism, and other non-material phenomena. He helped to found the Society for Psychical Research in 1882, and published *Phantasms of the Living* (1886), *Science and a Future Life* (1893), *Human Personality and Its Survival* (1903).

After 1870 there was also a perceptible growth of philosophical pessimism, as the theories of Schopenhauer and von Hartmann became known in England through James Sully's *Pessimism* (1877) and two books by the American expatriate Edgar Saltus, *The Philosophy of Disenchantment* (1885) and *The Anatomy of Negation* (1886).

Philosophical writing merged on one side into theology,

on the other side into science. The writing which dealt
with religion was partly concerned with the conflicting
opinions within the Church of England, first brought to a
focus by the *Tracts for the Times* between 1833 and 1841.
A leading contributor was John Henry Newman, and he
went on to a series of important and beautifully written
books, especially the *Apologia Pro Vita Sua*. The other
strong tendency, toward "higher criticism" and a rational
interpretation of the scriptures, was also centered in a
publication by a group of authors, *Essays and Reviews*
(1860). The influence of Kantian philosophy was brought
into the situation by a disciple of Carlyle, Frederick Denison
Maurice. He, in turn, was part of the "Christian Socialist"
movement which included Charles Kingsley, and it was
Kingsley's onslaught upon Newman's conversion to the
Roman Catholic church which evoked Newman's *Apologia*. Into this confused campaign of opposing forces Matthew Arnold stepped with his calm and apparently objective
analysis of religious concepts in *Literature and Dogma* and
St. Paul and Protestantism.

On the other side of philosophy, many of the great scientists were writing books so vivid in their material and so
exciting in the novelty of their theories that they were
read widely by the general public, and they strongly influenced the thinking of writers in other fields. There were
also able "popularizers" who helped to arouse interest and
to give the necessary elementary knowledge. Among the
most successful of the popularizers were Mrs. Mary Somerville *(The Connection of the Physical Sciences,* 1834), Hugh
Miller *(The Old Red Sandstone,* 1841, and *The Testimony
of the Rocks,* 1857), Robert Chambers *(Vestiges of the Natural History of Creation,* 1844), Philip Henry Gosse *(The
Romance of Natural History,* 1860), and George Henry
Lewes *(Seaside Studies,* 1858, *Studies in Animal Life,* 1862).

Great scientists who wrote books that were works of literature as well as being scientific treatises included Sir Charles Lyell *(Principles of Geology,* 1830-33), Charles Darwin *(The Origin of Species,* 1859, *The Descent of Man,* 1871), Alfred Russel Wallace, Thomas Henry Huxley, and John Tyndall. Later in the century, as scientific research turned from geology and zoölogy toward the study of the human being, the important figures were Sir Francis Galton, whose studies in heredity provided material for the novelists, and Sir James G. Frazer, author of a great anthropological study of primitive religion, *The Golden Bough,* a mine of strange stories and symbols for recent poets.

Sometimes closely connected with works on science, at other times more concerned with social conditions and international politics, were the numerous and successful books of travel. Several of the great scientists thus gave the public a glimpse into their adventures: Darwin's *Voyage of the Beagle* became a classic, and Alfred Russel Wallace wrote equally vividly in *Travels on the Amazon and Rio Negro* and *The Malay Archipelago.* The archaeologists, too, could combine scientific research with exciting experiences, as Sir Austen Henry Layard did in his books about his excavations at Nineveh.

There were areas of the world still which were new and dangerous, so that the records of the explorers had all the fascination of the unfamiliar and the thrill of peril, as well as the satisfaction of solving mysteries. Some of these explorer-authors became popular heroes, such as Sir Richard F. Burton, who wrote a breath-taking account of his visit to Mecca disguised as a Moslem pilgrim, David Livingstone, the great missionary-explorer of Central Africa, and Henry M. Stanley. Later came Charles Montagu Doughty, with his magnificently-written *Travels in Arabia Deserta.*

Just as much interest and enthusiasm, however, went into narratives of travel in near and familiar lands. In the earlier Victorian years a procession of English authors crossed the

Atlantic to the United States, and usually aroused controversy on both sides of the ocean by the reports that they published. Mrs. Frances Trollope and Captain Marryat were among the first to deal with the subject; and then Dickens, with his *American Notes,* evoked especial acrimony because of his eminence as a novelist. Dickens wrote also *Pictures from Italy.* Thackeray refrained from making a book about his American tours, but he got into the same sort of trouble over his *Irish Sketch Book;* a longer journey, though not adventurous, to Greece, the Holy Land, and Egypt, provided material for *From Cornhill to Grand Cairo.* The most admirable book on the Near East was by a less famous author—A. W. Kinglake's *Eothen.* Mention should be made of two good books on India by the Hon. Emily Eden, *Portraits of the People* and *Up the Country.*

George Borrow's *Wild Wales* and *The Bible in Spain* show how closely the travel book approaches other types of narrative—the autobiography or even the novel; for these books by Borrow are not essentially different from his *Lavengro* and *The Romany Rye,* which are usually classified as prose fiction.

Many of the travel books imply the lively public interest in social conditions, governmental systems, and so on, which was part of the rapid growth of the "social sciences." The books on economic and political theories were important for their influence upon the writings of poets and novelists, as well as for their effect upon the thinking of the public and its translation into political action. The writers on these subjects were in their turn affected by the developments taking place in national and international affairs. Hence, some of the leading authors changed their opinions considerably with the lapse of time. Just as in religious thinking the writings of Newman showed his movement from the traditional Episcopalian doctrines to the High Church idea and then to Roman Catholicism, so the social theorists traveled step by step toward views which they did not originally foresee.

John Stuart Mill, for instance, began as the spokesman for the Utilitarians, and their creed of laissez-faire capitalistic enterprise was developed in his *Principles of Political Economy* (1848). His wider sympathies, however, began to show in his essay *On Liberty,* ten years later, and his *Representative Government,* and eventually his views were not far from Socialism. On the other hand, Thomas Carlyle, who had been a friend and admirer of Mill at the outset of his career, and who was (in a sense) just as extreme an individualist, moved in another direction. Carlyle's distrust of the intelligence of the masses and his belief in the value of firm leadership made him antagonistic to democratic processes, just as his peasant simplicity caused him to exalt the virtue of hard labor and loathe the crowds and the machinery and the spiraling wealth of modern capitalism. The violence of the Chartist movement completed Carlyle's breach with the "philosophical Radicals."

Mill's thinking was closer to the actual political trends of England and the United States for the past century, but his chilly reasoning had less appeal to readers than Carlyle's eloquent denunciations and exhortations. When Carlyle began to express his ideas of social philosophy he produced such an odd mixture of discussion and fiction in *Sartor Resartus*—a kind of novel without a plot—that publishers scorned the book. As his style became more and more eccentric the public gradually learned to like it, even though he irritated most people by his contemptuous attitude toward all their shibboleths. In *Past and Present* he idealized the handicrafts and the paternalism of the middle ages in contrast with the greed and mass-production of the competitive system. *Latter-day Pamphlets* showed the full extent of his reactionary ferocity; and later *Shoot-*

ing Niagara—and After was his attack upon the Reform Bill of 1867. He condemned Mill's economics as "the dismal science" because it implied that human beings were helpless slaves of economic forces.

The leading convert to Carlyle's beliefs was John Ruskin. Beginning as a rich business man's son and a scholarly critic of art, Ruskin seemed anything but a person to become concerned over social controversies. While writing his books on art history, *The Seven Lamps of Architecture* and *Stones of Venice,* he gradually developed his theory that great art can be produced only in conditions of freedom and self-respect. The drab life of the industrial cities and the ugly products of the factory convinced him that his own era lacked these conditions. His other important book on art, *Modern Painters,* brought him into touch with the Pre-Raphaelite movement and strengthened his love for the middle ages. When these views brought him into the camp of Carlyle he began to write on economic subjects.

Ruskin's literary style had been much admired for its careful and elaborate constructions and for its passages of richly poetic description. When he undertook to expound economics he schooled himself in a clear and simple manner of expression which proved effective for its purpose. *Unto This Last* and *Munera Pulveris* aroused such opposition when they appeared as serials in magazines that the editors discontinued them. In these books, *The Two Paths, Fors Clavigera,* and others, Ruskin revealed his movement toward a definitely socialistic creed. His analysis of social problems was often mingled with rather naïve ethical moralizing, but to his own time he was eminently successful in awakening social concern among an influential and idealistic class of readers.

An almost identical path was followed by William Morris, starting as a Pre-Raphaelite medievalist who thought that art should not concern itself with the commonplace affairs of everyday life, and reversing this theory when he decided that the equipment of daily living must be made individual and beautiful. His practical encouragement of handicraft arts and coöperative industries converted him to socialism, which he preached in his prose allegories, *A Dream of John Ball* and *News from Nowhere*.

It is a paradoxical fact that the violent and sometimes incoherent ideas of Carlyle, springing from his intuitive hatred of industrial capitalism, when harnessed to a more analytical study of economic problems by Ruskin, and tried out in practice by Morris, helped to father the English Fabian Socialist group, which allied itself with the Labor movement to become a political party, and in 1946 took over the actual remodeling of the English way of life.

Standing apart from these angry theorists, but just as deeply concerned over the materialism and the uncouthness of the time, was Matthew Arnold. With his lucid prose and restrained irony he tried to bring some reason and perspective to bear on the disputes. Just as he wrote his literary essays in the hope of making English readers aware of the currents of world literature, and wrote *Literature and Dogma* to propose a moderate form of religious faith which might survive in a scientific era because it dispensed with miracles and biblical infallibility, so in *Culture and Anarchy* he recommended the virtues of "sweetness and light" to replace the heat and confusion that swirled about him. As often happens to conciliators, he annoyed most of the factions; but his gift of phrase-making contributed to the language several permanent epithets, such as "Philistine" and "Hellenism."

The later years of the century produced no writer on social, political, or economic theory of stature to rival those already mentioned. Walter Bagehot published a standard book on *The English Constitution* which displayed it as a living organism rather than an abstraction, just as his *Lombard Street* drew upon his personal experiences in finance for a study of economic processes. Edward Carpenter represented the humanitarian idealism near the end of the century with his book of Whitmanesque free verse, *Towards Democracy*, and his prose work, *Civilization, Its Cause and Cure*. The writings of Sidney and Beatrice Webb influenced the new Labor movement. George Bernard Shaw did much to popularize radical ideas through the long prefaces of his plays, and even Oscar Wilde wrote a thoughtful essay on "The Soul of Man Under Socialism."

Alongside of the other social sciences, history was prominent in Victorian literature. The most admired historian in the earlier half of the era was Thomas Babington Macaulay, who set a fashion for a picturesque narrative style, full of vivid details, modeled upon the techniques of the historical novel. His series of "Essays" in the *Edinburgh Review*, though ostensibly book reviews, were actually short historical studies, and his practice in them led to his large work, *The History of England,* which occupied the last fifteen years of his life. Its five large volumes covered only the years 1680 to 1700. Its sound construction, careful detail, and easy but dignified style made it immensely popular. Almost alone among the leading authors he represented the prevailing political and social tone of the age— the complacent approval of material progress and the optimistic liberalism of the Whig party. Accordingly his writing was free from the agonized protests and from the groping but sometimes profound search for meaning which marked his contemporaries. He wrote efficiently about the surface of events, and he suited the temper of his readers so well that his anti-Tory interpretation of English history prevailed almost unchallenged in England and the United States for generations.

In the same years as Macaulay, Carlyle was also devoting

himself principally to history. He carried even further the use of fictional methods to heighten the vividness and dramatic intensity of his narrative, giving the reader a sense of immediate observation of the scenes depicted. Emerson termed the effect "stereoscopic." Carlyle's theory of "the hero" made him assert that "the history of what man has accomplished in this world is at bottom the History of the Great Men who have worked here." His first historical masterpiece, *The French Revolution*, was a joint biography of a group of leaders. His later and even more gigantic works, on Cromwell and Frederick the Great, were only slightly less picturesque because the subject-matter was not so violent. Carlyle based his histories on such full research that neither his eccentricities of style nor his prejudiced opinions could seriously affect their essential value.

The more academic historians wrote thorough and readable books, though none rivaled the artistic skill of Macaulay and Carlyle. A follower of Carlyle, James Anthony Froude, wrote with a vivid style, his greatest book being on the English Reformation period; but his work was marred by bias. Originally associated with the High Church movement, he had broken away, under Carlyle's influence, and in consequence of his book entitled *The Nemesis of Faith* he had to give up his Oxford fellowship. His history was bitterly anti-Catholic, and on the basis of Carlyle's theory of leadership he glorified Henry VIII.

Other historians attacked Froude's interpretation of events. W. E. H. Lecky, for instance, wrote his *History of England in the Eighteenth Century* to refute *The English in Ireland* by Froude. Lecky's chief books were a *History of Rationalism in Europe* and a *History of European Morals*. The most implacable enemy of Froude was Edward Augustus Freeman, author of a *History of the Norman Conquest*. The best example of impartial historical scholarship was Samuel Rawson Gardiner's lifetime work on the Civil War and Commonwealth era. Other important works were a *History of Christianity,* by Henry Hart Milman, *History of Greece,* by George Grote, *History of Civilization in England,* by Henry Thomas Buckle, *Constitutional History of England,* by William Stubbs, and *Short History of the English People,* by John Richard Green.

In contrast with all these long and ponderous books, the later part of the century saw many volumes of graceful historical essays. The Italian Renaissance was the chief subject of Walter Pater, John Addington Symonds, and "Vernon Lee" (Violet Paget); the eighteenth century was treated by Austin Dobson; and many odd byways of history were brought to life by Andrew Lang.

In spite of Carlyle's enthusiasm for biography, this branch of historical writing did not flourish among the Victorians. Countless large volumes of "Life and Letters" were published, but these were of the "official testimonial" type, usually written by amateurs or literary hacks, and their conventional laudations were made duller by the scrupulous avoidance of anything "degrading" or "scandalous."

Strangely, the best Victorian biographies dealt with the lives of authors, although their careers are usually less picturesque than those of men of action. The beginning of the period saw one biographical landmark, John Gibson Lockhart's life of his father-in-law, Sir Walter Scott. Another biography which fairly well overcame the handicap of family connection was George Otto Trevelyan's life of Macaulay, his uncle. On the other hand, Arthur Penrhyn Stanley was uncritically adulatory in his book about his old schoolmaster, Dr. Thomas Arnold. John Forster won fame with a rather pompous biography of his friend Dickens, and also wrote the lives of Goldsmith and Landor. Mrs. Gaskell used her experience in fiction to create a vivid and touching life of her friend Charlotte Brontë, but got into trouble for letting her imagination function too freely. Any deviation from strict standards of propriety aroused protest: Monckton Milnes's *Life of Keats* (1848) was condemned for lack of discretion in its treatment of the poet's love story. Toward the end of the period J. A. Froude foreshadowed the modern trend of biography by applying psychological analysis to the life and character of his old friend Carlyle; and his books on the subject were virulently attacked.

The two greatest examples of extensive biography based on historical research, on a scale comparable with Carlyle's, were James Spedding's *Bacon* and David Masson's *Milton*. Among the few significant studies of foreigners were G. H. Lewes's *Life of Goethe* and the monographs by John Morley on Voltaire and Rousseau. Morley also served as editor of the *English Men of Letters* series, brief biographies by able critics, which proved so successful that before the end of the century it was imitated in a number of other "series," bringing biography in cheap and concise form to a wide public.

The "short biography" was not clearly recognized during the Victorian period as a distinct literary form; but circumstances produced some examples of it. Macaulay's essays often assumed this form, and it was used in Carlyle's *Heroes* lectures and in Thackeray's two lecture series, *The English Humorists* and *The Four Georges*. Later in the century many historians and critics wrote articles of this type for the magazines and collected them into volumes, such as Leslie Stephen's *Studies of a Biographer* and Walter Bagehot's *Biographical Studies*.

Autobiography was not conspicuous in the Victorian age. Though almost all the writers expressed their personal ideas and often revealed their characters while doing so, they seldom chose their own lives as the ostensible subject. Newman's *Apologia* is a conspicuous exception; but it too was intended to be a vehicle for controversy, and did not undertake a balanced account of the author's whole career. Probably the best autobiography, strangely enough, was that of the reticent John Stuart Mill. Ruskin covered the first half of his own life rather unevenly in *Praeterita;* and Carlyle's *Reminiscences,* published after his death, were also incomplete. Herbert Spencer wrote a large autobiography, but it is not particularly interesting. The most objective Victorian autobiography was Anthony Trollope's, and it brought temporary discredit to his memory by its candor. Literally scores of lesser Victorian authors, journalists, actors, artists, lawyers and others published volumes of recollections, which are an inexhaustible source of information for the literary scholar, but have no merit as artistic writing.

Perhaps the same reasons which caused the dearth of good autobiography were also responsible for the almost total absence of a more distinctly literary *genre,* the personal essay. During the Romantic generation this had been the outstanding type of prose; and the continued expansion of the magazines gave wide opportunity for the publication of such essays in the Victorian age. Two forces, however, militated against it. One was the intellectual seriousness of the time; most of the writers mentioned in this section were so deeply concerned with argument and demonstration that the informal essay would have seemed to them to be trivial and pointless. The other foe of the essay was the novel. Some of Dickens's *Sketches by Boz* were in the tradition of Lamb and Hazlitt, but he soon discovered that in fiction he could make more profitable use of his material. Thackeray was by nature cut out to be an essayist. His *Paris Sketch Book, Book of Snobs,* and many other writings during the first ten years of his career were of this type; and after making his fortune with novels he returned happily to essay-writing in *The Roundabout*

Papers, which are the best Victorian example of the true informal essay. The only other mid-Victorian who could achieve quite the subtle blend of humor, pathos, sympathy, and irony was Thackeray's Scottish friend, Dr. John Brown, author of *Horae Subsecivae* and *Rab and His Friends.*

In the last quarter of the century the traditional informal essay was brought back to prominence by another Scotsman, Robert Louis Stevenson, who had enough leisure to be thoughtful without wishing to be instructive; and from that time onward the essay flourished. A special category, the "nature essay," was best represented by Richard Jefferies. Oscar Wilde, in *Intentions,* wrote witty, paradoxical essays; Andrew Lang wrote urbane ones; Alice Meynell wrote fastidious ones. Most of the late-Victorian essayists, however, were dealing chiefly with literary topics, and so they will be discussed in a separate section on criticism.

J. M. Robertson, *Modern Humanists* (London, 1891); *Modern Humanists Reconsidered* (London, 1927); J. Hunt, *Religious Thought in England in the Nineteenth Century* (London, 1896); L. Stephen, *The English Utilitarians* (3v, London, 1900); E. Halévy, *La formation du radicalisme philosophique* (3v, Paris, 1901-04; trans. as *The Growth of Philosophic Radicalism,* London, 1928); E. Albee, *A History of English Utilitarianism* (New York, 1902); A. W. Benn, *The History of English Rationalism in the Nineteenth Century* (2v, London, 1906); J. McCunn, *Six Radical Thinkers* (London, 1907); G. P. Gooch, *History and Historians in the Nineteenth Century* (London, 1913); J. T. Merz, *A History of European Thought in the Nineteenth Century,* III, IV (Edinburgh, 1913-14); W. L. Davidson, *Political Thought in England: From Bentham to John Stuart Mill* (London, 1915); E. Barker, *Political Thought in England: From Herbert Spencer to Today* (London, 1915); M. M. Waddington, *The Development of British Thought from 1820 to 1890* (Toronto, 1919); W. R. Sorley, *History of English Philosophy* (Cambridge, 1920); A. K. Rogers, *English and American Philosophy Since 1800* (New York, 1922); G. H. Busey, *The Reflection of Positivism in English Literature to 1880* (Urbana, 1926); E. Neff, *Carlyle and Mill: An*

Introduction to Victorian Thought (New York, 1926); R. W. Murray, *Studies in the English Social and Political Thinkers of the Nineteenth Century* (2v, Cambridge, 1929); D. C. Somervell, *English Thought in the Nineteenth Century* (London, 1929); J. M. Drachman, *Studies in the Literature of Natural Science* (New York, 1930); H. A. L. Fisher, "The Whig Historians," in *Proceedings of the British Academy*, XIV (1930); E. Butterfield, *The Whig Interpretation of History* (London, 1931); C. Brinton, *English Political Thought in the Nineteenth Century* (London, 1933); *The Social and Political Ideas of Some Representative Thinkers of the Victorian Age*, ed. F. J. C. Hearnshaw (London, 1933); B. Russell, *Freedom vs. Organization, 1814-1914* (London, 1934); S. Maccoby, *English Radicalism, 1832-86* (2v, London, 1935-38); L. E. Elliott-Binns, *Religion in the Victorian Era* (London, 1936); R. Metz, *A Hundred Years of British Philosophy* (London, 1938); B. E. Lippincott, *Victorian Critics of Democracy* (Minneapolis, 1938); B. N. Schilling, *Human Dignity and the Great Victorians* (New York, 1946); A. W. Brown, *The Metaphysical Society* (New York, 1947); H. Jackson, *Dreamers of Dreams* (London, 1948).

THOMAS CARLYLE (1795-1881)

>>

Though born ten to twenty years earlier than his Victorian contemporaries, Thomas Carlyle outlived many of them; and his literary career began no sooner than theirs. Born at Ecclefechan in Dumfriesshire, Scotland, on December 14, 1795, he was the eldest of nine children of a mason, from whom he inherited his independence and sense of integrity. His devoted parents gave him all the education possible within their means, and he was ready for the university at the age of thirteen. From 1809 to 1814 he was a student at Edinburgh University, where some of the boys recognized his intellectual leadership. Upon leaving the university without taking a degree, he became a mathematical master at Annan Academy (where he had received his secondary education) and two years later changed to a school in Kirkaldy.

Finding teaching unsuited to his temperament, he left his post to go to Edinburgh in 1818. Here he spent the most comfortless years of his life. When he had entered the university, it had been with the intention of becoming a minister, but his inability to accept the tenets of the church prevented him from taking orders, and by 1818 he had lost his Christian faith. Tortured by dyspepsia and lacking money, he was forced to take private pupils and write hack articles for a living. In 1822 he went through a profound spiritual crisis, mastered his morbid despondency, and adopted an affirmative, defiant attitude to life.

During this time he became interested in continental literature and learned German

THOMAS CARLYLE

well enough to admire the works of Goethe, Richter, and Fichte. He translated Goethe's *Wilhelm Meister* into English, and wrote a *Life of Schiller*. In 1824 he took a trip to London and Paris, and formed a contemptuous opinion of most of the literary men he met, as well as sneering at the shallowness and materialism of the whole urban culture. Returning to Scotland, he settled at a farm belonging to his brother, and in 1826 published his first book, the *Life of Schiller*.

After a rather stormy courtship he married Jane Baillie Welsh, a talented young woman with a personality as strong as his own. She had been brought up in surroundings socially superior to Carlyle's. He was publishing essays in the *Edinburgh Review,* under the editorship of Francis Jeffrey, and some of those on German literature won the respect of Goethe and resulted in correspondence with him. Carlyle's "Essay on Burns," perhaps his most sympathetic piece of criticism, appeared in the *Edinburgh* in 1828, after he had moved to his wife's lonely farm at Craigenputtock.

There the Carlyles lived for seven uncomfortable, poverty-stricken years. He wrote *Sartor Resartus* in 1830 and spent three years in trying to find a publisher for it. When it finally appeared serially in *Fraser's Magazine* it puzzled and annoyed its readers. Emerson, however, who had recently visited Carlyle, persuaded an American firm to publish it as a volume. In the disguise of a fictitious German philosopher, "Dr. Diogenes Teufelsdröckh" (Godborn Devildung), Professor of Things in General at the University of Weissnichtwo (Don't know where), Carlyle told some of his intellectual and spiritual autobiography and presented an ironical "philosophy of clothes": as clothing reflects the wearer's taste, so his life reflects the nature of his mind. Through this grotesque fiction Carlyle satirized the shams of modern life, and went on to a mystical argument for the reality of God under the changing symbols of religious forms.

In his previous essays his prose had been direct, but he now developed a strange style, based on German and Greek constructions, with echoes of Scottish dialect, and rhetorical devices of rhythm, repetition, inversion, and even typography, calculated to produce startling emphasis. It was a kind of rugged prose-poetry that came to be known as "Carlylese."

In 1834 the Carlyles moved to London and took a house in Cheyne Row, Chelsea. Carlyle was welcomed by Mill and other radicals who admired his iconoclastic views; but for several years he earned nothing with his writing. He

5 CHEYNE ROW

THE
SOUND-PROOF
ROOM

was engaged upon an ambitious history of the French Revolution, and made up his mind that if it was not successful he would give up authorship and probably emigrate to America. Although he suffered a grievous set-back when the manuscript of the first volume was accidentally burned, he grimly rewrote it. Upon publication in 1837, the book gained wide fame. At his best when interpreting character as manifested in action, Carlyle brought out the dramatic power of the events with vivid description and thrilling suspense. A combination of ironic wit and deep human sympathy provided the emotional atmosphere, and Carlyle's mystical philosophy was always in the background. In spite of being a work of thorough historical research, it can best be described as a prose epic.

Each year between 1838 and 1841 Carlyle delivered a series of lectures, which proved more profitable than *The French Revolution.* Only the fourth series, *On Heroes and Hero-Worship,* was issued in book form. Herein he expressed his belief that in every age there were only a few great men, who, through the power of intellect and character, became leaders and shaped the course of history. The idea was echoed in America by Emerson in his *Representative Men.* Carlyle's lectures revealed a growing distrust of the value of democracy, which seemed to him to put power in the least competent hands.

At the age of forty-five Carlyle was emerging from poverty and neglect. Many leading authors had become his friends, and even in London society he was accepted as an amusing novelty, with his flood of opinions, his boisterous humor, and his carefully retained Scots accent.

In 1839 and 1843 he expanded his ideas on current social and political problems in *Chartism* and *Past and Present.* These gave offense to his friends among the Utilitarians by his condemnation of their doctrine of laissez-faire, and he shocked a wider public by assailing all the material progress represented by modern industry, transportation, and mass-produced appliances.

His second large historical work was *The Life and Letters of Oliver Cromwell* (1845), less episodic than *The French Revolution* but also less picturesque. Carlyle's theory of "heroes" made him believe that biography was the essential form of historical writing. In 1850 came *Latter-Day Pamphlets,* one of his most denunciatory books, which gave general offense and evoked the accusation that he favored despotism. *The Life of John Sterling* followed in 1851. This biography of a brilliant young man who had been his most ardent disciple was his gentlest book, but aroused further opposition by its attitude toward organized religion.

In that year he visited France with the Brownings and began to map out his *History of Frederick the Great,* an interpretation of a monarch whom he admired for his courage and strong leadership. Work on it occupied the next thirteen years. His constant stomach trouble made him irritable, so that noise or interruption infuriated him. His married life was a perpetual nervous strain, for his wife was unreasonably jealous and in constant danger of mental collapse. Although each admired and loved the other deeply, they often quarreled and caused each other pain.

Two visits to Germany, as well as vast research, were necessary for the completion of *Frederick the Great,* which was published in six volumes from 1858 to 1865. This work brought his fullest measure of fame and respect; Emerson called it the greatest book ever written. Carlyle's ideas had already been adopted by such influential writers as J. A. Froude and John Ruskin. Now praise and honors were accorded him in both England and Germany. In 1866 he became Lord Rector of Edinburgh University (an honorary position); when he was in Scotland in connection with his inauguration his wife died suddenly in London.

Carlyle never fully recovered from the shock. His grief and loneliness were intensified by remorse for the unhappiness he had caused his wife. Deprived of her intellectual stimulation, he found writing more and more difficult; and failing health hastened his withdrawal from social life. He worked on a book of *Reminiscences* dealing with his early days, and his final assault upon democracy was *Shooting Niagara—and After,* condemning the Reform Bill of 1867. After becoming an almost legendary character as "the sage of Chelsea," he died on February 4, 1881, in the house that had been his home for forty-seven years.

Bitter feeling was aroused when Froude published his friend's *Reminiscences* and *Letters.* Carlyle had given exaggerated, ungracious pictures of many people, including himself, and Froude's injudicious interpretations made the effect all the worse. Recent years have gradually brought a juster view of Carlyle's character and his relations with his wife.

His significance in literature was not so much for original philosophy as for integrity and courage. His attacks on sham and cant made him a sort of disturbing conscience to the complacency of his time, proclaiming woe like an Old Testament prophet.

His beliefs were sometimes inconsistent and chaotic, though his sincerity gave them force. His thinking was a mixture of his inherited Calvinism with the romantic primitivism that stemmed from Rousseau and the metaphysics of the German philosophers. The arguments over Carlyle are merely one aspect of the vast ideological conflicts that have filled the subsequent century. The supremacy of "will and idea," which was one of his axioms, originated in Hegel, from whom also in various ways sprang the theories of both Karl Marx and Adolf Hitler. Carlyle would not have agreed with either of them. Through Ruskin and Morris, his influence was strong in the shaping of the English Labor Party.

In spite of Carlyle's gloomy portents of destruction for modern materialistic civilization, the effect of his work was stimulating rather than depressing. His slogan of "the eternal yea" encouraged his readers to believe in the superiority of intuition and personality over intellectualism. His creed of Work and Duty, painful though it was to an era of facile optimism, may still have a prescription for the present day.

I. W. Dyer, *A Bibliography of Thomas Carlyle's Writings and Ana* (Portland, Me., 1928); *Works,* ed. H. D. Traill (30v, London, 1896-99; Centenary edition); *Letters to Mrs. Basil Montagu and B. W. Procter* (London, 1881); *Correspondence of Carlyle and Emerson,* ed. C. E. Norton (2v, London, 1883); *Letters, 1814-36,* ed. C. E. Norton (4v, London, 1886-88); *Correspondence Between Goethe and Carlyle,* ed. C. E. Norton (London, 1887); *Letters to His Youngest Sister* (Boston, 1899); *New Letters,* ed. A. Carlyle (2v, London, 1904); *Carlyle intime: Lettres à sa mère,* ed. A. Carlyle (Paris, 1907); *Love Letters,* ed. A. Carlyle (London, 1909); *Letters to Mill, Sterling, and Browning,* ed. A. Carlyle (London, 1923); M. D. Conway, *Thomas Carlyle* (London, 1881); J. A. Froude, *Thomas Carlyle* (4v, London, 1882-84); D. Masson, *Carlyle Personally and in His Writings* (London, 1885); R. Garnett, *Thomas Carlyle* (London, 1887; Great Writers); C. G. Duffy, *Conversations with Carlyle* (London, 1892); J. Nicol, *Thomas Carlyle* (London, 1892; English Men of Letters); J. A. Froude, *My Relations with Carlyle* (London, 1903); J. Crichton-Browne and A. Carlyle, *The Nemesis of Froude* (London, 1903); W. S. Johnson, *Thomas Carlyle: A Study of His Literary Apprenticeship* (New Haven, 1911); L. Cazamian, *Carlyle* (Paris, 1913; trans. E. K. Brown, New York, 1932); D. A. Wilson, *The Truth About Carlyle* (London, 1913); A. Ralli, *Guide to Carlyle* (2v, London, 1920); D. A. Wilson, *Life of Thomas Carlyle* (6v, London, 1923-34); N. Young, *Carlyle: His Rise and Fall* (London, 1927); B. H. Lehman, *Carlyle's Theory of the Hero* (Durham, N. C., 1928); O. Burdett, *The Two Carlyles* (London, 1930); W. H. Dunn, *Froude and Carlyle* (London, 1930); A. C. Taylor, *Carlyle: sa première fortune littéraire en France* (Paris, 1930);

Carlyle et la pensée latine (Paris, 1938); E. Neff, *Carlyle* (New York, 1932); C. F. Harrold, *Carlyle and German Thought* (New Haven, 1934); "The Nature of Carlyle's Calvinism," *Studies in Philology*, XXXIII (1936). 475-86; L. M. Young, *Thomas Carlyle and the Art of History* (Philadelphia, 1939); R. Wellek, "Carlyle and the Philosophy of History," *Philological Quarterly*, XXIII (1944). 55-76.

THOMAS BABINGTON MACAULAY (1800-1859)

>>

Essayist, historian, and statesman, Thomas Babington Macaulay was born at Rothley Temple, Leicestershire, on October 25, 1800. His father, a former governor of the

African colony of Sierra Leone, had become a violent opponent of slavery and was active in a group of intellectual philanthropists working to abolish the slave trade throughout the British colonies. Tom Macaulay's youth was spent at Clapham, a suburb of London. Precocious and gifted with an amazing memory, he was regarded as a youthful prodigy. At a private school near Cambridge his range of reading became immense. In 1818 he entered Trinity College, Cambridge;

THOMAS BABINGTON
MACAULAY

during his college days he displayed classical attainments and won the Chancellor's medal for poetry twice, but he grew to hate mathematics. His mental training being somewhat one-sided, he developed certain faults which later became apparent in his writings, such as a dislike of facing abstract intellectual problems and a lack of philosophical grasp.

Though his father was a strong Tory, Macaulay became an uncompromising Whig through his associations with Charles Austin and other gifted fellow-students. In the Union Debating Society his activities not only prepared him for a career in Parliament but influenced his literary style as well. In 1824, after receiving his degree, he became a fellow of Trinity College. Since his father's business had failed, he undertook tutoring and any other available ways of earning money to help support his brothers and sisters.

His career as a writer had begun before he left the university, for he had contributed lyrics and essays to *Knight's Quarterly Magazine*. In March, 1825, he suddenly gained a literary triumph with a single article, an essay on Milton in the *Edinburgh Review*. Although contributions to that periodical were never signed, it was so closely connected with high Whig social and political circles that the authorship of the able essay was soon known. Thus introduced to the leaders of his party, Macaulay at once became popular for his brilliant and easy conversation.

In 1826 he was called to the Bar, but soon gave up law in favor of politics. He was made a Commissioner of Bankruptcy in 1828; and two years later Lord Lansdowne, who had been favorably impressed by the stand taken by Macaulay in his essays on the controversial theories of James Mill, secured him a seat in Parliament. His success in the House of Commons was immediate, for he was a magnificent orator with complete faith in his own views and an incredible fund of information. The first measure he championed was the removal of civil disabilities of Jews; and although he was at the time a member for a "pocket borough" he vigorously supported the Reform Bill of 1832. Throughout these years he was contributing essays to the *Edinburgh*

Review on literary and historical subjects. Each essay was nominally a review of a newly published book, but actually was an extensive survey of Macaulay's own ideas of the subject.

In 1832 he was made a commissioner on the Board of Control; but he was so loyal to his family's cause of abolitionism that he was willing to resign his post the next year in order to oppose a ministerial measure for emancipation which he considered inadequate. He was then appointed to a position on the Supreme Council of India, and went to that country to stay for four years. Responsibility for the government of India having just been assumed by the English crown, Macaulay devoted himself to reforming the Indian Penal Code, as well as organizing a sound educational system. In his leisure moments he read the Greek and Latin classics, a great deal of Italian and French literature, and some German. From Thucydides, Tacitus, and Livy he received an inspiration to write living history.

Shortly after his return to England in 1838 he made a tour of Italy, and as a result wrote the highly popular *Lays of Ancient Rome*. He was soon reëlected to Parliament, and from 1839 to 1841 was Secretary for War in the cabinet of Lord Melbourne. The essays that he had contributed to the *Edinburgh Review* were collected and published in 1843. Macaulay had regarded them as ephemeral, but he was obliged by general demand to make a book of them. About five years later he issued the first two volumes of his *History of England,* a work to which he had devoted much time, both in research and in actual writing. As a result of its great success he was elected Lord Rector of Glasgow University and a Fellow of the Royal Society. He declined a professorship of history at Cambridge.

In 1855 the third and fourth volumes of the *History* were published; the next year ill-health obliged him to withdraw from the House of Commons, and he was made a peer in 1857, taking the title of Baron Macaulay of Rothley. On December 28, 1859, he died at his London home, Holly Lodge. The fifth volume of the *History* was edited and published in 1861 by his sister, Lady Trevelyan.

As a poet Macaulay produced a small group of vigorous narrative poems that long remained popular, particularly with young people. He followed the methods of Walter Scott in rhythmic swing and objective directness; but the mechanical form and the declamatory style were monotonous and there was a total lack of poetic subtlety.

His prose style was much admired for clearness, wit, and fluency, but it, too, tended to be monotonous. His essays, though uneven in quality, were masterly character-sketches of the political and literary celebrities that he described. Depending upon his prodigious memory, he was not always accurate as to details; and the opinions that he expressed with utter confidence were based upon strong personal prejudices.

As early as 1828 Macaulay had stated a theory that historical writing should be made pictorial and vivid, and in his great *History of England* he carried out his idea. His plan was to write a living account of the affairs of his country from the Revolution of 1688 to the death of George III; but he did not foresee the time and effort required. So detailed a history has seldom been produced: he devoted five volumes to the fifteen years following the Revolution, and if he had proceeded on the same scale his complete plan would have occupied fifty volumes and kept him at work for a hundred and fifty years. With unflagging thoroughness and infectious interest he narrated the events and portrayed the participants. Never before had history offered such lifelike characterizations. It may be described as brilliant reporting; the quality of interpretation or insight was absent.

Macaulay's intense Whig convictions colored both the *History* and the *Essays* so strongly that he can be regarded as largely responsible for the anti-Tory attitude in the teaching of English history and literature down to the present time.

Works, ed. Lady Trevelyan (8v, London, 1866); *Complete Writings* (20v, New York, 1898-1900; Whitehall edition); F. Arnold, *The Public Life of Lord Macaulay* (London, 1862); G. O. Trevelyan, *Life and Letters of Lord Macaulay* (2v, London, 1876); J. C. Morison, *Macaulay* (London, 1882; English Men of Letters); A. S. G. Canning, *Lord Macaulay, Essayist and Historian* (London, 1882; rev. ed., 1913); J. Morley, "Macaulay," in *Critical Miscellanies,* I (London, 1886); R. C. Jebb, *Macaulay* (London, 1900); D. H. Macgregor, *Lord Macaulay* (London, 1901); A. R. Hassard, *A New Light on Lord Macaulay* (London, 1918); S. T. Williams, "Macaulay's Reading and Literary Criticism," *Philological Quarterly,* III (1924). 119-31; S. C. Roberts, *Lord Macaulay, the Pre-eminent Victorian,* English Association Pamphlet 67 (1927); W. C. Abbott, "Macaulay and the New History," *Yale Review,* XVIII (1929). 539-57; A. Bryant, *Macaulay* (London, 1932); C. Firth, *A Commentary on Macaulay's "History of England,"* ed. G. Davies (London, 1938); R. C. Beatty, *Lord Macaulay: A Victorian Liberal* (Norman, Okla., 1938).

JOHN HENRY NEWMAN (1801-1890)

>>>

One of the most perfect masters of English prose in the Victorian period was also one of the most influential forces in its religious discussions. John Henry Newman, the son of a banker, was born in London on February 21, 1801, and was brought up earnestly in evangelical Christianity. At the age of fifteen he experienced a religious "conversion" that included a belief that he must never marry. In that year he entered Trinity College, Oxford, where he made a high record of scholarship. His poem, *St. Bartholomew's*

Eve, was printed anonymously when he was twenty. In 1822 he became a fellow of Oriel College, and two years later was ordained a clergyman of the Church of England and became curate of St. Clement's Church in Oxford. He was made Vicar of St. Mary's in 1828, and as this was the official University church he gained a strong influence over many undergraduates.

From 1826 to 1832 he was also a tutor at Oriel College, until he resigned over a disagreement about the relationship of religious and academic duties.

JOHN HENRY NEWMAN

The winter of 1832-33 was spent in a long Mediterranean tour with his friend Hurrell Froude. Newman had a severe illness in Sicily and was in a nervous, unhappy state of mind during the whole tour, but he wrote his best lyrical poems at this time, notably "Lead, Kindly Light." On his return to England he published his first book, a work of religious history.

In July, 1833, he heard John Keble preach on "National Apostasy" and was so deeply stirred that he began the publication of a series of *Tracts for the Times,* which came out during the next seven years. These and his sermons, also published at intervals, formed the heart of the Oxford Movement that reasserted the direct descent of the Church of England from the Church of Rome. In 1836 he became editor of the *British Critic,* a High Church magazine. His emphasis upon Catholic observances became more distinct until in 1841 *Tract 90* aroused excitement by positively stating that the Thirty-nine Articles of the Anglican faith were not inconsistent with Roman Catholicism. The Bishop of Oxford requested him to discontinue the tracts, and the next year Newman resigned from St. Mary's and withdrew to the village of Littlemore, where he lived for three years almost as a hermit, painfully thinking out his religious problems. Finally, in October, 1845, he was received into the Roman Catholic Church and soon afterwards went to Rome to enter the priesthood.

After coming back to England in 1848 he undertook various religious activities, and published a novel, *Loss and Gain,* showing how Oxford students had responded to the "Tractarian" movement (as it was coming to be called, with reference to his *Tracts for the Times*). At this time there was intense public excitement in England over the establishment of the Catholic hierarchy, and Newman was the object of bitter attacks. From 1854 to 1858 he was Rector of the newly-established University of Dublin. His lectures there, published as *The Idea of a University,* presented his ideals of education. While in Dublin he also published his second novel, *Callista,* an historical romance of early Christianity.

When he returned from Ireland he founded a Catholic college at Edgebaston, near Birmingham, and remained there for the rest of his life. Although he had become widely respected for his simple sincerity, he was still an object of some suspicion. A magazine article by Charles Kingsley in 1864 accused him of having said that "truth for its own sake need not be, and on the whole ought not to be, a virtue of the Roman clergy." Newman issued a reply, and Kingsley retorted with an angry attack. As a result Newman wrote *Apologia Pro Vita Sua,* an autobiography that narrated his changing religious opinions with logic, candor, and dignity. In 1868 he published a long philosophical poem, *The Dream of Gerontius,* and in 1870 a detailed exposition of his theological views, *The Grammar of Assent.*

Having disagreed with the papal authorities on certain policies, he was for a time out of favor with Rome, but upon the accession of Pope Leo XIII he was made a cardinal in 1879. In spite of frail health he lived to his ninetieth year, dying on August 11, 1890.

The two principal axioms of Newman's religious thought were apparently paradoxical: that spiritual truth is entirely intuitive and cannot be rationally expounded, and that therefore a central and authoritative church is essential to unite all such believers instead of leaving each individual to interpret religion as he pleases. To Newman the dilemma was between utter skepticism and unqualified faith. For twelve years he tried to establish a *via media* (middle road) between the individualism of the Protestant view and the authoritarianism of the Roman Church, but his logical mind could not be satisfied with a compromise.

His literary work was always subservient to his religious earnestness. Even his two novels were written to present religious issues. In view of the later controversy with Kingsley it is interesting to compare his *Loss and Gain* with Kingsley's *Yeast* and his *Callista* with Kingsley's *Hypatia.* In each instance the two novels present opposite interpretations of similar material. Newman was not skilful in the technique of fiction, and his novels are significant only for their relationship to his ideas.

The austere beauty of his few poems suggests that he might have been a great poet if he had chosen that career. In the bulk of his work, however—the *Tracts for the Times, The Idea of a University,* and the *Apologia*—he was writing expository and controversial prose that is nevertheless to be classified with great literature because it all carries the stamp of his honest, sensitive personality. His style was clear and unaffected, in contrast with the studied manner-

isms of many contemporaries, such as Macaulay and Carlyle. The subtle charm and gentle but inflexible character
that had fascinated the Oxford students listening to his
sermons came to be recorded in his pages with equal effect.
Newman had been emotionally and imaginatively molded
by romanticism ever since his childhood love of Walter
Scott. He is thus linked to Carlyle, Ruskin, Arnold, the
Pre-Raphaelites, and others who in their various ways
sought to promote outward beauty and inward spirituality
in opposition to the bleakness of evangelical Calvinism and
the materialistic ugliness of industrialism, utilitarianism,
and physical science.

J. Rickaby, *Index to the Works of J. H. Newman* (London,
1914); *Works* (40v, London, 1874-1921); (in process, New York,
1947-   ); *Letters and Correspondence,* ed. A. Mozley (2v, London, 1891); *Correspondence with Keble and Others* (London,
1917); F. W. Newman, *Contributions Chiefly to the Early History
of Cardinal Newman* (London, 1891); E. A. Abbott, *The Anglican Career of Cardinal Newman* (2v, London, 1892); L. F. F.
Goyau, *Newman: sa vie et ses oeuvres* (Paris, 1901); A. R. Waller
and G. H. S. Barrow, *John Henry, Cardinal Newman* (London,
1901); W. Barry, *Newman* (London, 1904; Literary Lives); R. H.
Hutton, *Cardinal Newman* (London, 1905); H. Bremond, *Newman* (Paris, 1906; trans. as *The Mystery of Newman,* London,
1907); C. Sarolea, *Cardinal Newman and His Influence on Religious Life and Thought* (Edinburgh, 1908); W. Ward, *The Life
of Cardinal Newman* (2v, London, 1912); B. Newman, *Cardinal
Newman* (New York, 1925); J. J. Reilly, *Newman As a Man of
Letters* (New York, 1925); J. D. Folghera, *Newman apologiste*
(Paris, 1927; trans. as *Newman's Apologetic,* London, 1929); E. B.
Burgum, "Cardinal Newman and the Complexity of Truth,"
Sewanee Review, XXXVIII (1930). 310-27; J. L. May, *Cardinal New-
man* (London, 1930); W. Meynell, *Cardinal Newman* (London,
1930); G. G. Atkins, *Life of Cardinal Newman* (New York, 1931);
F. L. Cross, *John Henry Newman* (London, 1933); J. M. Flood,
Cardinal Newman and Oxford (London, 1933); J. E. Ross, *John
Henry Newman* (New York, 1933); J. Guitton, *La philosophie
de Newman* (Paris, 1933); H. Tristram, *Newman and His Friends*
(London, 1933); F. R. Cronin, *Cardinal Newman: His Theory*

of Knowledge (Washington, 1935); F. Tardivel, *La personalité littéraire de Newman* (Paris, 1937); C. F. Harrold, *John Henry Newman* (New York, 1945); J. Moody, *John Henry Newman* (New York, 1945); W. E. Houghton, *The Art of Newman's "Apologia"* (New Haven, 1945); E. Ruggles, *Journey into Faith: The Anglican Life of J. H. Newman* (New York, 1948).

JOHN STUART MILL (1806-1873)

>>

John Stuart Mill is one of the rare examples of a son who gained equal fame with his father in the same career, and one of the still rarer examples of a child prodigy who achieved much in later life. He was born in Pentonville, a district of North London, on May 20, 1806. His father was James Mill, well known as a philosopher, economist, historian, and radical politician, who was a friend and colleague of Jeremy Bentham in his psychological researches.

JOHN STUART MILL

James Mill started teaching his son to read Greek at three, and by the age of eight the boy had translated many of the Greek prose writings into English. He was similarly initiated in history, logic, and political economy, and was trained according to his father's theory that one must challenge every statement and demand evidence.

At the age of sixteen he was appointed a clerk in India House, where his father was an official. In the same year young Mill organized his own ideas into what he called a "religion" based upon his studies of Bentham, Condillac, Helvetius, and other theorists, and founded the "Utilitarian Society" with a few friends. He thus supplied a convenient name for Bentham's system of ethics.

By this time he was writing extensively for newspapers and magazines, and at nineteen he founded the Speculative Society, which was intended to give practice in discussion and debate. He was beginning to be dissatisfied with the strictly mechanistic views of his father, and so he decided to appreciate poetry and the other arts and to sympathize with personal emotion, instead of disapproving of such weaknesses. His political philosophy became more humane. In 1836 he was appointed head of the India Office department that conducted relations with the native states, thereby gaining experience in practical application of government and diplomacy.

From 1835 to 1840 he was editor of the *London Review,* which presented the Radical point of view. During this time he was working upon a fundamentally new study of logic; six years went to the writing of his first book, *A System of Logic,* which came out in 1843. It was followed the next year by *Essays on Some Unsettled Questions in Political Economy.* Ever since he had been about twenty-four there had been a devoted friendship between him and Harriet Hardy Taylor, whom nobody else regarded as possessing either charm or ability, but whom Mill idolized. Mrs. Taylor's affection for Mill caused her to leave her husband, and while Mill was writing his most important book, *The Principles of Political Economy,* she helped him constantly. The publication of this book in 1848 established Mill as the leader of the laissez-faire school of economics, derived from Ricardo; but afterwards a growing concern with human values, attributed by Mill himself to Mrs. Taylor's influence, led him to allow more significance to Socialist theories.

He married Mrs. Taylor in 1851, and during the next seven years they planned and partly wrote the works which remain the most readable of Mill's writings from the literary point of view—*On Liberty, Thoughts on Parliamentary Reform, Representative Government, Utilitarianism,* and *The Subjection of Women.* From 1856 to 1858 he was head of the examiner's office in India House; the East India Company was in the process of being dissolved, and Mill wrote a defense of its administration of India, opposing the transfer of authority to the Crown. Refusing a seat on the new executive council, he retired on a pension, and went to live in the south of France, where his wife died the next year.

In rapid succession he published the essays that he had been working on during the preceding decade. He was persuaded to be a candidate for Parliament in 1865, and although he refused to conduct a campaign he was elected and held his seat for three years. During this time he helped to organize the first Women's Suffrage Society, and presented its petition to Parliament.

After his death, which occurred at Avignon on May 8, 1873, his stepdaughter published his *Autobiography,* which revealed the human side of a man whose professional writings had been somewhat colorless and grim. As the final spokesman of the political and social views derived from the Industrial Revolution, Mill expressed everything that was abhorrent to the eloquent romanticists of his time. An agnostic in religious questions and an empiricist in philosophy, he made uncomfortable assertions in a manner that was seldom graceful. His theories, widely argued in his own day, have been modified by later writers, but they remain largely relevant to present-day thought. He felt just as strong a crusading spirit for his beliefs as the idealists and humanitarians felt for theirs, but his severely rational style had so much less appeal that modern readers seldom enjoy it.

N. MacMinn, J. R. Hainds, and J. M. McCrimmon, *A Bibliography of the Published Writings of John Stuart Mill* (Evanston, Ill., 1945); *Letters*, ed. H. S. R. Elliot (2v, London, 1910); H. A. Taine, *Le positivisme anglais: étude sur Stuart Mill* (Paris, 1864; Engl. trans., 1870); M. Marston, *The Life of John Stuart Mill* (London, 1873); W. L. Courtney, *The Metaphysics of J. S. Mill* (London, 1879); *Life of John Stuart Mill* (London, 1889; Great Writers); A. Bain, *John Stuart Mill: A Criticism* (London, 1882); C. M. Douglas, *John Stuart Mill: A Study of His Philosophy* (London, 1895); *The Ethics of John Stuart Mill* (London, 1897); C. L. Street, *Individualism and Individuality in the Philosophy of J. S. Mill* (Milwaukee, 1926); O. A. Kubitz, *The Development of J. S. Mill's System of Logic* (Urbana, 1932); M. A. Hamilton, *John Stuart Mill* (London, 1933); R. Jackson, *An Examination of the Inductive Logic of J. S. Mill* (London, 1941).

JOHN RUSKIN (1819-1900)

>>>

Among the Victorian aesthetic critics John Ruskin was the greatest. Born in London on February 8, 1819, he was the only son of Scottish parents. His father was a wealthy wine-merchant, and both parents were determined to make their son into a genius; they began to teach him from an early age to love literature and painting. In spite of their cultural interests, they had rigid religious views, and their son was brought up under an unfortunate mixture of indulgence and moral austerity. Being kept away from other children, he received much of his education in the form of extensive travel, first in the British Isles and later on the Continent. From fifteen to seventeen he attended a day-school in London, and then took some literature courses at King's College. He also received training in drawing.

When the naïve and gentle boy became a "gentleman

commoner" at Christ Church, Oxford, at the age of eighteen, he was somewhat ridiculed as a "prig"—especially when it was known that his mother had moved to Oxford to keep watch over him. As his early training had not been thorough, his undergraduate days were undistinguished, except for his winning the Newdigate Poetry Prize. Ill-health (apparently brought on by disappointment in a love affair) caused an interruption of two years, spent in European travel, and so he did not receive his degree until 1842.

Ever since he was fifteen he had been writing for publication: essays on geology for a natural history magazine and on architecture for the *Architectural Magazine,* as well as bits of verse for *Friendship's Offering* and the *London Monthly Miscellany.* He thought seriously about becoming a poet.

JOHN RUSKIN

He had early become enthusiastic over the paintings of J. M. W. Turner, which seemed to him the only satisfactory embodiment of the natural beauty of clouds and mountains that he had learned to love. In 1836 *Blackwood's Magazine* published an attack upon Turner's' pictures and Ruskin started to compose a reply. This grew into an extensive book which he had ready for publication soon after he received his university degree. The first volume of *Modern Painters,* "by a Graduate of Oxford," was published in 1843. It had developed from a defense of Turner into a comprehensive treatise on the principles of art.

Literary fame thus came to Ruskin at the age of twenty-

four. The book attracted notice for three reasons: its unorthodox estimation of the popular painters of the day,
its confident approach to deep aesthetic problems, and the
startlingly beautiful and eloquent style in which it was
written. The second volume came in 1846, and three additional volumes followed at intervals until 1860, though
he was writing his other major books during the same years.

The primary importance of *Modern Painters* lay in its
emphasis upon the association of art with life. Ruskin
sought to show, by pointing out the superiority of the best
contemporary landscape painters over the ancients, that
the spiritual element in art was more important than the
merely sensuous. This interpretation became a revolution-
izing force in Victorian artistic taste.

While working on the second volume he felt the need of
a fuller knowledge of Renaissance art, and thoroughly explored the Italian galleries, becoming specially fascinated
with Venice. The architecture as well as painting and
sculpture impressed him and formed the subject of his
second great work, *The Seven Lamps of Architecture*, published in 1849. His theory was that all true art is illuminated
by the seven principles of sacrifice, truth, power, beauty,
life, memory, and obedience.

In his personal life, meanwhile, he encountered misfortune. When a grand-daughter of Walter Scott refused his
proposal of marriage he was so distressed that his parents
gave him permission in 1848 to marry Euphemia Gray, the
daughter of old family friends. Though he had known her
since her childhood and had written for her a fairy-tale,
The King of the Golden River, seven years before, their
natures proved so incompatible that the marriage was an-
nulled in 1854. Soon afterwards she married John Everett
Millais, one of Ruskin's young Pre-Raphaelite protégés.

His essay on *Pre-Raphaelitism,* published in 1851,
brought the whole strength of his authority to support the

new movement. The public consequently began to admire and to buy the paintings, and the Brotherhood regarded Ruskin as their hero. When his next book, *The Stones of Venice,* was published between 1851 and 1853 the Pre-Raphaelites adopted the chapter "On the Nature of Gothic Architecture" as their gospel.

Ruskin's books were having a direct influence upon the English architecture of the time. The country was prosperous and much building was going on. Ruskin's glowing eulogies of medieval design stirred the imagination of the reading public. As a result, inferior and inconsistent adaptations of the Gothic style prevailed in the construction of residences and public buildings alike.

From being studies of purely aesthetic matters, his books had gradually become concerned with social themes, until *The Stones of Venice* was greeted by Carlyle with enthusiasm as seconding his own views. Beginning with the axioms that art must be based on truth and that the greatest art is that which includes the greatest ideas, Ruskin decided that great art can flourish only in a good moral and social environment, and that art must be for the many, not for the few. As beauty was absent from the everyday life of his own time, he concluded that the conditions of that life must be at fault. Industrialism, mass-production, city slums, were symptoms of an existence without love, joy, or self-respect. Therefore his aesthetic philosophy suddenly became a dynamic social theory, in opposition to both the laissez-faire of current economics and the materialism of current science. The inevitable consequence of his new doctrine was a search for ways to remodel society in the direction of a beautiful and meaningful life for all. In 1854 he joined the Christian Socialists in conducting the Workingmen's College, at which he taught drawing for seven years. At that same date he began to deliver public lectures, and by 1857 these were emphasizing the moral and social aspects of art—*A Joy Forever, The Political Economy of Art,* and others. By 1860 he ended his writing on strictly artistic subjects.

His lecturing and his writing of magazine articles affected his literary style. He had become famous for his long rhythmic sentences encrusted with adjectives, a form marvellously adapted to the creating of beautiful pictures in the medium of words. Now that he was addressing a different public and for different purposes he gave up his poetic prose in favor of simpler and more emphatic phrases.

His new radical views gave such offense to his former admirers that in 1862 the editors of both the *Cornhill* and *Fraser's Magazine* were forced by the protests of their readers to suspend two groups of Ruskin's essays that they started to print. The material was then published by Ruskin in a volume entitled *Munera Pulveris.* Other controversial books at this time were *The Two Paths* and *Unto this Last,* a treatise on wealth which he considered the best statement of his views. His persuasive methods slowly wore out the public opposition, until *Sesame and Lilies,* a discussion of woman's place in the social system, in 1865 gained all his old popularity.

His father, who had been grieved by the revolutionary trend of his opinions, died in 1864, leaving him a fortune equivalent to half a million dollars. This he began to spend freely in support of movements that he championed. In 1871 he founded the Guild of St. George, in connection with which he started agricultural settlements, industrial projects, and a museum of art and science in Sheffield. *The Ethics of the Dust, The Crown of Wild Olive,* and *Time and Tide* were among the books in which he expounded his views on such needs as a national system of education, economic coöperation, and old-age pensions.

Ruskin became Slade Professor of Fine Arts at Oxford in 1870 and retained the chair for nine years. His lectures drew immense attendance of students. On the theory that principles and practice must go hand in hand, he founded a school of drawing at Oxford. During these years he also held the widest public attention with *Fors Clavigera,* a series of letters nominally addressed to the English working men.

After 1878, when he suffered from the first of several attacks of brain fever, he withdrew to a beautiful home that he had bought in the Lake District. In his last twenty years he produced nothing of importance except *Praeterita: Outlines of Scenes and Thoughts,* a beautiful and revealing autobiography that showed hardly any sign of mental decay. He died at his home overlooking Coniston Lake on January 20, 1900.

Although hampered by prejudices and emotionalism that made him exaggerate many statements, Ruskin served his generation worthily as a prophet. As might be expected from his upbringing, he was ever a preacher and a teacher; he regarded all his works as educational in purpose. His earlier books aroused the English public to its first genuine interest in art, and provided aesthetic principles that were basically sound, even if the moral implications were over stressed. Political leaders regarded his proposed social reforms as Utopian, but subsequent legislation has followed the course that he indicated.

The style of his first period produced some of the finest poetic prose in English. It was a carefully cultivated manner, with echoes of its many sources, from the Bible to Carlyle—overtones that added to the rich beauty of the effect. His art studies had made him a master of the technique of drawing, as shown by his own illustrations of natural and architectural forms, but he never essayed original painting. Instead, he used his skill to create pictures in the reader's imagination by his words. His later work, with its simpler style, was more human also in its sympathies, but it is now somewhat dated by the very fact that so many of the ideas for which he was pleading have come to be accepted as obvious.

T. J. Wise and J. P. Smart, *Bibliography of the Writings of Ruskin* (London, 1893); *Works*, ed. E. T. Cook and A. Wedderburn (39v, London, 1903-12; Library edition); *Letters to Charles Eliot Norton*, ed. C. E. Norton (2v, New York, 1905); *Solitary Warrior: New Letters*, ed. J. H. Whitehouse (London, 1929); *Letters to Francesca Alexander,* ed. W. C. DeVane (Boston, 1931); *Letters to Bernard Quaritch,* ed. C. Q. Wrentmore (London, 1939); *The Order of Release: John Ruskin and Effie Gray,* ed. W. James (London, 1947); J. M. Mather, *John Ruskin: His Life and Teaching* (London, 1883); E. T. Cook, *Studies in Ruskin* (London, 1890); W. G. Collingwood, *The Life and Work of John Ruskin* (2v, London, 1893; rev. ed., 1900); R. de la Sizeranne, *Ruskin et la religion de la beauté* (Paris, 1897; Engl. trans., 1899); J. A. Hobson, *John Ruskin, Social Reformer* (London, 1898); A. Meynell, *John Ruskin* (London, 1900; Modern English Writers); M. H. Spielmann, *John Ruskin* (London, 1900); J. Bardoux, *Le mouvement idéaliste et social dans la littérature anglaise au XIXe siècle: John Ruskin* (Paris, 1901); F. Harrison, *John Ruskin* (London, 1902; English Men of Letters); W. Jolly, *Ruskin on Education* (London, 1907); C. H. Herford, "Ruskin and the Gothic Revival," *Quarterly Review,* CCVI (1907). 77-96; A. Chevrillon, *La pensée de Ruskin* (Paris, 1909); A. Wingate, *Life of John Ruskin* (London, 1910); A. Earland, *Ruskin and His Circle* (London, 1910); E. T. Cook, *Life of Ruskin* (2v, London, 1911); A. C. Benson, *Ruskin: A Study in Personality* (London, 1911); J. R. Morley, *Ruskin and Social Ethics* (London, 1917); *Ruskin the Prophet and Other Centenary Studies,* ed. J. H. Whitehouse (London, 1920); J. A. R. Marriott, "Ruskin's Economics," *Cornhill Magazine,* LIV (1923). 403-14; A. Williams-Ellis, *The Tragedy of John Ruskin* (London, 1928); D. Larg, *John Ruskin* (London, 1932); H. Ladd, *The Victorian Morality of Art: An Analysis of Ruskin's Aesthetic* (New York, 1932); H. Gally, *Ruskin et l'esthétique intuitive* (Paris, 1933); R. H. Wilenski, *John Ruskin* (London, 1933); H. B. Hagstotz, *The Educational Theories of John Ruskin* (Lincoln, Neb., 1942).

CRITICISM

>>>

In contrast with extensive and significant books on almost every other possible subject, the Victorian period
contributed surprisingly little of first rank in criticism.
There was no critic as penetrating as Coleridge or Hazlitt,
no single piece of writing as crucial as Wordsworth's preface to *Lyrical Ballads* or Shelley's *Defense of Poetry*.

This dearth of great criticism coincided with a vast increase in the output of book reviewing and literary history.
A number of important periodicals, weekly, monthly, and
quarterly, were devoted wholly or in part to literary discussion; and the expansion of the daily newspapers allowed
much more space than ever before for similar material.
For the first time the "literary critic" became a recognized
professional classification, and beside him appeared the
dramatic critic, the musical critic, the art critic. Mass production and professional competence did not result in the
independence of judgment, the courage of conviction, and
the philosophic cogitation which are needed for great criticism. Apart from the reviews of current books in periodicals,
most of the writing on this subject took the form of literary
history and biography, sponsored by the universities—
where research in this field was newly developing—and
by a wide range of scholarly societies, the Shakespeare Society, the Chaucer Society, the Browning Society, and others.

Several authors showed promise of becoming major
critics, only to be deflected into writing on subjects of
more practical or controversial nature. Carlyle first
emerged as an authority on German literature. Macaulay's

essays were contributed to the *Edinburgh Review* in the guise of book reviews, though actually they were historical and biographical studies. The greatest works of English criticism between 1830 and 1860 were concerned not with literature but with art—Ruskin's three monumental books; but thereafter Ruskin too moved away into other fields.

The only Victorian critic of literature who made a serious effort to formulate general principles was Matthew Arnold, and even he never wrote a book on the subject comparable to his works on religious and social topics. His critical system has to be pieced together from the separate studies of authors in the two series of *Essays in Criticism,* from his *Study of Celtic Literature,* from his treatise *On Translating Homer,* and from various prefaces to anthologies. Perhaps because of this fragmentary presentation, his critical theories can be accused of inconsistency or of inadequate demonstration. On the other hand, his gift of phrase-making enriched the critical vocabulary with "sweetness and light," "high seriousness," "criticism of life," "the best that has been thought and known in the world," "sweet reasonableness," and other effective phrases. His theory of "touchstones," while dangerously subjective, was important in emphasizing austere standards of judgment; and his enthusiasm for various foreign authors helped to counteract the insular tendency in English thought. In general, his insistence that criticism should be concerned with the relationship of literature and life was consistent with Ruskin's theories of great art as the outgrowth of great social eras.

Perhaps partly as a result of Arnold's attention to continental authors, a new generation of critics soon afterwards developed with a marked adherence to the French school of criticism. Sainte-Beuve, who had been one of Arnold's enthusiasms, was much admired, as was Gautier. In contrast, therefore, with Coleridge and his school, who had been influenced by the German philosophers to attempt large and profound aesthetic theories, these English critics of the French school were more impressionistic, inclined to express personal preferences rather than philosophic concepts. They wrote gracefully and enriched their prose with picturesque images.

The most important was Walter Pater, who wrote about painting and architecture as well as about literature, and who came to be regarded as the apostle of "art for art's sake." This theory had been the motivating force of the Pre-Raphaelite Movement, and in another way it had been promoted by Arnold's attacks on the "Philistinism" and the "Hebraism" of contemporary culture. Pater certainly fulfilled one of Arnold's ideals by reasserting the "Hellenistic" element; but his proclamation of the ecstasy of artistic and intellectual experience was scarcely consistent with Arnold's insistence upon "high seriousness." Pater's own early admiration had been for Ruskin, and he had a vein of moral austerity; but his eclectic artistic passions, his recommendation to "burn always with a hard gem-like flame," as well as the lavish richness of his style, were seized upon by younger critics as justifying a complete divorce of literary art from ethical and moral concerns.

This "aesthetic" school was led by John Addington Symonds, Oscar Wilde, and Arthur Symons. The witty insolence of Wilde, as well as his personal excesses, aroused strong public opposition, whether in the form of ridicule or of disgust. The conflict over the asserted immorality of recent literature had been aroused by Robert Buchanan's essay on "The Fleshly School of Poetry" (1871), an attack on Rossetti and Swinburne, both of whom angrily replied. Pater's "paganism" was satirized by W. H. Mallock in The New Republic (1877), and later Wilde's aesthetic pose provided material for burlesque in W. S. Gilbert's operetta Patience. Thus the "Cyrenaic" critical theories of Pater merged into the extreme epicureanism of the "decadent nineties" and the influence of Sainte-Beuve and Gautier was replaced by that of other French authors— Baudelaire, Verlaine, Rimbaud, who fostered the theories known as "symbolism."

Many competent critics were writing during the later decades of the century. Eneas Sweetland Dallas wrote two good books on aesthetics—*Poetics* (1852) and *The Gay Science* (1866). Theodore Watts-Dunton, for years the principal reviewer for the *Athenaeum,* had an influence far more extensive than is indicated by his publication of books. The best example of his critical writing reprinted in volume form was *Poetry and the Renascence of Wonder.* William Ernest Henley was leader of the "virile" group in the eighties and nineties, striving to offset the preciosity of the aesthetes. A more soberly intellectual circle, the positivists, was represented in critical writing by Frederic Harrison and John Morley. Morley and Augustine Birrell, a critical essayist of polished wit and grace, later gained prominence in politics. Andrew Lang, Leslie Stephen, Austin Dobson, and Edmund Gosse wrote countless brief biographical and appreciative essays which came out first in periodicals and then were collected into books. George Saintsbury wrote literary history with such vigor of style and confidence of assertion that it was of real critical importance. Edward Dowden was another prominent literary historian.

Several of the poets ventured into the field of criticism, though none but Arnold relinquished poetry in its favor. Swinburne in his later life wrote copiously about literature, chiefly the Elizabethan dramatists but also about Dickens, the Brontës, and other contemporaries. As might be expected, his prose style was flamboyant and his loves and hates were violent. George Meredith's essay on *Comedy and the Comic Spirit* was one of the most noteworthy single items of critical theory. Robert Bridges wrote extensively on topics of vocabulary and poetic form.

J. M. Robertson, *Essays Toward a Critical Method* (London, 1889); G. Saintsbury, *History of English Criticism* (Edinburgh, 1911); L. Rosenblatt, *L'idée de l'art pour l'art dans la littérature anglaise pendant la période victorienne* (Paris, 1931); A. J. Farmer, *Le mouvement esthétique et "décadent" en Angleterre, 1873-1900* (Paris, 1931); C. R. Decker, "The Aesthetic Revolt Against Naturalism in Victorian Criticism," *Publications of the Modern Language Association,* LIII (1938). 844-56.

WALTER PATER (1839-1894)

>>

Walter Horatio Pater, the essayist who desired to "burn with a hard, gem-like flame" in his appreciation and interpretation of beauty, was born at Shadwell in East London, on August 4, 1839, the son of a physician. After attending Enfield Grammar School and King's School, Canterbury, he entered Queen's College, Oxford, in 1858, with some purpose of studying for the Church. While there he fell under the influence of such men as Benjamin Jowett, and started to read Plato. He later became an admirer of Goethe, and among contemporary writers Ruskin had a strong appeal to him. By the time he received his degree he had become skeptical toward religion, and instead of being ordained he accepted a Fellowship at Brasenose College.

WALTER PATER

A visit to Italy in 1865 led him to become interested in the Renaissance. He also found himself in sympathy with the "Art for Art's Sake" movement of Gautier, Swinburne, and others. During the next few years he wrote a number of essays on literature and history for the *Westminster Review* and the *Fortnightly Review*. In 1873 the principal essays were collected into a volume entitled *Studies in the History of the Renaissance,* which delighted a few readers, particularly those of Pre-Raphaelite sympathies, but shocked others, including Jowett, by its avowal of "pagan" and "hedonistic" views. Pater's academic prospects may have been damaged by the doubts that were thus aroused with regard to his morals.

Between 1875 and 1880 he did notable work on the art and philosophy of the ancient Greeks. At this time he wrote *The Child in the House,* an imaginative psychological study that probably contained a good deal of self-portraiture. Having decided that writing was his principal interest, he gave up all tutorial work in 1880, though retaining his fellowship at his college. The next five years were devoted chiefly to writing *Marius the Epicurean,* a work of fiction that was at the same time a study of Classical culture and a declaration of Pater's own creed of beauty. Lacking a plot, it cannot be called a novel; long essays, dialogues, even bits of translation, are interspersed. It is a sort of imaginary biography, or even perhaps a veiled autobiography, since Marius is evidently Walter Pater transported to second-century Rome. Written in an ornately beautiful style, the book was hailed by the leading "Aesthetes" as a gospel.

Imaginary Portraits, his next work, indicated by its title that it used the same method as *Marius,* except that it consisted of four short studies instead of a single long one. *Appreciations* (1889) was a collection of his literary essays, and included an important "Essay on Style." Retaining his close association with Oxford, Pater gave a series of lectures there and published them in 1893 as *Plato and Platonism*. He died unexpectedly at his home in Oxford on June 30, 1894. *Greek Studies* and *Miscellaneous Studies* were published posthumously.

A shy, quiet man, Pater was by nature contemplative and was not at all concerned with contemporary social or political issues. His writings were controlled by his ideal of beauty, the essence of all art, that which is perceived through the soul rather than through the mind. Since his aim was to suggest the beauty and the spirit of the works of the masters about whom he wrote, he cultivated a style of cumulative richness and sonority. For all its delicacy of touch, his style was full of melody, austere and at the same time highly ornamented. His long, involved sentences are regarded by some as beautiful and by others as needlessly difficult.

C. A. and H. W. Stonehill, "Walter Pater," in *Bibliographies of Modern Authors*, series II (London, 1925); *Works* (10v, London, 1910; Library edition); E. Gosse, "Walter Pater, a Portrait," in *Critical Kit-Kats* (London, 1896); F. Greenslet, *Walter Pater* (New York, 1903; Contemporary Men of Letters); A. C. Benson, *Walter Pater* (London, 1906; English Men of Letters); T. Wright, *The Life of Walter Pater* (2v, London, 1907); E. Thomas, *Walter Pater: A Critical Study* (London, 1913); A. J. Farmer, *Walter Pater As a Critic of English Literature* (Grenoble, 1931); A. Symons, *A Study of Walter Pater* (London, 1932); E. B. Burgum, "Walter Pater and the Good Life," *Sewanee Review*, XL (1932). 276-93; T. S. Eliot, "Arnold and Pater," in *Selected Essays* (London, 1932); H. H. Young, *The Writings of Walter Pater* (Lancaster, Pa., 1933); J. G. Eaker, *Walter Pater: A Study in Methods and Effects* (Iowa City, 1933); L. Cattan, *Essai sur Walter Pater* (Paris, 1936); F. Olivero, *Il pensiero religioso ed estetico de Walter Pater* (Turin, 1939); R. C. Child, *The Aesthetic of Walter Pater* (New York, 1940).

OTHER CRITICS

>>>

Walter Bagehot (1826-1877). Most influential for his writings on economics and government, Bagehot was also a distinguished literary critic. A prosperous banker, he was an unofficial adviser of Gladstone and other politicians. As editor of the *Economist* from 1860 to 1877 he wielded wide influence, and also with his monumental books, *The English Constitution* (1867), *Physics and Politics* (1869), and *Lombard Street* (1873). His essays on literature were collected after his death as *Literary Studies* and *Biographical Studies*. He wrote with analytical impartiality and epigrammatic ease.

E. I. Barrington, *Life of Walter Bagehot* (London, 1914); W. Irvine, *Walter Bagehot* (New York, 1939).

Augustine Birrell (1850-1933). A successful lawyer, Birrell entered Parliament in 1889, where he made a reputation as a witty speaker and became one of the group of Liberal intellectuals who shaped party policy. He served as Minister for Education and later as Chief Secretary for Ireland. Birrell wrote biographies of Charlotte Brontë, Hazlitt, and Marvell, and a series of volumes of polished, mildly satirical literary essays—*Obiter Dicta* (1884), *Res Judicatae* (1892), *Men, Women, and Books* (1894), and others.

Sidney Colvin (1845-1927). Equally noted as a critic of art and of literature, Colvin was Professor of Fine Art at Cambridge and later was in charge of Prints at the British Museum. An intimate friend of R. L. Stevenson, he edited Stevenson's letters, and wrote biographies of Landor and Keats as well as books on art.

E. V. Lucas, *The Colvins and Their Friends* (London, 1928).

Edward Dowden (1843-1913). Born and educated in Ireland, Dowden served as Professor of English Literature at Trinity College, Dublin, and became a leading Shakespearian authority. His biography of Shelley (1886) was also a standard work, and he published several volumes of critical essays.

Letters of Edward Dowden and His Correspondents, ed. E. D. and H. M. Dowden (London, 1914).

Edmund Gosse (1849-1928). Somewhat pompous and opinionated, Gosse was a friend of most of the leading authors of his time. After writing several books of undistinguished poetry, he became recognized as an authority on Scandinavian and French literatures, as well as English. He did much to promote Ibsen's works in England. His prolific literary essays and reviews, especially on English literature of the seventeenth and eighteenth centuries, were collected in a long series of volumes. His recollections of childhood, published anonymously in 1908 as *Father and Son,* is a minor classic of autobiography. Having served as librarian for the House of Lords, he received a knighthood in 1925.

P. Braybrooke, *Considerations on Edmund Gosse* (London, 1925); E. Charteris, *Life and Letters of Edmund Gosse* (London, 1931).

Frederic Harrison (1831-1923). An authority on legal matters, Harrison was a champion of trades unions and an enthusiastic proponent of Comte's Positivist philosophy. As well as biographies of Cromwell, William the Silent, Ruskin, and Chatham, his chief books included *The Meaning of History* (1862), *The Choice of Books* (1886), *Early Victorian Literature* (1896), *Byzantine History in the Early Middle Ages* (1900).

A. Harrison, *Frederic Harrison: Thoughts and Memories* (London, 1925).

Richard Holt Hutton (1826-1897). As editor of the *Spectator* from 1861, Hutton had great influence on Liberal thought. His earnest, independent reviews and his essays on political, religious, and scientific topics were collected in several volumes—*Studies in Parliament* (1866), *Essays Theological and Literary* (1871, 1888), *Modern Guides of English Thought in Matters of Faith* (1888), *Aspects of Religious and Scientific Thought* (1899), and others.

J. Hogben, *R. H. Hutton of "The Spectator"* (Edinburgh, 1899); G. C. LeRoy, "Richard Holt Hutton," *Publications of the Modern Language Association,* LVI (1941). 809-840.

Andrew Lang (1844-1912). A Scottish-born scholar, Lang gave up a fellowship at Oxford to become a London journalist. His amazingly prolific and versatile authorship included novels, poetry, translations of Homer, research in Scottish and French history, anthropological studies of primitive religion, and numerous collections of fairy tales. His literary articles and reviews were collected in a series of volumes including *Letters to Dead Authors, Books and Bookmen, Old Friends, Essays in Little, Letters on Literature.* His romantic imagination, whimsical humor, and graceful style gave charm to all he wrote.

R. L. Green, *Andrew Lang* (London, 1947).

John Morley (1838-1923). Coming to London in 1859, Morley served successively as editor of several magazines and newspapers, especially the *Fortnightly Review* (1867-1883) and the *Pall Mall Gazette* (1880-1883). He became prominent as a Positivist and a political radical. Entering Parliament in 1883, he was made a cabinet minister only three years later, remained a prominent leader of the Liberal party, and in 1908 was created a Viscount. Morley was editor of the "English Men of Letters" series of literary monographs, and his own biographical and critical works included lives of Voltaire, Rousseau, Diderot, Burke, Cobden, Walpole, Cromwell, and Gladstone, as well as volumes of shorter studies.

Recollections (2v, London, 1917); J. D. McCallum, *Lord Morley's Criticism of English Poetry and Prose* (Princeton, 1921); S. Ali Khan, *Life of Lord Morley* (London, 1923); J. H. Morgan, *John, Viscount Morley* (London, 1924); F. W. Hirst, *Early Life and Letters of Lord Morley* (London, 1927); F. W. Knickerbocker, *Free Minds: John Morley and His Friends* (Cambridge, Mass., 1943); W. Staebler, *The Liberal Mind of John Morley* (Princeton, 1943).

George Edward Bateman Saintsbury (1845-1933). After some years as a schoolmaster and as a reviewer for London papers, the *Academy* and the *Saturday Review,* Saintsbury in 1895 became Professor of English Literature at Edinburgh University. A man of vast reading and strong opinions, he wrote books which are stimulating and enlightening in spite of peculiarities of style and occasional errors. His works include *Dryden* (1881), *A Short History of French Literature* (1882), *Nineteenth-Century Literature* (1896), *A Short History of English Literature* (1898), *A History of Criticism* (1900-1904), *A History of English Prosody* (1906-1910).

A. B. Webster, *George Saintsbury* (Edinburgh, 1934).

Leslie Stephen (1832-1904). Though he had entered the priesthood of the Church of England, Stephen gradually developed rationalistic views which obliged him to withdraw from it. Meanwhile he had become a journalist, contributing to the *Saturday Review,* the *Cornhill Magazine,* and the *Nation.* He helped to found the *Pall Mall Gazette* (1865) and in 1871 he became editor of the *Cornhill.* He edited *The Dictionary of National Biography* from 1882 to 1891, and wrote many articles for it. His writings on free-thinking had a sincerity and dignity that did much to gain public respect for those views. His important books included *Free Thinking and Plain Speaking* (1873), *History of English Thought in the Eighteenth Century* (1876), *The Science of Ethics* (1882), *An Agnostic's Apology* (1893), *Social Rights and Duties* (1896), several series entitled *Hours in a Library* (1874-1890), two series of *Studies of a Biographer,* and a number of separate biographies. He was knighted in 1902.

F. W. Maitland, *Life and Letters of Leslie Stephen* (London, 1906).

John Addington Symonds (1840-1893). After a brilliant career at Oxford, Symonds's health broke down, and he spent most of his later life in Switzerland and Italy. In addition to his authoritative work on *The Renaissance in Italy* (7v, 1875-1886), he wrote *An Introduction to the Study of Dante* (1872), *Studies of the Greek Poets* (1873-1876), *Shakespeare's Predecessors in the English Drama* (1874), and biographies of Shelley, Sidney, Jonson, and Michelangelo.

H. F. Brown, *John Addington Symonds: A Biography Compiled from His Papers* (2v, London, 1895); Van W. Brooks, *John Addington Symonds: A Biographical Study* (New York, 1914).

HUMOR

One of the widely-circulated misconceptions about Victorian authors is that they were solemn and humorless. On the contrary, no other period of English literature had a wider range of humorous writing.

It is specially notable that almost all the major authors showed that they possessed some type of humor. Carlyle made much use of boisterous, contemptuous laughter; Macaulay and Matthew Arnold were adept in ironical wit. Among the poets, Robert Browning indulged sometimes in the grotesque humor which mingles the ridiculous with the grim and horrible, as in "A Soliloquy of the Spanish Cloister" and "Holy Cross Day." There is a mellower strain of laughter in many of his monologues, such as "Christmas Eve," "Up at a Villa—Down in the City," "The Flight of the Duchess," and "Fra Lippo Lippi." Tennyson has touches of real rustic humor in his dialect monologues, "The Northern Farmer" and "The Northern Cobbler." Swinburne wrote a group of irresistible parodies of contemporary poets (including himself).

Humor is an integral part of the Victorian novel. Dickens began his career with the intention of being a humorist, and the comic characters and incidents are the best-remembered parts of all his novels. Thackeray wrote chiefly humorous sketches for the first ten years of his career, and maintained an attitude of ironical comedy in most of his fiction. Trollope achieved sustained high comedy in *Barchester Towers* and wove a few comic episodes into most of his other books. Even the serious-minded George Eliot created quaint and mirthful rural characters, such as Mrs.

Poyser in *Adam Bede* and the Rainbow Inn patrons in *Silas Marner*. Thomas Hardy also showed the comic side of English rustic life. George Meredith based his whole method of fiction upon the theory that he set forth in his essay on "The Comic Spirit." Among less eminent novelists, Marryat, Surtees, and Lever all owed much of their popularity to their humorous scenes.

Earlier Victorian drama produced no outstanding comedy merely because it produced no plays of any literary distinction. One must remember that the London theater throughout the period depended largely on farces; these plays, seldom good enough to get into print, were enjoyed by both the public and the professional authors, and had a strong influence upon the comic techniques of novels and other literary works. The revival of drama in the later years of the century centered largely in comedy, from the sentimental domestic plays of Tom Robertson to the witty satires of Wilde and Shaw.

With this wide distribution of humor through all forms of literature, it is not surprising to discover that many writers devoted themselves primarily to comic work. *Bentley's Miscellany, Punch,* and other periodicals depended on their writings. A group of brilliant caricaturists, including George Cruikshank, Richard Doyle, John Leech, and Charles Keene, helped to set the style and promote the popularity of comic books and magazines. Works like Gilbert à Beckett's *Comic Histories of Rome and England,* illustrated by Leech, show that burlesque was invading a wide territory.

The opening years of the Victorian period were dominated by a group of humorists who had reacted against the serious emotionalism of the Romantic movement. The novels of Theodore Hook were full of horseplay, and were initiated by Henry Cockton in *Valentine Vox, the Ventriloquist* (1840) and *Sylvester Sound, the Somnambulist* (1844).

Another popular humorous novelist was Cuthbert Bede, who wrote a farcical story of Oxford student life, *Mr. Verdant Green* (1853).

Another type of early Victorian humor was represented by *The Ingoldsby Legends,* some in verse, some in prose, in which the Rev. R. H. Barham achieved grotesque effects by exaggerating the gruesome details of the Gothic "tale of terror."

Thomas Hood was perhaps the most typical humorist of the early Victorian years. A friend of Keats and his circle, he had hoped to be a serious poet; but the necessity of earning a living drove him to humor, and he started a series of "Comic Annuals." Combatting disease, he ground out his "whims and oddities," full of atrocious puns, until his premature death in 1845.

The staff of *Punch,* to which Hood was an early contributor, provides almost a roster of the leading humorists from 1841 onwards. The editors, Mark Lemon, Shirley Brooks, Tom Taylor, and F. C. Burnand, all produced quantities of funny stuff, including scores of burlesques for the stage. Douglas Jerrold, the chief contributor until 1857, won greatest popularity with *Mrs. Caudle's Curtain Lectures.*

All this comic writing was rather monotonously produced by formula. Much more original and characteristically English was the cult of nonsense, which was started by Edward Lear's collection of "limericks," *The Book of Nonsense,* in 1846, followed by his volumes of longer poems, *Nonsense Songs, Stories, etc.,* 1871, and *Laughable Lyrics,* 1877. Though ostensibly for children, these books gave delight to adults also by their imaginative freedom and their tendency to parody the solemnities of life and literature. In the same category is Lewis Carroll, whose jargon poem, "Jabberwocky," in *Through the Looking Glass,* has actually added new words to the language. *The Hunting of the Snark,* Carroll's longest nonsense poem, tantalizes readers who tend to interpret it as some sort of allegory.

Other mid-Victorian poets also wrote farcical tales. William E. Aytoun and Theodore Martin collaborated in *The Bon Gautier Ballads,* some of which were mock-heroic extravaganzas, others parodies of current poetry. This book formed a model for *The Bab Ballads* of William S. Gilbert (1869). The untrammeled burlesque in Gilbert's poems, the inconsequent anticlimaxes, and the facile rhymes, made his work very popular, and Gilbert later used the themes of several of his ballads as plots for the comic operas which he wrote for the music of Arthur Sullivan. Gilbert's songs in these operas are classics of light satire and neat rhyming.

In the special field of parody the leading poet was Charles Stuart Calverley, whose witty style had been formed through translating Latin poetry. As a parodist, his example was followed by Arthur C. Hilton and James K. Stephen.

The elegant type of light satire known as *vers de société* was written at the beginning of the Victorian period by Winthrop Mackworth Praed, and later by Frederick Locker-Lampson, Andrew Lang, and Austin Dobson.

W. S. Lilly, *Four English Humourists of the Nineteenth Century* (London, 1895); J. B. Priestley, *English Humour* (London, 1929); R. B. Ince, *Calverley and Some Cambridge Wits of the Nineteenth Century* (Cambridge, 1929); G. Kitchin, *A Survey of Burlesque and Parody in English* (Edinburgh, 1931).

PRINCIPAL HUMORISTS

>>>

Richard Harris Barham (1788-1845). A clergyman of the Church of England, Barham became a canon of St. Paul's Cathedral. When *Bentley's Miscellany* was founded in 1837, he began to contribute to it under the name of "Thomas

Ingoldsby." Sometimes in prose and sometimes in fantastically-rhymed verse, his *Ingoldsby Legends* were a burlesque of Gothic medievalism, and shocked some critics by the unsentimental ridiculing of death, crime, torture, and even religion.

R. H. D. Barham, *Life and Letters of the Rev. R. H. Barham* (London, 1870).

Charles Stuart Calverley (1831-1884). For the first twenty years of his life Calverley's name was Blayds, until his father resumed the original name of the family. A brilliant student at both Oxford and Cambridge, he became a lawyer but spent his later years as an invalid in consequence of a fall. As well as excellent translations of Greek and Latin poetry, he published in 1872 *Fly Leaves,* a volume of witty satirical verses and parodies.

"Lewis Carroll"(1832-1898). In his professional career the Rev. Charles Lutwidge Dodgson was a tutor at Christ Church College, Oxford, and author of technical mathematical books. A shy man, he found his chief friendships among little girls; and for one of them, a daughter of the dean of his college, he wrote *Alice's Adventures in Wonderland,* which was published in 1865 and won popularity with adults as well as with children

ALICE'S ADVENTURES IN WONDERLAND.

BY

LEWIS CARROLL.

WITH FORTY-TWO ILLUSTRATIONS BY JOHN TENNIEL.

London
MACMILLAN AND CO.
1866.

[*The Right of Translation and Reproduction is Reserved.*]

FIRST EDITION
TITLE-PAGE

for its mixture of whimsical fantasy and elusive satire. *Through the Looking Glass* followed in 1871, and a quaint poem, *The Hunting of the Snark,* in 1876. Dodgson never formally admitted his identity as "Lewis Carroll."

S. H. Williams and F. Madan, *A Handbook of the Literature of the Rev. C. L. Dodgson* (Oxford, 1932); S. D. Collingwood, *Life and Letters of Lewis Carroll* (London, 1898); L. Reed, *The Life of Lewis Carroll* (London, 1932); F. B. Lennon, *Victoria Through the Looking Glass: The Life of Lewis Carroll* (New York, 1945).

William Schwenck Gilbert (1836-1911). Son of a minor novelist, Gilbert became a lawyer and eventually a magistrate. In 1861 he had begun to contribute humorous ballads to a paper called *Fun,* illustrating them with his own drawings. Having used the pen-name "Bab," he collected his poems under the title *Bab Ballads* (1869) and *More Bab Ballads* (1873). In 1866 he began writing theatrical burlesques, and between 1874 and 1878 five of his satirical comedies were staged in London. Meanwhile in 1871 he had written the libretto for an operetta, *Thespis, or the Gods Grown Old,* for music by Arthur Sullivan. Four years later they collaborated in *Trial by Jury,* which set the pattern for gay and good-humored satirical operas on contemporary life and ideas—*The Sorcerer, H. M. S. Pinafore, The Pirates of Penzance, Patience, Iolanthe, Princess Ida, The Mikado, Ruddigore, The Yeomen of the Guard,* and *The Gondoliers.* In later years Gilbert wrote several librettos for other composers. Knighted in 1907, he was accidentally drowned in 1911.

E. A. Browne, *W. S. Gilbert* (London, 1907); S. Dark and R. Grey, *W. S. Gilbert: His Life and Letters* (London, 1923); H. Pearson, *Gilbert and Sullivan: A Biography* (London, 1935).

Thomas Hood (1799-1845). Trained as an engraver, Hood in 1821 became assistant editor of the *London Magazine,* which brought friendship with Lamb, de Quincey, and other members of the group. His early poems were charming pieces in the Keats style; later his *Dream of Eugene Aram* was a grim tragic ballad and *The Song of the Shirt* a bitter social protest. He also published two humorous volumes, *Whims and Oddities,* as early as 1826-27, and in 1830 he brought out *The Comic Annual,* which was so successful that for the rest of his life he had to grind out vast quantities of comic verse and prose, studded with egregious puns. After writing the *Comic Annuals* until 1839, he edited the *New Monthly Magazine* from 1841 to 1843, and established *Hood's Magazine and Comic Miscellany* in 1844; but his health had already given way, and he died the next year.

T. and F. Hood, *Memories of Thomas Hood* (2v, London, 1860); W. Jerrold, *Thomas Hood: His Life and Times* (London, 1907).

Douglas William Jerrold (1803-1857). The son of an actor, Jerrold was a midshipman from his tenth to his twelfth year, and then became a printer. His first play was produced when he was eighteen, and he continued actively writing plays till the end of his life. Except for one tragedy, *The Painter of Ghent,* his dramatic works were melodramas and comedies. He contributed to many magazines and established several papers, being notably successful as editor of *Lloyd's Weekly Newspaper;* but he was best known as a member of the staff of *Punch* from its foundation. His most popular volumes of humorous prose were *Men of Character* (1838), *Cakes and Ale* (1842), *Punch's Letters to His Son* (1843), *Mrs. Caudle's Curtain Lectures* (1846). A very small man, of quarrelsome temper, Jerrold was militantly radical in politics.

W. B. Jerrold, *Life and Remains of Douglas Jerrold* (London, 1859); W. Jerrold, *Douglas Jerrold* (2v, London, 1914).

Edward Lear (1812-1888). Through his ornithological drawings Lear became a friend of the Earl of Derby, and to amuse the Earl's children drew the absurd illustrations for his own limericks, published as *The Book of Nonsense* (1846). In later life he lived chiefly in Italy and traveled widely through the Near East as a landscape painter. He wrote books about his journeys, but was famous chiefly for the limericks and the *Nonsense Songs and Stories*, such as "The Jumblies," "The Pobble That Had No Toes," and "The Owl and the Pussy-cat," sharing with Carroll the distinction of giving nonsense a recognized place in English literature.

A. Davidson, *Edward Lear: Landscape Painter and Nonsense Poet* (London, 1938).

LITERATURE FOR CHILDREN
>>

Until the Victorian era, few books were written specially for children. During several centuries English children were given such existing books as chanced to be written in a fairly simple style and with some adventurous or fantastic element in the story. Thus, luckily for themselves, the children early encountered the *Morte d'Arthur, The Pilgrim's Progress, Gulliver's Travels,* and *Robinson Crusoe,* and the influence of those books upon English style and thought was greatly enhanced thereby. For smaller children a few "Mother Goose" nursery rhymes sufficed.

Toward the end of the eighteenth century stories and poems began to be written for children, with a strongly educational and moralistic purpose which overshadowed any elements of entertainment. Maria Edgeworth's juvenile stories partly emancipated themselves from these shackles, but even in the early Victorian period the most approved writer for children was Mrs. Mary Martha Sherwood, whose most famous book, *The Fairchild Family,* unctuously described corpses and funerals amid lectures on sin and punishment.

Early in the Victorian era, however, the fairy-tale gained recognition as suitable reading-matter for children, with translations of the collections of Perrault, the Grimm brothers, and Hans Christian Andersen. A great improvement occurred about the middle of the century with the establishment of several pleasant magazines for young people (the *Monthly Packet, Aunt Judy's Magazine, Good Words for the Young,* the *Boys' Own Paper*) and annuals (*Chatterbox*), with cheerful stories and suitable illustrations. Improved methods of book production also made possible the publication of children's books with charming illustrations (often in color) at reasonable prices. Such artists as Walter Crane, Kate Greenaway, and Randolph Caldecott (born within seven months of each other) strongly influenced the type of book for which they drew pictures.

Prestige came to children's literature also through the fact that several of the major Victorian authors contributed to it. Browning wrote *The Pied Piper of Hamelin,* Ruskin *The King of the Golden River,* Dickens *A Child's History of England,* and Thackeray *The Rose and the Ring.* More remarkable was Charles Kingsley, whose fairy-tale, *The Water Babies,* may well outlive his novels and his polemical writings. Although *The Water Babies* is full of philosophical symbolism and satire far above the heads of children, the fantasy and humor and kindliness of the book make it a true classic for childhood. Kingsley also wrote about Greek mythology for children in *The Heroes* and about science in *Glaucus* and *Madam How and Lady Why.*

In 1865, two years after *The Water Babies,* another scholarly gentleman wrote a fantasy for children that proved even more successful—*Alice's Adventures in Wonderland.* It was followed in 1871 by a sequel, *Through the Looking Glass.* Here again there are satirical overtones that a child cannot grasp; and it is ironical that the interspersed parodies of the old didactic poetry for children are now famous when the originals are forgotten. But Lewis Carroll's strange power of intimacy with children enabled him to appeal to their imagination and interest. Like Edward Lear in *The Book of Nonsense* twenty years before, Carroll understood that children can delight in humor if it is sufficiently fantastic and inconsequential.

Another serious writer who turned to the production of children's books was George MacDonald, the Scottish novelist and mystic. As well as many short fairy stories, he wrote

Ranald Bannerman's Boyhood, At the Back of the North Wind, The Princess and the Goblins, and a sequel to the latter, *The Princess and Curdie.* As in the books of Kingsley and Carroll, there are hints of the author's adult philosophical notions.

As might be expected, women wrote some of the most popular books for children. Though these retained some traces of the religious and didactic quality of the earlier type, they had enough humor and sympathy to avoid smugness. Mrs. Margaret Gatty was prominent for *Parables from Nature* and *Aunt Judy's Tales;* she was followed by her daughter, Mrs. Juliana Horatia Ewing, whose best books were *Jackanapes, Daddy Darwin's Dovecot,* and *The Story of a Short Life.* Other books in the same general style, such as *The Little Lame Prince,* were written by Dinah Maria Mulock (Mrs. Craik); the blind Irish writer, Frances Browne, was author of *Granny's Wonderful Chair* (1857); and a little later the most popular author for children was Mrs. Mary Louisa Molesworth, with *Tell Me a Story, The Cuckoo Clock,* and many others.

It is noteworthy that almost all the important Victorian books for children, mentioned above, were written during the middle twenty years of the period, from about 1855 to 1875. This is consistent with the idealization of the happy family which was at its height during the mid-Victorian era.

In addition to books for young children, the Victorian age developed definite categories of books for boys and girls in the teens. The type of the books for girls, strongly sentimental in cast, was established by the novels of Charlotte Mary Yonge, such as *The Daisy Chain.* One of her most prolific followers was Mrs. L. T. Meade.

The books for boys descended in some measure from the later books of Captain Frederick Marryat—*Masterman Ready* and *The Children of the New Forest.* Stories of ad venture in far corners of the globe were written by Robert M. Ballantyne, Captain Mayne Reid, and William H. G. Kingston. Almost every period of European history was covered in the eighty books of George Alfred Henty. Boys of the later Victorian years probably gained more of their geographical and historical knowledge from these authors than from text-books. Much of the "empire-building" spirit which sent young Englishmen into all corners of the globe, whether for big-game hunting or administration, was inculcated through the schoolboy reading of thrilling books about frontier lands and about the glories of English adventurers in the past.

Character-building books of another sort were those which dealt with life in the great English schools. The fame of *Tom Brown's School Days* (1857), by Thomas Hughes, has lasted until the present. Among numerous writers who followed the same model may be mentioned the Rev. F. W. Farrar, author of *Eric, or Little by Little* (1858) and *St. Winifred's, or the World of School* (1862).

Later in the century, juvenile literature gained new distinction through works by first-class authors. Robert Louis Stevenson glorified the adventure-story for boys in *Treasure Island;* Andrew Lang's wide scholarship and poetic style added value to his long series of *Fairy Books;* and Rudyard Kipling opened a new world for the child's imagination in *The Jungle Books.* A new era in poetry for children was initiated by Christina Rossetti's *Sing-Song* (1871) and Stevenson's *Child's Garden of Verses* (1885).

H. A. Watt, "Some Tap-Roots of Victorianism," *Sewanee Review,* xxxvi (1928). 292-301; F. J. H. Darton, *Children's Books in England* (Cambridge, 1932); P. Hazard, *Les livres, les enfants, et les hommes* (Paris, 1932; Engl. trans., Boston, 1944); P. James, *Children's Books of Yesterday* (London, 1933); M. Kent, "The Art of Nonsense," *Cornhill Magazine,* cxlix (1934). 478-87; G. König, *Die viktorianische Schulroman* (Berlin, 1937); E. S. Turner, *Boys Will Be Boys* (London, 1948).

BIBLIOGRAPHY

>>

GENERAL BIBLIOGRAPHICAL AIDS

Bibliographies of Studies in Victorian Literature, 1932-44, ed.
W. D. Templeman (Urbana, 1945).
Bibliographies of Twelve Victorian Authors, ed. T. G. Ehrsam and
R. H. Deily (New York, 1936).
Cambridge Bibliography of English Literature, iii, ed. F. W. Bateson (Cambridge, 1940).
Carter, J. *Binding Variants in English Publishing, 1820-1900*
(London, 1932).
Parrish, M. L., *Victorian Lady Novelists* (London, 1933).
Sadleir, M., *Excursions in Victorian Bibliography* (London, 1922).
"Victorian Bibliography," *Modern Philology,* xxx (1933)—. Compiled successively by W. D. Templeman, C. F. Harrold, and A.
Wright.

SOCIAL HISTORY

Bott, A., and I. Clephane, *Our Mothers* (London, 1932).
Cohen, V., *The Nineteenth Century: A Biographical History*
(London, 1932).
Cumington, C. W., *English Women's Clothing in the Nineteenth
Century* (London, 1937).
Dance, E. H., *The Victorian Illusion* (London, 1928).
ffrench, Y., *News from the Past, 1805-87* (London, 1934).
Harling, R., *Home: A Victorian Vignette* (London, 1938).
Hobhouse, C., *1851 and the Crystal Palace* (London, 1937).
Holden, A., *Elegant Modes in the Nineteenth Century* (London,
1935).
London Miscellany: A Nineteenth-Century Scrapbook, ed. R.
Harling (London, 1937).
Peel, D. C., *The Stream of Time: Social and Domestic Life in
England, 1805-61* (London, 1932).
Perugini, M., *Victorian Days and Ways* (London, 1932).

Quennell, M. and C. H. B., *A History of Every-Day Things in England*, III-IV (London, 1933-34).

Quennell, P., *Victorian Panorama* (London, 1937).

Wellman, R., *Victoria Royal: A History of Victorian Art and Life* (New York, 1939).

Wingfield-Stratford, E., *The Victorian Tragedy* (London, 1930) [American title, *Those Earnest Victorians*].

———, *The Victorian Sunset* (London, 1932).

Wyndham, H., *Victorian Parade* (London, 1935).

LITERARY HISTORY AND CRITICISM

Brandes, G., *Main Currents in Nineteenth-Century Literature*, IV (London, 1905).

Brownell, W. C., *Victorian Prose Masters* (New York, 1901).

Burdett, O., *The Beardsley Period* (London, 1925).

Cambridge History of English Literature, XII-XIV, ed. A. W. Ward and A. R. Waller (Cambridge, 1915-16).

Chapman, E. M., *English Literature and Religion, 1800-1900* (London, 1910).

Chesterton, G. K., *The Victorian Age in Literature* (London, 1913).

Chew, S. C., "The Nineteenth Century and After (1789-1939)." *A Literary History of England,* ed. A. C. Baugh (New York, 1948), pp. 1109-1605.

Cruse, A., *The Victorians and Their Books* (London, 1935).

Cunliffe, J. W., *English Literature During the Last Half-Century* (New York, 1923).

———, *Leaders of the Victorian Revolution* (New York, 1934).

Dobree, B., and E. Batho, *The Victorians and After* (London, 1938).

Dowden, E., *Studies in Literature, 1789-1877* (London, 1882).

Eighteen-Sixties, The, ed. J. Drinkwater (Cambridge, 1932).

Eighteen-Seventies, The, ed. H. Granville-Barker (Cambridge, 1929).

Eighteen-Eighties, The, ed. W. de la Mare (Cambridge, 1930).

Elton, O., *A Survey of English Literature, 1830-80* (2v, London, 1920).

English Poets, IV-V, ed. T. H. Ward (London, 1894-1918).

English Prose Writers, V, ed. H. Craik (London, 1896).

Great Victorians, The, ed. H. J. and H. Massingham (London, 1932).

Harrison, F., *Studies in Early Victorian Literature* (London, 1895).

——, *Tennyson, Ruskin, Mill, and Other Literary Estimates* (London, 1899).

Jackson, H., *The Eighteen-Nineties* (London, 1914).

Kennedy, J. M., *English Literature, 1880-1905* (London, 1912).

Knickerbocker, W. S., *Creative Oxford: Its Influence on Victorian Literature* (Syracuse, 1925).

Kunitz, S. J., and H. Haycraft, *British Authors of the Nineteenth Century* (New York, 1936).

Le Gallienne, R., *The Romantic Nineties* (New York, 1925).

Lucas, F. L., *The Decline and Fall of the Romantic Ideal* (Cambridge, 1936).

Magnus, L., *English Literature in the Nineteenth Century* (London, 1909).

Miles, J., *Pathetic Fallacy in the Nineteenth Century* (Berkeley, 1943).

Morley, H., *Of English Literature in the Reign of Victoria* (London, 1882).

Morris, L., *The Celtic Dawn: A Survey of the Renascence in Ireland* (New York, 1917).

Oliphant, M. O. W., *The Victorian Age in English Literature* (2v, London, 1892).

Routh, H. V., *Towards the Twentieth Century* (London, 1937).

Saintsbury, George, *Essays in English Literature, 1780-1860* (2v, London, 1890-95).

——, *Corrected Impressions* (London, 1895).

——, *A History of Nineteenth-Century Literature* (London, 1896).

Scudder, V. D., *Social Ideals in English Letters* (New York, 1898).

Shorter, C. K., *Victorian Literature* (London, 1897).

Walker, H., *The Age of Tennyson, 1830-70* (London, 1897; Handbooks of English Literature).

——, *The Literature of the Victorian Era* (Cambridge, 1910).

Williams, S. T., *Studies in Victorian Literature* (New York, 1923).

INDEX

≫≫

(**Bold-face** page numbers indicate main reference.)

(1)